THE CATHOLIC CHURCH
In
FAIRFIELD COUNTY
1666 - 1961

THE CATHOLIC CHURCH *In*

FAIRFIELD COUNTY 1666-1961

Stephen Michael DiGiovanni

WILLIAM MULVEY INC.
NEW CANAAN, CT.

William Mulvey Inc.
72 Park Street
New Canaan, CT 06840

Library of Congress Cataloging-in-Publication Data

The Catholic Church in Fairfield County, 1666–1961.

Bibliography: p.
1. Catholic Church—Connecticut—Fairfield County—
History. 2. Fairfield County (Conn.)—Church history.
I. Title
BX1415.C8D54 1988   282'.7469   88–42590
ISBN 0–934791–12–0

Printed in the United States of America

EPISCOPO ET FRATRIBUS MEIS
DIOECESIS BRIDGEPORTENSIS

Contents

ACKNOWLEDGMENTS

The history of the Catholic Church in Fairfield County did not begin with the establishment of the Diocese of Bridgeport in 1953. Catholics have lived in this county since colonial times. As their numbers increased through immigration, they succeeded in firmly establishing their ancestral Church in the southern most portion of Yankee New England. This book is the story of the development of the Catholic Church in Fairfield County from colonial times until the arrival of Bridgeport's second Bishop, Walter W. Curtis, in 1961. It is a general view of the Church's work within the county to provide the Catholics of the Latin Rite with the basic necessities of Catholic life, and, once those basic necessities had been assured, the efforts of its clergy, religious, and laymen and women to strengthen the faith and to affect the society in which they lived by their active Catholic faith.

I wish to express my gratitude to all who have aided me in the preparation of this work. In particular I would like to thank the Most Reverend Walter W. Curtis, Bishop of Bridgeport, for providing me with the time and opportunity to research and write this book. My special thanks goes to Mr. William Mulvey, whose generosity and encouragement have made this publication possible. I am also grateful to Msgr. Porter White of Baltimore, Msgr. John Horgan, Diocesan Archivist, Msgr. John Toomey, P.A., Pastor of St. Thomas the Apostle Church in East Norwalk, Msgr. William Genuario, P.A., Pastor of St. Catherine of Siena Church in Riverside, and the Rev. Peter Cullen, Pastor of St. Aloysius Church in New Canaan for their valuable suggestions and encouragement. I must also thank

ix

Msgr. James Leary, Rev. William Millea, and Don Paulson who served as proof readers. My special thanks goes to Mrs. Madeline Carroll who labored for many weeks over the first draft of this book as a proof reader and editor. I would also like to thank Al Bifano for his assistance at the beginning of this project, as well as Ernest and Deborah Marsan and their family for their generous friendship during the two years of research and writing. I am also indebted to Brother Randal Riede, C.F.X., for his constant support and encouragement during my research.

In writing this book I worked in the Secret Archives of the Vatican, Vatican City State, the Archives of the Sacred Congregation de Propaganda Fide in Rome, Italy, the Archives of the Generalate of the Congregation of the Missionaries of St. Charles Borromeo in Rome, Italy, the Archives of the Archdioceses of Baltimore, Boston, Hartford, the Archives of the Diocese of Bridgeport, the Archives of the Center for Migration Studies on Staten Island, the Archives and the historical collections in the Memorial Library of Notre Dame University in Notre Dame, Indiana, the Archives and collections of the Nyselius Library of Fairfield University in Fairfield, Connecticut, the Archives of the School Sisters of Notre Dame in Wilton, Connecticut, the Archives of the Sisters of Mercy in West Hartford, Connecticut, the Bishop's Room in the Burroughs Public Library in Bridgeport, Connecticut, the Geneology Room in the Norwalk Public Library in Norwalk, Connecticut, the Danbury Public Library in Danbury, Connecticut, the Ferguson Public Library in Stamford, Connecticut, the Rare Book Collection of the Pequot Public Library in Southport, Connecticut, the Fairfield Historical Society, the collections of the Lockwood House and of the Lockwood Matthews Mansion Museum, both in Norwalk, Connecticut and the Archives of the Scott Fanton Museum in Danbury, Connecticut. I am very grateful to the staffs of all of these institutions for their generous, courteous and patient assistance.

I'm especially grateful to the New York Public Library for granting permission to reprint the Thomas Nast engravings. These are from the Print Collection, Miriam & Ira D. Wallach Division of Art, Prints and Photographs, The New York Public Library, Astor, Lenox and Tilden Foundations.

FOREWORD BY
BISHOP WALTER W. CURTIS

History chiefly records past events, their causes and their consequences.

However, history also teaches. We learn how to avoid the mistakes of the past and how to duplicate or continue the successes of our ancestors.

History, indeed, inspires. Thrilled by the deeds of our physical or spiritual forebears, we apply to ourselves the words of the Lord: "Go thou and do likewise." (Lk. 10:37)

This history of Catholics in Fairfield County, Connecticut written by the Reverend Stephen M. DiGiovanni, H.E.D., gives us in large outlines a view of, in his own words, "the story of the development of the Catholic Church in Fairfield County from Colonial Times until the arrival, in 1961, of Bridgeport's Second Bishop, Walter W. Curtis."

I am indebted to Father DiGiovanni for setting aside so many months of his young life to preparing for us this history that we may indeed learn to duplicate or continue the successes of the past.

Rather than detailed items (left for the most part to the footnotes), we have here a history in bold strokes which allows us to cover many decades in a short space of time.

Read with your heart as well as with your mind and then you will also learn and be inspired by what you read. For example, the persecution which early Catholics underwent in the State of Connecticut, both because of their faith and also because they were new arrivals facing the opposition of the settled people, can remind us that we still today have that same conflict between those who have been established here in Fairfield County and immigrants who come to be with us. We need to be reminded of the words of Scripture: "You, too, were once aliens in a strange land." (Lev. 19:34)

Mindful that we build upon the past, let us build with faith and virtues.

Walter W. Curtis, S.T.D.
Bishop of Bridgeport

INTRODUCTION:
CATHOLIC ROOTS IN
FAIRFIELD COUNTY

Colonial Fairfield

Fairfield County was established on May 10, 1666, while King Charles II ruled England and her possessions and while John Winthrop was the Royal Governor of the Colony of Connecticut.[1] Five towns were then extant within the county: Stratford, Norwalk, Stamford, Greenwich and Fairfield, the last served as the business and governmental center of the county for over one hundred years; it was there that the county court convened twice each year. It was governed by the same charter and laws, forged by an unbreakable bond between Church and State, that ruled the rest of the Colony of Connecticut. The Colonies of Connecticut and New Haven (Quinnipiack) were founded by men and women of sturdy Puritan stock who came from England by way of the Massachusetts colonies. They came to America and established settlements in order ". . . to advance the Kingdome [sic] of our Lord Jesus Christ, and to enjoy the liberties of the Gospel, in purity and peace . . ."[2], and, ". . . that they [might] inioye [sic] *Christe* [sic] in his ordinances, without dis[turbance]."[3] These founders held a theory of government similar to that of their neighbors in the Massachusetts Bay and Plymouth Colonies: the prime reason for government was to protect and further the cause of true religion. The form of religion they considered to be true was that which would come to be known as Congregationalist.

These colonies were founded as sacred experiments, established to create utopian societies based upon Reformation principles and creeds. From their inception, therefore, a commingling of ecclesiastical and civil powers existed, along with a deep distrust of all that was contrary to the Standing Order—especially Catholicism.

New England: A Beacon of the Reformation

The unfriendly atmosphere toward Catholicism that existed in colonial Connecticut was not a singular creation of the English colonists. From the time of Henry VIII and his schism from the Roman Church, a ferocious and highly successful persecution of Catholicism was carried on throughout the English realm. It was only natural that the hatred and fear of all things Catholic, instilled in the hearts of the colonial founders prior to their departure from England, should be brought with them to the New World along with their other possessions.[4]

More than any other English possessions in North America, the New England colonies developed a theology and historical worldview that was thoroughly xenophobic. Works such as Edward Johnson's *Wonder—Working Providence of Sions Savior* published in 1654, Increase Mather's *Order of the Gospel* published in 1700, and Cotton Mather's *Magnalia Christi Americana* published in 1702 popularized the belief that the New England colonies were established by God as mankind's second chance to live the Gospel in a pure form, with no less a destiny than to become the beacon of the Reformation to the world. According to these colonial divines, the only form of religion and government acceptable to God was that of the Puritan fathers.

The laws of the colonies in Connecticut reflected this elitist view. They were designed as barriers to intruders and as supports for a system of government and religion intolerant of dissent.[5] The Puritan founders were thoroughly honest and straightforward regarding their intolerance of other religious groups. They believed that God had established their colonies as a holy experiment for His newly chosen people. Any who declined to support the civil or religious creeds of the colonies as established by God through His General Court,[6] could not be allowed to enjoy the rights and privileges of a citizen,[7] hold an elected post, or be allowed the ministrations of a clergyman.[8]

The Congregational Church alone was sanctioned by law in the early Connecticut colonies and remained the established state church in Connecticut until the ratification of the State Constitution in 1818. Throughout the colonial period, all inhabitants of the colony were bound by law to support financially the established church, regardless of the individual's faith. This support took the form of a universal, forced tax. Relief from this tax was granted to members of Protestant churches other than the Congregational during the early eighteenth century, but was not extended to Catholics until the 1818 Constitution.[9] Attendance at Congregationalist sabbath services of all inhabitants of the colonies was also mandated by law, except for those dissenting Protestant churches that were approved by the civil authorities.[10]

Few Catholics in Colonial Connecticut

Few Catholics existed in colonial Connecticut; fewer lived in Fairfield County prior to the American Revolution. In response to questions from the British Privy Council concerning trade and religion in the colony, the colonial governor replied that in 1680 the majority of men in the colony were Congregationalists and Presbyterians, with ". . . four or five Seven–day men, in our Colony, and about so many more Quakers." No other dissenters are mentioned.[11] In 1743, only one "Papist" was reported in Stratford.[12] Irish, French, Spanish, and Portuguese names are found in the colonial town records, newspaper advertisements, and tombstones, but no evidence that they were Catholics exists.

The largest group of Catholics to settle within Fairfield County during the colonial period was the Acadians from Nova Scotia, and they did so involuntarily. By the Treaty of Utrecht, France ceded Nova Scotia to England in 1713. As the fear of renewed hostilities between France and Britain grew during the century, British authorities expelled the French inhabitants from their land and transported them to British holdings, lest they become a threat to the British cause. In accord with this decision, 7,000 Catholic Acadians were forcibly transported from Nova Scotia and resettled within the British colonies to the south.

Connecticut had been prepared for the possible arrival of these "French Neutrals," as they were known, by the General Assembly in 1755. After destroying their homes and property, the British transported 400 Acadians by ship to Connecticut, landing them in New London in January and May 1756. By an act of the General Assembly, provisions were made for the distribution and care of these people throughout the colony. The Assembly instructed the selectmen of each town to treat the French Neutrals with all due consideration and to ". . . take care of, manage and support them as tho' they were inhabitants of such town, according to the laws of this Colony." They were not, however, to be regarded as guests—they were definitely prisoners. The instruction to the selectmen continues, that they were to ". . . prevent such French people making their escape out of this Colony."[13]

Sixty–eight Acadians were settled throughout Fairfield County in accord with the orders of the General Assembly.[14] The inhabitants of Newtown were very generous in their treatment of the Acadian family settled among them. In April, 1756, the town appropriated funds which were used to care for the French family settled there. A committee was instructed

> . . . to take a view and pitch upon a place to build a small house for the neutral French family among us, and to allow them as much land for the use of and benefit of a garden as they shall judge, the Town bearing the expense thereof.[15]

Even though bereft of the ministrations of any Catholic priests, the Acadians seem to have maintained their faith and practices while in Connecticut. The Church of England minister in Stratford, the Rev. Mr. Winslow, reported that there were few dissenters from the Standing Order in that town in the late eighteenth century,

> . . . except a few families of French Neutrals, of inconsiderable notice, who were in the beginning of the war dispersed from Nova Scotia, and remain inflexibily tenacious of their superstitions. But there is not the least danger of any influence from them. It is rather hopeful that if they are not themselves, their posterity may in time be brought off from their errors, though hitherto they will not suffer any efforts of this kind.[16]

A number of Irish had immigrated to the British colonies prior to the American Revolution.[17] Most came to the New World in one of two ways: as transported criminals, or as redemptioners—indentured servants who exchanged passage to the colonies for servitude, usually for a period of three years. Once arrived in Connecticut, they would be sold off to speculators who disposed of them throughout the colonies. An advertisement publicized the sale of such servants in Stamford in 1764:

> Just Imported from Dublin in the Brig Darby, A Parcel of Irish Servants, both men + women, + to be sold cheap by Israel Boardman, at Stamford.[18]

Some of these Irish must have been Catholic, but the total lack of documentation does not allow any certain estimates of their number to be made.[19]

Full Citizenship Denied Catholics in Connecticut

The fear that the colonial authorities in Connecticut held of pollution from contact with Catholicism or other churches considered to be unwholesome led to the formulation of protective laws and oaths whose ferocity far out-weighed the actual threat.[20] Public office and suffrage were limited to freedmen who were landowners. Since land could be owned only by members of the Established Church, Catholics were effectively barred from active influence in the colony's public and economic life. Oaths were required of all naturalized citizens and elected public servants prior to the assumption of their official responsibilities in order to prove the allegiance of officials to the English Crown and to the Established Church. The only recorded instance of a Catholic who actually took the oaths in Fairfield County was that of Dr. François Forgues of Fairfield in 1774. Whether Forgues ever had any allegiance to the Church is not known. Whatever his sentiments toward the Church may have been, they were not sufficiently favorable to prevent him from taking the form of the oaths published in Connecticut in 1766, clearly condemning the Church and its doctrines as unwholesome to colonial life.

François Forgues was born in Toulouse, France of Catholic parents on January 10, 1739, and baptized into their ancestral faith at the parish Church of St. Nicholas de Toulouse.[21] While serving his government as a surgeon in the French colonies during the French and Indian War, Forgue was taken prisoner by the British. Following the war he settled in the town of Fairfield, in the British colony of Connecticut where he eventually married Sarah Dennie–Thompson, the daughter of a prestigious local family. It may safely be assumed that the doctor had ceased practicing the Catholic faith while in the colonies, either due to the lack of any organized church life, or simply because of a lack of faith. In any event, he must have cut all allegiance to his family faith; he must even have denied his Catholic roots by the time of his marriage since it would seem highly unlikely that a prominent Yankee family such as the Thompsons would have consented to the marriage of their daughter to a papist.

A son, Francis,[22] was born of this union, and by the spring of 1774 Doctor Forgue petitioned the General Assembly that he might become a naturalized citizen and be

admitted to the privileges of His Majesty's subjects within the Colony, and that his son Francis Forgue jun[io]r, born in this Colony, may be capable of inheriting, and the real estate by him the said Francis the elder already purchased may be confirmed to him, notwithstanding his being born out of the allegiance of the King of Great Britain.[23]

Citizenship could be had only after the swearing of the prerequisite oaths of allegiance and supremacy of the King of England as well as the oath of abjuration of the Roman Catholic faith. The form of the oaths taken by the doctor was published in Connecticut in 1766. After swearing allegiance to the king and denying the doctrine falsely attributed to the Catholic Church by some Protestant reformers concerning the lawful murder of kings or rulers deposed or excommunicated by the pope, Doctor Forgue was obliged to deny the authority of the pope or any prelate over the English realm. He then continued,

I, Francis Forgue, do solemnly and sincerely in the presence of God profess, testifie [sic] and declare, that I do believe that in the sacrament of the Lord's Supper there is not any transubstantiation of the elements of bread and wine into the body and blood of Christ, at or after the consecration thereof [sic] by any person whatsoever; and that the invocation or adoration of the Virgin Mary or any other saint, and the sacrifice of the mass, as they are now used in the Church of Rome, are superstitious and idolatrous. And I do solemnly, in the presence of God, profess and testifie and declare, that I do make this declaration and every part thereof in the plain and ordinary sense of the words read unto me, as they are commonly understood by English Protestants, without any evasion, equivocation, or mental reservation whatsoever, and without any dispensation already granted me for this purpose by the Pope or any authority or person whatsoever, and without any hope of any such dispensation from any authority or person whatsoever, or without thinking that I am or can be acquitted before God or man, or absolved of this declaration or any part thereof, although the Pope or any other person or persons or power whatsoever should dispence [sic] with or annul the same, or declare that it was null and void from the beginning.[24]

If the abjuration of his parents' faith had any effect upon Doctor Forgue, it was never recorded. Toward the end of his life, however, he manifested a certain brand of indifferentism toward all religions, judging each to be of equal merit. Joking with friends he said that when a man died God would inquire as to his religious faith. God accordingly asked,

Job what are you? A strict Presbyterian.—Then go among the Presbyterians.—to another, what are you—an Episcopalian—then go among the Episcopalians.—finally—to Dr. Forgue, what are you—I am nothing—You go where you please.[25]

The doctor died in 1783 after a life of service to his adopted country during the Revolutionary War and to his community as a physician and public official. His remains were interred in the Old Burial Ground in Fairfield, with a simple stone which bore testimony to the fact that he had served his town well as a physician and citizen. The religious details on the stone were of common usage, referring to Forgue as having fallen asleep in Christ, along with a phrase relating the accepted belief in Christ and the afterlife: "To him to die was Gain to others Loss. This Life is Nought, Eternity is ALL." Nothing was said of his personal belief or religious life, if, indeed, such existed. The oaths that Forgue was required to swear exemplify the paraonia felt within the colony toward any form of religion that allowed prelates or popes to delimit the freedom of any individual or which might disturb the status quo. Regardless of the Doctor's ultimate religious convictions, he provides an example of how unwelcome and how restricted was the life of any Catholic within the colony at this time.

Warnings against Catholics from Pulpit, Press, and School

Although few in number, disenfranchised by law, lacking priests or churches, and scattered throughout the colony, Catholics and Catholicism continued to be the subject of strong hatred and vitriolic writings by Protestant divines prior to and following the American Revolution.

The sermons of the Puritan ministry provided the primary source of knowledge about Catholicism during the seventeenth and eighteenth centuries. Increase and Cotton Mather, Jonathan Edwards, Charles Chauncy, Jonathan Mayhew, and other Boston divines preached unceasingly about the dangers of the "Romish" Church. The Saybrook Platform of 1708, designed as a tool of reform for the Congregational Church within Connecticut, set the standards of ecclesiastical polity in the face of increasing pressure from members of dissenting Christian faiths for full participation in colonial life. In order to stem the threat to the Established Order, the Saybrook statement reaffirmed the religious principles of the founding Puritan fathers, decried popery and Catholic belief, and established Connecticut as a bastion of Puritan orthodoxy for the subsequent 150 years.

Various books were published concerning New England history as the final unfolding of the Reformation ideal. Numerous catechisms and school books taught the children of the colonies the basics of elementary education, while instilling in them a love for the Protestant ideal and a fear of Catholicism. One such lesson in the "New England Primer" relates John Rogers's imagined exhortation to his children. A martyr who died for his Protestant faith in England in 1554, Rogers instructs his children from the stake:

> Abhor that errant Whore of Rome [The Catholic Church], + all her Blasphemies; And drink not of her cursed Cup, obey not her decrees.[26]

Anti–Catholic sentiments also could be found in the halls of higher academe in Puritan New England. Harvard University received a bequest from the estate of Judge Paul Dudley in 1750 to underwrite a series of lectures. Every third lecture of the four–year cycle was, as his last will and testament directed,

> . . . to be for the detecting & convicting & exposing the Idolatry of the Romish Church, Their Tyranny, Usurpations, damnable Heresies, fatal Errors, abominable Superstitions, + other Wickednesses in their high Places; + Finally, that the Church of Rome—That Mystical Babylon, That Man of Sin, That Apostate Church spoken of, in the New Testament.[27]

The theory became quite well–developed, that to be foreign—anything other than of Puritan, or at least of Protestant Anglo-Saxon stock—was to be dangerous; to be Catholic was to be traitorous. America was to be a Protestant country, founded on Reformation principles and the political acumen of its Puritan fathers. This concept would continue to plague the growth of the Church throughout the nineteenth and twentieth centuries, not only in Connecticut, but throughout the entire country, as will be seen in the subsequent chapters. This anti-Catholic fear, so prevalent in pre–revolutionary America, dissipated only as the need for manpower grew and as alliances with Catholic nations formed when the colonies entered into their war of independence against Britain.

Catholics and the American Revolution

The pragmatic accommodation of the colonial government toward the Church is clearly seen in actions by the Continental Congress prior to the revolution. In June, 1774, the English government enacted the Quebec Act. Anxious lest the French Canadians support the revolutionary tendencies of the American colonists, the crown granted, among other things, the freedom and legal protection of the Catholic Church in Canada. The American colonists were aghast. In accord with the anti-Catholic sentiments of the colonists, the Continental Congress adopted the Suffolk Reserves on September 17, 1774, which condemned the Quebec Act as ". . . dangerous in an extreme degree to the Protestant religion and to the civil rights and liberties of All Americans."[28]

Alexander Hamilton, the American Revolutionary statesman, responded to the Quebec Act as did Congress:

> Roman Catholics, by the reason of implicit devotion to their priests and the superstitious reverence they bear those who countenance or favor their religion, will be the voluntary instruments of ambition and ready to second oppressive designs against other parts of the Empire.[29]

In October of that year, Congress addressed letters of protest to King George III and to the British people, expressing their revulsion that Parliament could see fit to establish by law, . . . a religion fraught with sanguinary and impious tenets; . . . which deluged your island in blood, and disbursed impiety, bigotry, persecution, murder, and rebellion through every part of the world.[30]

Ironically, five days later, in an effort to secure the assistance of the Canadians in their enterprise of revolution, the Continental Congress penned an "Address to the Inhabitants of Quebec," stating that differences of religion should not be allowed to bar mutual cooperation in a common cause of liberty. Congress tempted the Canadians with the promise of religious liberty for their Catholic faith in return for their support against England. The infuriated Canadians did not respond.[31]

The Rev. Daniel Barber of Simsbury later recalled the sentiments of many in Connecticut and the other colonies following the Quebec Act. In *The History of My Own Times*, Barber recalls that most felt the King to be a traitor who

> . . . had broken his coronation oath; was secretly a Papist; and whose design it was to oblige this country to submit itself to the unconstitutional powers of the English monarch, and . . . be given up and destroyed, body and soul, by that frightful image with seven heads and ten horns [the Catholic Church]. The real fears of Popery, in New England, had its influence; it stimulated many timorous pious people to send their sons to join the military ranks in the field, and jeopardize their lives in the bloody contest. The common word then was, 'No King, no Popery.'[32]

The fear that Catholics were traitors to the American cause was commonly held. Thomas Paine vented his anger, stating that Parliament had subverted the Protestant religion in the colonies by establishing the Catholic Church in Canada. He wrote,

Admit that Ministry by the power of Britain and the aid of our Roman Catholic neighbors. . . . The wealth, and we may add the men, particularly of the Roman Catholics, will then be in the power of your enemies.[33]

The success of the revolutionary venture depended very much upon the unity of the colonial forces and the alliances with the Catholic powers.

George Washington understood this when he addressed his troops at Cambridge, Massachusetts, in November, 1775. In anticipation of the fifth of November, Guy Fawkes Day, when an effigy of the pope and the devil were traditionally burned both in England and in the colonies, the General rebuked the American soldiers for their mockery of the religion held by those countries whose assistance was essential to the revolutionary cause.[34]

France had supplied the Americans with funds and war materiel for nearly two years prior to its official entry into the war as a colonial ally in 1778; Spain followed the next year but as an ally of France, not of the colonies.[35] Strengthened by the French alliance, the American forces united themselves, paying little heed to religious differences when faced with a common foe. Daniel Barber wrote of the common cause which led Catholic and Protestant to fight side by side,

. . . though stimulated by extremely different motives: the one acting through fear, lest the King of England should succeed in establishing among us the Catholic religion; the other equally fearful, lest his [the King's] bitterness against the Catholic faith should increase till they were either destroyed, or driven to the mountains and waste places of the wilderness.[36]

Catholics played a generous part in the revolutionary struggle, especially once much of the anti–Catholic bias was softened because of the alliance and the presence of foreign Catholic troops in the colonies.[37] Under the command of the Count de Rochambeau, the French forces passed through Fairfield County, camping at Ridgefield and Newtown during late June, 1781.[38] Their presence, along with that of numerous Irish Catholic troops, displayed a discipline and dedication to the revolution which effectively weakened the belief that Catholics could not be faithful to American ideals.

In order to impress this upon the mind of the newly elected first president of the American Republic, Bishop-elect John Carroll and representatives of the Catholic laity addressed a letter to General Washington following his election in 1789. They wrote that equal rights were due to American Catholics as the price owed, ". . . the blood spilt under your eyes, and for our common exertions for . . . defence, under your auspicious conduct—rights rendered more dear to us by the remembrance of the former hardships."[39] The president replied on March 12, 1790:

As mankind become [sic] more liberal they will be more apt to allow, that all those who conduct themselves as worthy members of the community are equally entitled to the protection of civil Government. I hope ever to see America among the foremost nations in examples of justice and liberality. And I presume that your fellowcitzens [sic] will not forget the patriotic part which you took in the accomplishment of their Revolution, and the establishment of their Government; or the important assistance which they received from a nation in which the Roman Catholic faith is professed. . . . may the members of your society [the Catholic Church] in America, animated alone by the pure spirit of Christianity, and still conducting themselves as the faithful subjects of our free Government, enjoy every temporal and spiritual felicity.[40]

Limited Freedom for Catholics in Post–Revolutionary Connecticut

The prevailing political wind in America following the Revolution favored religious toleration and the separation of church and state. This was embodied in the first amendment to the Constitution of 1787 in its proscription of an established religion. Nonetheless, established churches remained in seven of the original states for years, while Catholics were granted the full rights of citizenship in only five states.

The Standing Order in Connecticut had no intention of changing its religious policies following the Revolution. The war, however, had dislodged more than political theories and governmental institutions. It had raised the cry for freedom of conscience in matters religious, while declaring the sole means of such freedom to be the disestablishment of religious creeds and churches. Men like John Locke, Thomas Paine, and Ethan Allen called for such a religious revolution, that would free man's conscience in accord with his natural rights.

Echoing the radical Protestant concept of religion as merely a personal relationship between the individual and his god, they insisted that the law held no sway in the realm of religion and conscience.

The rigors of Calvinist theology and morality held by the Standing Order were no longer acceptable to many in Connecticut. After exposure to the concepts of popular sovereignty, deism, and freedom of conscience popularized during the American and French Revolutions, religious dissenters from the Standing Order began to unite within Connecticut. They called for religious toleration and full rights for all, based upon the acceptance of republican ideals rather than religious creeds, and for the disestablishment of the Congregational Church by the state.

Connecticut passed acts of toleration in 1784 and 1791. The former granted Protestant dissenters immunity from the obligatory tax for the support of the Congregationalist clergy if they could provide a document proving membership in a regular religious society recognized by law. The 1791 act extended this privilege to all Christians within the state if they could present such a document of church attendance to the clerk of the local Congregational church.[41]

Not all agreed that such toleration and easing of the Standing Order was wise. In "The Duty of Americans in the Present Crisis," delivered on July 4, 1798, the Rev. Timothy Dwight, President of Yale, reminded the Connecticut citizenry of their Puritan roots, and of their obligation to do battle against untruth in order to preserve the republic, which was the creation of their Puritan forefathers.

Aware of the influence of deism within Connecticut, popularized by such works as Ethan Allen's "Oracles of Reason" in 1784, and Thomas Paine's "The Age of Reason" in 1794, Dwight lashed out against the infidelity of the present age, so eager to accept new ideas. Americans should not forget their Protestant roots and obligations, lest the strength and success of the Revolution falter and prove fruitless. If Americans failed in their vigilance, foreign untruths would infect American ideals. The most perfidious of untruths—both political and religious—were those held by the Church of Rome. Dwight stated:

> Three unclean spirits, like frogs, are exhibited as proceeding out of the mouth of the Dragon or Devil, of the Beast or Romish Government, and of the False Prophet, or, as I apprehend, of the regular Clergy of that Hierarchy.

wealth, and industry of these larger, colonial towns were Yankee, while the general atmosphere and social life were rural, protective, and wary of all that was foreign. With the heavy migration of American–born sons from the state, those towns whose economies were based upon mills or factories were loathe to give the few available jobs to immigrants, most of whom were Irish Catholics.[10] The general atmosphere of the larger towns was unfriendly to most foreigners and often overtly hostile to Catholics.

Bridgeport and Norwalk were exceptional in their treatment of these early Irish immigrants. Bridgeport, a relatively new town, was, for the most part, free from much of the Yankee prejudice and fear of innovation that marked life in the major towns of colonial origin within the county. Norwalk had always tended to be a community willing to accept change and outsiders, unlike many of the neighboring towns. During the 1830's and 1840's, a number of new factories requiring both skilled and unskilled laborers were opening in Bridgeport and Norwalk, as seen in the employment notices in the *Republican Farmer* and the *Norwalk Gazette* of the period. Economic opportunity, combined with a citizenry eager to promote economic growth and tolerant of foreigners, attracted these early Irish Catholics to settle in Bridgeport and Norwalk.

Plans for the construction of a church in Bridgeport began in earnest with the purchase of land by the town's Catholics in 1836. When this site proved to be unacceptable to Bishop Fenwick during his visit to the city on June 7, 1837, a second parcel of land was procured on the corner of Arch Street and Washington Avenue. Construction of St. James Church was begun in August, 1841 by the Catholic community of 250 persons. Having received the financial and moral support of the larger Protestant community of Bridgeport,[11] St. James was dedicated as the first Catholic church in Fairfield County, and the first brick church in the state, on July 24, 1842 by Bishop Fenwick.[12] The bishop recorded the event as follows:

Said early mass in the Parlour of Mr. Moran's house. All the family assisted consisting of his Brother & wife & his own wife with several neighbors. After breakfast repaired to the church. Rev's Mess'rs Smyth had already celebrated Mass in it. At ten OC'[loc]k proceeded to the blessing as prescribed by the Ritual, assisted by Rev'd Mess'rs Smyth & Brady. Dedicated it to God under the patronage of St. James, Apostle. After the dedication Rev'd Mr. John Brady sang High Mass assisted by the choir of New Haven. At the Gospel Rev. Mr. John Smyth preached a very good discourse appropriate to the occasion. The Church in

3

Bridgeport is a snug handsome Brick Building about 60 feet in length & 40 in width, finished off in a very pretty style with a spacious gallery for the Choir & a convenient sacristy in addition to the length. It Stands on elevated ground & overlooks the City of Bridgeport. It is built in the Gothick [sic] style. Its present debt is about 1500 Doll[ars] which in a year or two can be easily liquidated.[13]

Catholic Immigration Increases

The development of manufacturing and of railroads during the 1840's and 1850's brought many new immigrants to Connecticut. The need for laborers in the newly opened mills was so great in areas during the 1840's that long black wagons called "slavers" were sent to the area farms in search of workers.[14]

Between 1840 and 1850, the population of Fairfield County had risen by nearly 10,000 persons, from 49,917 to 59,775, of which more than half (5,499) were of foreign birth, the vast majority coming from Ireland, along with increasing numbers of French–Canadians and Germans. Bridgeport exemplified both the growth and predominance of the Irish in the county. Its population had grown from 3,294 in 1840 to 7,560 in 1850, with one out of every seven of its inhabitants an Irishman.[15]

Faced with such an unexpected hoard of immigrants, the Church authorities in Connecticut, as elsewhere in the United States, found themselves with enormous practical problems. The first Bishop of Hartford, William Tyler, expressed this to the authorities of the Society for the Propagation of the Faith at Paris when he wrote,

The Catholics are without exception, Irish who have been driven out of their country by poverty. A great number arrive every year. They readily undertake the hardest labour to make a living, and readily contribute to support the priests who serve them. But they are poor and need help to build churches, school-houses and to establish religious institutions.[16]

The Catholic communities of Norwalk, Stamford, and Danbury were in need of such assistance by the late 1840's. As their numbers increased, they felt the need for a religious life more regularized than was provided by the infrequent visitations of the Rev. Michael Lynch of Bridgeport, whose far-flung mission included all of Fairfield County and part of Litchfield County. Norwalk's Catholics numbered 75 by 1844; Danbury's 60 or 70 by 1849; and Stamford's between 15 and 25 by 1846.

4

Fearful lest such odious false doctrines of Europe infect and weaken the infant American Republic, Dwight instructed the heirs of the Puritan founding fathers that God's will in America could be accomplished if its citizenry performed four duties. The first was to keep holy the Sabbath; he informed his listeners that the Protestant religion and liberty were the ". . . meat and drink of the body politic. . . ." The second, was a separation from the enemy, lest the chosen be defiled. This was a natural result of mankind's highest moral duty, which was political, urging all citizens to the third duty, unity. The final duty was ". . . unshaken firmness in our opposition."

All were to fight for the lives and liberty of their wives and children, and to preserve the faith of their Protestant fathers, upon whose Reformation ideals and political acumen God had established America. The faithful American was to continue defending God's nation, ". . . that our children may inherit these glorious blessings, be rescued from the grinding insolence of foreign despotism, and saved from the corruption and perdition of foreign atheism."[42]

Such pleas against religious toleration were not strong enough to withstand the dissatisfaction of many Protestant dissenters within Connecticut, who banded together to form the Democratic–Republican party. By 1816 this new party supported a platform of reform and disestablishment of the Congregational Church within the state, and succeeded in electing Oliver Wolcott to the governorship the following year on the American Toleration and Reform Ticket.[43]

In May, 1818, a resolution was passed by the General Assembly calling for the framing of a new state constitution to replace the royal charter of 1662. The Connecticut Constitution of 1818 disestablished the Congregational Church as the state church within Connecticut and granted religious liberty and full rights of citizenship, at least to its Christian inhabitants, regardless of creed. With the attainment of religious liberty and full civil rights, the possibility of developing normal church life and religious practice was at last open to Catholics within the state.

The Church Organizes in New England

The Rev. John Carroll, who had served as the head of the Catholic missions in the United States since 1784, was consecrated the first Bishop of Baltimore in August, 1790. To him fell the task of organizing the Church considered by many an

American to be controlled by foreign powers hostile to republican ideals. Bishop Carroll recognized the impossibility of administering a diocese stretching the length of the new republic. Hampered by the scattered settling of Catholics and by a lack of priests, Bishop Carroll requested that the Holy See divide the Diocese of Baltimore. In 1808, Baltimore was raised to the dignity of an archdiocese, and the Dioceses of Bardstown, Philadelphia, New York, and Boston were created.

Following their consecration in Baltimore in the Fall of 1810, the Bishops of the new dioceses met with Archbishop Carroll and his coadjutor, Bishop Neale, to determine a concerted program of action, to normalize and unify Catholic discipline and practice within the United States. The result of their two–week consultation was the issuance of the two series of resolutions which were made binding throughout the province.

Bishop Jean Louis Lefebvre de Cheverus carried these resolutions back to his newly erected Diocese of Boston, which encompassed all of New England. Cheverus had arrived in Boston in 1796 in order to work among the city's Catholics along with the Rev. Francis Matignon. Both men had been assigned to Boston by Bishop John Carroll to heal a conflict which had arisen between the Irish and French Catholics, and to strengthen the faith of the small Catholic colony against the hostilities of the Puritan Bostonians. From this period of the assignment of these two missionary priests dates the beginning of the permanent establishment of the Catholic Church in New England.

The Catholic population of Bishop Cheverus's diocese was very small. By 1814 there were approximately 2,000 Catholics in all of New England.[44] Since the majority of these Catholics, along with the clergy, were either French or Irish immigrants, the Church took on a decidedly foreign appearance, raising suspicions among Protestant New Englanders. The improvement of relations between Protestants and Catholics, along with their missionary efforts among the various Indian tribes, proved to be the most memorable works of Bishop Cheverus and Father Matignon. The beginning of organized church life in Connecticut would come only through the efforts of Bishop Cheverus's successor, the Jesuit, Bishop Benedict Fenwick.

Benedict Fenwick was a native son, born in Maryland in 1782. He received his education in Georgetown College and at St. Mary's Seminary in Baltimore, entered the Jesuit novitiate at Georgetown, and was ordained a priest in 1808. After working in various parts of the country, Father Fenwick arrived in Boston as its second bishop in December, 1825.

New England still presented little prospect for a flourishing church life. Archbishop Carroll and other bishops felt that the Dioceses of Boston and New York should be united, since the cities were so close and the Catholic population of New England so small, which, as one bishop wrote to Rome,

> . . . would render the position of the Bishop of Boston hardly dissimilar from that of a parish priest; a situation truly discouraging for a prelate of an active mind, and little honorable to the Episcopacy.[45]

Upon his arrival in Boston, Bishop Fenwick found his extensive diocese to be staffed by 3 priests, serving 10,000 Catholics in only 9 ramshackle churches. He worked strenuously to attract vocations to the priesthood and to secure the ministrations of foreign clergy to work with the growing number of immigrants then settling in New England.

The Church Grows in Connecticut

Connecticut during the early nineteenth century was beginning to change from an agricultural to a manufacturing and industrialized state. Many of the native Yankees were moving away from the poor farm land to the newer territories of the west. Attracted by the early canal and railroad projects of the 1820's and 1830's, by mining and quarry work, and by an increasing demand for domestics, Irish immigrants, many of them Catholic, began to arrive in the state in greater numbers. Since these employment opportunities were scattered throughout the state, the immigrant communities supported by them were also scattered and isolated one from another, thus complicating any effort by the Church on their behalf.

The largest community of Catholics in Connecticut during the late 1820's was to be found in Hartford. The exact number of Catholics then in the city is unknown, but by 1831 there were 120 communicants.[46] It was here that Bishop Fenwick established the first Catholic church in Connecticut: Holy Trinity, appointing its first resident rector on August 26, 1829, the Rev. Bernard O'Cavanagh, with jurisdiction over all Catholics within the state. Father O'Cavanagh's appointment marks the beginning of the Church's organization in Connecticut; Hartford was the center from which all early missionary efforts within the state would proceed.

Catholics in Fairfield County

The number of Catholics within Fairfield County was also beginning to grow as a result of immigration. Based in New Haven, where the second Catholic church in the state was established in 1832, the Rev. James McDermott visited the small Catholic communities scattered throughout Connecticut. By 1835 he estimated that of a total population of 220,955 in the state, 720 were Catholics. Within Fairfield County, Father McDermott counted 125 Catholics residing in Bridgeport and Norwalk—the towns that would become the missionary bases of the Church's endeavors within the county.[47]

Since Bridgeport was the home to the larger Catholic community, with approximately 100 adults by 1836, it was decided that that town should be the site of the first Catholic church in the county. Land was purchased in that year; the church was erected in 1841, by which time the Catholic population had increased to approximately 250 persons. On July 24, 1842, a small brick Gothic church on the corner of Washington Avenue and Arch Street was dedicated by Bishop Fenwick, under the patronage of St. James the Apostle, as the first Catholic church in Fairfield County. The founding of the church of St. James in Bridgeport and the presence of the Rev. Michael Lynch as the first resident rector, provided the Catholic residents of Fairfield County with at least the benefits of periodic priestly ministrations throughout the year.

By 1842 the rector of Bridgeport had responsibility for the spiritual well–being of the small Catholic communities of Derby and Norwalk in addition to Bridgeport.[48] The needs of the Catholics in other towns, such as Stamford and Greenwich, were also met by the rector of Bridgeport and by Jesuit priests of Fordham College.

Conclusion

As the number of Catholics in Connecticut increased, the ineffectiveness of his distant administration became more and more obvious to Bishop Fenwick in Boston. Convinced of the importance of the division of his large diocese, Fenwick petitioned the fathers of the Fifth Provincial Council of Baltimore in 1843 to erect a new diocese within New England.[49] Rome approved the recommendation of the council and erected the Diocese of Hartford on November 28, 1843 with responsibility for the Catholics residing within the States of Rhode Island

and Connecticut, under the guidance of its first Bishop, William Tyler.

Following the division of his diocese, Bishop Fenwick wrote to the Society for the Propagation of the Faith in Paris, thanking them for their continued financial support which had greatly assisted the Church in New England during his incumbency. He wrote that it was their generosity,

> . . . which has furnished the means of carrying on the work with so surprising a rapidity that a New Diocese even has emerged in the midst of this Wilderness, & Catholic Churches are now scattered where, a few years back, Catholics had not dared to show their faces.[50]

With the division of Boston, the development of the Church in Connecticut could begin in earnest. When appointed to Hartford, Bishop Tyler could count a total of 4,817 Catholics, 3 priests, and 4 churches in Connecticut. Within a short time the number of his faithful would increase rapidly, primarily as a result of immigration, taxing the bishops's slim resources and calling for increased churches, priests, religious, and schools.

CHAPTER I

AN IMMIGRANT CHURCH:
IRISH CATHOLIC FOUNDATIONS
(1842–1872)

> The New Englander has a character, many of the features of which I admire; and dare I venture upon a prophetic calculation I would say, that the land of steady habits will, before the lapse of half a century, be a land in which the Catholic Church will extensively flourish.[1]

As reflected in the prediction of John England, the Bishop of Charleston, South Carolina, New England was thought to offer splendid prospects for the rapid development of the Church during the nineteenth century. While the Church's growth was expected, the rapidity of that growth due to immigration astounded Church authorities. The Roman Catholic Church received more of these immigrants than did any other religious denomination in the United States. During the period from 1830 until 1920, prior to the restrictive immigration laws, the United States received an estimated 20,119,443 immigrants. Of this number, approximately 9,318,494 professed to be Catholic.[2] Connecticut received its share of the immigrant population, but not until the 1840's when the state entered into a new period of economic development.[3] The state's economy, following the revolution, remained an agricultural one.[4] Possessing neither abundant natural resources nor adequate power sources for industry, manufacturing enterprises were limited to the production of goods requiring imported materials and little power.[5] As a result, Connecticut provided little appeal early in the century to either immigrant or native son.

The early years of the Church in Connecticut were years dedicated to the establishment of the foundations for normative Catholic life and to the defense of its predominantly Irish constituency against anti–Catholic rhetoric. Hartford's second bishop, Bernard O'Reilly, pinpointed how such a life could be established, and supplied a succinct outline for the work

1

of his administration and those of his successors through the 1860's:

> We can do little without sufficient number of priests, and we cannot save the children, without a Catholic education. All the influences which are here are against our religion's [influences], and . . . it is only by great zeal, purely Catholic education and sufficient number of priests, that we can save our own and make progress against heresy.[6]

Though the pastoral program of the early bishops of Hartford was limited by the Church's slim financial resources and inadequate number of priests, the establishment of normative Catholic life included the founding of missions and the construction of churches, regular sacramental practice, preaching, and religious education of the young.

Cradles of Catholicism in Fairfield County: Bridgeport and Norwalk

Attracted to the state by work on canals, quarries and early manufacturing, small groups of Irish Catholics began to settle within the larger towns during the late 1820's. Bridgeport and Norwalk, located on Long Island Sound and close to New York City, offered economic opportunities in trading and manufacturing, and became the two centers from which Catholic life would develop within Fairfield County.

By 1830 Bridgeport counted 17 Catholics, who gathered in the house of James McCullough, on Milne Street, to celebrate Mass with the Rev. James Fitton during one of his missionary visits through the state.[7] Norwalk's first Catholic resident was Michael Cooney, a hat dyer, who arrived in Norwalk with his family in 1828. William Donahoe, a chandler, arrived the following year with his family of six persons. Clement Burns, a potter, arrived shortly after, as did the families of Farrell Gillooly, Paul Bresnan, James Conners, John Conners, Edward Conners, and the Brennans. In 1833, with a congregation of about 25 Catholics, the Rev. James McDermott celebrated the first Mass in Norwalk at the Cooney home on Water Street.[8]

These towns were neither the largest nor the most prosperous within the county in 1830. Bridgeport, which was not then an incorporated city, claimed only 2,803 inhabitants, while Norwalk, 3,790. The largest towns in the county were Fairfield, the center of county government since colonial times and a very wealthy town with 4,246 inhabitants; and Danbury with 4,331, sustained by a thriving hat industry.[9] But the citizenry,

These scattered Catholics willingly sacrificed in order to enjoy the benefits of their religion. The Catholics of Bethel, for instance, often walked over 20 miles to Stamford with the visiting priest in order to hear Mass. The growing Catholic community in Norwalk walked over 14 miles to Bridgeport each Sunday. They would walk as far as Jarvis Hill,

> . . . and there, quietly removing the shoes from their feet, trudged zealously on as far east as the old Fairfield and Bridgeport division line, where, before entering the house of God [old St. James Church], they would replace their shoes, and dust their travel-soiled wardrobe, so that no disrespect should be done the sacred place from whence, after their morning sacrifice . . . they would turn their faces toward their fourteen miles westward home.[17]

Norwalk's Catholic community petitioned Bishop Tyler in 1848 for a resident priest. Impressed by their petition and by the representation of the interests of the Norwalk community by Paul Bresnan, John Hanlon, John Foley, Terrence Reynolds and Farrell Gillooly, Bishop Tyler visited Norwalk to assess the needs of the Catholics there, celebrating Mass for them in the Town House. As a result of this visit, and because of the splendid prospects for growth of the Church in the town, the Rev. John Brady was charged with the spiritual care of the Catholics of Norwalk, along with those in Danbury, Stamford, and neighboring towns the following year, becoming the second resident priest in the county.

A site on Chapel Street was secured by Terrence Reynolds that year, and a committee was established for the solicitation of funds for church construction from non–Catholic members of the community. Heading the committee was Paul Bresnan, who decided that the success of the fund–raising would be assured only if the assistance were secured of the Rev. Dr. William Cooper Mead, Rector of St. Paul's Episcopal Church on the Norwalk Green. The Episcopal minister knew Bresnan, and, as the historian of Norwalk relates, asked Paul Bresnan,

> '. . . how is it you come to me first? Why not go to the Congregational minister, Dr. Hall?' Paul, who was always ready promptly replied, 'Well, Doctor, we know you to be an off–shoot of the parent stock.'[18]

Both the Revs. Mead and Hall headed the list, and the Protestant majority of Norwalk followed their lead generously.

A small wooden clapboard church, with Gothic finials, and steeple, was dedicated in Norwalk under the patronage of Mary the Mother of God on January 28, 1851 by Bishop Bernard O'Reilly.[19] The bishop had dedicated a small Gothic clapboard chapel in Stamford two days earlier to serve the Catholic community there that was subject to the canonical mission in Norwalk and its rector until 1854.[20]

Nativist Fears in Connecticut

The rapid growth of the foreign and Catholic population in the country did not go unnoticed by the American–born population. Fearful of the Church's growth in America, the alarm was sounded by the Protestant clergy and press warning of the insidious influence of Catholicism upon American liberty and institutions. When the English government granted full rights to English Catholics in 1829, many in America expressed fears concerning the growth of the Church in Protestant countries. When the American bishops met in the same year in Baltimore to evaluate the Church's growth over the previous fifty years and chart a course for her continued development in the United States, America's native sons cried out in horror.

Connecticut residents became especially alarmed when the Catholic Bishop of Boston not only established a Catholic church in Hartford with a resident priest but also began the state's first Sunday school and Catholic newspaper.[21] Catholic literature began to appear in the state, producing converts from Protestantism and exercising a positive influence upon many American–born residents concerning the Church. One such apologetical work appeared in Hartford in 1831, entitled, "A Brief Sketch of the True Religion." The author, Thomas Brigden, was a recent convert to Catholicism from the Presbyterian Church, and addressed a series of letters to his readership explaining his conversion and the truth of the Catholic Church.

Bridgen told his readers that a choice had to be made by those in America between Catholicism and Protestantism, since a plurality of religions could never be pleasing to Christ. The basic question was,

> . . . which of the two should surrender? The Children [Protestantism] to the Parent [Catholicism]? Modern to Ancient, or Ancient to Modern? Man to God, or God to Man? Your reply to these interrogatories will, I think, amply decide the important question. It now remains for us individually to decide for ourselves, which we are in reason and conscience bound to prefer.[22]

The number of converts to Catholicism was increasing within Connecticut as the Church began its advance within the state.

The conversion of members of the Barber family, many of whom were Protestant clergymen, raised more than eyebrows within Connecticut Yankee circles. Jerusha Booth–Barber of Newtown converted along with her husband and children, all of whom later entered religious life to the consternation of many. Newtown was also the home of Mrs. Joseph Nichols who not only converted to the Church but also offered her substantial estate in Newtown to Bishop Fenwick of Boston in 1830.[23] Conversions to Catholicism of such prominent members of Yankee society did not go unnoticed by the Protestant majority.

The various Protestant churches united throughout the country in order to stop the spread of Catholicism in America.[24] Spurred on by a flood of anti–Catholic literature and sermons by leading Protestant clergymen, Americans came to believe that the immigrants were the Church's advance guard. Choreographed by the Jesuits, led by the Church's hierarchy, funded by Europe's Catholic princes, the ever-rising flood of Catholic immigrants would soon destroy all that was American, all that was free, leaving the republic prey to the alleged depravities of Catholicism.

On the evening of August 11, 1834, a well–organized group of Americans burned down the Ursuline Convent and school in Charlestown, Massachusetts. Alarmed by a series of anti-Catholic sermons, these native citizens were led to strike out against the Church and to root out the Catholic evil from their midst. The event shocked the entire nation, but the remorse and lament were shortlived, as the anti–Catholic press continued in its vocal crusade to save America. Two of Connecticut's native sons wielded considerable influence in the anti–Catholic crusade: the Rev. Lyman Beecher, and the Rev. Horace Bushnell.[25]

Beecher, whose preaching in Boston precipitated the arson in Charlestown, responded to the burning of the Ursuline convent with a tract entitled, "Plea for the West." After reaffirming his belief that America was the chosen instrument of God for the salvation and liberation of the world, he observed that the center of God's salvific work was to be the American West. It was there that the Catholic princes and the pope had fixed their gaze, sending the immigrant poor as the first wave of an army bent upon the conquering of the Mississippi Valley. Beecher warned,

But if, upon examination, it should appear that three–fourths of the foreign emigrants [sic] whose accumulating tide is rolling in upon us,

7

are, through the medium of their religion and priesthood, as entirely accessible to the control of the potentates of Europe as if they were an army of soldiers, enlisted and officered, and spreading over the land; then, indeed, should we have just occasion to apprehend danger to our liberties. . . . A tenth part of the suffrage of the nation, thus condensed and wielded by the Catholic powers of Europe, might decide our elections, perplex our policy, inflame and divide our nation, break the bond of our union, and throw down our free institutions.[26]

The Rev. Horace Bushnell repeated the anti-Catholic sentiments of his colleague from New Haven in his numerous writings. In 1835, he published "Crisis in the Church." This tract opens with the praises of the American Republic, not only as the home of true liberty but also as the stage upon which Protestant truth would do battle with the evils of Catholicism—the new triumphing over the old. The glories of Protestant truth, according to Bushnell, are manifest in the glories of the republic, since, ". . . we [American Protestants] represent Christianity and the Protestant faith; we are also the depositaries [sic] . . . of that light which is to illuminate the world." However, he continued, the forces of evil were mustering at the borders of the great Protestant experiment in liberty which was America, taking the three–fold form of slavery, infidelity and romanism.

Bushnell repeated the already popularized belief that the immigrants were the unwitting advance forces of the Vatican. He added a new twist, however, to the charge that the Church was allied to European absolutist monarchies of the time. He singled out one of the Catholic organizations which supported the Church's missionary efforts in America—the St. Leopold Society—as

. . . the society, which is flooding our country with Jesuits, erecting nunneries and establishing schools in all the western valley.

Bushnell unmasked what he considered the duplicitous actions of the Church as having been designed, not for the salvation of the American people, as might appear, but for the destruction of liberty and the enslavement of the nation:

They [the Catholic hierarchy] flatter the people to believe that their religion is greatly changed. It has no longer any spirit of persecution; it does not even forgive sins, but only prays for their forgiveness; nay, if you will trust the priests, it is the most eminently democratic religion in the world! It draws in parents by means of their children, and children it allures by gratuitous education; for the church is also patroness of knowledge as well as of democracy! In the mean time, Catholic emigrants are pouring into the country, in a manner altogether unexampled.

8

Every one of them and their descendants are meant to be our enemies, and most of them probably will be.[27]

Such inflammatory writings[28] invariably led to less academic conflicts between Catholic immigrants and Protestant native sons. Anti–Catholic agitation in Philadelphia and New York held the public's attention during the summer of 1844, when Orange–Catholic riots left Irish Catholics dead and injured and Church property destroyed in Philadelphia. New York Catholics received less severe treatment only as a result of the orders of Archbishop John Hughes that his Irish–Catholic congregations protect their churches against nativist attack with canon and armed guards.

As the Irish Great Famine (1845–1852) began forcing more and more starving Irish to American shores, Bushnell continued his vitriolic anti-Catholic writings.[29] In his most famous anti–Catholic tract, "Barbarism the First Danger," published in 1847, the great Connecticut divine put forth his most eloquent appeal to the American public. America must awaken and respond to this threat by improving the education of those immigrants settling in the American West. The immigrants must be properly educated, Bushnell continued, in order that they might be properly formed as Americans, faithful to true religion. It was America's duty to rescue the immigrants from their past, their ignorance and superstition—in short, their barbarism, which, as he stated, was the perfect medium for the development of Catholicism. He warned his readers, ". . .OUR FIRST DANGER IS BARBARISM—Romanism next."[30]

Such writings, so odd–sounding today, were accepted during the last century as gospel truth. Since communication was difficult between different areas of the country, or even between various towns within the same state, the testimony of prestigious public and religious leaders was accepted readily by the Yankee citizenry. They could see for themselves the increasing immigrant population, and the rise of the Catholic Church within their own neighborhoods, and were often very willing to accept the interpretation of events given them by vocal Protestant clergymen: America was threatened by all that was foreign— by the immigrant who took their jobs and threatened America's economy, and by the Roman Church, which had designs on America's liberty.

The rapid and seemingly ubiquitous growth of the Catholic Church within the county led to a certain uneasiness at the beginning of the 1850's, and some isolated attacks upon the

9

Church as a foreign intrusion. A group of unsympathetic citizens disturbed Catholics worshipping in the old court house in Danbury in 1851, and made the purchase of property in the town by the Catholic bishop impossible. The situation necessitated the purchase of the property by three Protestant bankers, sympathetic to the Church, who later transferred it to the Catholic bishop.[31] St. Mary's Church in Norwalk was set on fire and the gilded cross atop its roof pulled down by unfriendly citizens in September, 1854.[32]

Despite these instances, the majority of the Catholic population continued to exist without much interference or molestation, other than a few unfriendly articles in local newspapers.

The Church Grows with Immigrant Arrivals: 1850–1860

The decade 1850–1860 was an extremely important one for Connecticut, both socially and economically: socially, because the once homogeneous Yankee society ceased to exist as a result of immigration; economically, because of the displacement by industry of agriculture as the basis of the state's economy. In 1850, the total foreign population in the state was 38,374. By 1860, it had increased to 80,696 in a total state population of 460,147.[33] During this decade, the majority of the state's native–born population remained in the rural areas, while the majority of the immigrants gravitated to the cities that offered job opportunities in the developing industries. The largest immigrant group within the state by 1860 was still the Irish, with a total of 55,445 persons. English immigrants followed with a total of 8,875, while the Germans held third place with 8,353.[34] Fairfield County recorded an increase in population of 17,700 persons during the decade, third highest in the state after New Haven and Hartford Counties, with Bridgeport as the largest city in the county.[35]

Since most of these immigrants were Catholic, it was in the larger cities of Bridgeport, Norwalk, Danbury, and Stamford that the Church established its original missions.[36] The resident rectors of these city missions were given the care of the Catholics within their city and in the surrounding towns and villages. A rudimentary form of church organization was established by Hartford's second bishop in 1854. Bishop Bernard O'Reilly divided Fairfield County into four districts, each centered on the Catholic church within one of the four major cities of the county: Bridgeport's St. James Church, Norwalk's St. Mary Church, Danbury's St. Peter, and Stamford's St. John Church.

The bishop's resources and manpower were slim, a fact that limited the effectiveness of the Church's ministry within Rhode Island and Connecticut in these early years.[37] As the number of Catholics rapidly increased during the decade, two more missions were established: Bridgeport's St. Mary Church was founded in 1857, and Newtown's St. Rose of Lima in 1859.

Despite their poverty, these early Irish immigrant Catholics succeeded in building eight chapels by the end of the decade—one in each of the five major towns and three smaller chapels: one in Fairfield—St. Thomas (1853); in Greenwich—St. Mary (1859); and in Westport—Our Lady of the Assumption (1860).[38] These were dependent upon the rectors of the five missions in the larger towns of the county.[39] Other towns within the county had Catholic communities that also were visited by these priests, but still lacked church buildings by 1860. These towns were visited periodically by the rectors of the larger missions for the celebration of Mass and catechetical instructions. As the number of resident priests and churches increased, the need for Catholic education for Catholic children was recognized as essential to normative Catholic life.

Catholic Schools in Connecticut

Bishop O'Reilly had regularly listed Catholic education as essential to Catholic life within his diocese, second only to the founding of churches. Even though funds, women religious and priests were all in short supply within the diocese, the Church began to open Catholic schools in order to educate the young and to protect them from the anti-Catholic, Protestant teachings often found in the public schools of the state.

Education in Connecticut had always been supervised by the Congregational Church until 1798 when the State Assembly established an independent school society to oversee education. Monies provided by the Connecticut School Fund, established in 1795 by the sale of the Western Reserve lands, were to assure the provision of a general education in the common schools throughout the state. Following the reforms and leadership of Henry Barnard during the 1850's, the state's common schools began to flourish.

The schools were not, however, free from religious influence. Developed within a predominantly Protestant society, the public educational system naturally followed time-honored methods of education that included the moral education and formation of the students, Bible readings, school prayer, and visits by the local Protestant clergy. Attempts to rid the common schools of any denominational character or influence were often met by violent reactions.

As the membership in the Catholic Church steadily increased because of immigration, more and more of its younger members began to attend the common schools. Church authorities became increasingly concerned about the influence upon Catholic children of the clearly Protestant teachings and prayers offered in the state's schools. The necessity of establishing Catholic schools was emphasized by the Church authorities in the decrees of the first six Provincial Councils of Baltimore, held between 1829 and 1846. As nativist sentiment and attacks upon the Church became much more frequent and violent, the absolute necessity of establishing parish schools was emphasized by the fathers of the First Plenary Council of Baltimore in 1852.

The decrees of the First Provincial Council of New York, which also affected Connecticut, clearly reflected the fears of the American bishops concerning the strong Protestant influence present within the public school system. Such an influence, so often hostile towards Catholicism, the hierarchy contended, would be deleterious to the Catholic faith of immigrant Catholic children. Rome agreed that unless Catholic schools were established, Catholic children might be lost to the Church and be left prey to religious indifferentism. At the same time, however, the Roman authorities were loath to express their fears officially and suggested to the bishops of the New York Province that they make no public mention of the "very grave" dangers to which Catholic children were exposed in non–Catholic schools. Rather, they were simply to ". . . employ prudence in their present exasperation, since it would be better to prescribe as a rule the sound instruction of Catholic youth" rather than publicly condemn the state schools, and so avoid public, and possibly violent, confrontations with Protestants and American authorities.[40]

In a letter written in 1856 to the Propagation of the Faith in Paris, the second Bishop of Hartford, Bernard O'Reilly, expressed the need for Catholic schools in his diocese in order to combat the efforts made by Protestants to convert Catholic orphans and students in the common schools. He wrote:

Catholic schools are nearly as necessary as our Churches, the education of the state is entirely Protestant; if we wish to save our children, it is imperative that we have Catholic schools. Our enemies are entirely active, and they do their best to do harm to our holy religion, so for

12

our part, we must be prepared every day, as a soldier, to defend our own.[41]

One of the most vocal supporters of the public school system in Connecticut at the time was the Rev. Horace Bushnell of Hartford. His theory of public education was markedly religious, but Protestant. Children were to receive a moral formation in the public schools, based upon Protestant moral principles and religious tenets. Religion had an obvious part to play in the public school education of American children, Bushnell believed. It was, however, to be the Protestant religious beliefs alone that could be sanctioned in public schools, since America was touted to be a Protestant nation. Bushnell had expressed his theory of education in his "Discourses on Christian Nurture" in 1847:

> . . . the child is to grow up a Christian. In other words, the aim, the effort and expectation should be, not, as is commonly assumed, that the child is to grow up in sin, to be converted after he comes to a mature age, but that he is to open on the world as one that is spiritually renewed, not remembering the time when he went through a technical experience, but seeming rather to have loved what is good from his earliest years.[42]

This he expanded in his 1853 attack upon the Catholic efforts to establish parish schools, entitled, "Common Schools; A Discourse on the Modifications demanded by the Roman Catholics."

Beginning with the scriptural citation from the Book of Leviticus in which God commands Israel to have one law for both stranger and native-born alike, Bushnell states that America is a Protestant country. Americans, nonetheless, have generously opened their doors to any and all, regardless of national origin or religious beliefs, imparting citizenship, suffrage, and the right to own property to all. In return, these welcomed strangers are expected to become part of American society, blending with all others. Despite the generosity of Protestant America, Bushnell continued, the Catholics alone proved ungrateful, since they preferred separation to entrance into mainstream American life:

> They [Catholics] require of us either to give up our common schools, or else . . . to hand over their portion of the public money, and let them use it for such kind of schools as they happen to like best; ecclesiastical schools, whether German, French or Irish; any kind of schools but such as are America, and will make Americans of their children.[43]

For the Church authorities, the prospect of losing Catholic children because of Protestant teachings in public schools far

13

outweighed the pressure and sometimes violent reactions resulting from Protestant rhetoric such as Bushnell's. The Church's prime duty was to confirm the Catholic faith of its youth, not to serve as an instrument of assimilation into American society. The Church was to safeguard the faith of Catholic Americans, not transform Catholics into Protestant Americans. Catholic schools would be the means by which American Catholic children could be instructed in all that was American, while remaining faithful to the Catholic creed of their forefathers. It was generally held among Catholics that parish schools were needed in order to spare their children the ridicule, the anti–Catholic rhetoric, and Protestant teachings that became more and more the common fare offered in the common schools, especially as the Know–Nothing Party gained power in the state during the 1850's.

The religious education of Catholic children was further hindered by the poverty of the majority of Catholic parents that forced most Catholic children to work in factories. This left little free time for their education.[44] The religious formation of Catholic children, therefore, was dependent for the most part upon the parents and upon Sunday school classes that were established in all of the churches throughout the Diocese of Hartford by the late 1840's.[45]

Catholic Schools in Fairfield County

Bishop O'Reilly expressed the urgent need for Catholic schools within the Diocese of Hartford in his 1854 diocesan report. He wrote,

If we wish to save to God and to religion the rising generation, we will, even at a sacrifice, organize for their education Catholic schools.[46]

Catholic schools were begun in Fairfield County during the 1850's. All were small, taught by lay men and women. St. James in Bridgeport opened a school in 1851. It began in a private home taught by a laywoman with about 25 students. A small school house was built in 1853 but burned in 1859. St. Mary Church in Norwalk opened a day school in August, 1855, in two small rooms, added to the rear of the clapboard church following a fire.[47] Originally intended solely for religious instruction, the rooms were converted to serve as a Catholic grammar school in the spring of 1856. A night school was begun in 1859, but proved a short–lived enterprise.[48] St. Peter in Danbury began a school in 1857, conducted in the church by lay teachers.[49]

The only town in Fairfield County that expressed strong disapproval at the opening of a Catholic school was Norwalk. Already informed of the Church's alleged efforts against public schools by the work of the local editor,[50] Norwalk's citizenry took a dim view of the establishment of a Catholic school in their own town. The editor of the *Norwalk Gazette* reflected the anger of his fellow citizens in an editorial entitled, "Sectarian Schools." The object of Catholic schools, the editor opined was,

> . . . to draw the children of that faith from our Union School, where as one objected to us—the souls of the children were jeopardized by the reading of the Protestant Bible and the morning Prayer of the Principal. We are sorry to see any such thing rooted, for it can prove but a failure, as a Society which cannot keep their poor from famishing except by Protestant aid, will not be likely to sustain a Sectarian School, if they could, it would only tend unnecessarily to embitter the prejudices already existing against them.

The editor called for a closing of the Catholic school by the members of St. Mary's, and continued:

> When sectarianism is introduced into our public Schools, it will be plenty of time to withdraw their children from them. If the poor deluted [sic] creatures who find a home and assylum [sic] on American soil, cannot consent to accept our Country and its Institutions as they find them—we think they had better return by the first Packet.[51]

The majority of Catholic children attended the common schools during the 1850's.[52] Catholic attendance at the free public schools continued to be high during the subsequent decade, especially as a result of the Civil War. Deprived of the bread winner who was a casualty or a draftee of the Union effort, few Catholic families could spare the small fee required by the lay teachers of the Catholic schools.[53] Their poverty was such that in some cases Catholic widows of Union servicemen were forced to send their children to the Catholic orphanages.[54] Unable to support their children, these parents could hardly afford to provide them with a Catholic education, no matter how trifling the cost.[55]

The churches within the state, and the diocese itself, had been hard hit financially by the Civil War. Funds normally used to liquidate debts, and to build churches and needed schools were diverted to assist those Catholics reduced to penury by the War.[56] By 1866, therefore, there were only four Catholic

15

schools within Fairfield County, each with individual departments for boys and girls; all had relatively low attendance.[57]

The Roman authorities, however, continued to emphasize the importance of Catholic education for all Catholic children within the Diocese of Hartford.[58] Bishop McFarland lamented the fact that the majority of Catholic children were attending the public schools. He, nonetheless, continued to emphasize that money and religious sisters were imperative to the realization of the Roman directives for Catholic schools.[59]

Such a rapid growth of the Church prompted many to work politically for the stemming of the immigrant tide and a reduction of the Church's influence within the state.

The Know–Nothing Party in Connecticut

Slavery, temperance, and immigration were the major political issues of the 1850's. Connecticut was not politically stable by the middle of the century. The political parties were weak, and their sometimes questionable political alliances often led to ineffective policies. Add to this a strong dose of political dabbling by ministers throughout the state preaching a civic gospel, and the stage was set for the success of any party offering quick, popular solutions to unpopular problems. In July, 1853 the "Know–Nothing Party" began its Connecticut work. The party first presented itself as a secret society. When its members were asked concerning the party's beliefs they claimed to "know nothing"—hence its name. The party first called itself the "State Council of Connecticut." The innocuous title did not long disguise the principles of the party, as seen in its constitution:

> Its object shall be to resist the insidious policy of the Church of Rome, and all other foreign influences against the institutions of our country, by placing in all offices in the gift of the people, whether by election or appointment, none but native–born Protestant citizens.[60]

The Know Nothings saw the Church as a political machine with religious trappings, composed primarily of the poorer, immigrant classes who were easily controlled by priests. The priests in turn, were controlled by the bishops, who were subject to the Vatican. To grant suffrage to the mass of arriving Catholic immigrants would, in the view of the nativist, give control of the ballot boxes and the United States government to the powers in Rome.[61]

Local papers within Fairfield County and elsewhere in the

16

state at first tended to treat the new party as little more than a joke.[62] This changed dramatically late in 1854 with the death of the Rev. John C. Brady in Hartford, when many of the depravities credited by the Know–Nothings to the Catholic Church, appeared real and close to home.

Fr. Brady had served as a dedicated priest at St. Patrick's Church in Hartford for a number of years. However, after some dispute with Bishop O'Reilly, he was removed from his position in November, 1854, and died a few weeks later of cholera. A public row concerning his burial followed with an extremely vocal group of parishioners insisting that their pastor be interred directly in front of his church. The bishop objected that there was not sufficient space for a grave in front of the church because of the proximity of the street and prohibited the burial as planned. Despite the bishop's objections, the congregation forcibly buried Brady's remains near the front door of the church.

All of this would have had little effect in Fairfield County—a world away from Hartford—if not for the articles of the Norwalk, Stamford, and Bridgeport papers, reporting that Brady had been a respected member of the Norwalk and Stamford communities, having built the first Catholic churches in both towns, and served as the founding rector of Norwalk.[63]

The truth of the Know–Nothing claims appeared to be borne out in this conflict that the press represented as pitting the Roman Catholic hierarchy against a dedicated man and against the democratic rights of his congregation.

Norwalk took especial umbrage at the Hartford incident. Since Brady had served as the first rector of the town, the local press interpreted the Hartford events as a direct attack against its citizenry, as if a native son had been wronged. Despite the fact that he was a Roman Catholic priest, the *Norwalk Gazette* reported that he had ". . . the very general respect of our citizens."[64] Throughout November and December of 1854, the paper continued to carry not only reports of the Brady affair, along with those of "escaped nuns," citizens whose rights allegedly had been trampled upon by priests and bishops, but also notices of the growing strength of the Church in America.

In its November 28, 1854, number, the Norwalk paper quoted the *Hartford Courant*, which had wrongly surmised that the crux of the entire Brady affair had been over the right of the congregation to hold title to church property, steadfastly denied by the Catholic bishop. Brady, according to the paper, had sided with the congregation, thus precipitating his removal. Despite the fact that nothing of the sort ever occurred, the paper continued:

> It is one of the cheering signs of the times that the people and priests connected with the Romish Church are beginning to look into the titles to their property, and are beginning to think that they have, or ought to have, some control over wealth which they have accumulated. The movements in different parts of the country show that a leaven is at work that will not easily by checked.[65]

Trusteeism, or the owning and administration of church property by laymen, had been a problem for the Church in America for years. Tendencies to usurp the authority of bishops and rectors in church administration and teaching and to transform church missions into personal possessions, led the Church to officially require that the title to all church property be in the name of the local bishop.[66]

Such a rule was the opposite of that practiced by most Protestant congregations in the country at that time, whereby the individual congregations held the title to the church's property, controlling church administration, and hiring and dismissing their ministers at will. The Brady incident presented a fine example of the allegedly un–American nature of the Catholic Church: a foreign church, led by foreign powers with foreigners as communicants who had no rights, and whose land was owned, not by those who paid for it, but by those who administered it.

The Know–Nothing Party was served very nicely in Fairfield County by this incident, and by the reports in the local press, since, for the first time, the Church was presented as attacking one who had been well respected locally. No longer was the threat of Romanism a distant one; it had touched home. No longer did it repress the stranger; it attacked a one–time neighbor. Therefore, the Brady incident made the threat of the immigrant and his church very real in Fairfield County and clearly outlined a way to effectively disarm the Catholic Church: deny suffrage to the immigrants, and change the property laws for Catholic churches within the state.

The Know–Nothing party had its chance to raise this issue in the Connecticut gubernatorial election of 1855, when it succeeded in capturing the office for its candidate, William T. Minor of Stamford. In his inaugural address to the General Assembly, the newly–elected governor outlined his program for the state, which took a dim view of Catholic immigrants. Describing them as "tinctured with the social infidelity of continental Europe," and "many of them blind followers of an ecclesi-

18

astical despotism [the pope]," Minor dismissed the larger portion of immigrant arrivals as unfit for American citizenship. The root of the state's problems was seen to be the granting of citizenship and suffrage to immigrants whose loyalties were questionable. The governor continued:

> But as a matter of policy connected with the privilege of citizenship to be conferred upon the alien, we have the right to enquire how far the allegiance due from the members of the Romish Church to their spiritual head is compatible with the allegiance due their adopted country.[67]

Since the success of papal interference in American affairs hinged upon the ballots of the immigrants, according to the governor, then a longer period of naturalization was deemed warranted. In order to protect United States citizens from possible foreign violence, the governor also advocated the disbanding of all militia companies in the state consisting of foreign-born troops.

Praise for the governor's address was nearly universal by the press of Fairfield County, with only Bridgeport's *Republican Farmer*, of all the papers in the county's larger towns, sounding a condemnatory note. William S. Pomeroy, editor of the *Farmer*, denounced Minor's address as historically inaccurate, un–American, and fallacious. America was founded, not by Americans, as Minor would have his constituents believe, but by immigrants. Full liberty, Pomeroy continued, had been found, not in the Puritan colonies, but only in Catholic Maryland. Pomeroy found Minor's distaste for Catholic immigrants to be too much, and his desire that a "thoroughly American feeling" pervade Connecticut to be dangerous. Pomeroy closed his editorial aware that Americans undoubtedly would choose to believe the vitriolic sensationalism of Governor Minor and the powerful Know Nothings instead of reason and historical facts:

> Of course, as good christian people, we shall all then give glory, first to the 'Father and Son,' and then to ex-Captain Minor and the Know–Nothings.[68]

The *Farmer* noted that the flag over the Hartford State House had been raised "Union down" the day of Minor's inauguration—a foreboding omen for the state and, ". . . a slight indication of the position in which the Know–Nothing party will be after the next State election." But, before that election, both the Church and the immigrant found the Minor years (1855–1857) to be rough going.

Advocating a longer residency period for aliens and more stringent naturalization laws, Minor and the state legislature succeeded in limiting suffrage within the state to those who could read the constitution and the laws, revoking the power of the state courts to naturalize aliens and disbanding six state militia companies composed of foreign-born troops, all of which were Irish.

The major legislative attack upon the Church in the state was passed by the General Assembly on June 25, 1855. It dealt with the ownership and title of ecclesiastical property. The legislation primarily denied the Church the right to corporate ownership. No longer could the Church's lands be held in the bishop's name, in accord with Church legislation and practice. The legislature, sympathetic to the nativist cause, required that all Church property be held by the respective church congregations. The only church subject to this legislation was the Roman Catholic, all others were exempted by name.

The effects of Know–Nothing rule upon the Church's life in Connecticut were real. Normal Catholic life in the Diocese of Hartford was disturbed by the Know–Nothing administration. The diocese remained without a bishop for nearly two years following the death of Bishop O'Reilly in 1856, since the bishops of the province declined to submit names to Rome for a successor until the political atmosphere in the state became less hostile to the Church.[69]

But the more important effect was one not intended by the nativists. The various legislative acts neither stemmed the immigrant tide nor permanently disabled the Church. The legal restrictions placed upon the Church and the moral buffeting of the immigrants by the press, instead of weakening the Church and scattering the immigrant congregations, tended to produce a community that banded together, closing its ranks and uniting around the Church. As their American neighbors read papers filled with stories and editorials against them and their Church, the Catholic immigrants could do little else but stand united.

The Norwalk and Stamford papers were particularly bitter in their reports on the Church in America, carrying anti–Catholic reports in nearly every issue during Governor Minor's years in office.

The Church Continued to Grow: 1860–1870

By the end of the decade, the Know–Nothing Party had lost all power and influence, and the protectionist and anti–

Catholic sentiments that they had championed appeared silly when compared with the more pressing question of slavery. However shortlived the Know–Nothings' rule, the effects of their hatred and legislation were long lasting, at least among the Catholics of the state. Their Church and native land denounced by the ruling party, local politicians, Protestant clergymen, and their own neighbors, Irish Catholics were deeply hurt and reacted in a normal manner by creating their own society within which they could find protection and strength with the Church at its center.

New churches were built and the first Catholic schools were opened in Bridgeport, Norwalk, and Danbury. Social, spiritual, and self-help societies began to form under the Church's auspices, touching all aspects of life, offering the Catholic immigrant the social respect, protection, and communal assistance denied by neighbors in the larger society.

The prejudice of many toward the Church and the immigrant quieted during the years of the Civil War. Slavery appeared as the greater threat to the Union than did the designs of an unseen pope, while the need for his immigrant envoys in battlefield and factory far outweighed any potential threat which they were thought to pose to the American Republic.

Practical necessity alone was not responsible for the lessening of prejudice in both the state and the country during the war. The service of Catholic immigrants in the field served as ample proof to many that Catholics of foreign birth could indeed be loyal Americans, willing to defend their adopted country. Governor Buckingham reinstated militia companies composed entirely of foreign–born troops. The Irish regiment—known as "The Fighting Ninth"—and the German militia, including the German Rifle Company from Bridgeport, sent thousands from Connecticut to defend the Union.[7]

The example of the Catholic clergy and religious during the war, both in the field and at home, also drew the attention of many native-born Americans. Bishop McFarland spoke out frequently supporting the Union, encouraging his Catholic flock to defend the principles of their government, and blessing the northern troops. He followed the example given by Archbishop John Hughes of New York, who was sent by the Union Government to secure the support of Catholic European leaders for the Union cause.

By their support of the troops and government efforts, the local clergy also manifested a distinctively pro–Union tone. The sole exception in Fairfield County was that given by the rector

21

of St. Mary's Church, Norwalk, who, during a military parade along West Avenue early in the war, refused to show the flag in front of the church, lest the Church's neutrality in the military conflict be compromised.[72] In the field, the dedicated service and courage of the Catholic chaplains and religious sisters working as nurses resulted in a number of converts and praise for their patriotism. The Bishop of Hartford reflected on the influence of the dedicated religious in the field when he wrote,

> There is a lessening of anti-Catholic prejudice. More than one Protestant soldier on the field of battle and in hospital, about to die, has asked for the consolation of a Catholic priest or a Sister of Mercy.[73]

An "Irish" Catholic Church

By the end of the Civil War, the majority of the Catholic population of the Diocese of Hartford was composed of Irish immigrants—nine-tenths of the Catholic population, according to Bishop McFarland. They were, for the most part, according to the bishop, ". . . attached to their faith and attentive to their obligations, even though rather dirty and ignorant." The remainder of the Catholic population was composed of German, French, and Italian immigrants, whom the bishop described with an equally critical eye as having ". . . a tint of irreligion and infidelity, and who are generally grossly ignorant of the mysteries of their religion."[74] Bishop McFarland was far from being a bigot. Rather he was a realist, who acknowledged that his people were mainly immigrants who had arrived in America with little or no formal education, expecting little more than a life of hard work and grinding poverty. He saw that poverty, the vices attendant upon that poverty, and the recent immigration of his people, as the prime evils to be overcome. He saw them as weak, prone to exploitation by employers, and as being ". . . indulgent in intemperance or to other faults, and exposed to great temptation."[75]

The war had not helped Catholics in Connecticut financially. Many mills not involved in war production had closed because of a lack of manpower, reducing many families to begging. With the losses from the battlefield a number of homes were broken. Mothers, unable to support their children were often driven to give up their children to asylums.[76] One Catholic woman from Norwalk wrote to the Vatican asking for financial assistance for her children, since her husband had been killed during the war. She wrote:

I am now alone, thrown on the wide world with three . . . children, what will become of me if your protecting arm does not protect me; this miserable poverty grinds me almost to despair; let me entreat you, therefore, to hold my petition in consideration.[77]

Despite their poverty and lack of education, these Irish Catholics sacrificed to build up the Church in Connecticut. Bishop McFarland spoke of the dedication of the Irish Catholics to the Church in his report to the Society for the Propagation of the Faith in Paris in 1867:

It is only during the last twenty years that the Catholic faith has spread and implanted itself . . . and in this work of propagation the first pioneers were almost exclusively poor Irish immigrants. They were the ones who at the cost of their first sweat and with the inexhaustible resources of their fecund poverty, put up our first Church buildings. But, as one can easily guess, churches, rectories, and schools were built in wood with as much simplicity as economy.[78]

St. James in Bridgeport had been established in 1842 as the first mission in Fairfield County. By 1860, that number had risen to six, each with its own church, land, and resident priest, who was assigned to care for the needs of the Catholics within the larger towns and those in the surrounding villages.[79] By 1870, five of the smaller missions had built their own chapels, raising the total number of chapels and churches to eleven.[80] Of these, nine were simple wooden chapels. St. Augustine, formerly St. James, in Bridgeport was the only stone church in the county, and St. Mary, in Norwalk, had only just completed the basement of its new stone church.

The establishment of this immigrant church was no easy task. Prescinding from any obstacles found outside the Church, those within the local communities themselves were formidable enough to retard, if not foil, any plans for development and growth. Faithful there were in abundance. In 1850, the Diocese of Hartford, comprising the states of Rhode Island and Connecticut, counted 30,000 members; by 1870, 200,000. During that period, the number of Catholics in Fairfield County had risen from approximately 1,100 to 15,000.[81] The rapidity with which the body of the faithful grew, in itself, was a formidable obstacle to proper and adequate administration and ministry. The fact that the majority of the faithful were impoverished and ill–educated added to the practical problems of establishing missions and building churches in order to provide normative Catholic life for them. These early church communities desperately needed priests and funds in order to staff and build churches necessary for the normal practice of the faith.

Most of the priests who ministered to the Irish Catholic congregations within Fairfield County, as elsewhere in the country, were Irish. Numerous petitions exist from the early bishops of Hartford to All Hallows College in Dublin, begging for priests and seminarians willing and capable of missionary work in Connecticut and Rhode Island. In 1860, there were 52 priests working within the Diocese of Hartford, of which only five were American–born.[82] By 1870 the number of priests had risen to 95, of which 20 were American–born.[83] Of the eight priests serving the 15,000 Catholics of Fairfield County in 1870, most were of Irish birth.

Some of the funds and ecclesiastical appurtenances necessary for religious life were provided by the various European missionary societies in Paris, Vienna, Munich, and Rome. The greatest portion of the burden, however, fell upon the shoulders of the local communities. Often unable to contribute financially, the Irish Catholics donated their labor to excavate church basements and build schools and churches in order to provide some secure form of religious life at least remotely reminiscent of that which they left in their native villages. In order to maintain and bolster their religious beliefs and traditions, the Irish Catholics formed various self-help and religious societies.

By the end of the Civil War, the Catholic communities located in the various towns of Connecticut had become the centers of Catholic social and spiritual life. Having closed their ranks in response to the adverse feeling expressed in the local press and from Protestant pulpits and oftentimes unwelcome in social societies during the late 1850's, Catholics began a ghetto–like existence. They created societies and organizations that provided spiritual nourishment as well as the social benefits and prestige denied them in the larger community because of their Catholic faith.

Library and literary societies, Rosary, Scapular, Altar Societies, the Children of Mary, Benevolent Societies, St. Vincent de Paul Societies, and the Third Order Franciscans[84] were founded by the local clergy in nearly all of the churches in Fairfield County soon after their establishment, in order to meet the spiritual and social needs of their congregations. Such associations bolstered the Catholic identity of these small congregations, while at the same time they assisted their spiritual growth.

Since Ireland proved to be the ancestral homeland for most

Catholics by mid–century, a society grew up that was distinctly Irish in its makeup and purpose: the Ancient Order of the Hibernians (AOH). The AOH was first introduced into Connecticut by way of Bridgeport, where the state's first division was organized on March 6, 1869. The AOH flourished under the leadership of its first president, James Davitt, under the standard of "Friendship, Unity and Christian Charity."[85] Membership was limited to practicing Catholics of Irish birth or ancestry who were called upon to enter into programs of charity for the aged, sick, blind, and infirmed. The Order, therefore, united Irish nationalism with Catholic practice and bolstered the Catholic and Irish identity of its members while performing needed services for the Catholic community.

Another society that developed at the same time in Fairfield County was the Catholic Total Abstinence Society. The problem of alcoholism had proven to be very serious among the ranks of the immigrants in America by the middle of the nineteenth century. The problem was never adequately addressed until the temperance movement was launched in Ireland by the Rev. Theobald Mathew in 1838. A priest of great personal dynamism and dedication to his apostolate, Fr. Mathew's missions and preaching brought thousands in Ireland and Scotland to take the pledge against alcohol. The American bishops, aware of the tremendous danger of alcoholism among the Church's immigrants, condemned intemperance in 1843, and called upon Catholics in America to abstain from immoderate drinking.

Fr. Mathew visited America in 1849 and traveled through 25 states preaching his gospel of temperance. His work produced amazing effects—he converted over 600,000 people to total abstinence! He toured Connecticut, preaching in various large towns, and impressed Protestants and Catholics alike. Bridgeport's P.T. Barnum was so moved by the priest's dedication that he donated $500 to Fr. Mathew's temperance work, in return for which Barnum received a gold watch with the inscription,

'Presented by Father Matthews [sic] to P.T. Barnum, Esq. as a trifling mark of personal esteem, + as a grateful recognition of his zealous labors in the promotion and advocacy of Temperance.'[86]

Connecticut's first Catholic Abstinence Society was established in Hartford as the result of Fr. Mathew's visit to that city. Following Hartford's lead, churches throughout the diocese were urged to establish similar associations. The original five churches within Fairfield County all counted temperance societies by the early 1860's. The male members of the congregations were usually divided into three separate temperance societies according to age: older men, younger men, and adolescent "Temperance Cadets."

Cries for prohibition within the state had been heard from many a Protestant minister and group for years. They found support from the Whigs and the Free Soil Party that succeeded in passing a prohibition law in Connecticut in 1854. Since the temperance issue became entangled with the growing anti–immigration sentiments, the alleged habitual drunkenness of the Irish Catholic immigrant provided ammunition for those favoring more stringent immigration and naturalization laws, as well as a curbing of the Church's growth in Connecticut.[87]

Even after the weakening of such public anti-Catholic sentiment, the Church continued to form the center of life for Catholics. It offered community support and nourished the identity of its members, especially as Catholic immigrants from countries other than Ireland began to arrive in ever greater numbers during the later years of Bishop McFarland's rule.[88] Bridgeport and Norwalk, the two original centers of Catholicism in the county, were towns that attracted an ever-growing number of Catholic immigrants during the late 1860's and early 1870's.

Immigration had slowed during the years of the Civil War. Following the Union victory in 1865 the immigrant numbers again rose in response to peace–time and to the opportunities afforded by the post-war industrial economy in the North. Ireland continued to supply the greatest number of immigrants.[89]

Therefore, the Church quite naturally took on a distinctly Irish flavor, which continued and intensified as the Irish moved up the economic and social ladder and made their presence felt and seen in business and politics and in statements of stone and mortar. Irish immigration continued to outstrip all other arriving groups in Connecticut through the 1880's. As the numbers grew, the need for larger, more substantial churches of stone, replacing the earlier wooden structures, grew along with it. Since the majority of the local Catholic communities was Irish, a distinctive Celtic profile dominated Church administration, Catholic identity, and even building decoration of Catholic churches of the period.

Bridgeport built two new churches for the resident Catholic community. St. Augustine, which replaced the old St. James, opened its doors on St. Patrick's Day, 1869. The new St. Mary's was dedicated in October, 1877, replacing the older wooden structure on Crescent Avenue. They were the largest churches in the city and identified themselves as of Irish patronage, even though they were not national missions; they were open to all Catholics, regardless of national origin or culture. Since the majority of Catholics in the area were of Irish descent, however, the two became generally identified: to be Catholic was to be Irish. This was reflected by the national origin of most local rectors, by the majority of any given congregation, and by the shamrocks in stucco and marble that adorned their sanctuaries.[90]

Norwalk's St. Mary's Church was replaced by a larger stone edifice in 1871, and decorated with shamrocks inside, both on the altar and in decorative stucco bosses in the ceiling, and outside with shamrocks of Kelly green on the steeple above each clock face.[91] Stamford's new St. John's opened in 1886; Danbury's St. Peter's in 1875; and Newtown's St. Rose of Lima in 1883.[92] All bore the stamp of Irish Catholicism, and all were strong, stone statements that the Irish Catholics were to become a permanent, major force to be reckoned with in the local communities of Fairfield County.

The only other groups of immigrants with substantial Catholic numbers in Connecticut were the Germans, who in 1860 numbered 8,353, and by 1870, 12,443; and the French Canadians, numbering 3,145 in 1860 and 10,840 by 1870.[93] The majority of these newer, non–English–speaking immigrants were Catholic. The presence of a Catholic church in Norwalk helped to commend that town as a possible home for the Matthews family in 1876. One of the reasons why this wealthy Protestant family was attracted to Norwalk was the presence of the Church, which signaled the presence of immigrants who could be employed as domestics. As Florence Matthews recalled in her diary,

> So many large country places were isolated and lonely, it greatly increased the domestic problem. But Norwalk had a Catholic Church nearby and a village only a mile away at each side of us, and yet it was truly rural.[94]

Norwalk felt itself to be so cosmopolitan as to attract immigrants of even the highest social standing. Rumors circulated that the recently dethroned Emperor Louis Napoleon of France had considered Norwalk as his new home. Since Norwalk boasted a Catholic Church, Pope Pius IX also was rumored to be interested in settling there following the fall of Rome in 1870.[95] Both were rumored to have been interested in the Lockwood Mansion, the agents of which estate did, in fact, visit the Archbishop of New York and the Bishop of Hartford

27

inquiring about rumors of a possible sale of the land to the Pope.[96]

Conclusion

The rapid growth of the Catholic population within Connecticut and Rhode Island prompted the Holy See to divide the Diocese of Hartford in 1872. Rhode Island Catholics then became the subjects of the newly elected bishop of Providence, leaving Hartford's bishop the care of those Catholics within the boundaries of Connecticut.

The care of the ever–growing Catholic community in Connecticut, however, required more than merely administrative readjustment. Since the Catholic immigration of the later nineteenth century would prove to be predominantly non-English–speaking, coming from other than Anglo-Saxon countries, conflicts more serious than mere linguistic differences would make the Church's work all the more complex. Bishop McFarland had observed in 1866 that the prejudices of non-Catholics ". . . are directed as much to the nationality, the poverty, and ignorance of our people as to their catholicity."[97]

The Catholic Irish immigrants took great pride in the churches they had built in Connecticut. It was they who had done battle against anti–Catholic prejudice and poverty, establishing churches and schools on a firm foundation that would serve future generations of Catholics in the state. It was they who had succeeded in proving that a Catholic, even of foreign birth, could be a loyal, patriotic, and productive American.

As the number of non–English–speaking Catholic immigrants increased during the subsequent decades, however, the antagonism toward them, of which Bishop McFarland spoke, came to be exercised by those within as well as outside the Church. The "new immigrants," as they came to be called, would be seen by native-born Americans as a threat to the country; to Catholics of Irish heritage they were perceived as a threat to the Church in America. For the Catholic Irish in Connecticut, the Catholic Church was theirs, established by their struggles and sacrifices. The subsequent decades of the Church's growth in Connecticut, so intimately linked to the immigration of the period especially within Fairfield County, would be marked by occasional clashes between cultures and races within the same Church.

CHAPTER II

THE "NEW" CATHOLIC IMMIGRANTS
(1880–1930)

The Catholic immigrants who arrived in Fairfield County during the last decades of the nineteenth century and the first decades of the present century did not always find a warm welcome from either the American–born Protestant community or from their American coreligionists of different ethnic backgrounds. The Protestant majority often viewed these Catholic, non–Anglo–Saxon arrivals as threats to what was regarded as the Protestant American Republic. The Connecticut Catholics, predominantly of Irish birth or descent, often viewed the Catholic non–English speaking immigrants from eastern and southern Europe as threatening the American Catholic Church that they had built. It had been the Irish immigrants who had laid the foundations for the Church in Connecticut, and who had fought the battles to defend it as compatible with American institutions. By the 1870's they had established a stable Church and had proven themselves faithful Catholics and loyal Americans. The newcomers appeared to the Catholic Irish majority and their Protestant fellow citizens as an eloquent confirmation of the allegations made during previous decades that the Church of Rome was indeed foreign to America.

Despite such prejudiced views, the Catholic Bishops of Hartford staunchly supported the new immigrants' desires for churches of their own. The pastoral programs of these bishops in favor of the immigrants demonstrated that they were willing to go to great lengths to bolster and preserve the Catholic faith of the arriving immigrants.

Programs to train American–born seminarians abroad and to enlist the help of European–born priests and religious revealed the pastoral concern of Hartford's "Irish" Bishops for the arriving immigrants. Despite the practical obstacles, such as the prejudice of native–born Catholics and those of rival ethnic groups, national and provincial tensions among the immigrants themselves and the lack of capable priests, Fairfield County proved to be a welcome home for the thousands of arriving Catholics, since it provided, not only job opportunities, but an atmosphere that promoted and nurtured the religious traditions and cultural identities of the various Catholic ethnic groups.

Bridgeport, with more national churches than any other city in the state, was the prime example of a city whose Catholic leaders and faithful offered sanctuary and opportunity to the immigrant Catholics. It was in Bridgeport that the first national churches were formed for the respective immigrant groups that settled in the county. It was there that the diocesan policies concerning national churches were tested and the pattern for the establishment of national parishes worked out as a paradigm for the other national groups within the county. Despite the problems, failures, and nationalistic antipathies among the immigrants, the Church in Fairfield County proved itself successful in its ministrations in favor of the Catholic immigrants and allowed those immigrants to leave a living legacy of their faith to the subsequent generations of Connecticut Catholics.

Catholic immigrants arriving in this country during the decade ending in 1880 totaled 604,000. That number more than doubled during the subsequent decade, adding 1,250,000 foreign–born Catholics to the ranks of the Church in America. The estimated 6,259,000 Catholics in 1880 increased to 8,-909,000 by 1890. By 1920, the Catholic population was estimated at 20,000,000, mainly the result of immigration. Such an enormous increase presented the American church leaders with extraordinary practical problems concerning the pastoral care of so large and diverse a body of faithful.[1]

The United States was considered mission territory by the Church authorities in Rome and was placed under the jurisdiction of the Church's missionary department of the Roman Curia, the Congregation "de Propaganda Fide" until 1908. Because of this, the Church's pastoral and canonical legislation was limited to local circumstances and conditions in America. For instance, there were no canonically established parishes in the United States, as was common in other countries. Each church bore the status of a mission, with its own respective territory. Since no canonical parishes existed, there could be no pastors, only rectors, charged with the care of those Catholics living within the mission's boundaries. Rectors, therefore, had only delegated authority since they were not canonical pastors. This proved to be an unsatisfactory system to a number of priests who preferred the security afforded by the canonical status of irremovable pastor to the possibility of frequent transfers according to the will of the bishop. Rome received numerous complaints concerning this problem as well as petitions by various immigrant groups claiming that large numbers of immigrant Catholics were being lost to the Church because of the lack of adequate pastoral care by local bishops and clergy.[2]

As the number of non–English–speaking Catholic immigrants increased in America, the question of establishing national churches for them arose. Since these national churches would be established within the territorial boundaries of previously existing missions, the question of jurisdiction and rights of the rectors of the national and territorial missions also arose. Were national churches independent missions, or merely succursal chapels of the established English–speaking mission? Were the newly arrived immigrants to assimilate immediately, becoming Americans and learning English overnight, or were they to be allowed to use their native languages and customs in the practice of their faith? The question of the place of nationalism in religion was very real. The tensions that developed between the various immigrant Catholic groups over these issues of nationalism called for provisions as yet untried in the canonical and pastoral practices of the Church in America.

Developing a Pastoral Plan

In the late 19th century, the question of the pastoral care of non–English–speaking Catholic immigrants was—and still is—a complex problem for the Church in America. The problem was cultural as well as linguistic. The newer Catholic immigrants required a church staffed by priests capable of speaking their languages. They also required an institution capable of forming a community whose life and worship reflected the cultural heritage and national background so beloved by the newly-arrived immigrants. To them, America was a foreign land. It was only natural, then, that upon their arrival they hoped to find comfort in the Catholic faith they had practiced in their homeland.

But the Church in America, which had been formed and long dominated by Irish Catholics, presented a foreign appearance and practice to these newer Catholic immigrants. Practical questions arose from the meeting of a basically Irish–American Catholicism and the ever–increasing number of "new" non–English–speaking Catholic immigrants. Should these newcom-

31

ers belong to the territorial missions where English was employed, or should they be granted their own national churches? Would these national churches be independent of the territorial missions? Where would the clergy and religious women capable of speaking the numerous languages be found? How far could the spirit of old–world nationalism, so much a part of each immigrant group, be allowed to influence their practice of the Catholic faith in America? Was the Church to assist these immigrants in the process of Americanization or to bolster their individual national identities, thereby effectively establishing individual national enclaves of Catholic foreigners within the country? It had been the Irish Catholics who had sacrificed to establish the Church in Connecticut. They had succeeded in proving that the Catholic Church was not foreign to America, and that a Catholic could be a loyal American. The "new" immigrants seemed to threaten this hard-won victory. The primary question, therefore, was: Is the Catholic Church in America foreign or American?

Tensions between the various Catholic immigrant groups and American–born Catholics were intensifying by the 1880's. The German Catholics were the first group of non–English–speaking Catholic immigrants to protest forcefully to Rome concerning the pastoral care accorded them in America by what they called the "Irish" clergy. Their numerous protests and complaints were summarized by two questions sent to Rome by Bishop Kilian Flasch of LaCrosse, Wisconsin, in 1885. His questions dealt with the relationship between succursal chapels, established for national groups, and independent or territorial missions.[3]

Bishop Flasch presented Propaganda Fide with two questions: first, whether several independent missions, distinct from territorial missions because of language and national groups, could exist within the same neighborhood or territory; and second, whether a local bishop would offend "the mind of the Church" if he were to require the children of immigrants to remain as members of their parents' church until they had attained their legal majority or married.

The Propaganda officials responded quite calmly to the apparent tensions developing because of national differences in religion in America. In December, 1885, a letter was sent to members of the American hierarchy by the prefect of the Propaganda, asking their opinion upon the questions presented by Bishop Flasch concerning parochial jurisdiction and national missions. Sixteen prelates replied. All but one agreed that a number of different churches could exist within the same neighborhood, distinct and independent of each other, established according to language and national groups. They agreed that independence from territorial missions could be granted these national churches. To the second question they answered that the children of the immigrants should attend their parents' church, lest they elude their parents and not attend church at all.[4]

The problem was much more involved than simply providing clergy capable of speaking foreign languages. Yet, for a number of American bishops and clergy, language was the only question when dealing with the Catholic immigrants from eastern and southern Europe. Cultural problems, and the role of the immigrants' culture in the practice of their faith, were minimized if not ignored.

This was expressed by Archbishop John Ireland of St. Paul and Bishop John Keane of Richmond, in a report which they sent to the Roman authorities on December 9, 1886. In responding to the growing tensions among the national groups in America, and particularly against the protests of numerous German Catholics in America, they wrote:

> The only question that can be considered is this: the question between the English language, which is the language of the United States, and the German language, which emigrants from Germany have brought to the United States. Why Germans so often give to this question another form, as to indicate that there is a conflict of races in America between the Germans and the Irish, we do not know.[5]

The American bishops were aware of the delicacy of their situation. They were still striving to prove the compatibility of the Catholic Church with American institutions and ideals, while disproving any claims that the Church was "foreign." The addition of millions of foreign-born Catholics by the end of the century, insisting upon the usage of their languages and customs, provided a serious dilemma for the American Church authorities. The American archbishops expressed their sentiments and fears in a letter to Rome in 1886:

> If the Church of God wishes to make true progress among us [in America], it cannot depend exclusively upon European emigration, but must fix deeply its roots elsewhere than this alone. Therefore, the Church will be neither Irish, nor will it be German, but AMERICAN, and even more, ROMAN; since there is neither Jew, nor Greek . . . but all are one in Christ Jesus.[6]

The Propaganda settled down to consider a possible solution to the problems of providing pastoral care for the Catholic immigrants in America in April, 1887. The final decisions of the April meeting took the form of answers to the questions presented to the Propaganda by Bishop Flasch in 1885, since they formed the core of all subsequent controversy and debate concerning the pastoral care of the immigrants. National missions were to be erected for the salvation of souls, and could be independent of other churches, even when in the same territory. These national churches were to enjoy the same rights as those of the territorial missions. Taking into account the shifting population in America, and the resultant changes in local circumstances, the consultors left much freedom of implementation to the discretion of the local bishops. The local bishops were to decide concerning the membership of immigrant children in their parents's church. While the important question concerning the future of national churches should immigration to America cease was raised, it was not answered by the consultors in 1887. The potentially disastrous effects of nationalism in religion were not considered by Rome until 1897, when national churches were declared to be only a temporary solution to a temporary problem, which would cease to exist once immigration from any individual country ceased.

The questions of assimilation, the foreign appearance of the Church in America, and the use of the language and culture of the respective immigrant groups in their religious practice would continue throughout the century up to the present day. The American hierarchy would be split by these questions, with John Ireland of St. Paul, Minnesota, leading the prelates favoring rapid, forcible Americanization of the immigrants, and Michael Corrigan of New York, leading those in favor of a natural assimilation, allowing for the immigrants' use of language and culture in their religious life.

For Rome, the primary concern was the salvation of souls; the Americanization and assimilation of the Catholic immigrants into American culture was not seen as an essential part of the Church's mission. This was reflected in the Propaganda decision concerning the establishment of national churches, and in the approval of the apostolic efforts in favor of Catholic immigrants by Simon Peter Paul Cahensly, founder of the St. Raphael Society for the Protection of the German Catholic Emigrants, and of Bishop Giovanni Scalabrini, founder of the Missionary Congregation of St. Charles Borromeo, to supply Italian missionaries to work among Italian immigrants and the Italian St. Raphael Society.

Whether Rome liked it or not, the nationalistic sentiments of the immigrants in America were playing an ever–increasingly important part in the maintenance of the faith of many Catholic immigrants. In some cases, it was very difficult to distinguish the motivating forces for the various religious manifestations of numerous immigrant groups: Were they manifestations of religious faith or merely of national sentiment with religious overtones? By the end of the century, the national sentiments of these various immigrant groups in the United States were seen as no longer serving religion, but as threatening the unity of the Catholic Church in America.

Nationalism and Religion

As a result of the nationalistic controversies during the late nineteenth century among the Catholics in the United States, the Holy See discovered that in order to provide effectively for the spiritual needs of the Catholic immigrants in America, the Church could not be party to any national interests. The primary goal of the Church's plan for the immigrants was the preservation of their Catholic faith, regardless of their nationality. Special arrangements and provisions were to be made for language differences and cultural expressions of their faith. The Church, however, was not to align her preaching or her apostolic work with any single national group or national interest. The Church's duty was not to maintain or serve the national identity of any group—whether "American" or "foreign." Her duty was to "save souls."

This was re–emphasized in 1892 in a circular letter from the prefect of the Propaganda Fide to the American hierarchy. He wrote that private interests could not be honored or served by the Church, especially in the nomination of bishops. He continued,

> The Holy See has in mind that in the United States the various nations of Europe that are seeking a new home should form one sole nation. This is the only viewpoint that the Holy Congregation [of Propaganda Fide] can approve, having studied the situation and, therefore, it cannot encourage the maintenance of original national groups in their new home.[7]

This same sentiment was repeated in the instructions to Archbishop Francesco Satolli upon his appointment as the first Apostolic Delegate in the United States in 1892. He was instructed to do whatever proved necessary to promote the faith of the

Catholic immigrants in America, while at the same time encouraging them to blend into their new country, socially and politically.[8]

Archbishop Satolli had the opportunity to apply this principal when the French–Canadians of Danielsonville, Connecticut, complained that the Bishop of Hartford was neglecting them. Bishop McMahon had assigned a French–speaking priest of Irish ancestry to attend to their needs, but they preferred a priest from Canada. The apostolic delegate wrote reminding them that they had freely chosen to leave their native land, and that it was impossible to expect the same provisions for the preservation of their language in this country as might be obtained in their native land. They were instructed to obey the bishop and to accept the French–speaking priest provided.[9]

Even the provision of national churches was deemed a temporary concession to the newly arrived Catholic immigrants, affording the use of native language and custom in order to preserve the faith, not to bolster nationalistic sentiment. This was emphasized in the 1897 decision of the Propaganda officials concerning a group of French–Canadian Catholics in Saginaw, Michigan, who preferred to attend the English–speaking church rather than the national church provided for them. Since the rector of the national church protested, the prefect of the Propaganda responded—in favor of the immigrants' choice to abandon the national church once able to speak English.

Mieczyslaw Cardinal Ledóchowski communicated the decision of the Propaganda in a letter to the Apostolic Delegate, stating that the provision for national parishes, distinct from territorial churches because of language, was ". . . an exceptional distinction, which must cease with the disappearance of the cause . . ." which, of course, was immigration itself. He continued, "The abolition of such quasi–parishes in the United States will have to be done with much prudence and slowness."[10] The decision was repeated in a circular to the American bishops from the Apostolic Delegate, in which he emphasized the right of any Catholic immigrant capable of speaking English to attend the local English–speaking churches instead of his national church.[11]

Practical Obstacles

The local implementation of the Roman decisions concerning the pastoral care of the immigrants in America was often far from simple, especially in regard to the large number of non–English–speaking Catholic immigrants. A lack of zealous priests and religious sisters capable of speaking the requisite languages and willing to work among their co–nationals in this country was a major problem. Desperately in need of priests capable of speaking the languages of their resident Catholic immigrants, local American bishops gladly accepted any European priest who presented himself for employment. Quite often, such vagabond clerics were a source of great scandal. Fleeing their own European bishops, or traveling to America without the release of their superiors in order to seek their fortune, such clerics scandalized many an immigrant congregation by means of dishonest or immoral practices. The problem was compounded by many European bishops who regarded the American priest shortage as the perfect opportunity to rid themselves of troublesome clerics.[12] By the end of the nineteenth century, the Roman authorities forbade any American bishop to employ priests from eastern and southern Europe unless such clerics received permission from the Congregation of Propaganda Fide in Rome and could present bonafide credentials and testimonial letters from their bishop or superior in Europe. Connecticut's bishops improved the number and quality of their priests capable of speaking the languages of the immigrants in the state by sending American seminarians to study in Europe and by visiting European dioceses and seminaries in search of acceptable priests.

The many zealous priests and religious who came to America bearing legitimate permissions often found the establishment and administration of national churches in America a near impossible task. Untrained in administration and oftentimes baffled by American finances, real estate procedures, or church fund raising, not a few immigrant priests found themselves unsuccessful in their attempts to establish and maintain a national church.

A lack of adequate funds with which to build national churches, schools, and other buildings needed to form vibrant parishes for the Catholic immigrants was another serious problem. Since the majority of arriving immigrants were extremely poor and often unused to contributing for the support of the Church, having come from countries in which the Church received state subsidies, the income necessary for the establishment and maintenance of parochial facilities was extremely difficult to come by.

Added to this was the obligation to build a parochial school for each mission in the country, placed upon the church leaders by the Third Plenary Council of Baltimore in 1884. Rectors were given two years to implement this decree, which meant that major funds from each mission and diocese had to be siphoned off the total income. Each diocese also was required to establish a seminary, providing another drain upon already strained diocesan finances and another block to projects such as national churches.

Internal factions within the respective immigrant communities often contributed to the difficulties of establishing national churches. Rivalries whose roots were found in ancient village or sectional differences among the immigrants themselves often hindered the establishment of churches or divided existing national church communities. Despite such obstacles the Church did establish national churches and also defended the Catholic immigrants and their rights to be in America.

Catholic Immigrants in Connecticut

The Diocese of Hartford was able to overcome successfully the obstacles to the establishment of national churches because of the determination of the immigrant groups themselves to establish such churches and use their own languages and cultures in their worship and religious life. The dedication of the clergy and religious—both immigrant and American–born— was guided by the strong pro–immigrant policies of the bishops who ruled the diocese during the years of greatest immigrant arrivals in Connecticut: Bishops Lawrence S. McMahon (1879– 1893), Michael Tierney (1894–1908), and John J. Nilan (1910– 1934). Bishops McMahon and Tierney, who was raised in Norwalk, were both immigrants; Bishop Nilan was of immigrant stock. All, therefore, were sympathetic to the sufferings and needs of the Catholic immigrants within their diocese.

The policies of each of these bishops in favor of the Catholic immigrants in Connecticut were based, ultimately, upon the fundamental ecclesiastical principle of pastoral solicitude for the salvation of souls. The role of the Church was not to perpetuate the nationalistic sentiments of each respective immigrant group in America. Rather, the Church in Connecticut, following the Roman instructives, would allow the establishment of independent churches, employing the respective languages and cultural manifestations of each nationality, insofar as the Catholic faith of the immigrants was bolstered and maintained by such specialized provisions. The Church was to employ every means possible in order to maintain the Catholic faith of the immigrants, so long as the unity of the Church was likewise maintained.

The Bishops of Hartford also defended the immigrants, opposing those inside and outside the Church who demanded the immediate, forcible Americanization of the new arrivals, or who condemned the Church as foreign and threatening to America. One such group, the American Protective Association founded in Clinton, Iowa, in 1887 to protect America from all that was foreign and Catholic, established strong followings in many Connecticut industrial towns, especially Norwalk and Bridgeport, at the turn of the century. Their anti-Catholic attacks were successfully parried by the preaching of members of the clergy, such as the Rev. James O'Donnell, Rector of St. Mary's, Norwalk, and the Rev. John Rogers, Rector of St. Mary's, Bridgeport. The diocesan newspaper launched its own defensive salvos against attacks on Church and immigrant, especially when it sensed a united effort between the APA. and the Republican Party to reduce the Church's influence on school boards and city posts by electing their men. During the city elections of the early 1890's, for instance, the *Connecticut Catholic* warned Bridgeport's Catholics to be wary of the Republican candidates who were united to the APA. whose title should be the society of "American Prejudicial Asses," and whose motto was "Ignorance, Fanaticism, and Forgery."[13]

Various Protestant churches also entered into immigrant work, often mixing their preaching with the same anti–Catholic attacks bandied about earlier in the century. The Fairfield County Baptist Association sent missionaries among the arriving immigrants in order to free them from the alleged errors of the Roman Church and to assist them in becoming Christian, productive members of Protestant America. A number of the Protestant missionaries working among Catholic immigrants were ex–Catholic priests who had converted to Protestantism, such as the Rev. DeCarlo, who opened a Baptist mission to the Italian community in Norwalk, and the Rev. Ceretta, who labored in Bridgeport. These men attempted to "Christianize and Americanize" their Catholic co–nationals by offering them material assistance and the gospel of American Protestantism. Often led by abject poverty rather than religious conviction, or confused by liturgical rites alarmingly similar to those familiar to the Roman Catholic, some Catholic immigrants joined these various Protestant churches. On the whole, however, the success of these efforts was meager when compared with the money expended on such missions.[14]

The Protestant ministers of Danbury unanimously supported the principles and work of another anti–Catholic group, the "Guardians of Liberty." Founded at the turn of the century by Charles Haines, ex-congressman from New York,[15] its purpose, as stated in its constitution, was to prevent the appointment to any political or military office of ". . . any person who openly or secretly concedes superior authority to any foreign political or ecclesiastical power whatsoever."[16] On May 1, 1912, the Guardians held a public meeting in Danbury, at the Methodist Episcopal Church. Attended by the pastors of all the local Protestant churches, the society's representatives, Charles Haines, Dr. Augustus Barnett, an ex–Philadelphia clergyman, and T. Benton Wilgus of West Virginia, once again sounded the warning against the Vatican, the Knights of Columbus—a secret military force which was allegedly arming the Catholic immigrants— and the un–American doctrines of the Roman Catholic Church. Condemned by the Vatican through James Cardinal Gibbons of Baltimore, the Guardians received a series of verbal thrashings from the Rector of St. Peter's in Danbury, the Rev. Walter Shanley, again supported by the Catholic press.[17]

In a letter to the editor on the evening following the Guardian meeting at the Methodist Episcopal Church, Fr. Shanley wrote:

> May the first, 1912, and the Methodist Episcopal Church . . . and the Philadelphia minister, and the railroad builder, and the Rev. Mr. Marsland [Rector of the Methodist Episcopal Church] will go down in history, associated with the most pitiable exhibition of bigotry and malicious calumny that Danbury has ever witnessed.[18]

Although the Diocese of Hartford and her clergy bore a distinctly Celtic stamp throughout this period of intense immigration, the open–minded policy and generous provisions in favor of the arriving Catholic immigrants provided an atmosphere both attractive and conducive to the settlement of large numbers of Catholic "new immigrants" within Connecticut.[19]

By the end of the nineteenth century, the City of Bridgeport was well-known as the most "cosmopolitan" of Connecticut's urban centers because of the multi–national flavor of its citizenry. The city had the largest number of immigrant groups in the state. The Church in Bridgeport also bore the most universal of images within the state, counting a wide variety of national groups among its congregations.[20] As a result, the first national churches in Fairfield County were organized in Bridgeport.

The establishment of national churches in Fairfield County,

as elsewhere in the country, was no easy task. The problems and successes of each national group in Bridgeport were similar to those experienced by the immigrant groups in other cities within Fairfield County. The national churches in Bridgeport provided the paradigm for the development of national churches throughout county. By the time smaller cities in Fairfield County began founding national churches, important developments had occurred within the state. The number of clergy and religious able to speak the numerous languages was greater; the intensity of national and factional differences lessened; the pattern and program of establishment perfected to a greater degree than was possible during the founding of these earlier, precursory national churches in Bridgeport.

The establishment of national churches and the subsequent defense of the Catholic immigrants by the Church formed the two essential parts of the Church's pastoral program for the Catholic immigrant in Connecticut. The first phase was the product of necessity—the establishment of normative Catholic life for the Catholic, non–English–speaking immigrants. Churches, clergy, and religious sisters were needed to provide the basics of Catholic life and were supplied by the diocesan and local clergy so far as practical circumstances allowed. The lessons learned from the establishment of Bridgeport's national churches served well to guide the Catholic immigrant communities and clergy in the other towns within the county.

Antipathies toward the Catholic immigrants grew along with the immigrant numbers by the turn of the century. Renewed efforts were made to effect new restrictive laws to curb the number of immigrant arrivals and, consequently, the influence of the Church that was growing so rapidly because of the immigrants. The Church responded on the diocesan and local level by defending the Catholic immigrants and their rights to come to America. Connecticut's bishops and clergy went beyond the traditional defense of the rights of their Church to exist in a democratic society. By the turn of the century they claimed that America should welcome the Catholic Church, with all its immigrant members, since the fortunes of "one nation under God" were dependent upon the success of Christ's "one, holy, Catholic and Apostolic" Church.

The Germans of St. Joseph

Prior to the organization of national churches within Bridgeport, the majority of non–English–speaking Catholic immigrants settled in the city's East Side, joining with other Catholics at St. Mary Church, which gained the title "Mother of Seven Daughters," since seven parishes were organized from the original establishment, five of which were founded for immigrant congregations.[21]

The first national church to be organized within Fairfield County was St. Joseph in Bridgeport, founded for the growing Catholic German community. The earliest Germans in Bridgeport settled on the East Side, around the Waltersville School, on Kossuth, Pembroke, Hallet, and Hamilton Streets.[22] The Rev. Joseph Schaele of St. Boniface Church in New Haven was assigned to attend to the needs of the few German and French Catholics in Bridgeport in December, 1874. By 1877 the German and French Catholics formed a sufficiently large community to require the construction of their own church. It was a "frame church of an English Gothic style," with a seating capacity of 250, located at 43 Madison Avenue.[23] St. Joseph Church retained its status as a mission of St. Boniface Church in New Haven until 1886, when it was established as an independent national church, with the title "St. Joseph German Canadian Church." At the time the mission was formed, some 700 German Catholics and 500 French Canadian Catholics numbered among its communicants, and the duties of its rector were extended to include the Bohemians, Hungarians, and Slovaks of the city.[24]

In 1890 a school was begun in a rented hall for sixty–one students taught by lay teachers. By 1893 this arrangement proved insufficient for the needs of the parish and was closed in June of that year. Land was purchased in 1900, and a four–room frame school building was opened by the Rev. Hubert Dahme in September, 1901, for 140 students, taught by three School Sisters of Notre Dame.[25]

By the turn of the century most of the other national groups originally assigned to the care of St. Joseph had succeeded in establishing their own churches, leaving this "German Canadian Church" with a markedly Teutonic complexion. In September, 1901, Bridgeport's German Catholic community played host to the more than 2,000 delegates of the German Central Verein and the German American Young Men's Catholic Societies of North America. Sunday September 8, Bridgeport witnessed the parade of German Catholic delegates through town as they marched to St. Augustine's Church where a pontifical Mass was celebrated for them by Bishop Tierney. Later in the day a larger parade was organized as a sign of Catholic unity and strength, with participants of every Catholic society from throughout the state and New York marching with the German delegates and city officials.

The purpose of the week long meetings was ". . . to attempt to unify all Catholic organizations in order to stem bigotry, assure rights and maximize effectiveness . . ." of Catholic organizations in the United States.[26] This idea of uniting all Catholic societies in the United States regardless of nationalistic sentiments and loyalties, was first put forth by Bishop Hortsmann of Cleveland and received the strong support of the Diocese of Hartford. Bridgeport and the resident German Catholic community, therefore, became instrumental in the initial efforts in this country to unify Catholic activity for the benefit of all Catholics in America, an idea that would ultimately lead to the formation of the American Federation of Catholic Societies and the National Catholic Welfare Conference.[27]

The Slovaks of St. John Nepomucene and Sts. Cyril and Methodius

The responsibility for the spiritual welfare of the Catholic Slovaks, Hungarians, Polish, and Ruthenians was given over to the Rev. Joseph Formanek in 1890. He was assigned as the assistant at St. Mary's in Bridgeport and held services for these Catholic immigrants in the church's basement. Fr. Formanek had been brought to Bridgeport by members of the Hungarian community, a fact that would prove abrasive to the delicate factional balance within the Slovak community.[28] As their numbers grew, however, each of these groups would desire to establish its own church, staffed by its own priests, in order to manifest the strength of their Catholic faith and to bolster their own national identities and cultures in a foreign land. The establishment and maintenance of such churches for the "new immigrants," those arriving from eastern and southern Europe, would be no easy task.

The Slovak settlement in Bridgeport had its origins in 1879 with the arrival of Joseph Mrazik and his family from Slovakia, then a part of the Austro–Hungarian Empire. His home on Willard Street became the center for the early Slovak community, since through Mrazik's assistance the newcomers were able to find food, clothing, housing, and employment.[29] As the community grew, its center was moved to Sedlar's Hall at 83 Willard Street. It was here that a number of early Slovak societies were organized: The Society of St. John Nepomucene, founded in 1887; the Society of St. Stephen, in 1888; and the St. Joseph

Society Branch 19 of the First Catholic Slovak Union, also in 1888.[30]

In April, 1889, the "Slavonian Catholic Society of Bridgeport, Connecticut" sent a petition to the Bishop of Hartford, reporting they had purchased land in Bridgeport on which they intended to build a church, and requesting the bishop's permission to solicit funds in order to pay for the land.[31] The bishop flatly refused his permission, stating,

> The Bohemians and Slavs ought to be satisfied with what is granted to other Catholics. No other people has asked me to give to people that I do not know a letter with my official seal, to collect as they please. . . . If the Bohemians and Slavs cannot build a church as other Catholics do, namely, by acting under their own pastor, they had better give it up. They will never get any more authority from me; though if they act like other Catholics, I will help them all I can.[32]

In 1890 the reported 1,200 Catholic Slovaks of the East Side renewed their petition to the Bishop for permission to begin a parish.[33] They diligently continued their efforts to secure funds sufficient for the payment of the purchased property. Money collected among the community during Slovak services at St. Mary's was watched over by the lay leaders, among whom was Michael Simko, one of the original petitioners to the bishop, and in whose house much of the organization and counting of funds took place.[34] Bishop McMahon acceded to their wishes and appointed the Rev. Joseph Formanek to serve as their rector. An election was called by Fr. Formanek to choose trustees, a parish secretary, and four ushers, one to represent each of the four major groups within the parish, the Slovaks, Hungarians, Poles and Czechs.[35] The community continued to worship at St. Mary's until November, 1891, when the basement church of St. John Nepomucene was completed.[36]

St. John's, the first Catholic Slovak mission in New England, was to provide the pattern for the formation of national churches for the newly arriving eastern and southern European immigrants in Fairfield County. It would also serve as a clear example of the deleterious effects of nationalism and factionalism in religion that would plague so many of these latter immigrant groups during their early efforts of parochial organization. Divisions already were developing during Fr. Formanek's administration. A lawsuit was brought against the church, the nature of which is unclear. The church was judged liable for damages, the payment of which provoked controversy within the church itself, dividing the congregation, the trustees, and the rector.[37]

The divisions within the mission were made "crystal clear"

to the newly appointed rector, the Rev. Francis Pribyl in 1897. Fr. Pribyl received an anonymous letter and telegram from Bridgeport threatening him if he dared come to the city and take possession of St. John's.[38] The already tense situation was worsened by Fr. Pribyl himself, who dismissed the trustees in September, 1897, claiming them to have been irregularly elected and guilty of "neglect of duty and malfeasance in office. . . ."[39]

Having ejected the elected trustees of the church, Fr. Pribyl very effectively gave offense to the members of the various national societies to which they belonged. The results were disastrous. Since Fr. Pribyl's dismissal of the trustees had been seen as an act of prejudice against the various national groups, those so offended began to agitate among the parishioners to have him removed from office.[40] The result was the excommunication of the three men primarily responsible for the agitations, since they had ". . . given grave scandal to the faithful and being detrimental to religion, instigating riots and disturbances . . ." against lawfully constituted ecclesiastical authority.[41] Since the majority of the men who belonged to the church were fellow society members of the three men censured by the Bishop, the excommunications had little immediate effect, other than rendering impossible the election of non–society members as trustees.[42]

Fr. Pribyl resigned in 1899 and was replaced by the Rev. Joseph Kossalko, a Slovak, and by a Polish priest, the Rev. Joseph Culkowski, who was sent to assist the new Rector in the process of re–establishing peace among the various national groups in St. John's.[43] Since the Societies of St. John and St. Stephen failed to grasp the seriousness of the situation, Bishop Tierney threatened to include all members under the ban unless the societies expelled the censured men from their membership. In September, 1899, when the two societies refused to comply with the Bishop's demands, they also were placed under interdict and excluded from normal church life. Not until June, 1900, did the societies and the excommunicated men comply with the demands of Bishop Tierney and receive full absolution from the incurred censures.[44]

Fr. Kossalko had worked for the excommunications of the three men and of the parish societies, which resulted in strained relations between rector and parishioners. By 1905, the rift had widened, and the congregation elected the one–time excommunicated men to the positions of parish trustees and secretary, an election which Fr. Kossalko was powerless to stop without further insulting his people.[45]

In April, 1907, representatives of the Society of Saints Cyril and Methodius, composed of members of St. John's Church, met with Bishop Tierney to ask his permission to establish a new congregation for the Slovak community of Bridgeport.[46] The need for a new mission was alleged to be the small size of St. John's Church, making it unable to service the large Slovak community of Bridgeport, then reportedly numbering about 8,000. However, the society was anxious to purchase an even smaller frame church—the old St. Mary's on Crescent Ave.—recently evacuated by the newly formed Polish mission of St. Michael. The reasons for the petition were other than the seating capacity of the church. Internal factions, problems in Fr. Kossalko's administration and pastoral practice, and his refusal to erect a parochial school numbered among the motives for the Slovaks's request.

The members of Fr. Kossalko's congregation also had notified the Apostolic Delegate in the United States, Archbishop Diomede Falconio, OFM, of their rector's administration and divisive practices.[47] The Delegate had his own questions concerning Fr. Kossalko. The priest had sent a circular letter to the American bishops containing grave and groundless accusations against the promoters of a Slavic congress that was to be held in Scranton, Pennsylvania. Anxious for more information about the priest, the Delegate wrote to Bishop Tierney for his opinion.[48] Bishop Tierney responded before he had been apprised of the problems at St. John's by the representatives of the congregation, and reported to the delegate that Fr. Kossalko appeared to be a zealous and capable priest. The Bishop viewed Fr. Kossalko's circular as containing nothing of an alarming nature, since it appeared,

> . . . only to present another phase of the restlessness that is quite general throughout the country on account of difference in language, political sentiment and nationalistic tendencies. This restlessness is a natural result of the association of so many different nationalities under one government but will become less pronounced as the various people grow accustomed to the new order of things in which they live.[49]

Archbishop Falconio informed Bishop Tierney of the complaints against Fr. Kossalko, which were confirmed by the representations made to the Bishop by members of St. John's. Fr. Kossalko's own disobedience of the Bishop's order to build a parochial school, his attempts to thwart the Bishop's census of Slovaks in Bridgeport by forbidding his supporters from co-operating, and his submission of false data also bore witness to the truth of the accusations made about the priest's administrative practices.[50]

Finally, convinced by the chorus of accusations against Fr. Kossalko and of the real need for another Slovak church in Bridgeport, Bishop Tierney met with the diocesan consultors on October 10, 1907, and decided to divide St. John's and to establish the Church of Saints Cyril and Methodius.

Fr. Kossalko protested the decision to the Apostolic Delegate, and, on November 27, 1907, opened canonical proceedings against Bishop Tierney on the grounds that the division had violated canon law and the priest's parochial rights.[51] The Delegate communicated his decision to Bishop Tierney on January 17, 1908, in favor of the parochial division.[52] Fr. Kossalko was subsequently removed as the Rector of St. John's and replaced by the Rev. Desiderius Major in 1908.[53]

The Rev. Matthew Jankola was assigned as the first rector of Saints Cyril and Methodius in November, 1907, and gathered his congregation in the old frame St. Mary Church on Crescent Avenue. It was on this site, originally given to the city by P.T. Barnum for use by religious groups, that Fr. Jankola and his congregation built the present church, which opened on March 23, 1913.

With the division of St. John's and the formation of the mission of Saints Cyril and Methodius in 1907, the Slovak community was able to manifest its strong devotion to the Church by developing vibrant, impressive parishes.[54] During the pastorate of the Rev. Matthew Jankola, a school and convent were completed by 1912, and a basement church opened in 1913.[55] Under the leadership of the Rev. Andrew Komara the community of St. John's parish opened a "model school," in September, 1913, complete with gymnasium, bowling alleys, baths, library, hall, stage, and assembly rooms, which also served as a social and civic center for the parish.[56] Father Komara also opened an industrial school in 1927, and the first Catholic day nursery with the help of George Eames of the Singer Sewing Machine Company.[57]

Fr. Komara strongly opposed the desire of many of his congregation to create a Slovak enclave capable of resisting the influence of the larger American society. He constantly encouraged them to learn English and to Americanize some of their traditions in order to adapt gradually to their adopted country.[58] St. John's also nurtured the vocations of a number of priests. The Rev. Stephen S. Grohcol, a member of St. John's, was ordained in June, 1914, and was "the first native of New England of Slavonian extraction to be ordained to the priesthood."[59]

During the twenty–fifth anniversary celebration of the founding of St. John Nepomucene Church, the strong faith and devotion of the Catholic Slovaks was emphasized by the Rev. John Kubasek of Yonkers, who stated,

> . . . we [Slovaks] are Catholics by faith, Americans by allegiance, and Slovaks by birth, and we are proud of all three, because each one of these in its own sphere only helps to perfect the other. . . . The strong Faith of the Slovaks of Bridgeport is but a new proof of what religion can inspire, what enduring monuments it can create.[60]

The French of St. Anthony

The 500 French Canadian Catholics who attended St. Joseph German Canadian Church in Bridgeport were encouraged by their rector to organize their own church soon after St. Joseph had attained its independent status in 1886.[61] Following the advice of their Swiss–born rector, the Rev. Theodore Ariens, thirty members of the colony formed the Société de Saint Jean Baptiste on October 1, 1887, with the sole purpose of establishing an independent mission for the French Catholics of Bridgeport.[62] The community was composed of some Swiss and Parisian French, but the greater majority was of French–Canadian or Acadian origin. Following the closure of various industries in New Hampshire, and especially of the Silver Plating Shop in Meriden in the early 1880's, their numbers grew throughout Connecticut. Large French communities began in Waterbury, New Haven, Danielsonville, and Bridgeport, the members of which were employed in various trades and manufacturing occupations.[63]

The French–Canadians in Connecticut had shown themselves to be strong in national pride, at times belligerent toward the Bishops of Hartford in their demands for parishes and French–speaking clergy of Canadian origin. Those of Danielsonville were especially vocal. They petitioned Rome and the Canadian bishops for aid, claiming that the Bishop of Hartford had refused to respond to their plea for French–speaking priests. The reality of the matter was quite different than the French petitioners had suggested to the Roman authorities.[64] A resident French–speaking priest had served that community for years. The problem was that he was of Irish extraction; the French–Canadians of Danielsonville demanded one of their own. The tensions were increased by various petitions of the Canadian hierarchy to Rome which simply repeated the accusations and impossible demands of the Danielsonville community.[65]

The policies of the bishops of Hartford had been far from prejudiced or half–hearted on behalf of the French–Canadians in Connecticut, or on behalf of any other Catholic immigrant group. Because of the practical concerns of the diocese, especially a lack of funds and a shortage of reliable foreign–born priests, the American bishops were forced to employ American–born or Irish–born priests capable of speaking the required languages and willing to minister to the different language groups.

Bishop Lawrence McMahon had expressed his open–minded policy towards Catholic immigrants in 1887 during a meeting of the Congress of French Canadians of Connecticut. The Bishop was accused of mistreating the French–Canadian people by opposing the employment of French–Canadian clergy and the training of clergy abroad. The Bishop replied, in French:

> Send them to me. . . . That they are Canadian, Irish, or German makes no difference to me. . . . I am the father of all. Send me your children . . . poor and intelligent . . . who have the disposition to the priesthood, and I will take charge of their education.[66]

The French–Canadians of Bridgeport were far from belligerent toward their Bishop as had been their co–nationals in Danielsonville. Under the continued guidance of the Rev. Theodore Ariens and of the Rev. Joseph Cartier, Rector of the French Church of St. Louis in New Haven, they had successfully obtained the permission of Bishop McMahon to form a parish committee. They met on March 6, 1892, at Bridgeport's old Post Office Building, then known as the Grand Army of the Republic Hall, and elected Nelson Bonneau and Joseph Bousquet as their first trustees.[67]

With Bishop McMahon's permission, St. Anthony's was organized on December 23, 1892, as a mission of New Haven's French Church of St. Louis, and visited once a week for Mass by Fr. Cartier or one of his curates. The congregation first gathered for Mass in a rented store on Fairfield Avenue, then in the Grand Army of the Republic Hall. As the community grew, the need for larger quarters led to the decision of December 24, 1892, to purchase property for the construction of a church. A parcel of land on Colorado Avenue was purchased on December 31 from the P.T. Barnum estate, at the cost of $3,346.00.[68]

The prestige of Bridgeport's Catholic French community was enhanced in October, 1893, when St. Anthony's played host to the eighth annual convention of Connecticut's French Canadians. Having grown and prospered, Bridgeport took its rightful place as one of the centers of French settlement in the state, while St. Anthony's displayed its strength of numbers, organization, and importance among Connecticut's French Catholic immigrant communities.

On December 4, 1894, the newly constructed frame church of St. Anthony was dedicated by Bishop Tierney. St. Anthony's became the fifth French mission in the diocese of Hartford on June 21, 1896, when it was granted independent status,[69] and received its first resident rector in the person of the Rev. Joseph Senesac.[70]

The need for Catholic education was felt almost immediately at St. Anthony's. Sunday school classes were organized and directed by lay teachers beginning in 1898.[71] As the number of transient boarders decreased, replaced by an ever–increasing number of resident families, the Rev. Joseph DeSaulniers observed the need for a Catholic school for his French congregation, and opened the first grammar school classes in 1902, with an enrollment of 125 children, taught by three lay teachers.[72] In 1904 Sisters Louis Yvonne and Anne Philibert, Daughters of the Holy Spirit, were employed to teach the children in the church basement that had been remodeled by the parishioners to serve as classrooms for the eighty students.[73]

The stability of the French community of St. Anthony was manifested in the generous use of their church and facilities accorded the various other Catholic immigrant groups in the city during the periods of organization and construction of their own respective churches. The Hungarians of St. Stephen used St. Anthony's during the year 1899–1900; the Lithuanians of St. George in 1907; and the Slovenians of Holy Cross from 1913 through 1915.

The Hungarians of St. Stephen, St. John, and Holy Trinity

By the beginning of this century Fairfield County had become the home for the second largest Hungarian community in the United States, which had formed in the West End of Bridgeport during the last years of the previous century.[74]

The religious allegiance of the Hungarian community was much more diverse than was that of most other immigrant groups. They adhered to the creeds professed by the Roman and Eastern Rite Catholic Churches, the Jewish synagogue, the Hungarian Reformed Church, and the Church of Christ (originally begun as the Hungarian Reformed and Evangelical Church).

The Catholic Hungarian community itself was composed of members of both the Latin (Roman) Rite and Catholics of the Eastern Rites. Both groups were fully Catholic, and professed an identical creed, yet followed their own ancient liturgical and ecclesiastical traditions, which necessitated the establishment of individual churches, the formation of separate church communities, and the employment of separate clergy able and sanctioned to minister to the needs of the faithful according to their respective traditions.

Due to the general lack of clergy, the care of all Bridgeport's Hungarian Catholics, of both Eastern and Latin Rites, originally was given over to the Rector of St. Joseph's Church, until the arrival of the Rev. Joseph Formanek as assistant at St. Mary's in 1889. Fr. Formanek had come to Bridgeport as the result of the encouragement of members of the local Hungarian community, but was given expanded responsibility for the Slovak, Ruthenian, and Polish Catholics as well. These Catholics remained under his jurisdiction even after he became the first rector of the Church of St. John Nepomucene. National antipathies among these groups led many of the Hungarian Catholics of the Latin and Byzantine Rites to move out of the East Side of Bridgeport, and to clear and settle in the then uninhabited, wooded West End, forming their own solid and isolated enclave around Pine and Spruce Streets.[75] The larger community of Ruthenian Rite Hungarian Catholics, however, chose to remain in the East Side and eventually formed St. John the Baptist Church on Arctic Street.[76]

The Hungarian Catholics of the Latin Rite were organized into the mission of St. Stephen on December 1, 1897, and the spiritual welfare of its 500 original members was entrusted to the Rev. George Csaba, its first rector.[77] Under Fr. Csaba's leadership the community of St. Stephen prospered. Until the original St. Stephen's on Spruce Street was completed in 1901, the community worshiped in the churches of St. Peter and later St. Anthony. A school was opened in 1905 for 167 students, taught by three Sisters of the Holy Ghost.

Following Fr. Csaba's death in December, 1905, the strength of various factions within the Hungarian community threatened the church's unity. So strong were the divisions within the community itself, which were bolstered by the administrations of the succeeding rectors at St. Stephen's, that by 1914 Bishop Nilan feared the possibility that nearly half of the Catholic

Hungarian congregation might be lost to the Church.[78] A general distrust of the American–born, or "Irish" clergy, hampered the efforts of the Bishop to secure an adequate supply of Hungarian–speaking priests.

Bishop Tierney's program of sending American–born seminarians to study in Hungarian seminaries was threatened during his successor's administration because of the insistence by the Hungarian congregation that only Hungarian–born priests minister to their community. In an editorial, the *Catholic Transcript* tried to explain the practice of foreign studies for American–born seminarians:

> It is not intended by this policy to place American priests over Hungarian congregations, but to supply mixed congregations, where Hungarians are numerous, with priests who can speak their language and keep them in the practice of their religion.[79]

The solution, however, was not found simply in the supplying of bilingual priests. The bond between the religious and national sentiments of the Catholic Hungarian urged him to search for a religious experience capable of evoking the specter of his homeland.

Bishop Nilan's fears were not unfounded, since the Hungarian Catholics fell prey to the work of the Hungarian Reformed Church and the various Orthodox Churches in the area. The problems within the St. Stephen community, however, were successfully overcome with the appointment of the Rev. Stephen Chernitzsky in May, 1914. He had served as the Pastor of the Hungarian parish of St. Ladislaus in South Norwalk for five years at the time of his Bridgeport appointment. He had united a divided parish in South Norwalk to produce an extremely energetic community during his short five–year pastorate.[80] Fr. Chernitzsky remained in office until his death in 1948, during which time he consolidated the parish, gaining for his Hungarian community national recognition as the most prominent and progressive Hungarian Latin Rite parish in the Northeast.[81] The Catholic Hungarians of the Eastern Rites organized their own churches during this period.

The pastoral care of the Eastern Rite Catholics in the United States posed a unique problem to the American bishops. The resources of the bishops were stretched to the breaking point. Attempting to care for the arriving immigrants of the Latin Rite, as well as working to build up the already established American–born congregations, many bishops saw little need for what they deemed to be special provisions for immigrants of the various Eastern Rites.

In 1895 the American archbishops petitioned Rome, asking that the arriving Eastern Catholic immigrants either be allowed or forced to subscribe to the Latin Rite in the United States.[82] The Apostolic Delegate, Archbishop Francesco Satolli, disagreed with the harsh, yet convenient, solution proposed by the American archbishops. Much more aware of the cultural and religious sensitivities of the Eastern Rite Catholics than his American counterparts, and cognizant of the schism of many from union with Rome as a result of what was termed "forced Latinization," the Apostolic Delegate cautioned Rome against any provision that would oblige these Catholics to abandon their ancestral religious traditions.[83]

The Holy See followed the Delegate's suggestion and, in 1897, decreed that such a change of rites be allowed in the United States, but was not obligatory.[84] Nevertheless, the Eastern Rite Catholics felt themselves possessed of a second-class status in the Church in America. Further Roman decrees subjected Eastern Rite clergy to the Latin Rite bishops and denied their married clergy the right to exercise their legitimate ministry in America. The superior attitude often exhibited by the Latin clergy toward their Eastern Rite brethren and the co-opting of many Eastern Rite Catholics into Latin congregations, bolstered their suspicions that they were being forcibly "Latinized" by their American co-religionists.

Hartford's situation was similar to that of other dioceses in the country that had large and growing communities of Eastern Rite Catholics. The American bishops were strapped for priests capable of speaking the needed languages, who possessed the required permissions for work in America and who were acceptable to the nationalistic sensibilities of each immigrant group. As a result, the American bishops found the cleric of the Eastern Rites to be a commodity more difficult to come by than his Latin counterpart, yet of equal importance. American bishops were often forced by necessity to accept immigrant priests who had arrived in their diocese without the ecclesiastical permission of their superiors. Rome issued numerous decrees prohibiting the American bishops from accepting such wandering clerics of both the Latin and Eastern Rites, since they were so often the cause of scandal and schism among the faithful. Yet the bishops' need for priests often left them with no choice other than to employ these men and hope for the best. Many foreign bishops availed themselves of that opportunity, providing the required permissions and letters of recommendation to their American counterparts. The results were often scandalous to the faithful and injurious to the Church in America.

By 1903 the situation with the Hungarian Catholics of both the Eastern and Latin Rites in America was such that the Austro–Hungarian hierarchy met in late March to pass obligatory resolutions concerning Hungarian immigrant priests. Concerned to "protect the ecclesiastical and national cause . . ." of their Catholic co–nationals in the United States, the Hungarian bishops agreed that only those priests who were judged to be politically and ecclesiastically irreproachable would be granted permission to emigrate to America. They refused, however, to prohibit the migration of unsuitable or troublesome clerics, deciding that they would receive only a "verbal dimissorial commendation" instead of the required written ecclesiastical permissions. They were, nonetheless, permitted to go to America.[85]

The obstacles to the successful establishment of normative Catholic life for the Eastern Rite Catholics in America were far from removed, either by the Roman decrees or by those of the Austro–Hungarian bishops. Since the Eastern Rite Catholic immigrants in the United States were without their own hierarchy until 1924, they were subject to the local Latin bishops, a situation that often times resulted in tensions and schism.

The tensions that developed between the Latin and Eastern Rite Catholics in Bridgeport were capitalized upon by the various Orthodox churches, which opened missions within the city to offer their services to any dissatisfied or confused Eastern Rite Catholics. As early as 1894 the Russian Orthodox in Bridgeport and other Connecticut cities began their work among the Greek Rite Catholics under the leadership of the Rev. Michael Balough.[86] By 1900, Bridgeport was home to one of the largest Orthodox missions to the Catholics of the Eastern Rites in the country and had taken in many of Eastern Rite Hungarian Catholics, the majority of whom attended Holy Ghost Russian Orthodox Church, then on Hallet Street. Unaware that Holy Ghost was not a Catholic Church, since the liturgical rites were very similar to those of the Ruthenian Rite, they continued as members of that church. Reports to the Roman authorities that a large number of Ruthenian Rite Catholics in Bridgeport had abandoned the Church resulted in the appointment of the Rev. Michael Jozkowicz to retrieve his co–nationals from what was termed a "quasi schism" in late 1900.[87] Once informed that Holy Ghost was not a Catholic church, the Ruthenian Rite Catholics returned to the Church, petitioned Bishop Tierney that Fr. Jozkowicz be named their rector,[88] and promised to turn over all ecclesiastical property to the Diocese of Hartford.[89]

Holy Trinity Church was organized in 1900 as the first Byzantine Rite Church in Fairfield County. Its first Rector was the Rev. Michael Jozkowicz, who ministered to all Eastern Rite Catholics in Bridgeport. The mission had grown from the St. John the Baptist Lodge, organized in 1860 by Hungarian Catholics of the Eastern Rite, then residing on the East Side of the city.[90] Prior to the completion of the church on the West Side in 1910, the lodge organized worship services in private homes, rented halls, the old Hawes Opera House, Sacred Heart and St. Mary's Churches on the East Side of Bridgeport.[91]

A second society, that of St. Elias the Prophet, was organized on September 2, 1900, by those Eastern Rite Catholics recently returned to the Church following their unintentional dalliance with the Russian Orthodox Church of the Holy Ghost. The purpose of this group, as expressed in its records, was to care for the Catholic faith of its members, and, eventually, to establish a church for the practice of their Eastern Rite Catholic faith.[92] Both societies came under the care of the Rector of Holy Trinity, but were divided geographically into colonies on the East and West Sides of Bridgeport. Since the larger Eastern Rite Hungarian community remained on the East Side, the second rector of Holy Trinity, the Rev. Eugene Volkay, resided on Kossuth Street and opened a small chapel on Pembroke Street in 1901 for the Eastern Rite Catholics in that area of the city.[93] On May 8, 1904, the Society of St. Elias the Prophet changed its name to "The Greek Catholic Church of St. John the Baptist." It served as the foundation for the Church of St. John the Baptist, founded in 1905, under the care of the Rev. Elias Gojdics, the second Eastern Rite church in Fairfield County.[94]

Relations between the Latin and Eastern Rite clergy in Bridgeport, as elsewhere in the United States, were not always cordial. Questions concerning jurisdiction and the administration of the sacraments to Eastern Catholics by Latin priests often led to disputes. The relations even among the priests and hierarchy of the Eastern Rites proved difficult in these early years in the United States. In 1902, Pope Leo XIII named the Right Rev. Andrew Hodobay as Apostolic Visitator to the Greek Catholics in the United States to represent the needs of the Eastern Rite Catholics to the American hierarchy. After four years, Bishop Hodobay was exhausted by the battles engaged in with his own Eastern Rite priests who either ignored or openly disobeyed his authority.[95] The Bridgeport and Norwalk missions were not exempt from such insubordination by members of the Eastern clergy,[96] which hindered their growth and stability even after a bishop had been assigned to them in 1907.[97]

The problems faced by Bishop Soter Stephen Ortynski as he attempted to establish normative Catholic life for the Ruthenian Catholics within the United States were enormous. The conflicting national factions, often troublesome clergy, and abrasive relations with the Latin Rite clergy all proved to be nearly overpowering. The *Catholic Transcript* spoke of the Bishop's problems and the sad state of affairs that had resulted among many Eastern Rite Catholics because of their excessive nationalistic fervor. Possibly overemphasizing the point from an "Irish" and Latin perspective, the editor of the paper wrote,

> The hundred odd priests scattered over his extensive diocese, though far enough apart to abide in peace, are not oppressively handicapped by the bonds of charity. The spirit of discord has learned the secret of annihilating distance in this age of wireless and the 'phone.' As for the people, we are told: 'They will often prefer to desert to the orthodox schismatics rather than run what they consider the risk of being Latinized, or brought under the influence of the Latin hierarchy.' If their own clergy cannot devise means for keeping these Greek Catholics in peace it were bootless for strangers [the Latin hierarchy] to undertake to hold them within the realm of peace and charity and fraternal love. Nationalism has proved a poor exchange for the Christian religion.[98]

Until the establishment of the Ukranian Greek Catholic Diocese of the United States in 1913, and the Greek Rite Diocese of Pittsburgh in 1924, the Catholics of the Eastern Rites in America continued to be under the jurisdiction of the Latin bishops.[99]

Once the diocese was established, the Hungarian Catholics of both Eastern and Latin Rites proved their dedication to the Church by developing vibrant, thriving parish communities throughout Fairfield County. In 1912, the parish of St. Ladislaus was dedicated in South Norwalk, and the Diocese of Hartford took the opportunity to voice its official praise of the Hungarian Catholics, stating,

> They [Hungarian Catholics] are industrious and hard–working. The erection of this becoming temple is an earnest expression of their determination to remain and to worship God according to the traditions and teachings of their native land.[100]

The Poles of St. Michael

The care of the Catholic Poles originally was given over to the priests of St. John Nepomucene Church.[101] Bishop Tierney assigned the Rev. Joseph Culkowski, a native of Poland, to serve the Polish community at St. John's in July, 1899. By December, the estimated 1,000 Polish Catholics on the East Side of Bridgeport were organized to form the Church of St. Michael the Archangel and placed under Fr. Culkowski's care as temporary administrator of the new mission.[102] Old St. Mary's Church on Crescent Avenue was purchased and served as the first Roman Catholic Church for the Polish immigrants in Bridgeport until 1907, when the present church was built on Sterling Street.

The formation of St. Michael's was as much the result of agitation by members of the Catholic Polish community of Bridgeport as it was the result of the pastoral solicitude of Bishop Tierney. The religious fervor of the Catholic Polish immigrants was outstripped only by their nationalism. They, more than any other Catholic immigrant group in America during the last century, came into conflict with authority—both civil and ecclesiastical. Such excessive nationalism in religious practice led to the only permanent Latin Rite schism from the Roman Catholic Church in America and the subsequent formation of a sect known today as the National Polish Catholic Church.

The first important rupture came in 1895 with the excommunication of the Rev. Anton Kowalski in Chicago. After entering into conflict with his bishop over parochial administration, Fr. Kowalski and a faction from his mission established their own church and subsequently were excommunicated. The second, and more important incident, occurred in Scranton, Pennsylvania, in 1897. Local Catholic Polish immigrants built a church, petitioned the Catholic bishop to staff it, but demanded control of the property. The bishop refused, demanding the deed in accord with church law. The Rev. Francis Hodur, a Polish priest in the diocese, who had been active in labor relations between Polish mine workers and unions, intervened, taking the side of the people against the bishop.

Fr. Hodur, supported by a faction of the faithful, built a church and carried on his priestly functions for his own community despite the protestations of his bishop. After losing numerous appeals to Rome, Fr. Hodur was finally excommunicated and united various groups of dissatisfied Catholic Polish immigrant groups, into his own church, based upon what was termed "democratic Catholicism."[103]

Hodur had been active in the labor struggles of the Polish immigrants within the Irish–controlled United Mine Workers Union. Arriving late in the century, the Polish laborers found many management positions filled by the descendants of earlier Irish immigrants. The exploitation of these newer immigrants by those of Celtic origins was real and often savage. Hodur justly and heroically defended his co—nationals against such exploitation and injustice at the hands of the Irish union bosses. The hatred for the Irish, however, which many Poles developed as a result of labor injustice, was all too often transferred and applied in areas where no anti—Polish prejudice or exploitation existed.

All too often insensitive to the practical limitations of the Church in America, the Polish immigrants demanded their own priests, as well as the right to control the administration of the churches established for them, lest they be forced to "submit" to any Irishman. The result was the development of a tendency among Catholic Poles to cry out for a church independent from the "Irish" hierarchy in America.

Bishop Michael Tierney of Hartford felt the sting of numerous unjust accusations against himself and his administration by various Polish groups, including the nascent community of St. Michael in Bridgeport.

At the instigation of the Rev. Lucian Bojnowski of New Britain, the Catholic Poles of Connecticut gathered in Meriden in October, 1899, to organize a mutual aid and social society in an attempt to stabilize and unite the factions within the greater Connecticut Polish community. The result was the establishment of a united organization, but one whose membership professed open hostilities toward the Roman Catholic Church.

In his report to the Bishop, Fr. Bojnowski repeated the words of one speaker at the meeting who stated,

> I was born a Pole, not a Catholic, and, therefore, the Catholic religion has no significance among us: We ought to strive for that which the most liberal and socially minded hold as a goal.[104]

Fr. Bojnowski's retort was a call for a Catholic union that would unite the Polish community, supported by members of the Bridgeport and New Britain Polish communities. Fr. Bojnowski also received the support of the Bishop, who approved the establishment of a Polish Catholic Union within the diocese on October 6, 1899.[105]

The division among the delegates at the Meriden meeting accurately described the divisions felt in all Polish communities in the country. Bridgeport's was no exception. Problems between those supporters of independence from the local bishop and from all things "Irish" and those loyal to the Church led

58

to demonstrations during 1898 and 1899 and culminated in the establishment of St. Michael's under the temporary administration of a Polish priest, the Rev. Joseph Culkowski. This was an attempt to meet the real needs of the Catholic community of Polish immigrants while uniting the community and undermining the strength of the hostile faction.[106] The effectiveness of the Bishop's move was limited.

With the establishment of the new mission and the purchase of old St. Mary's Church, St. Michael's received its first rector in February, 1900. The Rev. Witold Becker, a native of Poland, had been employed by Bishop Tierney while still a student at the University of Louvain, Belgium. His appointment to St. Michael's, however, was not received with universal acclaim by the members of the local Catholic Polish community, nearly half of which left the church as a result of the new rector. Fr. Culkowski had been appointed only as temporary administrator, yet members of the community took a dim view of his transfer, effected without their consent or consultation.[107]

Fr. Becker successfully overcame most of the divisions within his congregation. He diligently worked among his people and built up a strong, loyal following by returning many to church membership. He established church societies and Sunday school classes, reduced the original church debt considerably, purchased land, and secured loans in order to build a new church. His work was cut short in July, 1906, by his sudden death, at the age of 32 years, after a four–day bout with ptomaine poisoning.[108]

Prior to Fr. Becker's death, Bishop Tierney entered into discussions with the Conventual Franciscans of the newly formed Polish-American Province of St. Anthony in order to secure their assistance in the Church's work among Catholic Polish immigrants of the diocese. The need for Polish priests in the diocese was great. The Bishop had made numerous appeals and visits to European seminaries and bishops asking for their help, and continued to send many American–born seminarians to study in Europe in order to learn the languages of the Catholic immigrants resident within the diocese. However, the need for priests far outweighed the supply.[109] The agreement reached with the Franciscans by the time of Fr. Becker's death, therefore, assured a constant supply of Polish–born and Polish–speaking priests for the Polish community of St. Michael.[110]

One of the reasons why Bishop Tierney decided to employ the Polish Franciscans was the strength of Polish nationalistic fervor of the Catholic Poles that led them to demand only Polish–born priests for their church. So strong was this fervor that the Bishop was forced to terminate his program of seminary studies for American–born priests in Poland, since it was viewed by the Catholic Poles as an Irish plot to steal Polish parishes by staffing them with non–Polish priests.[111]

The result of the employment of the Polish Franciscans led to a split within the community at St. Michael's, the schism of a group of Catholic Poles from the mission, and the eventual establishment of St. Joseph National Polish Catholic Church by the dissatisfied faction in 1907. This was through no fault of Bishop Tierney. The problems and subsequent schism at St. Michael's were the results of the excessive nationalism and anti–Irish prejudice of some of the members of the Catholic mission to the Poles in Bridgeport, not the lack of pastoral care on the part of the Catholic clergy.

Following Fr. Becker's death in 1906, St. Michael's was entrusted to the temporary care of the Rev. George Glogowski, who remained for the month of July. The Rev. Felix Baran, OFM, was then named the first Franciscan Rector of the mission. Already assigned to a church on Long Island, he was unable to take charge of St. Michael's immediately and sent the Rev. Leon Wierzynski as a temporary replacement, who remained until December, 1906.

Fr. Wierzynski had built up a following among the congregation during his stay at St. Michael's. When Fr. Baran was able finally to take charge of St. Michael's, the supporters of Fr. Wierzynski began to demonstrate publicly against the Bishop's decisions. They disturbed church services,[112] physically blocked the departure of Fr. Wierzynski and the arrival of the Franciscans, nearly causing a riot, sent a committee to Hartford to protest to the Bishop himself, and finally protested the actions of Bishop Tierney to the Apostolic Delegate in December, 1906.[113]

In his response to the dissatisfied members, the Delegate repeated the Vatican's instruction to the American bishops, reminding them that it was the prerogative of the local bishop to appoint rectors for the good of the individual parishes and not according to the private interests of individual groups.[114] The Delegate concluded his letter,

> Therefore I would advise and urge you to show yourselves obedient and submissive to your ecclesiastical superiors, and to show by your hearty cooperation with the Father appointed as pastor of your church, that you appreciate the attention shown by the Right Reverend Bishop for the welfare of your parish.[115]

Submissive to an "Irish" bishop, who had disregarded their demands concerning the affairs of a Polish mission, they could not be. So, on the evening of February 18, 1907, a group of about 500 dissatisfied Roman Catholic Polish immigrants from St. Michael's Church met in Sedler's Hall on the corner of Hallet and Wheeler Streets. The principal figure at the meeting was the excommunicated Catholic priest, Francis Hodur, who convinced his angry audience to abandon their ancestral Catholic faith, break with Rome, and to establish a National Polish Catholic Church in Bridgeport.[116]

He glossed over the major differences between the faith of the Roman Catholic Church and that held by the newly founded Polish Catholic Church and convinced his audience that their departure from allegiance to Rome would be of no major consequence since the beliefs of the two Churches were identical. Hodur told his audience that as members of his church they, and not their priest, would handle the administration of their parish. They would select their own pastor, instead of being forced to depend upon a non–Polish bishop. The majority of those present at the meeting voted to support Hodur, and a committee was chosen to canvas the Polish community in Bridgeport to solicit funds for a new church.[117] St. Joseph National Polish Catholic Church was organized by those who had protested to the Apostolic Delegate.[118] The schismatic congregation completed a wooden church on California Street in 1908, and continued to worship there until the present building on Harriet Street was completed in 1936.

Once the divisive faction within the community removed itself, the development of normative Catholic life among the Poles of Bridgeport continued rather smoothly. Fr. Baran arrived at St. Michael's in 1907 and began to continue the work begun by the first rector, Fr. Becker. As the Catholic community continued to grow at St. Michael's, the small wooden church on Crescent Avenue proved too small.[119] The church was sold to the newly organized Society of Sts. Cyril and Methodius in September, 1907. Fr. Becker's plans for a church were approved and the cornerstone laid by Bishop Tierney on September 2, 1907, on the Sterling Street property,[120] purchased by the former rector.[121] The church was completed and ready for use by the congregation in late May, 1908. A school also was opened in September, 1907, for 125 students, presided over by two Franciscan Sisters from Trenton, New Jersey.[122] The school flourished and, after numerous renovations and site changes, settled in the present school building, which opened in September, 1920.

The Italians of Holy Rosary

On December 10, 1888, Pope Leo XIII addressed an apostolic letter to the American hierarchy concerning the spiritual and material plight of the Italian immigrants in the United States. A lack of familiarity with language and culture was the common lot of all immigrants in America. To this universal obstacle was added the more insidious danger of the "padrone" system of contract labor. Promised passage to America and a job in exchange for a contract agreement, thousands of Italians found themselves literal slaves once they arrived in the United States, forced by unscrupulous fellow countrymen to perform the most wretched work for the lowest pay.[123] The result of such poverty and degradation was described accurately by the Pope:

> It is to be deplored that so many unfortunate Italians, forced by poverty to change their residence, should rush into evils which are often worse than the ones they have desired to flee from. For very often to labors of various kinds that take away the life of the body, there is added the ruin of souls.[124]

For the Church in America, the pastoral care of the Italians presented problems peculiar to the Italians themselves. Their numbers alone created an almost insurmountable practical obstacle to the provision of adequate pastoral care. Added to the language problem was that of the innumerable Italian dialects. Another obstacle was provided by the provincial loyalties of the Northern and Southern Italians, which often led to divisions within the congregations. A priest hailing from the northern provinces often couldn't be understood, and therefore, not accepted by his Southern Italian congregation. The poverty and often transient status of many Italian immigrants made the establishment of normative Catholic parochial life among them difficult. Not only unable and unaccustomed to support a church, in many cases they were unwilling to contribute to their local parish. Arriving from a country only recently united by the revolution of 1870 against the Papal States, many Italian immigrants bore marked anti–clerical views that kept them far from the institutional Church in America.

Rome had been very interested in the plight of the Italian immigrants in America from the early 1880's. Having received numerous reports that Italians were being lost to the Church in America in great numbers, the officials of Propaganda Fide requested the American Bishops to discuss the "Italian Problem," as it came to be known, during the Third Plenary Council of Baltimore in 1884.[125]

The American bishops preferred to deal with the Italian immigrants in the broader context of the pastoral care of all Catholic immigrants arriving in the country. Implying that the vast majority of Italians arrived in America with precious little love for the Church, the Americans wrote the Pope, and suggested that the solution to the Italians' weak faith was to be found in a beefing up of the pastoral care offered them prior to their departure for America.[126]

Rome was rather uninterested in the Americans' discussion concerning the possible causes of the Italians's alleged weakened devotion to the Church. The possibility that millions could lose their Catholic faith upon migrating to America pointed out clearly to Rome that the solution, as well as the problem, now was to be found in America.[127] Rome's solution was the adoption in 1887 of the plan of Bishop Giovanni Battista Scalabrini of Piacenza, Italy. It provided for the foundation of a lay institute, which came to be known as the Società San Rafaele, to assist the Italian immigrants from departure to arrival in the new world.[128] Its clerical counterpart was a religious congregation of Italian priests, the Congregation of St. Charles Borromeo, whose members would serve as missionaries to the Italian immigrants in the Americas. To foster the apostolate to the Italian immigrants and to aid the nascent immigrant pastoral societies, the Pope wrote the American bishops in 1888, encouraging them to do all in their power to secure the faith of his fellow countrymen.

Bishop Lawrence McMahon of Hartford had begun to provide for his Italian subjects by the late 1880's. By the end of the decade he found the number of Italians in his diocese to be growing, with the largest colonies developing in New Haven and Bridgeport.[129] The Bishop's most pressing need in order to establish missions to the Italians, was a number of dedicated Italian priests.[130] Having already secured the assistance of priests for New Haven from Bishop Scalabrini's newly founded missionary congregation, Bishop McMahon pressed for another Italian missionary to be sent to the Italian community in Bridgeport. As the result of the Bishop's persistence, the Rev. Pietro Lotti was assigned to serve, temporarily, the Italian immigrants of Bridgeport who then numbered about 1,000 persons in May, 1891.[131]

Because of ill health, Fr. Lotti was replaced after a short period by the Rev. Carlo Bertorelli. At first, Sunday and festive Masses were celebrated in St. Mary's old convent, then at the old St. Mary's Church on Crescent Avenue (then being used as St. Mary's School) until late 1891, when a small wooden, frame chapel was constructed.[132] Since many Italians were transient residents, remaining in Bridgeport only so long as work on the railroad continued, Fr. Bertorelli's superiors found it impossible to continue the mission. Because of the poor response from the Italian community and the pressing need for Italian priests elsewhere, the Bridgeport mission was closed in July, 1892.[133]

The mission was re–opened in 1894 by another missionary priest of Bishop Scalabrini's congregation, the Rev. Beniamino Bertò, and placed under the patronage of St. Michael the Archangel. By 1894 the mission had attracted only 850 members from the rather substantial number of Italian immigrants then residing in the city.[134] Bertò continued to work among his co–nationals in Bridgeport, receiving financial support, not from his congregation, but from one of the local "Irish" rectors, the Rev. John Rogers of St. Mary's.[135] In 1896, the mission again closed due to a lack of support from the local Italian community and because of the need for good Italian priests in other parts of the state that already had established, responsive Italian congregations.

By the turn of the century, new Protestant missions opened for the Italians in Bridgeport and in Norwalk. The main field of their labors was the large, nominally Catholic, Italian population within these cities that remained substantially unchurched. The Bridgeport mission was the Evangelical Italian Calvary Congregational Church on Center Street, organized in 1902 and presided over by the Rev. Carlo Ceretta who provided services and Sunday school in both English and Italian for those under his care.[136] Ceretta, a former Catholic priest, had been laying the foundations for a secure Protestant mission in Bridgeport for some time prior to its formal organization in June of that year.[137] Another Protestant mission to the Italians of Bridgeport was organized by the Second Baptist Church on the corner of Kossuth and Arctic Streets. It enjoyed a large attendance by members of the local Italian community.[138] One of the Protestant missionaries spoke of their work among the Italian Catholics in 1901:

> It is not a hard matter to Christianize and Americanize the Italians when they come here, if the [Missionary] Association will only furnish the men and the money to do it.[139]

Even though the Protestant missions had slow beginnings, the very idea of Protestant proselytizing among the pope's fellow countrymen was a disturbing one for the Catholic clergy.

Following the closure of St. Michael's Italian mission in 1896, the Italian community had been cared for by the ministrations of the Rev. Stephen Csaba of St. Stephen's Hungarian Church as well as at St. Mary's and St. Augustine's. In 1901, the Rev. Bernard Donnelly, assistant at Sacred Heart Church, was assigned ". . . the charge of the Italians with jurisdiction over the entire city.[140] With the advent of new Protestant missions to the Italians it was deemed necessary once again to attempt a permanent, independent Catholic establishment for them in the city.

In early January, 1903, another Scalabrinian missionary, the Rev. Gaetano Ceruti, was sent to re–establish the Catholic mission among the Italians of Bridgeport.[141] On January 18, Fr. Ceruti celebrated Mass in the basement church of St. Mary's on the East Side and organized a committee for the establishment of a permanent mission among the Italians of Bridgeport. Following the meeting on the 18th, Fr. Ceruti purchased land and a house on East Washington Avenue, ". . . with 18 rooms on two floors, one of which will be transformed for use as a church, while the other will serve as the priest's residence . . ." The total purchase cost was $12,000, half of which he secured from a local bank, the balance promised by members of the Italian community, which numbered nearly 5,000 persons.[142] He issued a handbill on January 23, announcing that the Catholic mission to the Italians would again be opened and that Mass would be celebrated every Sunday and Monday in the basement of St. Mary's Church. All other religious services—baptisms, marriages, sick calls and counselling—could be arranged with him at St. John's Rectory on Brook Street, where Ceruti was temporarily residing. The handbill continued, inviting all Italian men of twenty–one years and older to join the Italian priest for an organizational meeting on January 25.[143]

On February 13, 1903, the Italian mission was legally incorporated under the title of "Our Lady of Pompeii." A small wooden frame church was built alongside the two–story house and solemnly dedicated by Bishop Michael Tierney on March 20, 1904. The rectors of the local territorial churches were present, along with a number of their parishioners, as a sign of solidarity and support for the nascent Italian community.[144] Despite the auspicious inauguration, all was not secure for the Italian mission, the third newly built national church in Bridgeport since the opening of the century.[145]

By the turn of the century, the Scalabrinian missionaries in Connecticut, as elsewhere in the United States, were experiencing serious internal problems. Problems arose since they had overextended themselves and accepted the responsibility for too large a number of Italian missions in the country. The missionaries also found themselves to be shorthanded, since a number of their Italian–born priests chose to serve under local diocesan bishops once in America, rather than renew their commitment to the missionary congregation. Added to this was the fact that the administrative and organizational abilities of many of the Italian priests proved unequal to the problems posed by their impoverished Italian congregations. The congregations themselves often were divided by provincial loyalties, which made unified actions impossible, while rendering the collection of necessary funds from people unaccustomed to supporting their churches even more difficult.

The Bridgeport mission reflected some of these problems. In 1904 the estimated membership at Our Lady of Pompeii was 3,000 Italians, while the total receipts for the year totaled only $1,278.72. With a debt of $9,000, and expenditures of nearly $4,000 for the year, the prospects for financial solvency were dim at best. By the end of the following year the debt had increased to over $26,000, while the receipts barely covered operating costs. Even though the number of members was substantial for a newly established church, the regular reception of the sacraments and participation in church activities was also low, as far as church records are able to reveal.[146]

By late 1904, Bishop Tierney seriously considered the possibility of entrusting all of the Italian missions within the diocese to the care of diocesan priests, twenty of whom spoke Italian, having studied in Rome.[147] Any such plans concerning the Bridgeport mission were forestalled by a fire which partially destroyed the Church of Our Lady of Pompeii on the night of January 9, 1905.[148]

Even though the church was restored and rededicated by Bishop Tierney on March 26, 1905, the consolidation and development of the mission continued to be slow because of the provincial conflicts among the members of the congregation and inadequate leadership on part of the priests.[149]

The entire situation became intolerable when Fr. Ceruti entered into a literary battle in the local press that simply aggravated the sensibilities of his congregation. Fr. Ceruti's actions pushed the Bishop to write to the priest's superiors and request a replacement.[150] Since the Missionaries of St. Charles were already short of priests, they were forced to employ an Italian diocesan priest for the Bridgeport mission.

On December 13, 1906, the Rev. Angelo De Toro was assigned as the new rector of Our Lady of Pompeii Church. Although not a member of Bishop Scalabrini's missionary congregation, he received their support. Since Bishop Tierney had experienced problems from itinerant European ecclesiastics in the past, he insisted that the new rector be subject to supervision by Bishop Scalabrini's missionary congregation, even though he was a diocesan priest.[151]

Italian immigration to Bridgeport increased, with a second wave of immigrants arriving between 1905 and 1910, which built up the already established communities on the East Side and North End of the city.[152] With the increased population came increased problems at Our Lady of Pompeii, stemming from provincial loyalties and frictions within the congregation. In an attempt to defuse such provincial factions, endemic to the Italian churches in Connecticut, and, in some cases, to relieve the local Italian churches from inept administration, Bishop John Nilan entered into a program suggested by his predecessor: replacing Italian–born rectors with American–born priests capable of speaking Italian.

On August 17, 1916, Bishop Nilan appointed the first of three successive American–born priests of Irish descent as the pastors of Our Lady of Pompeii, which had come to be known as Holy Rosary Church. The Rev. Michael Keating served until 1924, the Rev. Thomas Sullivan until 1927, and the Rev. Joseph Daly until 1938. The administrations of these men proved to be successful. Since they were not of Italian birth or lineage, they were freed from the provincial loyalties that had divided the Italians from each other and from their earlier Italian–born rectors. They could speak Italian, were familiar with Italian customs, since they had studied in various seminaries in Italy, and were provided with Italian–born assistant priests. These pastors were able to unite the Italian Catholics of Bridgeport, stabilize the financial situation of the parish, build the present church on East Washington Avenue, and begin the organization of the Church of St. Raphael, the second national church in Bridgeport for the Italian community.[153]

The Lithuanians of St. George

The Catholic Lithuanian church in Bridgeport had its origins in the St. George Lithuanian Benefit Society, organized in 1892 by the Rev. Joseph Zebris and led by Petas Bezgelis, Juozas Ruzgis, and Anupras Cimelius.[154] The Lithuanians as a group tended not to forge bonds with any other immigrant groups, preferring their independent national identity to any possible benefits garnered from united efforts with other groups.[155]

Bridgeport's Lithuanian community was among the smallest in the state. In fact, in a census of Lithuanian families made by the Rev. Joseph Zebris in 1896, the Lithuanian community in Bridgeport is not even mentioned. By February, 1907, when the independent mission of St. George was established, there were only 283 members enrolled, including children and fourteen Poles.[156]

Prior to the organization of their own church, the Lithuanians worshipped at Sacred Heart, St. Michael's, and St. Anthony's Churches. They had established themselves in the area around Summer Street, and Park, Main, and Myrtle Avenues; and it was here, in the early summer of 1907, that land was purchased by the Rev. Matthew Plavzinaitis, ". . . far from any other Catholic Church and . . . far enough from any saloon, and wholesale of liquors."[157] On October 13, 1907, Bishop Tierney dedicated a small wooden–frame church under the patronage of St. George for the Catholic Lithuanian community of Bridgeport. The ceremonies were followed by a parade of Lithuanian Catholics from throughout the state, including members of the St. George's Lithuanian Society, the St. Alanilus Lithuanian Lodge, and the Great King John Sebaskey Lithuanian Society of Bridgeport.[158]

The stability of the newly established mission was threatened by internal divisions, the frequent change of administrators, debt, and battles with nearby missions concerning membership. The first pastor of the church was not named until 1911. Prior to that time, three priests had served as temporary administrators and either resigned or were replaced due to illness or administrative problems. From July, 1910, until the appointment of the Rev. Matthew Pankus as the first pastor, St. George's was served by the priests of Sacred Heart Church.[159] The community, small though it was, found itself divided, as were the other Lithuanian communities in the state, over questions concerning the importance of ethnicity and its relationship to the Church.[160]

Bishop Tierney had spelled out clearly the field of activity and the limits of St. George at the time of its establishment. In September, 1907, he wrote the Rev. Victor Paukszto, the second administrator of St. George, that the church had been established,

> . . . exclusively for the benefit of the Lithuanian Catholics of that city [Bridgeport] and therefore only the Lithuanian language is to be used

in the sermons, instructions, announcements, etc. . . . . These regulations
are necessary to preserve proper discipline and safeguard the spiritual
welfare of souls.[161]

Such restrictions were necessary, not simply for discipline,
but to preserve peace between neighboring missions.[162] With
so many national groups within the city, the administration of
the sacraments to a person of one ethnic background by a
priest of another nationality often sparked fierce battles among
the members of the clergy themselves. Because of this, church
regulations were established restricting the ministrations of any
immigrant priest to Catholics of his own nationality. Such restrictions appear trivial today, but at the turn of the century when
national loyalties and prejudices ran deep, they proved the
only way to maintain unity and peace among the various groups
within the Catholic Church.[163]

Such was the problem at St. George's. The Rev. Paukszto
had begun preaching in Polish as well as Lithuanian at St.
George's, attracting some Polish Catholics and incurring the
wrath of the rector of St. Michael's Church that had been established to serve the Polish community. Fr. Paukszto claimed that
his actions were justified by the presence of Lithuanians who
spoke only Polish, but the true reason was financial necessity.
Since his Lithuanian congregation was too impoverished to meet
the interest payments on the church's debt, the added income
garnered from the Poles was his only hope of solvency. In
order to justify his actions further, Fr. Paukszto wrote the
Bishop, accusing the Rector of St. Michael's of poaching within
St. George's territory, collecting funds from the Lithuanians
for the Polish church.[164]

The Rector of St. Michael's repaid his Lithuanian counterpart
in kind, writing Bishop Tierney that he was amazed at the
splendid changes occurring in the modern world, ". . . and
amongst them Lithuanians change into Poles, and Poles into
Lithuanians."[165] He complained that Fr. Paukszto continued
to hold Polish services, stealing the one–time members, and
income, of the Polish church.[166]

Fr. Paukszto resigned in January, 1908, after an administration of only five months. He was replaced by the Rev. Lewis
Woitys, who remained over two years, but whose term also
was marred by financial and factional difficulties.[167] Following
Fr. Woitys's administration, the parish was placed under the
care of the Rev. Timothy Sweeney, assistant at Sacred Heart
Church. The placing of the Lithuanian mission under the care

of a territorial parish was an attempt to diffuse the factional strife within the community, relieve the tensions between the Poles of St. Michael's and the Lithuanians of St. George's, brought about by the crossing of national lines by the previous administrators, and to improve the financial status of the mission.

It was not until the appointment of the Rev. Matthew Pankus as the first resident Pastor of St. George on April 2, 1911, that the prospect of real stability, both financial and spiritual, appeared possible for the Bridgeport Lithuanian community. Fr. Pankus finally liquidated the old debt on the original wooden church and property, purchased land and a house for a rectory, and succeeded in constructing the present brick church, which was dedicated on June 29, 1924.[168] Fr. Pankus united and increased the membership in his congregation dramatically during his long administration. The efficacy of his efforts was revealed by the editor of the *Catholic Transcript* on the occasion of the dedication of the lower church of St. George in 1912:

> The Lithuanian people of Bridgeport are industrious, law–abiding and religious. The strong Christian faith in which they were nourished in their native land abides with them in their new home. They promise to constitute a most desirable element in the Catholic progress of Connecticut.[169]

The Slovenians of Holy Cross

Catholic Slovenians began to settle in Bridgeport by the beginning of this century. Since their homeland had been divided among the Italians, Austrians, and the Hungarians prior to the War, the Slovenians did not feel isolated entirely upon their arrival in the city. The foundations established by the Hungarian settlement on the West Side of the city served well as a buffer community for the arriving Catholic Slovenians. The Catholic Hungarian Church, St. Stephen, became the center of life for the newly–arrived Slovenians as well as for the larger Hungarian community.[170]

The Slovenians had difficulty in adjusting to American life and business practices. This resulted in the emigration to their native land of a large portion of Bridgeport's Slovenian community by the outbreak of World War I. This number increased following the war and the establishment of Yugoslavia as an independent country. Bridgeport's Slovenian community, therefore, was neither large nor stable, factors that would prove crucial in the development of a Slovenian church.

The national sentiments of the Slovenians in Bridgeport were also an important factor that determined their relationship with other immigrant groups. Most of Bridgeport's Slovenians came from the area of Prekmurje in Yugoslavia, which had come under the rule of Hungary prior to the war. An effective program to crush Slovenian culture and nationalism had been pursued there for years. Since the public use of the local language was allowed by the foreign government only in the local village churches, the loyalty to the Catholic Church professed by the Slovenians came to be a sign of their national heritage as well as their religious fervor. While their relationship with the larger Hungarian community in Bridgeport was peaceful, for the most part, it was marked by some animosity, especially after the Slovenian community began to work for its own, independent national church.[171]

In December, 1910, Fr. Edmund F. Neurieher, the Pastor of St. Stephen's, went to New York in order to secure the assistance of the Franciscans of the Slovenian Province. The meeting resulted in the regular visits of the Rev. Anselm Murn, OFM, to the Slovenian Catholic community of Bridgeport, which began on the Feast of the Holy Name of Jesus and continued until the founding of Holy Cross Church.[172]

The regular, if infrequent, visits of the priest from New York proved to be insufficient for the needs of the growing Slovenian community in Bridgeport. By 1912, the Rev. Kazimir Zakrajsek, OFM, a Slovenian Franciscan in New York, secured the assistance of a newly arrived Slovenian priest, the Rev. Michael Golob. A meeting was held in Zigler's Hall in Bridgeport on December 8, 1912, for those Catholic Slovenians of the city interested in forming a Slovenian parish. The meeting was conducted by Fathers Anselm Murn, OFM, and Michael Golob. Fr. Golob agreed to work in Bridgeport and, through the intercession of Fr. Zakrajsek and the petition from the Catholic Slovenians of Bridgeport to Bishop Nilan, received permission for a mission to the Slovenians to be centered at St. John Nepomucene Church. The Franciscan described the series of events that led to Fr. Golob's appointment, as well as the seeds of animosity between himself and the Hungarian priest of St. Stephen when presented with the prospect of a Slovenian church in Bridgeport:

> There [in Bridgeport] Slovenians from Prekmurje lived in a Hungarian neighborhood. Bishop originally was not favorably inclined [to them] because the Hungarian pastor convinced him that they [Slovenians

from Prekmurje] were not Slavs but Hungarians speaking a 'dialect.' I went there quite often. Since I had there a good friend in person of the Slovak pastor I was able to induce him to accept Father Golob as his assistant. Thus he [Golob] was in a position to go slowly and somehow secretly he did organize people, prepare a census in order to show to the Bishop how many are they. I have sent to the Bishop also the Slovak [pastor] and thus we did succeed.[173]

Fr. Golob celebrated the first Mass for the Slovenians at St. John Nepomucene on Christmas Day, 1912. According to Fr. Golob,

Slovenian people in the West End of the city rented on Christmas Day (1912) special street cars and traveled to the Slovak church of St. John Nepomucene where they had the first Mass and sermon in Slovenian.[174]

Since St. John's was on the East Side of the city, and the Slovenian community in the West End, Bishop Nilan decided that Slovenians should gather for Mass in the basement of St. Anthony's Church on Colorado Avenue. Not only would this prove more convenient for the community, but would also give the community the opportunity to prove its desire for and ability to build and support its own parish.

Opposition to the Slovenian Mass and the early plans for a national church was quick in manifesting itself. Most of the opposition came from the Hungarian Catholics of St. Stephen's where the Slovenian community had worshipped since its arrival at the beginning of the century. Since the removal of the Slovenian Catholics from the Hungarian parish would result in a substantial decline in the parish's income, St. Stephen's could hardly be expected to look upon such a move with delight. Also, some Catholic Slovenians opposed the new parish, since they preferred to continue worshipping at St. Stephen's. Their severe poverty diminished their ability to contribute to the construction of a new church. Despite the opposition, the plans for the new church continued. On January 29, 1913, the Society of St. Joseph was formed, and the majority urged that the society join the national mutual aid society, the American Slovenian Catholic Union (KSKJ).[175]

Since the Slovenians did not feel welcome at St. Anthony, they hastened to organize a committee to direct the foundation of their own church by February, 1913. The committee was composed of two representatives from each parish in Slovenia that had members within the Bridgeport Slovenian community.[176] On June 7, 1913, Fr. Golob was named the pastor of the newly established Slovenian national parish of the Holy Cross, which was legally incorporated on June 13.

Almost immediately after the formation of the church committee, rumors began to circulate that threatened the unified actions of the Catholic Slovenians. Having heard that the Hungarian church would soon receive a Slovenian priest, members of the Slovenian community began to grumble that the construction of an independent Slovenian church would be a useless waste of their hard–earned money. The provincial loyalties of each group, as well as the national antipathies felt between the Hungarian and Slovenian communities, all played their part in rendering the collection of funds for the new church more difficult. Fr. Golob lashed out at his congregation on July 13, 1913, concerning these problems:

> I know for sure that until I am delegated by the Bishop to serve Slovenians, at no other place a Slovenian Mass will be celebrated. If you can get somebody for your region to take care of you, I will then step down.[177]

The difficulty of collecting funds from a divided community was made more acute by the return of over 300 Slovenians to their homeland prior to the war, which reduced the Bridgeport community to approximately 800 members.[178] Nevertheless, land was purchased on Pine Street in August, 1914, for $3,850, and construction on the church was begun the following July. The church was completed and dedicated on November 28, 1915.

Problems arising from the national sentiments and animosities between the Hungarian community and the Slovenians of Holy Cross intensified. So intense were the attacks upon Fr. Golob that he resigned his pastorate in July, 1922. Despite the protestations of devotion to their pastor by the members of Holy Cross, which resulted in his reinstatement, rumors and accusations that he was "Pan–Slav" required the Bishop to intercede personally. Bishop Nilan addressed the congregation of Holy Cross on June 29, 1924, concerning the necessity of peace and unity within the Church. The response of the people is not documented. It must have been insulting to the Bishop, because the following Sunday Fr. Golob announced that the Mass would be a votive Mass of the Sacred Heart, ". . . in reparation for the grievous offences to the Most Revered Bishop past Sunday. . . ."[179]

73

The Slovenian population continued to decrease after the war as many returned to Europe. Despite the fluctuating membership and the animosity of some within his parish, Fr. Golob succeeded in developing a number of strong parish societies, regularize the Catholic life of his congregation, and, eventually, overcome all problems and divisions within his parish.[180]

Continued Immigration: Source of Connecticut's Problems?

Besides the establishment of national churches, the Catholic Church in Connecticut defended the Catholic immigrants. The success of the national churches may have been responsible for the growth of the foreign–born Catholic population within Connecticut, which continued at a phenomenal rate throughout the first two decades of the twentieth century. Catholic immigrants were drawn by Connecticut's industrial economy, and, to some extent, by the atmosphere created by the Church that was favorable to the immigrants' respective religious and ethnic needs.[181] Connecticut passed the 1,000,000 mark in population by 1906, of which an estimated 350,000 were Roman Catholics.[182] Bridgeport ranked as the most industrialized city in the state by 1910, thirty–third among the seventy–five most industrialized cities in the nation.[183] The growing economic importance of the city was mirrored by Bridgeport's population increase during the first decade of the century, the most dramatic of all cities in the state. In 1900, the city's population was 70,996, which jumped to 102,054 by 1910, primarily the result of foreign immigration.[184]

By the turn of the century, Connecticut was no longer the secure Yankee enclave it once had been, and many Connecticut residents were unhappy because of this change of events. The blame for all of the state's social ills was awarded to the newer immigrants. The present appeared threatened by the immigrants, who took jobs for the lowest wages and created social problems in the cities. The future stability of the state and its economy also appeared endangered as the sons and daughters of the immigrants began to assume leadership positions in business, government, and education.[185]

Concern over the mounting foreign population, the social transformation, and attendant problems in the cities unnerved many "old stock" Connecticut residents. In the spring of 1908, Governor Rollin Woodruff questioned leading Connecticut citizens concerning major social problems in the state. In his answer, J. Moss Ives, a noted Danbury attorney, named immigration as the greatest possible threat to the stability of the state, voicing the views held by many of his contemporaries. A man of flawless character, free from bigotry and a supporter of the Church, Ives nevertheless asked the basic question, "Will old New England, her standards of learning, her ideals, her customs, and her laws survive the constantly increasing influx of alien blood."[186]

Moss's fears resulted from the social evils—the ghettos, the abject poverty, disease and crime—that were the immediate result of such large–scale shifting of populations. Yet for many others, the arrival of the foreign–born proved to be objectionable on racial and religious grounds.

Immigration Restrictions

The works of Henry Adams and especially John Fiske, of Middletown, Connecticut, had worked well to create the attractive nineteenth–century myth of Anglo–Saxon Protestant superiority that influenced America's life, its view of history, its education and racial attitudes for decades.[187] New England was the "Third England," the last bastion of the democratic principles and virtues native to the ancient Anglo–Saxon and Teuton, which was threatened by the alleged genetic, cultural, and religious impurities of the arriving immigrants.[188] Calls for legal restrictions to immigration had been heard for years, usually with little result. Since the restrictions were aimed primarily against the recent arrivals, the bulk of which were from eastern and southern Europe, the Church saw such moves as direct attempts to stem its growth in America. The Lodge Bill of 1896, backed by Henry Cabot Lodge, a one–time student of Henry Adams, was a case in point. Attacking the bill as unjust, the Church authorities in Connecticut and elsewhere labeled the bill as "prejudiced and unfavorable to the Church. . . ."[189]

Having arrived in America with little financial resources, usually unskilled and ignorant of English, most immigrants gathered together in colonies, mainly within the larger urban areas. The resultant overcrowding, crime, disease, and the immigrants' general ignorance of language, clannishness, and religious and cultural practices that appeared alien to Americans, tended to confirm and strengthen the native Americans' phobia for all things foreign. Since earlier movements during the nineteenth century had proved ineffective in stemming the arrival of foreigners and the development of the Church, it was deemed more productive to convert the Catholic foreigners into productive, Protestant Americans.[190]

Discouraged by the large number of unnaturalized immigrants, programs designed to teach the immigrants English, personal hygiene, certain marketable skills, and the virtues of American democracy were begun throughout the country.[191] Still trying to prove itself compatible with American institutions, the Church praised such efforts and canonized the values of the Republic as being in harmony with those of the Church, while at the same time emphasizing that the Catholic need not be transformed into a Protestant in order to be a productive American. In an editorial entitled "What Catholics owe their Native Land," the *Catholic Transcript* demonstrated that the discipline and teaching of the Church led Catholics to be the best of citizens. Lest the Anglo–Saxon mythical history of Adams and Fiske go unchecked, the paper recalled that Catholics were among America's founders:

> The American Catholic loves the nation with a patriotic fervor. He treasures it as a rich inheritance. He proudly recalls, for the inspiration of himself and the edification of his children that Catholic science combined with Catholic philanthropy to rescue the land from the unknown; that the first sound that broke the Sabbath stillness of its oldest city summoned Catholic souls to prayer; that its Catholic priests explored its trackless rivers and Catholic pioneers felled its virgin forests and established its ancient cities; that freedom of worship was a contribution which the Catholic colony of Baltimore made to civilization; that on every battlefield from Lexington to Concord to Manila to Santiago Catholic soldiers did their duty with hearts as pure as the stars, pouring out blood as rich as the stripes of the flag of freedom. They signed the Declaration of Independence; they aided in the building of the Constitution; their wisdom illumined the senates; their judges kept pure the streams of justice; their industry, their ingenuity, their knowledge, their thrift, their courage aided substantially in the material prosperity of the country. We profess an inextinguishable faith; we are citizens of an indestructible Republic.[192]

The Church Defends the Immigrants

A new twist to the Catholic apologetic was employed in the Catholic press and pulpit in Connecticut at the turn of the century. Led by a clergy predominantly of Irish descent, with the bulk of its congregation composed of immigrants of eastern and southern Europe, the Church in Connecticut emphasized two themes prior to the first World War. The first had been suggested during the previous century: America was neither the handiwork nor the personal possession of the Anglo–Saxon or the Protestant alone. It was the second theme that showed a new boldness in the Church's leadership in Connecticut. No longer were Connecticut Church leaders content merely to emphasize the Church's compatibility with American institutions. They baldly stated that the continued strength of America and of her liberties was directly dependent upon the strength of the Roman Catholic Church in America. A goodly part of that strength came from arriving Catholic immigrants.

The Church was prepared to assist in the Americanization of her immigrant faithful—to a point. In fact, Rome had instructed the American hierarchy to do so during the previous century lest old–world loyalties threaten the growth and unity of the Church in America by socially and politically isolating large portions of its membership from mainstream American life.[193] Yet the ultimate goal of the Church was the preservation of the immigrants' Catholic faith, not the preservation of the immigrants' respective culture or national sentiments, nor of their Americanization. Lest the Church and her immigrant members remain on the fringe of American society, the Church had to encourage the slow adaptation of the immigrants to the American way of life. Neither the process of adaptation nor the American way of life could be tolerated, however, if either meant the loss of the immigrants' Catholic faith. A precarious balance had to be struck between encouraging the abandonment of old–world loyalties in order to melt into the surrounding society, while employing old world cultures and languages to strengthen the Catholic faith. On the local parish levels, this balance was not always achieved and resulted in excesses of national fervor on the part of the immigrants or prejudiced administration fostered by American–born Catholics. Nevertheless, the Church in Connecticut fought to defend its immigrant members' rights to maintain their culture and their ancestral faith while participating fully in American life. The Rev. Thomas Duggan, editor of the *Connecticut Transcript* was particularly vocal in defending the Catholic immigrants. Despite the support of the Church in Connecticut, the immigrants continued to confront American–born prejudices through the early twentieth century.

A stinging editorial entitled "Hyphenization" appeared in the *Catholic Transcript* in October, 1915. It decried the excesses of the Americanizing campaign in Connecticut as well as the condescending attitude of the American Anglo–Saxon intelligentsia that categorized naturalized Americans and their offspring according to their ethnic background. It was they who had the effrontery, according to the paper, to grant these new immigrants only a half citizenship as "German–Americans," or "Irish–Americans." The editorial continued sarcastically,

Let it be understood then that America belongs to Anglo–Protestantism. If it ever escapes from the domination of that element, it will be through the apotheosis of usurpation and the triumph of outrageous intrusion. We hear lots about the amalgamation of the races and the begetting of a distinctively American type. In the minds of many who use the word, to amalgamate means to make like unto ourselves. It means that the amalgamated must have cast off what was distinctive and takes on what we approve and what we affect. They must think our thoughts, accept our standards, repudiate what we condemn regardless of their own judgement and the rulings of their own conscience. Do this or be hyphenated. There is no alternative.[194]

The Catholic Church: Foreign or American? Again!

Distrust of the Church was growing stronger as the country's entrance into World War I drew nearer. Since the Church's membership was largely foreign–born and its highest authority was in Rome, the Church in America again came under attack as an agency subversive to the American Republic. The *Christian Science Monitor,* for example, claimed that the Vatican sent the names of episcopal candidates in the United States to Berlin for approval prior to issuing the appointments, ". . . in order that the Kaiser might pass upon the capabilities of the men named of advancing German propaganda in America."[195] In early March, 1918, the country's legislators in general, and Maryland's in particular, were informed that the number of Catholic servicemen in the American armed forces was too high, presenting the country with the real threat of a takeover of its government by the Pope at whose command these enlisted Catholic men would begin the revolt.[196]

Distrust of the immigrant and his Church also was growing in Fairfield County. Bridgeport's foreign–born population had increased as the war–related industries of the city grew. As the distrust of the foreigners and the push for Americanization intensified, the various Catholic immigrant groups exhibited their loyalty to their adopted country in numerous public displays, patriotic rallies, and religious services. The most significant of these public displays was choreographed by the Rev. Andrew Komara, the Pastor of St. John Nepomucene Church, who arranged for ex–President Taft to address the Catholic Slovak community of Bridgeport in March, 1917. The President praised Fr. Komara for his work among the Slovaks of Bridgeport and assured his audience that they had a place in the society of their adopted country. In the face of the claims of European governments that naturalized American citizens were considered by them to be the subjects of their native land, Taft reiterated that a naturalized citizen was a full American.[197] The effect of the President's address to Bridgeport's Slovak community was very positive, since it ". . . strikingly illustrated the true expression of the local Slovaks in the face of the crisis which this country is confronting."[198]

With the country's entrance into the war, the Church voiced its solid support of the government's policies, encouraging all Catholics to sacrifice willingly for the war effort. Enlistment rallies arranged by local Catholic churches in Bridgeport, Norwalk, Danbury and other towns encouraged the immigrants to offer their services for the defense of the nation. The need to prove their loyalty as Americans was felt most keenly by the national churches. Examples of the loyalty to the American cause felt by the various national congregations can be seen in St. John Nepomucene and St. Joseph Churches, which acquitted themselves admirably, sending the highest number of volunteers into the service from any national church in the county. St. John's Slovak Church sent 177 of its young men,[199] while the volunteers from St. Joseph's German Church "flocked loyally to the cause of the Stars and Stripes."[200]

Despite the patriotic efforts of the Church during the war, it could in no way lessen the isolationist fervor and distrust of the foreigner that marked life in post–war America. The state's Catholic press continued to defend the rights of the Catholic immigrant against the almost–fanatical push to Americanize all foreign elements in the country.

Only Americans Welcome

Local communities throughout the state developed their own Americanization programs. Bridgeport, suffering from severe economic problems with the closure of many war–time industries, blamed much of its problems on the immigrant population. The head of the Bridgeport War Bureau, Judge George Wheeler, a staunch anti–Communist, stated that riots and unrest in post–war Connecticut were proof that ". . . some elements in the pot of Connecticut have not melted."[201] Any immigrant who was not a citizen, or who was unable to speak English, became suspect as a radical anarchist.

Catholic parochial schools, especially those attached to national churches, came under attack as centers of foreign subversion and intrigue. The state school board passed two resolutions concerning schools where classes were taught in a foreign language in the state. During its June 17, 1918, meeting, the board determined that attendance at any such school did not satisfy the compulsory school law. During its Feb 10, 1920, meeting, the board pointed out that only two schools still used foreign languages: one was a Catholic school, St. Joseph in Bridgeport; the other was a Lutheran school. By 1923, schools in Connecticut were obliged by law to teach only in English. Foreign languages could be taught only one hour per week.[202]

In order to crack down on the alleged subversive tendencies and movements of the immigrants in the city, Bridgeport hired Cleveland's one–time police chief with a salary of $25,000 to oversee the Americanization of the resident aliens. Bridgeport High School's Americanization classes were revamped with the help of an officer furnished by the War Department who insured strict military discipline in dealing with the "potentially danger- ous" immigrants.[203]

In 1919, Connecticut established the Department of Ameri- canization. The department received a budget of $50,000 to establish a state–wide program that would effectively transform the state's immigrant population into loyal Americans within two years. A battery of agents capable of speaking various for- eign languages toured the state, establishing local Americaniza- tion offices, distributing bilingual posters and showing a specially composed movie that touted the benefits of Americanization.

This intensified program to Americanize the immigrant had received a boost from the state's Republican governor, Marcus H. Holcomb, who expressed his belief that the unassimilated immigrant was a danger to the republic.[204] Despite protests from the local and Catholic press condemning the governor's sentiments, the general fear of the foreigner and his alleged intrigues, especially following the Bolshevik Revolution, contin- ued to bolster the Americanization programs.[205]

The National Catholic War Conference in Washington, D.C., instituted a nation–wide campaign in the spring of 1919 to promote citizenship among the Church's foreign–born mem- bers. The aim of the program was "to emphasize the mutual obligations of citizenship and to encourage and aid immigrants to become citizens."[206] The efforts stressed the obligations of citizenship, ". . . to offset such civic lethargy as is apparent in the neglect of politics and civic affairs."[207]

The True American: White, Protestant, Non–alcoholic

Two other movements grew in strength during the post– war period that were much motivated by a fear of the un–

Americanized foreigner: the Ku Klux Klan and the movement for Prohibition. The Klan, re–organized in Georgia in 1915, preached a radical doctrine of white, Protestant supremacy in America. All that was foreign—Black, Jewish or Catholic—came under its ban. The Klan was most active in New Haven, New Britain, and Stamford. Prohibition had been supported for decades by many Protestant churches as a means of curbing the effects of alcoholism. The epitome of the evils of alcohol was usually portrayed as residing within the Catholic immigrants who were slaves of both a foreign Church and "demon rum" and, therefore, dangerous to America.

The Church's position concerning the Klan and its hatred of foreigners was made clear in a talk given by the Rev. Richard E. Shortell, the Pastor of St. Mary in Ridgefield in 1921. He spoke to his audience of over 8,000 in Putnam Park, stating that Americanization should take place in this way,

> . . . let us commence by first Americanizing some Americans within our gates; let us commence it by Americanizing those Americans who, radical and disloyal, are seeking to put the supremacy of the mob, the cunning of the criminal and the defiance of authority above the sacredness of the law; let us commence it by Americanizing the American who in a venal press and degraded pulpit are striking at the heart of America, seeking to undermine her strength and unity by putting class against class and creed against creed. . . .[208]

During the elections of 1924, Stamford played host to one of the largest of the Klan's state meetings. It was organized by the Grand Dragon Harry Lutterman of Darien, and thousands of Klansmen appeared. The state's Republicans had refused to include an anti–Klan plank in their platform during the state convention and received the support of party members during the election. Stamford's Republicans were no exception, employing their Lincoln Republican Club as a front for all Klan activities in the area.

The local Democrats joined with their state confreres, labelling the Klan un–American. The *Stamford Advocate* published an advertisement signed by all the local Democrats denouncing the Klan and its supporters. The Klan published their own advertisement in response, pointing out the un–American names of the signatories of the Democratic broadside. The generally negative response to the Klan's bigoted action did not help the Americanist movement. Even though the Klan enjoyed only a brief period of popularity in Connecticut, with an estimated peak in state–wide membership of 15,000 in 1925, it had its effect upon popular thought and contributed to the fear of the immigrant.[209] By 1926, the Klan leadership had become divided and lost much of its political and popular strength, but it continued to maintain smaller local branches for a number of years in Stamford, Bridgeport, Darien, Greenwich, and Norwalk.[210]

Prohibition had been supported for years, primarily by many Protestant groups. The movement was not simply a religious one, but drew deeply from cultural, political, and economic undercurrents as well. The post–war period was ripe for such an attempt to legislate the prohibition of liquor sales and consumption in the state. Prohibition was touted as a means to reduce the urban crime and poverty of the immigrant laborer while enhancing his productivity in the work place. Because of this, prohibition was supported by employers and much of the old Yankee, Protestant population of the state. The Catholic Church in Connecticut had urged temperance throughout the previous century. By its support of temperance societies and unions, it had encouraged the faithful, both immigrant and American–born, to a more temperate lifestyle and voluntary total abstinence. The Prohibition movement received little support from the Church, however, since it was seen as a fruitless interference into the privacy of the majority of state residents whose lives were not marked by intemperance or the vices and problems usually associated with drink.

Later Arrivals

Such movements to legally restrict the immigrants or to forcibly Americanize them according to the current white, Anglo–Saxon pattern had little lasting effect. Catholic immigrants continued to arrive during the first two decades of the century. They found already established and flourishing Catholic communities in Fairfield County providing them with an environment both economically and religiously attractive. The smaller communities of Stamford, Norwalk, Danbury, Fairfield, and Stratford found themselves to be the homes of newly established colonies of foreign–born Catholics. Familiar with the national parishes already extant in Bridgeport, they petitioned the bishop for their own, new national churches. Bishop Nilan, continuing the program established by his predecessor, granted permission for the establishment of nine national churches within Fairfield County during his years of administration from 1910 until 1934. However, where the numbers of any national group did not justify the establishment of an independent national parish, or where such an independent church might undermine the security of an already established parish, Bishop Nilan demurred.

Such was the case of the Germans in Stratford who had attended St. James. If permission were granted for an independent church for Stratford's small German community, then the same privilege would have to be granted to the other national groups then resident in the town. The result would be the establishment of a number of small national churches, each with questionable financial security, that threatened to eventually dismember St. James by removing its congregation. Bishop Nilan wrote the Apostolic Delegate concerning his predicament, stating that

. . . it seems necessary to adopt a policy that will safeguard our parish organization and thus provide more effectively for the ultimate spiritual welfare of these people and their children.

Bishop Nilan preferred that the immigrants in the smaller communities attend the local territorial parishes staffed by American–born priests capable of speaking the needed languages,[211] or, in the case of the Poles and other Catholic groups, he allowed those living in smaller towns to belong to the national churches existing in the larger, nearby cities.[212]

Two other examples were those of the Catholic Italian communities of South Norwalk and Tunxis Hill in Fairfield. The Italian community in South Norwalk petitioned Bishop Tierney for their own church as early as 1903. Since the Italian community was small, the Bishop feared that their independence would hurt St. Joseph's Church, the only territorial mission in South Norwalk. The Bishop, therefore, asked the community to wait and to continue to attend St. Joseph until the Italian community grew sufficiently in number to support its own mission.[213]

In 1913, the Society of St. Vincent Ferrer was organized by John Pinto and other immigrants from Salerno as a mutual aid and religious society for immigrants from Salerno with a total membership of about fifty–five people. Land was purchased and a plan to construct a church was developed, despite the Bishop's prohibition. Internal divisions weakened the membership and slowed the building of the church, which was finally begun only in 1933. The society again petitioned the Bishop of Hartford for an independent parish and again was refused. The membership was considered too small, and, since it was restricted to only those from Salerno, it was too limited in its scope to be granted independence as a parish. The society also refused to turn over the property title to the Bishop, which was required of any established church in the diocese. The society simply continued to attend St. Joseph and, after some minor alterations, used their church as a social hall.[214]

The Italians of Tunxis Hill in Fairfield provided another example of a small group of immigrants who desired to organize their own church. By 1921, a group of Italians had petitioned the Roman Catholic Bishop of Hartford for a church. Because of the lack of Italian–speaking priests, and because of the small number of Italians requesting their own church, the Bishop doubted the practicality of such a project and declined to give his permission. The small group of Catholic Italians was encouraged to attend the local territorial churches in Bridgeport or Fairfield. It was at this time that a young Protestant Episcopal minister, the Rev. Joseph Racioppi, approached the Catholic Italians of Tunxis Hill and offered his assistance.

Father Racioppi, who had been born in New York and baptized a Roman Catholic, and who had entered the Episcopal ministry after studies in America and Europe, began his work among the Italians in the cellar of a private home on Marlborough Terrace. Able to speak Italian, he introduced himself to the Italians as an Episcopal priest who had come in order to establish a catholic church among them.[215] His services were those of the Episcopal Church, employing the Italian version of the Book of Common Prayer then in use. He was straightforward concerning the Protestant nature of his church. It cannot be known, however, whether the Italians understood that Fr. Racioppi was not Roman Catholic. He spoke their language, dressed as a Catholic priest, and promised them a church that would employ the doctrine, sacramental system, and ceremonies similar to those of the Roman Catholic Church. Since few of the Italians were educated, and fewer, if any, had ever come into contact with Protestants, it may be that they did not understand that Fr. Racioppi's Church was not the Church of their birth. According to Fr. Racioppi many of the sons and daughters of the founders of his mission, once they reached their majority, returned to the Catholic Church. His Church of St. Michael the Archangel was built by the Italians themselves and consecrated by Bishop Chauncey Bunce Brewster, the Protestant Episcopal Bishop of Connecticut, in 1922.

Bishop Brewster was of the "High Anglican" school. He encouraged the employment of liturgical ceremonial that was very close to that of the Roman Catholic Church, and subscribed to the view that the Protestant Episcopal Church was indeed as catholic as the Roman Catholic Church in its apostolicity, creed, and practice. The future bishop developed a keen interest and zealous concern for the welfare of the arriving southern and eastern European immigrants.[216] Both his apostolic zeal for the immigrants and his belief in the apostolicity of his church were evident in the development of the Protestant Episcopal Church of St. Michael in Fairfield, established in 1921 for the Italian community of Tunxis Hill.

The mission was established in conjunction with the work of Trinity Episcopal Church in Bridgeport. Through the aegis of the Rev. Frank Ernest Aitkins, a plan was developed to assist the Italians of Tunxis Hill with the aid of Fr. Racioppi, who had been sent by his Protestant superiors to the Roman Catholic Italians of Tunxis Hill, ". . . because there was a group of people who were not taken care of by the Church of their ancestors."[217]

According to Fr. Racioppi, the opening of the church was a sore point among the Roman Catholic clergy who regarded the establishment of such a Protestant church for Roman Catholic Italians as dishonest.[218] Since the Protestant Episcopal Bishop appeared to be "Roman" in his ministry, as was the ceremonial employed at St. Michael's, many of the Catholic clergy questioned whether the Italian immigrants were not simply confused concerning the nature of their Roman Catholic faith and that of the Episcopalian Church, that told the immigrants that it too was "catholic."

The *Catholic Transcript* for years had let loose with broadside attacks against Bishop Brewster's missionary zeal among the Catholic immigrants. In an article entitled "The Foreigners" in its number of June 27, 1907, the *Transcript* commented on a then recent utterance of the Episcopal Bishop of Connecticut concerning the scope of his Church's missionary work. Such work, contended the Bishop, was not designed to proselytize among the faithful of other communions. Rather it was a work among those with no faith. The Bishop continued,

'. . . where faith has been lost as in the case of some through reaction from authority or otherwise, and they are as sheep having no shepherd, have we not something to do?'[219]

The *Catholic Transcript* saw such work as nothing short of proselytizing and the stealing of Catholics by the Protestant Episcopal Church. The same article concluded with the editor's note,

It is not religion, but pride, misguided nationalism, and other unmentionable things that lead men to shake off obedience to duly constituted authority.

In his homeland, the foreign–born Catholic knew the priest, the altar, and the confessional as essential to his Catholic faith, the *Transcript* continued,

Under the new conditions that confront him here he looks for these in the land of his adoption. Rome alone has them. No other Church makes any pretense of having anything like them.[220]

Contrary to the statements of the editor of the *Catholic Transcript*, there were Churches that actively taught that they too were catholic and apostolic in their creed and practice. Various pamphlets in Italian printed during Bishop Brewster's years were designed to explain that the Episcopal Church was as catholic as the Roman Catholic Church. One such was prepared by the Rev. Carmelo DiSano, a Protestant minister, entitled, "Brief History of the American Church, or, the One, Holy, Catholic and Apostolic Church of Christ Jesus." The Italian pamphlet was published in Hartford and briefly explained the history of the Protestant Episcopal Church, which the author linked directly to Rome.

The pamphlet stated that in America true religion is protected by the American Constitution. It continued,

In practice we find that the religion of the United States is not the Roman Catholic religion, but a catholic religion, free from all the dogmas of the Papal Church. The American Church protests against false doctrine . . . against lies, and every thing which is truly contrary to the spirit of Christ's law. The citizen, and the stranger who lives within this grand Republic is free and independent in the practice of one faith or another.[221]

The pamphlet contained pictures of the church's ministers wearing vestments that were very similar to those used by the Roman Catholic Church. To the Italian immigrant, quite uninformed as to the subtle nuances employed in the pamphlet, the religion of America as portrayed in the pamphlet was identical to that of his ancestors in Italy.

Bishop Brewster encouraged the free usage of all expressions of religion that were traditional to the Catholic Italians since he understood and was sympathetic towards their ". . . love for large processional statues, their ornate altars or their special shrines."[222] An example of the Bishop's zeal to make his Italian congregation feel at home in the Protestant Church was the occasion of his visit to St. Michael's. While making some announcements to the congregation, Fr. Racioppi used the word "Eucharist." Bishop Brewster corrected him with the words, "Say Mass, Father, not Eucharist."[223]

The *Osservatore Romano*, the official Vatican newspaper, railed against the work of Fr. Racioppi in its issue of October 5, 1922, as his church celebrated its patronal feast on September 29th. Rome was astounded that such Protestant inroads into the Catholic Church could be made in the state that was the home of the Knights of Columbus.

Bishop Brewster was aware of the animosity that the Roman Catholic clergy felt toward him in regard to St. Michael's. During one of his visits to St. Michael's toward the end of his life he experienced some of the cultural manifestations of the Italians' faith. During the elevation of the host, the Italians set off fireworks. The octogenarian prelate was stunned by the entire effect, and commented to Fr. Racioppi, "Oh my God, I thought the Roman Catholics were coming!"[224]

Less than one year after the opening of St. Michael's Episcopal Church, the Diocese of Hartford established a mission under the Pastor of St. Thomas Church in Fairfield. Fr. Racioppi claims the Catholic mission was the direct Catholic reaction to the opening of St. Michael's.[225] This may have been the case, especially after the cutting words employed by the *Osservatore Romano* and the general impression that the Diocese of Hartford had come away with some egg on its face. Nonetheless, the Catholic Diocese's record of work among the Catholic immigrants is an impressive one, and cannot be tarnished by the excessive attention that the small St. Michael's group attracted by the press.

Conclusion

The effects of foreign immigration upon the Catholic Church in America lessened rapidly during the 1920's as the result of new legislation that effectively limited the number of arrivals in the country. Various bills were proposed during the first two decades of the century, but not until 1921 did the government succeed in establishing immigrant quotas, thus effectively limiting the number of annual arrivals to 357,803 persons of foreign birth. This total was further reduced in 1924 and again in 1927 to an annual total of 150,000 persons.[226] The implications of such laws for the Church in America were obvious.

The laws effectively cut off the source that had been the mainstream of its population growth in America for over a century.

1930 marked the centennial of the first Mass celebrated in Bridgeport by the Rev. James Fitton. That Mass had been celebrated at the home of James McCullough, an Irish immigrant, with a congregation of seventeen Catholics. The anniversary was a seemingly unimportant one to those outside the Church. For the American and foreign—born Catholics of Fairfield County, however, this hundredth anniversary of "Catholicity in Bridgeport" was a milestone of great importance. It served as a public statement that Catholics in the county had thrived during the previous century, had remained faithful to their ancestral faith while being loyal to their adopted country, and had become an important part of the life of Southern Connecticut.[227]

The Catholic Church in Connecticut had grown primarily as the result of foreign immigration. By the time of the centennial celebrations in Bridgeport, Catholics in Fairfield County had established forty—eight parishes and twenty—one parish schools. Bridgeport had twenty parishes, eleven of which were national parishes by 1930. With the legal restrictions placed upon immigration during the 1920's, and the depression of the 1930's, the immigrant source of numerical growth for the Church was greatly closed off. For the first time, the Church was able to focus attention and resources on areas of importance other than the pastoral care of the Catholic immigrants.

CHAPTER III

WOMEN RELIGIOUS AND CATHOLIC LIFE
(1876–1953)

Teaching was the original work of women religious in Fairfield County. By the turn of the century, the sisters' efforts were extended to hospital work and later to other fields and ministries. Though women religious did not begin working in Fairfield County until late in the nineteenth century, Catholics in the county had been affected earlier in the century by the work of religious sisters in the orphanages in Hartford and New Haven established by Bishops O'Reilly and McFarland. These cared for Catholic orphans from throughout the diocese, supported by a special diocesan collection taken at Easter and by contributions from the home parishes of the children.[1]

The first women religious to work in Fairfield County were the Sisters of Mercy, who established a mission in conjunction with St. John Church, Stamford, in 1876. From that time, women religious have served faithfully within the county primarily in the fields of education, hospital work, and social work.

The work of the sisters in Fairfield County was limited by the general diocesan plans, formulated by the respective Bishops of Hartford, and implemented under the direction of local priests. The sisters' initial role in parish life was to teach in Catholic schools and parochial catechism classes. Later, the need arose to provide sick and dying Catholics with the sacraments in the atmosphere of a Catholic hospital. In both instances, it was the bishop who invited the sisters into the diocese and who directed their work, usually under the watchful eye of the local pastor.

There were few women religious in leadership positions in the Church in Connecticut during the last century and the early decades of the present one. Those who were found themselves subject to the direction of a cleric.

In the church, all work within any diocese is subject ultimately to the bishop. This ecclesiastical principle, coupled with the private role of women in American society prior to the 1960's, accounts, in a large part, for the distinct lack of detailed documentation concerning the work of religious women.

The role of an American woman in the nineteenth century was far from a public one, since she was limited to the home as wife and mother. Dependent upon her husband for the necessities of life, she worked in and for her family. Hers was a private life; her public appearances usually were restricted either to those necessary for the fulfillment of her household duties, or to those social occasions when she was perceived as an ornament and compliment to her husband.

The role of the American religious sisters in the nineteenth century was not dissimilar to her lay counterpart, in that hers was a completely private life. Totally retired from society, she lived a quasi–monastic existence. Her only public appearances were those necessitated by her work in schools or hospitals. Her work was dependent upon the direction of her female superiors who, in turn, were responsible to the local pastor or bishop. As one School Sister of Notre Dame wrote in the "Chronicle of St. John Nepomucene Convent in Bridgeport," the work of the sister was to be done quietly and without fanfare:

> Though not productive of any noticeable results of a startling character, the work of the Sisters goes on quietly and we pray that our unassuming efforts may prove to be pleasing in the eyes of the good God.[2]

The result of such private dedication was effective: hundreds of schools were established in the state; thousands of children were taught; the sick and dying were cared for. Only on rare occasions were their works documented, in contrast to the detailed chronicling of the works of priests and bishops. Until the 1920's, detailed documents concerning convent life and the work of the sisters rarely existed, and then only by verbal testimony.

Nuns in Yankee New England

The first Connecticut–born woman to enter the convent was Jerusha Booth Barber. She entered the Visitandine Sisters at Georgetown, D.C., in 1820, taking the name Sr. Mary Augustina. Jerusha Booth was born in Newtown, Connecticut, on July 20, 1789, to a prominent Protestant family of that town. She married the Rev. Virgil Horace Barber, an Episcopalian minister, bore

90

him five children, and accompanied him during his ministerial career. Both Jerusha and her husband were deeply moved by the conversion to Catholicism and subsequent entrance into the convent in 1809 of Frances Margaret Allen, daughter of the Revolutionary War hero Ethan Allen. It was very influential in bringing about the conversion of the entire Barber family, important to the history of the Church in Connecticut since Hartford's first bishop, William Tyler, was a member of the Barber family, and likewise a convert.[3] Virgil, Jerusha, and their five children were converted to Catholicism in 1816 and later entered religious life.[4]

Regardless of the fact that Fairfield County had produced a vocation to the religious life so early in its history, there were few women religious to be found anywhere in New England in the early years of the last century. Nonetheless, anti–Catholic forces worked doggedly to impress upon the minds of the Yankee citizenry the dangers of the convent system during the last century. The renowned Connecticut–born minister, Lyman Beecher, proved himself the champion of the "Protestant Crusade," calling upon Americans everywhere to oppose convents and Catholic schools, since these were the weapons of the Catholic Church in its battle to conquer Protestant America.

Inspired by Beecher's warning against the growing immigrant and Catholic population in America, a well–organized mob attacked and burned the Ursuline convent in Charlestown, Massachusetts, on an August evening in 1834. Even though he denied his instigation of the affair, Beecher's proved to be the leading voice in the attack against the sisters.[5] In a letter written soon after the burning of the convent, Beecher spoke of the effect that the mob action would have upon the Catholic Church in New England:

It was a favorable providence, which called me back to speak in undaunted tones. . . . Before I left the tide turned [against the Catholics] and Catholicism forever in New England must row upstream, carefully watched, and increasingly understood and obstructed by public sentiment.[6]

Following the burning of the Charlestown convent, a number of anti–Catholic books appeared concerning convent life. Their alleged authoresses claimed to have escaped from Catholic convents and were now ready to reveal the true workings of the convent system to all who would listen. The contents of the books were as false as were the claims of the purported authoresses to have been real nuns. Nonetheless, the American audience was more than willing to listen to and believe the stories that Rebecca Theresa Reed told in her *Six Months in a Convent* (1835); and those of Maria Monk, in *Awful Disclosures of the Hotel Dieu Nunnery of Montreal*, (1836). Theodore Dwight of Connecticut, believed to be the author of the final version of *Awful Disclosures*, offered *Open Convents* to the public in 1836. It was graced with a preface by the inventor, Samuel B. Morse, who dubbed Dwight's work,

> . . . a valuable collection of evidence . . . showing, in the clearest manner, the hollowness and the depravity and the danger of the Convent system.[7]

These works portrayed convents as scenes of debauchery and murder, disguised by a facade of religious devotion and consecrated life. The effects of such books were much greater in forming American's views of the Church than those produced by the efforts of priests and bishops to prove to the public that the standard practice of Roman Catholic convents did not include sexual dalliance with clerics, the disposal of the bodies of the offspring of such illicit unions, or the secretive plotting of the overthrow of the Republic. These books were read and believed by hordes of Americans, ignorant of Catholicism and starved for entertainment. Attracted more by the pornographic and sensationalist stories than by the truth or falsity of the accusations, Maria Monk's work alone sold over 300,000 copies by the time of the Civil War.

Lyman Beecher's harangues against the growth of Catholicism in America were joined by those of many other Protestant divines, including another Connecticut minister, Horace Bushnell. In his *Crisis in the Church*, published in 1835, the Congregationalist pastor of Hartford's North Church echoed Beecher's warnings when he wrote that the Catholic Church,

> . . . is constantly advancing in its liberality and enlarging the sphere of its operations. More than six hundred persons of the church—Jesuits and nuns—are said to have landed on our shores, within the last year.[8]

As if aliens from a distant planet, these Catholic women religious were seen as essential to the success of Rome's efforts to dominate America, since it was to them that the formation and education of so many immigrant children was to be entrusted. Beecher gave voice to this view in his *A Plea for the West*,

Can Jesuits and nuns, educated in Europe, and sustained by the patronage of Catholic powers in arduous conflict for the destruction of liberty, be safely trusted to form the minds and opinions of the young hopes of this great nation?[9]

The inhabitants of Connecticut and Rhode Island were prepared well for the arrival of Catholic nuns by this anti–Catholic propaganda spouted from the pulpits of revered Protestant clergymen and circulated in the local press.

Sisters of Mercy in the Diocese of Hartford

The first women religious to arrive in the Diocese of Hartford were five Sisters of Mercy in the spring of 1851. Hartford's first Bishop, William Tyler, had sought the assistance of the Sisters of Mercy from Ireland[10] and the Sisters of Charity from Emmitsburg early in his administration.[11] Members of the latter community had agreed to work within the diocese provided that travel expenses and room and board be secured by the Bishop. Because of the poverty of his people, the Bishop was unable to secure the necessary funds, and the original plan for a school staffed by the Sisters of Charity never materialized.[12]

The first group to work in the diocese arrived in Providence, Rhode Island, on March 12, 1851. Mother Mary Xavier Warde, Sisters Mary Camillus O'Neil, Mary Joana Fogarty, Mary Josephine, and Mary Paula Lombard immediately became the objects of scorn by the local inhabitants. One of the sisters described their reception:

Indeed, had these women been guilty of some dreadful crime more pains could not have been taken by their friends to isolate them. No sooner had the Sisters taken possession of their poor, little cottage on Weybosset Street than the mob gathered, broke all the windows and hooted at the inmates. The inveterate hatred of the benighted people among whom their lot was cast never slumbered. Whenever they [the sisters] appeared on the streets their lives were in danger. To have their clothing soiled with mud or marked with chalked crosses was no uncommon experience.[13]

The response to the presence of the women religious in Connecticut varied from place to place, especially as the Know–Nothing Party grew in political power during the 1850's. Hartford received them with little fuss, simply noting their arrival and purpose in the local press.[14] In other towns, the propaganda made popular by Maria Monk had made a lasting effect. The residents of Norwalk were disturbed by the prospects of Catholic nuns in their midst. The *Norwalk Gazette* published a letter to the editor concerning nuns rumored to be in the town, entitled, "Have We a Nunnery Among us?" Appearing in the June 12, 1855 number of the *Gazette,* the letter alleged that a pair of convents existed within the town limits. The first was reported to be inhabited by ". . . innumerable Nuns caged up, of all ages and descriptions, but whether there are any 'vile monks' or 'friars' within, we have no means of knowing." The second convent was alleged to be "situated in a dark by–path, under the very shadow of one of our own church edifices." Known as the "Mayflower Nunnery," its denizens were only one or two "antiquarian nuns, and only a few of those Monks."[15] Even though written as a "lark," according to the editor, a wave of angry and frightened letters flooded the offices of the paper, penned by citizens fearful that such a diabolical institution as a Roman Catholic convent might indeed be within the town limits.[16]

The expression of such fears concerning the Church was not limited to the local press or Protestant pulpit. They were introduced into the local public school system as well. Protestant teachings, prayers, and Bible readings as well as visits by the local minister had always been a part of the public school curriculum within the state. Once these teachings began to include sentiments unfriendly to Catholics, the Church felt the need for Catholic schools. The obvious teachers for such parish schools were the religious sisters.

Religious Sisters for Fairfield County

Religious sisters were essential for the development of good parish schools. The year 1872, therefore, was an important year in the history of religious sisters and Catholic education in Connecticut. January of that year saw the division of the Diocese of Hartford and the formation of the Diocese of Providence which, henceforth, would take charge of Catholic life within Rhode Island. With his jurisdiction restricted to Connecticut, Bishop McFarland's immediate task was one of reorganization, consolidating his limited resources in order to meet the needs of his growing Catholic population in the state.

With the division of the diocese, Bishop McFarland moved the seat of his administration to Hartford. With him came Mother Mary Pauline Maher, Mother Superior of the Mercy Sisters in Providence, along with Mother Angela Fitzgerald, her assistant, to establish a new Motherhouse in Hartford. The

94

same year also saw the foundation of two other Mercy centers in Connecticut. These would soon provide the sisters necessary for the establishment of Catholic schools throughout the state, as well as those who would assist the poor, care for the sick and instruct adults.[17]

The Motherhouses at Meriden and Middletown were both formed by Sisters of Mercy from Ennis, Ireland. Of the eleven sisters who volunteered to serve in the new American missions, Mother Mary Agnes Healy was chosen to be the Mother Superior at Middletown. Her assistant, Mother Mary Teresa Perry, was to serve as the local superior to the mission house in Meriden, which became an independent Motherhouse in 1876.

Responding to the invitation of the Rev. Michael Tierney, Rector of St. John's in Stamford, Sister Mary Nolasco Sherman and two other Sisters of Mercy from Hartford arrived in late April, 1876, in order to administer the ". . . one, poor, small school house" that served as the local parish school.[18]

Stamford proved to be an excellent site for the first of the county's Catholic schools to be staffed by religious sisters.[19] Stamford was not a factory town. The town's children were able to ". . . remain longer in [the] schools and study a more advanced course than the children of most other small towns," since Stamford's children were usually not required to leave school in order to work in factories.[20]

The need for Catholic schools was still strong. Rome had emphasized this in its response to Bishop Galberry's diocesan report of 1877 and insisted that a diocesan synod be held in order to address various needs within the diocese, among which was the better organization of Catholic education within the state.[21]

The Hartford Synod also promulgated three educational decrees that would begin in earnest the organization of Catholic education in Connecticut. These decrees emphasized the necessity of parish schools. Since religion was seen as an integral part of a true Christian education, each church was to work to provide its young with Catholic schools. Rectors were to prescribe the books to be used in the schools, teach catechism to the children, and be deeply involved in the formation of the Catholic faith of the children of the local church. Since it was practically impossible to establish schools in every mission, rectors were to establish catechism classes, in addition to Sunday schools, for those Catholic children attending public schools. The rectors also were obliged to supervise the parish Sunday school.[22]

The synod also noted that the effectiveness of parish schools was to be bolstered by the teaching of religious sisters, a fact that had been emphasized in 1866 by the Second Plenary Council of Baltimore, and which was promulgated and reaffirmed by the Hartford synod. During the years between this second synod and Hartford's third in August, 1886, six new Mercy missions were opened in Fairfield County, all involved with Catholic schools and the religious education of Catholic youth.

The Mercy convent at St. Mary's in Norwalk opened in late February, 1879. Led by Sister Mary Evangelist Kerin, the sisters from Meriden first attended to the religious education of Catholic girls, with classes in the church basement. The sisters soon admitted boys to their instructions, later organized various religious societies, entered into work with sick and hospitalized Catholics, and began a school.[23] The local paper observed that,

If the attendance of the children of Catholic parentage is anything like general, the effect upon our public schools will be marked.[24]

The effect upon the public schools did prove to be substantial, since by 1881 St. Mary's School numbered 400 pupils.[25]

Bridgeport's St. Mary Church received the next Mercy convent, which opened on March 30, 1880. Even though a convent and school had been planned since 1875, it was not until the arrival of Sister Mary Agatha Boland and the Sisters of Mercy from Middletown that St. Joseph Academy was opened.[26] Housed in the old St. Mary's Church on Crescent Street—then one of the poorest sections of the city—the first Catholic school to be staffed by religious sisters in Bridgeport opened with 140 students, even though it was not a free school.[27]

St. Thomas Church in Fairfield opened the next convent in the county in 1882. Sister Mary Monica O'Sullivan and three Sisters of Mercy from Middletown began teaching in the parish school, which opened in September of that year with 130 students on the first floor of the remodeled rectory. The second floor served as the convent.[28]

St. Augustine Church in Bridgeport welcomed Sister Mary James Murray and the Sisters of Mercy from Hartford in September, 1884. A tuition academy for Catholic boys and girls opened in January, 1885 on the first two floors of the convent, with an opening enrollment of 155 students.

St. Peter in Danbury opened the next convent and Catholic school staffed by religious women in the county in 1885. Sisters of Mercy from Hartford, led by Sister Mary Bernard Feehan, began teaching in the then newly erected brick parish school the following year. The eight–room school opened in September, 1886, with a student population of 535, which rose to 600 during the next three weeks.[29]

St. Mary's Convent in Greenwich opened in August, 1886, with Sister Mary Monica O'Sullivan and two other Sisters of Mercy from Middletown. The old church on Williams Street was converted into a school for 150 Catholic students.[30]

The founding of these convents was important for the development of Catholic life, since the presence and work of religious sisters allowed for the expansion of parish schools within the county. Such a rapid increase in the number of missions for the Sisters of Mercy, then the only congregation of women religious working in the state, made the adequate training of teachers often impossible.[31] Most of the sisters had received high–school educations, but were left to train themselves or garner some little instruction from those members of their communities already seasoned by years of teaching.[32]

Rome continued to call for the establishment of additional parish schools in America as a necessary safeguard of the faith of Catholics.[33] Writing in 1883, Bishop John Lancaster Spalding informed Rome that, "Americans have a passion for education, which, one might say, is almost their religion." Even though the Bishop of Peoria was speaking on the topic of seminary education, his observations were applicable to general education in the country.[34]

Importance of Catholic Schools

The majority of the Catholic parents within the state did not send their children to Catholic schools by 1884. Of the estimated 40,000 Catholic children of school age within the Diocese of Hartford in that year, only 13,000 were enrolled in Catholic schools.[35] Education was seen as necessary by most, but Catholic education, especially when not free, proved far from universally popular within the state, especially among poorer Catholics.

The decrees of the Third Plenary Council of Baltimore, which ordered all missions within the country to establish schools within two years after the promulgation of its decrees of 1884, and those of the Third Diocesan Synod of Hartford, held in 1886, expressed the need for Catholic education. Those of Hartford, which reflected some of the local needs, addressed the problem of the Catholic attendance at public schools, and warned Catholic parents that a secular education could lead to the destruction of the faith of their children.[36]

Diocesan authorities in Hartford, however, made no concerted effort to organize the developing schools into a unified system. It was not until Hartford's third synod, which mandated the establishment of a diocesan school board in accordance with Baltimore III,[37] that any steps were taken to insure the proper training of its teachers, or standardize the curricula of the Catholic schools in the state.

The school board was composed of six priests. It included the Rev. Michael Tierney as its president and the Rev. William Slocum, rector of Norwalk, whose duty it was to visit and evaluate each of the Catholic schools within the state at set intervals and to examine the sisters and teachers for certification.[38] These examinations by the diocesan school board provided the basis for the teacher preparation programs offered after 1889 in the novitiates for the Sisters of Mercy and the Sisters of St. Joseph, then teaching within the diocese.[39]

By 1890 the quality of the education offered within the Catholic schools of the diocese had improved. This resulted in a corresponding rise in the student population. The paradigm for the curriculum and grading of each Catholic school was the program offered by the local public schools.[40] Once the Catholic schools could offer an education comparable to the public schools, and especially once they were able to prepare the students adequately for the public high school entrance examinations, the student populations began to rise.[41] The Catholic schools of Fairfield County reflected both the improvement and the increase in students: St. Augustine's in Bridgeport had 538 students divided into 24 grades; St. Mary's in Norwalk, 425 students in 17 grades; St. Peter's, Danbury, 600 students in 26 grades; St. John, Stamford, 345 students in 18 grades; St. Thomas, Fairfield, 152 students in 10 grades; St. Mary, Greenwich, 135 students in 8 grades.[42]

By 1894, Bishop Tierney could report that the majority of the Catholic students within the diocese were attending Catholic schools. Because of the efforts of the Bishop, his clergy, and the women religious who served as teachers, Catholic schools had been established, which were, by the end of the century, if not superior to the public schools, at least their equals.[43] By 1901 the diocesan paper bragged that, not only was the student population growing in the Catholic schools in the major towns and cities of Fairfield County, but that they had produced scholars who led their public school peers in the passage of the high school entrance examinations.[44] Among these schools, the foremost in academic performance and numbers was St. Peter's in Danbury. By 1900, the student population numbered

1,008, and the school was staffed by seventeen teachers.[45]

Further development of a diocesan school system came with the work of the Rev. Patrick McCormick. Assistant at St. Augustine in Bridgeport at the time of his appointment in 1906, Fr. McCormick saw the formation of a skilled teaching staff as the primary need of the Catholic schools of the state. His insistence upon a two–year novitiate for the teaching sisters within the diocese proved an important innovation for the provision of qualified teachers within the diocesan system. Fr. McCormick also inaugurated a Teachers' Institute, designed to instruct the teaching sisters in pedagogical method.[16] Fr. McCormick's work was continued by his successor, the Rev. William J. Fitzgerald. With the assistance of the Sisters of Mercy, who had united their Connecticut houses in 1911 at the request of Bishop Nilan, Fr. McCormick produced the Syllabus in 1914 that would guide Catholic education within the state for years.

Religious Sisters and National Parishes

Much of the diocese's energy was directed toward the welfare of the arriving Catholic immigrants during the later nineteenth and early twentieth centuries. In order to care for them, schools as well as churches were needed and were provided whenever possible.

Up until the turn of the century, the Sisters of Mercy had been the only religious congregation involved in Catholic education and religious instruction within Fairfield County. As the national parishes organized, other communities of religious women entered into the educational apostolate: The School Sisters of Notre Dame came to St. Joseph, Bridgeport, in 1901, and to St. John Nepomucene in 1913; the Sisters of the Holy Ghost taught at St. Michael in 1903, and at St. Anthony and St. Stephen Churches in 1905; the Sisters of the Most Precious Blood arrived at Our Lady of Pompeii in 1907; the Sisters of St. Francis, Minor Conventuals came from Buffalo to Bridgeport in 1908; the Sisters of St. Joseph of Rochester, New York, taught at St. Charles in 1909; the Sisters of Sts. Cyril and Methodius, founded by the pastor of that Bridgeport church, began work in Bridgeport in 1910; the Sisters of the Resurrection arrived at Stamford's Holy Name of Jesus Church in 1910.

The sisters' influence upon the life of any parish was immense. Their teaching and counselling of students influenced the lives and faith of many families throughout the county, especially within the larger cities. By the turn of the century, the sisters were no longer regarded as a luxury to any parish. So respected had they become among the Catholic and non–Catholic communities as the embodiment of all that was truthful and virtuous, that their endorsement was even sought for various products.[47] Even though Catholic schools were touted as the great tool for Americanizing the immigrants, affording, ". . . a much easier pathway for the foreigner to enter into American life than is the case in the public school," the reality was somewhat different.[48] For most of the Catholic immigrant groups, the maintenance of their language and their culture was considered to be the necessary safeguard for their Catholic faith in America. This was reflected in the schools established by the national parishes. So strong was the desire for a school at the Slovak Church of St. John Nepomucene in Bridgeport that a large number of the congregation petitioned the Bishop for permission to establish their own Slovak church with a parish school. The result was the establishment of Sts. Cyril and Methodius Church in 1907 and the school in 1908.[49] In order to provide teachers who would instruct their children in their native customs and language, the Rev. Matthew Jankola, later pastor of Sts. Cyril and Methodius Church in Bridgeport, founded the Sisters of Saints Cyril and Methodius, which received papal approbation in 1909 and staffed the Bridgeport school.[50]

The School Sisters of Notre Dame staffed the school at Bridgeport's German Church, St. Joseph, in 1901. The national roots of the students were strongly emphasized, with instruction, graduation ceremonies, and school entertainments conducted in English and German, even through World War I.[51] They also staffed the Slovak school of St. John Nepomucene in 1913.[52]

Sisters Affect Children's Religious and Moral Development

The desired effect of Catholic schools upon Catholic youth was one of moral formation. Public schools offered good academic training, but only the Catholic school offered the moral formation considered necessary for adult Christian lives. This was the battle cry in favor of Catholic education, repeated at school dedications and in the diocesan paper for years. At the dedication of St. Peter's new school, Monsignor John Synnott addressed Danbury's Catholics in November of 1908, giving the reason for Catholic schools:

Education must embrace morality. The child's soul and its relation to God are of the utmost importance. Morality and its relation to our fellowman is as important as any other teaching and, therefore, should receive as much consideration as any other. The schools is [*sic*] the Church of the child.[53]

The Church's duty and right to train children was emphasized by the Rev. Richard Shortell, pastor of Ridgefield, in his address to the graduates of St. John's in Stamford in 1912. The effects of young lives educated without the Church can be seen, Fr. Shortell said:

. . . the highway of life is strewn with more wrecks of human lives because of their . . . weakness in moral strength than because of their lack of mental culture and development.[54]

By the turn of the century a new trend was developing that affected education in general: the essential role of the parents as the primary educators and instructors of morality for their children was lessening in importance. By 1909 the editor of the *Catholic Transcript* spoke out against this trend that delegated the parental responsibility of raising the children to the religious women who were their teachers:

It is these religious women who are expected to see that the lessons of Christian Doctrine are mastered and the class for First Communion and Confirmation are prepared. The natural and most responsible guardians of the souls of the children hold themselves relieved of their paternal burden. . . . Pastors and teachers were never intended by the Church to take the place of the parents. . . .[55]

The Rev. William J. Fitzgerald, diocesan supervisor of schools, wrote a column in the Catholic paper under the pen name "Scholasticus," beginning in 1912. In January of that year he defined and limited the role of the Catholic school in the intellectual and moral formation of children.

. . . the School with the Home and the Church form a trinity of influence that combined make Christian character and develop the sense of duty and responsibility.[56]

The key to the successful application of such educational theories in the Catholic schools of the diocese was the adequate training of teachers allied with the dedication of those religious sisters who taught generations of Catholic children.

The further education and training of religious sisters teaching within the diocese was emphasized by the various diocesan school supervisors, the first of whom was the Rev. Patrick

McCormick. Under his successor, the Rev. Austin Munich, many teaching sisters had attended Catholic colleges and pursued summer courses at various academies and motherhouses.

Most of the teacher training in the convent, however, was without college credit. Newly professed Sisters of Mercy, for example, received only a basic instruction prior to teaching—lasting from July through January. They continued with night and summer courses while they taught. One Sister of Mercy who entered the convent in 1927 and was trained under this system, did not receive her Bachelor's degree until thirty years later, a common experience.[57]

St. Charles Borromeo Parish, established in 1902, on the East Side of Bridgeport, gives a fine example of the importance of Catholic education in the parishes of the early twentieth century and the dedication of the religious sisters who staffed the schools within Fairfield County. The East Side of Bridgeport was home to four national churches, two Eastern Rite churches, and two territorial churches by late 1907. St. Charles was established in 1902 as the second territorial church on the East Side, popularly known as the "Irish Church" by members of the national churches. It was the only mission in the diocese that built its school before the construction of a church. Since only St. Mary's Church had a school on the East Side at the turn of the century, most Catholic children attended the local public schools. The addition of a second Catholic school, therefore, was welcomed by the Catholic community, evidenced by the pledging of sufficient funds and material to build the school and equip the classrooms, prior to the formal opening of any fund drive by the parish.[58] Bricks for the proposed school were sold for $1.00 each in order to raise funds for construction.[59]

The school was given over to the care of the Sisters of St. Joseph from Rochester, New York. The original community of religious consisted of Sisters Mary Lucina Flaherty, who served as the superior of the convent; Agnes Miriam; Angelica; Eleanor; Severina; Melita; Cyrilla; and Mary Emelina. So welcomed were the sisters at St. Charles, that several students who had previously completed their sixth–grade courses, were willing to repeat the grade in order to come to St. Charles School and be taught by the sisters.[60] In order to encourage attendance at the new school, the Rev. William H. Lynch, the parish's first pastor, canvassed the East Side for students, regardless of ethnic background or parish membership.[61] The Sisters of St. Joseph remained at St. Charles until 1913, when the Sisters of Mercy took charge of the school, adapting the course of studies and discipline according to their own teaching traditions.

The curricula of the Catholic schools at the opening of the century were far from standardized throughout the diocese. Most were based upon those of the public schools, geared primarily to the passing of the public high–school entrance examinations by the Catholic school children.[62] The basic courses of reading, writing and arithmetic were offered. These were interspersed among other subjects and activities throughout the day, which varied from school to school. A curriculum, standardized throughout the diocese, was not to be had until 1914, when the Rev. William J. Fitzgerald, assisted by representatives of the various religious teaching communities, developed the Hartford Syllabus. This remained in force until revised by the Rev. Edward Flynn in 1926, and finally by the Rev. Austin Munich in 1935. The school schedule typical at that time was that followed at St. Charles School.

The school day opened at St. Charles with prayers, followed by Christian Doctrine, and then Religion, which consisted in the learning of prayers and the ten commandments. These were "hammered into the students."[63] The religion lessons were supplemented by the classes preparing the children for the reception of the sacraments as they grew older. Geography and History were next, after which followed Arithmetic. Two or three times a week, the children were then led into the school yard for exercise, which consisted in the swinging of "Indian clubs."[64] During World War I, the school exercises became much more regimented, the children's movements choreographed in time to a record, and the children marching ". . . in and out of school while Sister Rinalda played the 'Connecticut March' on the piano."[65] The afternoon classes consisted of English Grammar, which ". . . was pounded into us,"[66] sewing, and Dancing classes for the lower grades. This latter instruction was optional, since there was a charge of 10 cents per lesson.[67] Only a rudimentary form of Science instructions was offered. As one member of the class of 1927 recalled:

> There was no science. When an airplane passed over we'd run to the window in the fifth grade to see it. Then the sister would give us a quick explanation of flight. We'd go to the parks to gather wild flowers and do nature walks. That was the extent of science.[68]

The school children were all members of various religious societies, organized and supervised by the sisters. Originally

103

intended as means to further the children's devotions and frequent reception of the sacraments, the school societies also served a social function as the children grew older. The friendships forged during years together in St. Charles School, as in other Catholic schools, were nurtured during high school years in the still closely knit neighborhood. The parish provided a self–contained Catholic society for its members. The Catholic faith, taught and interpreted by the parish priests and sisters, provided its moral foundation; the religious societies and school provided a theater for social relationships. Speaking of her membership in the Holy Angels Society, one graduate of the class of 1915 recalled,

> We were anything but angels! Every Sunday afternoon there was a meeting [at Church], followed by ice cream at the drugstore. Children and nuns were so innocent then![69]

Teaching Sisters

The life of all religious sisters was a quasi–monastic one prior to the changes following the Second Vatican Council in the 1960's. There were some differences between the day–to–day schedules of the teaching and the nursing sisters, based upon their work, but on the whole their schedules centered upon their community life and work. Guided by their vows of poverty, chastity, and obedience, the insights of their mother foundress, community prayer, and a strong dosage of self–abnegation, the women religious worked diligently and with great self–sacrifice for the glory of God and the salvation of their fellow men and women. The individual sister was to be lost in a community life, shared by women who had been trained and formed to live all and to do all for God with no thought of individual happiness or glory. The concept of loving self–sacrifice, by which the sister would give up all pleasure and ambition in order to win the salvation of mankind, was one that guided the rule of life of most if not all of the religious orders of women. Far from being a punishment for any personal sins, theirs was a life lived in order to pay for the sins of others. The seemingly harsh rules, so often formulated in another age and country, appeared odd—if not repressive—when transferred to American society.

Most sisters were fully aware of the sacrifices required upon entering the convent. Sister Ignatia Marie Federici, RSM, recalled her entering the convent in 1929: "Knowing how life would be, we accepted the rules and the way of life." A member of the Sisters of Mercy—the first religious sisters to enter into the field of religious education in Fairfield County last century—Sister Ignatia Marie remembered the day she left her Norwalk home in order to begin her novitiate:

> I was the eldest in the family, and the day I left for the convent I started to cry and my father asked me why. My brother broke in and said, 'she's crying because she can't eat another meal here at home.' This upset my father, and he had to leave the room. My father would never interfere with my vocation, even though he knew these things would be painful.[70]

The evangelical prescription by Christ that His followers abandon father and mother and everything for His Kingdom was applied literally by the sisters. None was permitted to leave her convent without a sister companion, and then only to visit the sick after school hours. The parents of the sisters were allowed to visit them once a month at the convent. It was only during their vacation period that the sisters were allowed to visit their parents' home. Obliged to reside in the convent nearest their homes, the sisters were allowed only three visits to their parents. Each visit lasted only three hours, during which time the sisters were not allowed to eat a meal or receive any refreshments from their parents or relatives, other than water or tea.[71]

The Sisters of Mercy were prohibited from traveling further than a radius of ten miles from their convent for any reason, without special permission from the provincial superior in Hartford.[72] Never allowed in any public places other than school or church, the sisters were required to sacrifice rights that most people take for granted, such as the right to vote in local, state, and national elections. The sisters were not allowed to vote until June, 1953, when they received the permission of Bishop O'Brien and the General Council of their congregation.[73]

By 1930, the average salary of the teaching sisters within the diocese amounted to $300.00 per year, while that received by lay teachers was double the amount. Included in this were room and board, for which the sisters performed various other duties around the parish.[74]

The regimen within the convent usually was not relaxed. Beginning with Prayer and Mass every morning at 6:00, the teaching day was punctuated by community prayer in the convent. Unless a holy day or the name day of one of the sisters occurred, most were "silent days" in the Mercy convents, during which no talking was permitted within the house. Depending upon the severity of the local superior, meals were all taken in silence, with only one sister reading aloud from a book of an improving nature. Speaking was permitted only during the short recreation period prior to retiring in the evening.[75]

Most convents were composed of a series of small rooms—or cells—furnished with a bed, bureau, small desk, and chair. The shared bathroom facilities were at the end of the corridor. St. Charles convent—at one time the largest Mercy mission in the state—was considered innovative, if not luxurious, when it opened in 1922 since it provided sinks in the sisters' cells—the first convent in the state to allow such a convenience![76]

Leadership positions in parish schools were not usually open to the sisters. Of the 25 Catholic grammar schools within Fairfield County in 1941, only four of them had religious sisters as principals. The remaining 21, although staffed by sisters, were administered by the senior curate of the parish. The success and well–ordering of the school and convent, although the domain of the sisters, was determined by the pastor of the local parish. The relationship of the sisters with their pupils often reflected the relationship between the convent and the rectory.

Depending upon the disposition of the parish priests, especially the pastor, and their concern or disregard for the sisters, the life and work of those religious women in any given parish could prove to be either unendurably miserable, or remarkably productive. St. Charles in Bridgeport, again, provides an example of this dependence of the religious sisters upon the parish priests.

The Rev. Thomas B. Gloster, Pastor of St. Charles during the years 1939–1956, had little regard for the sisters who staffed the parish school. Often the sisters found themselves dependent upon the charity of the Catholics in the neighborhood for food, since the pastor refused to give them either food from the rectory or extra money, erroneously believing their niggardly salary to be sufficient to supply all their needs.[77]

During the same pastoral incumbency, the Rev. Edward Doyle, principal of the school, would secure permission from the provincial superior of the Mercies in order that the school sisters might attend educational conferences. The conferences never existed and the senior curate of St. Charles used the permission to treat the school sisters to supper at a local restaurant, without the knowledge of his pastor.[78]

The effect of the work of the religious sisters upon the children placed under their care was profound. "The Sisters of Mercy lived only to give the children the best they could give them," was the memory of one student at St. Charles.[79] Tough and exacting as they could be, these sisters proved their dedication and love for their children in varied ways.

Besides providing Catholic children with an elementary education that was equal, if not superior, to that offered by the local public schools, the teaching sisters fostered a Catholic identity within the hearts of their young charges. Through the efforts of the sisters in the schoolroom, classes in religious instruction, and membership in the various parochial societies, Catholic children became comfortable with, and attached to, their local churches.

The local parish church and school were more than mere institutions, and the priests and religious sisters proved to be more than staff members, since they became an intimate part of the lives of the children.[80] The sisters offered instruction, direction, and guidance to those in their care. They formed the children's outlook on the world as well as their consciences according to Catholic beliefs and practices. Seeking advice or guidance after graduating from their parish school, alumni often returned in order to meet with those sisters who had taught them. Salvatore Petriello graduated from St. Mary School in Bridgeport in the late 1930's. Before being sent overseas during World War II, he visited one of his former teachers, asking for her prayers and a medal to take with him overseas. Sister Leo gave him, instead, the cross she had received on her profession day, which proved to be ". . . a source of great strength for me during the war."[81] His was not an isolated case, but rather exemplified the special place that the sisters held in the hearts and lives of their students. Religious sisters also deeply affected those in their care in other fields.

Religious Sisters and Catholic Hospitals

Another apostolate entered into by religious women in Fairfield County was that of Catholic hospitals and health care. The need for Catholic hospitals in Fairfield County was met by the work of two congregations of religious women: the Daughters of Charity of St. Vincent de Paul, who opened St. Vincent's Hospital in Bridgeport in 1905; and the Sisters of St. Joseph of Chambery, who opened St. Joseph's Hospital in Stamford in 1942.

St. Vincent's Hospital was established as the second Catholic hospital in the state, the first being St. Francis Hospital in Hartford. The growing Catholic population of Bridgeport prompted the interest in the spiritual welfare of those Catholic patients then being treated in the one city hospital in Bridgeport at the turn of the century.

The Rev. James Nihill, the Rector of St. Patrick's Church, was responsible for the establishment of the hospital and the securing of the Daughters of Charity of St. Vincent de Paul as the institution's administrators and nursing staff. The praises of the Daughters of Charity were heard in Bridgeport even before the opening of the hospital. The speaker for the laying of the hospital's cornerstone spoke of them on November 8, 1903:

> This institution will be in the hands of the Sisters of St. Vincent de Paul. The name is synonymous with charity. These sisters have taken a vow to live and to work, to suffer and if need be to die for the sick and afflicted. . . . God has blessed their work everywhere.[82]

Led by Sister Laura Eckenrode, the first administrator, Sisters Vincent Mullany, Alice Cannon, Josephine O'Rourke, Gertrude Connoly, Jane Frances McCarthy, and Mary Grace Duffy arrived from Emmitsburg on May 16, 1905, to join with Sisters Bernard Orndorf and Raphael in the final preparations for the hospital opening on June 28, 1905. Although opened only a few days, the Daughters of Charity were praised in one of Bridgeport's papers:

> The Sisters are exceptionally experienced and trained in hospital work. Indeed it is an undisputed fact that many of them have had more extensive vital experience than have the majority of physicians. Their hearts are in their work and their gentle, patient, sympathetic faces are inspirational.[83]

By late 1914, the work of the sisters was hailed as having produced one of the best–equipped hospitals in New England.[84] The high standard of health care offered at St. Vincent's was assured by the sisters and the nursing staff trained by them. Soon after the opening of the hospital, Sister Laura Eckenrode opened a school of nursing to provide the hospital with a qualified staff. The school opened with 12 students, three of whom were men. By 1915, a separate nursing residence was constructed by the administrator, Sister Alice Cannon, which provided the hospital with additional room and a steady supply of trained nurses.[85]

The Daughters of Charity expanded their hospital apostolate to include work among the city's poor, the number of which grew as the armaments works in Bridgeport geared up for the First World War. A day nursery was begun on November 12, 1917, on Ogden Street in the East Side,[86] which was open to all in the city, regardless of creed.[87] The nursery was designed to meet the pressing needs of working mothers, who otherwise would be forced to surrender their children to public asylums since they could not adequately care for them.[88] The nursery was under the auspices of Bridgeport's Charitable Bureau and was staffed by the sisters. By late June, 1918, a shortage of sisters and the inability of the Bureau to pay full–salaried workers, forced the closure of the nursery,[89] which did not open again until the re–organization of the Bureau in 1920.

The work of the Daughters of Charity in Bridgeport in St. Vincent's Hospital and in the area of social work and religious education in the parishes had a great affect upon the Catholic life of the city. An editorial in the *Bridgeport Post* of 1937 summed up their work and their humility:

> The sisters seek no publicity. They ask no praise. Their aim in life is to serve the sick, the ignorant and the poor for the sake, not of man but of God.[90]

The second congregation of religious sisters to begin hospital work within Fairfield County was that of the Sisters of St. Joseph of Chambery. Founded in France in 1650, these sisters had established a reputation within Connecticut for fine administration and charitable work in their hospitals in Hartford and Waterbury. Besides teaching for a number of years and caring for orphans within the diocese, this congregation was the first in the state to direct a Catholic hospital.

Bishop McAuliffe's desire to found a Catholic hospital in the Stamford area found an able proponent in the Rev. Nicholas Coleman, then Pastor of the Church of St. John in Stamford. Having appreciated the need for a Catholic hospital for some time, Fr. Coleman began the search for available land and financial support for the project in 1937. The hospital opened on October 28, 1942, under the direction of Mother Sacred Heart, CSJ, assisted by Sisters Mary Christine, Mary Assisium, Francis Agnes, Elizabeth Mary, Mary Albina, Mary Stephen, Mary Andrew, Francis Agnes, Constance Marie, and Mary Teresita.[91]

No living quarters were provided for the sisters when they arrived in Stamford to prepare for the hospital opening in

1942. They found temporary lodging at Sacred Heart Academy, which was operated by their sisters in Stamford. The hospital sisters created a stir in the area. The sisters of the Academy were always formal in their dealings with the public and were removed from the life of the Stamford community because of their quasi–monastic lifestyle. Even though their rule was the same, the hospital sisters were more visible to the public than the school sisters because of the nature of their work:

> "We rolled up our sleeves and worked. People felt closer to the nuns at the hospital than to those at the Academy. People were always close to the nuns at the hospital. Our sisters who were here in Stamford before the hospital opened never met people, except on formal school occasions."[92]

One of the founding sisters of the hospital recalled that while working with a young man in the hospital's supply room and kitchen, she noticed that he constantly stared at her. Not a little uncomfortable, Sister Mary Assisium asked if there were any problems. He responded that there was none. He was simply amazed since she was the youngest nun he had ever seen. Having only had experience with the Sisters of Mercy in school, he thought that all nuns were ancient. "Nuns weren't around people much in those days."[93]

On October 12, 1942, the hospital sisters moved from the Academy into makeshift sleeping quarters in one of the hospital wards. Dissatisfied with the lack of proper housing, the sisters began to look for a suitable convent. A house and property next to the hospital was for sale, but the price was too high for the sisters. Determined to have the property, Mother Sacred Heart instructed her sisters to pray and bury medals on the property and around the house. Despite this act of simple faith on the part of the sisters, the property was sold and became a school. Years later, however, the sisters succeeded in acquiring the property and built the present convent on the site. Until that time, the sisters resided in an estate known as Caswell, given to the hospital by Mrs. Mary H. Gilmour and made ready for them by August, 1943.

Hospital Sisters

Despite the cramped and incommodious quarters, the sisters carried on a full convent schedule soon after the hospital dedication on October 28, 1942. Their morning began in chapel at

5:45 A.M. for prayers, 30 minutes of meditation and Mass. Work at the hospital began at 8:00 and continued until 11:45 when the sisters returned to their residence for prayer, lunch, spiritual reading in common, and 30 minutes in chapel. Work resumed at 2:30 P.M., and continued unbroken, except for supper, until the sisters retired for the evening at 8:00. During the period of recreation or communal reading, the sisters were expected to perform some type of handicraft, lest they be idle. This was their seven–day schedule with only minor changes during the summer months.[94]

A thirty–dollar monthly salary was paid to each of the sisters employed in the hospital. This was turned over to the community and used for the payment of personal needs and the running of the convent. The sum of each sister's personal clothing consisted of six white habits for use in the hospital and two black habits. The sisters were allowed to own little and depended upon the generosity of others. "Whatever was given never was to change our attitude of simplicity of life in living out personal poverty."[95]

Vacations and free time were not granted the hospital sisters until the 1950's, when Bishop O'Brien granted them two free days a month, which later became one free day per week. With no union guidelines for the sisters, no minimum number of weekly work hours was established. Theirs was an unvaried schedule that called for more working hours than those provided by their lay counterparts in the hospital. The forty–hour work week enjoyed by the hospital personnel was not extended to the hospital sisters until the late 1960's.[96]

The sisters employed in the schools enjoyed free time during the summer, broken only by teacher courses. But those sisters employed in the hospitals received no vacation until 1939 when Bishop McAuliffe rented a summer house for them in Higinam, Connecticut. He stipulated that the hospital sisters were to be assigned to a one–week vacation. During that time only a limited schedule was to guide the days in order to allow the sisters some time to relax. The sisters were, therefore, undisturbed by the ringing of bells, which normally punctuated the days in the convent and hospital, calling them to prayer, meals, and other community functions. Only one bell sounded in the vacation house on any given day, calling the sisters to Mass. "Otherwise the day was to be unstructured and the sisters 'on their own' for prayers."[97]

The quality of life within any convent depended upon the disposition of the superior and her relationship with the sisters under her direction. Mother Sacred Heart, the co–founder of St. Joseph Hospital, proved to be a remarkably talented and dedicated woman, a capable administrator, a compassionate nurse, and an amiable superior.

> Most superiors were suspicious of those under them. Mother was never suspicious of the nuns, believing that everyone was doing what they were supposed to do, unless proven otherwise.[98]

Exacting as administrator of the hospital, she was never harsh or cruel, understanding the strengths and limitations of the members of her staff. The rule followed by Mother in the convent at Caswell was similar in that it was faithful to the principles of her Order, yet flexible enough to allow for individual circumstances. "Mother was very open and different in regard to religious life. She gave everyone the freedom to grow" personally and spiritually.[99]

When the father of one of the sisters was ill, Mother granted her permission to be with her family. In accord with the rule of the Order, the sister was not allowed to stay at her family home, but was to reside in the nearby convent. The convent was overcrowded, and the visiting nun was given the room of one of the resident sisters who was forced to move. When Mother discovered this she granted the visiting nun permission to stay at her family home, rather than inconvenience another sister for a long period of time.

In Caswell, Mother Sacred Heart never enforced a rigid lifestyle. Since most of the sisters' time was spent in the hospital, Mother felt that what little free time was theirs should be enjoyable.[100] The Sisters of St. Joseph Hospital received the gift of a television in the early 1950's that they used at night before bed. The Mother Provincial, Mother Herman Joseph, took a dim view of such innovations and issued a decree that no convent of the Sisters of St. Joseph within her province was to possess any such device. After a debate with Mother Sacred Heart, the provincial superior compromised: the sisters at St. Joseph Hospital might keep the television, but were not allowed to watch the picture, they could only listen to the sound, and that only for the local newscast. For four months the sisters listened to television until Mother's patience was exhausted, and she decreed that the television would be fully used in her convent at Caswell. From that point on the hospital sisters hosted the sisters from Sacred Heart Academy to watch "I Love Mama" and other shows.

For the sisters under Mother Sacred Heart working at St. Joseph Hospital, "Religious life was not a burden. . . . We really felt that what we were doing would make a contribution to the Church. I suppose I entered because I felt I couldn't save my soul anywhere else."[101]

The early years of the hospital coincided with those of World War II. Even though the staff was reduced in numbers and their supplies limited because of the war, the hospital provided needed services to the Stamford community. During their first year of operations, 3,329 patients were treated, which rose to 4,736 two years later.[102]

The care offered by Catholic hospitals in Fairfield County, as elsewhere, bore a quality different from that offered in public facilities. The dignity of the individual as the image of God was foremost in the treatment of the patient at any Catholic hospital. As mentioned in the St. Joseph Hospital report of 1955,

> Over and above their technical excellence as nurses and their supervisory skills, the Sisters bring to their work a high spiritual purpose. All of their merciful ministrations are performed in the name of God and the welfare of humanity.[103]

Conclusion

As the needs of the growing Catholic population within Fairfield County increased during the century, the number of religious women to teach in Catholic schools, to establish parish catechetical programs, and to work in the field of Catholic health care also increased. Theirs was a quiet, constant service to their fellow Catholics that, although essential to Catholic life, was nonetheless unsung. When the first Bishop of Bridgeport arrived in Fairfield County in 1953, he found 451 sisters from 23 religious orders working within the newly established diocese. It is to these religious women, to their predecessors and successors in the various fields of apostolic labor, that the Catholics of Fairfield County owe a great debt not only for the establishment of the numerous institutions of education, healing, and spiritual renewal but also for the devoted example given and the sacrifices made for the upbuilding of the Church and the salvation of souls within Fairfield County.

CHAPTER IV

BISHOPS, PRIESTS, AND
CATHOLIC LIFE
(1829–1953)

Bishops and priests were essential to the development of normal Catholic life. During the early nineteenth century, provision of the essentials of Catholic life including the Mass, the sacraments, the preaching of the Gospel, and the teaching of the faith formed the core of the work of the clergy of Connecticut. By the late 1820's, Catholics were few in Connecticut; priests, nonexistent. The few Catholics within the state were scattered among the larger towns and villages. They practiced their ancestral faith as best they could without the regular ministrations of any priest, or the benefit of normative parochial organization.

By the 1870's, as the number of priests, churches and faithful grew, these basic needs of the Catholic people of Connecticut were being met regularly. Once the spiritual rudiments of Catholic life were provided, the clergy began to speak out on local moral, political, and social issues that touched upon the lives of Catholics. The Mass continued to be celebrated daily; the Gospel preached and the sacraments administered by the clergy; the faithful continued to gather for spiritual activities and church society meetings. A change was occurring, however, during the latter part of the nineteenth century that would continue throughout the next. As the number of Catholics in the state grew, the Church urged them to come out of hiding and to influence American society according to the Catholic social and moral principles learned in their local churches and Catholic schools. They were to take their rightful place as Americans: America was to be formed by Catholics—clergy and laity alike.

Connecticut: Beware the Priests

The citizens of the state had been well versed in the alleged crimes of the Catholic hierarchy in the old world. They believed that God had established a purer religion in the new world, embodied in the Congregational Church, controlled, not by the cleric, but by the will and faith of the congregation itself. Democracy was taught to be from God and, therefore, was the only form of government capable of leading one to perfection, whether in the realm of the state or the church.

A letter to the state legislature, published in Bridgeport's *Republican Farmer* in the summer of 1819, warned against the possible encroachment on the people's rights by the power–hungry ecclesiastic. The subject of the letter was the proposed tax exemption of the churches in the new tax laws that were then being formulated. After a brief outline of the alleged "democratic" origins of the Church under Christ and His Apostles, the author, employing the nom de plume "Luther," described the usurpation of the people's rights, property, and wealth by the Catholic clergy of the Middle Ages. God had re–established His apostolic church in America in Congregationalism, which was democratic in its polity. In order to preserve apostolic purity of faith and practice, the Congregational Church had been watched over by the General Assembly during colonial times. Even after the Constitution of 1818, it seemed natural that the state legislators should continue their vigilant duty and prevent the clergy from becoming too wealthy or powerful, lest America's apostolic democracy be compromised. "Luther" concluded,

> The corruption of the clergy will grow with their wealth. Some men, more ambitious, more able and more wicked than his [sic] fellows— some [Pope] Gregory, or [Pope] Boniface—will grasp the scepter of gold, and our children will be slaves, and our posterity 'hewers of wood and drawers of water' for a hundred generations.[1]

The general attitude was one of distrust for all clergy, regardless of their ecclesiastical loyalties, since the will to power appeared endemic to their profession. Vigilance on the part of the laity, therefore, was required lest their apostolic democracy be compromised or usurped by unscrupulous clerics.

For the Protestant resident of Connecticut, as elsewhere in America, the Roman Catholic clergy was the embodiment of all that was contrary to liberty and free–thinking. Agents of a foreign church, whose Inquisition and political machinations bore eloquent testimony to its abhorrence of liberty and democracy, the Catholic priests were to be feared and their progress in America blocked. Few Catholics were to be found in New England during the early nineteenth century, and they were attended to by a handful of priests. Nonetheless, the fear and hatred of the Church and her ministers as foreign and dangerous was solidly instilled in the Yankee mind by Protestant preachers and officials.

In a sermon preached in Norwalk in 1802, the Rev. Justin Mitchell expounded upon the text from the Gospel of Matthew that read, "And whosoever shall fall on the stone shall be broken." The stone, according to Mitchell, was the Protestant religion, which was the Kingdom of Christ, that ". . . had been attacked by all the cruelty which E[vil] and hell, could invent." The power of evil took the form of the Roman Church that attempted ". . . to extirpate the protestant church, or the K[ingdom] of C[hrist] and so fell on the stone." He continued, recounting to his congregation that the Roman Church,

. . . destroyed between 30 & 40 millions of the [Protestant] church, or K[ingdom] of C[hrist]. In one country they killed two thousand thousand [sic]. Some parts of Spain, were almost entirely depopulated.[2]

Faced with the prospects of mass slaughter as well as the deprivation of their American liberty, the Protestant residents of Connecticut could do little else than be wary of the wicked Roman cleric.

The quintessence of the evils of the Roman Church was to be found in the foreign Jesuit and those trained by the followers of Ignatius of Loyola. The great Yankee preachers of the seventeenth and eighteenth centuries had warned against the Jesuit as the agent of the pope and the enemy of pure Protestantism. The prophecies of these evangelical sages must have been seen as fulfilled when in 1789 a Jesuit, the Rev. John Carroll, was appointed as the first Catholic bishop in America. In 1825, the Yankee sanctuary of Boston received its second Catholic bishop, Benedict Joseph Fenwick, also a member of the Society of Jesus, with jurisdiction over all of New England. The progress of Jesuitical Popery in America had begun. Despite the apparent realization of Protestant fears concerning the establishment of the Church in New England, not much progress could actually be made without an adequate number of priests—especially American–born priests.

Obstacles to the Church

The problems faced by the Church in Connecticut were similar to those felt in other areas of the country, as reflected in the decrees of the various Provincial and Plenary Councils of Baltimore, celebrated during the nineteenth century. The major problems dealt primarily with ecclesiastical polity, property, and personnel within the Church, and anti–Catholic prejudice from without. All of these problems stemmed from the need for priests—especially American–born priests—who could establish normative Catholic life among the small, isolated Catholic communities within the country, while at the same time providing a convincing apologetic for the Church as an institution compatible with American ideals.

The American bishops found themselves in a very difficult situation. Granted the authority to establish the Church in America, they quickly found that their influence was often times undermined by the interference of European ecclesiastics. The nomination of bishops for the American missions was a perplexing problem. Bishop Jean de Cheverus of Boston expressed his dismay about foreign interference in the naming of bishops for America in a letter to Archbishop John Carroll of Baltimore. He wrote,

> It is certainly astonishing that Prelates in France or Ireland should recommend subjects for the Mission & be listened to rather than you & those you are pleased to consult.[3]

The American bishops were fearful that the naming of European clerics to American episcopal sees would confirm the anti–Catholic accusations that the Church was, indeed, a foreign institution. At the same time, it was felt that the appointment of foreign–born bishops to American posts could threaten the Church's unity in America by dividing the growing Catholic immigrant population along lines of nationalistic loyalties. The American bishops, therefore, did all in their power to apprise Rome of the true conditions and needs of the American missions. They were able to limit foreign interference in the matter of episcopal nominations to some extent, but possessed no control over the supply of American–born priests.

In order to remedy this problem, Bishop Fenwick opened his house as a seminary in Boston on July 3, 1826. His domestic seminary served as the training ground for some of the first of New England's priests, including Hartford's first Bishop, William Tyler. R.D. Woodley and James Fitton were the first to be instructed by their Bishop and were ordained the following year.

Bishop William Tyler: a Priest Shortage

The number of Catholics in Connecticut was far from large prior to the mass immigration from Ireland and Europe later in the century. By 1835, Bishop Fenwick reported an estimated 720 Catholics within Connecticut, whose total population numbered 220,955.[4] Hartford and New Haven had the only two resident priests within the state, and only one was American–born. The efficacy of the ministrations of the two priests, Fr. James Fitton and Fr. Bernard O'Cavanaugh, was hindered, since the Catholic population was scattered throughout the state. With no roads connecting the smaller towns and villages, travel by horse was slow at best, and visits by these priests were infrequent.

Not until the construction of St. James Church in Bridgeport in 1842 did Fairfield County receive its first resident priest. The Rev. Michael Lynch was given jurisdiction over the entire county as well as some outlying towns in Litchfield County. As more Irish Catholics began to settle within Fairfield County the need for resident priests increased. Bishop Tyler saw this first hand in the summer of 1848 when he traveled to Norwalk in response to the petition by the Catholics of that town to establish a mission with a resident priest. He celebrated Mass, baptized and administered the sacraments, and then visited the Catholics of Danbury.[5] Priests were needed in order to insure the strong establishment of the Church in Connecticut; the problem was locating them.

In August, 1844, Bishop Tyler wrote the rector of the newly established All Hallows College in Dublin, requesting priests for his diocese.[6] The plans of the Rev. John Hand for the establishment of a college that would provide Irish missionaries won the approval of Pope Gregory XVI on February 28, 1842.[7] The college provided a number of American dioceses with Irish priests who staffed the early missions.

The problems arising from the priest shortage in America were compounded by the activities of some priests who had immigrated to America for reasons other than the salvation of souls. The Councils of Baltimore had warned the bishops not to accept any priest into their service unless that priest carried with him the requisite permissions and letters of recommendation from his European or American superiors. The First

119

Provincial Council of Baltimore addressed the laity in its pastoral letter of 1829 concerning the need for American–born priests. American–born vocations would free the Church from dependence upon foreign–born missionaries, many of whom had brought disgrace to the Church in America:

> Neither would you desire, nor are we disposed any longer to permit, that priests who have been elsewhere held in disrepute, shall be received into our churches, to create schisms, to encourage strife, to perpetuate abuses, and to disseminate scandal; to degrade that which is holy, and to bring upon a religion that has emanated from God, that obloquy which belongs only to the vices that have been found in individual man.[8]

Necessity, however, often outweighed caution and the requirements of canon law. Bishops, desperate for priests, took their chances by accepting clerics who applied to them without the proper ecclesiastical permissions. The results were often disastrous and injurious to the Church. Bishop Tyler had experienced the ill effects of fortune–seeking, foreign–born priests soon after his appointment to Hartford. He wrote to the rector of All Hallows concerning potential candidates for the priesthood for his diocese:

> I hope these young men will make pious and disinterested priests as your account of them gives reason to expect. If so, with the blessing of God, they will do much here for the salvation of souls, but religion has already suffered much in this country from priests who were destitute of the proper spirit.[9]

All seminarians were required by the decrees of the Third Provincial Council of Baltimore to take an oath prior to subdiaconate to ". . . perpetually serve the mission to which they shall be appointed."[10] To this the Bishop of Hartford added the further requirement that those to be ordained were to stay with him in Providence for two weeks in order that he could be quite sure of their intentions and capabilities.[11] The majority of the priests sent from All Hallows proved to be more than satisfactory in their ministrations among the poor Catholics scattered throughout the diocese.[12]

The poverty of the Catholics in the diocese proved another formidable obstacle to the development of the Church in Connecticut, second only to the lack of priests. Bishop Tyler described the abject poverty of his diocese in a letter to the Propagation of the Faith of Paris, in 1847:

> I have not vestments, chalices, etc. for them [three new priests from All Hallows]. I wish to send these newly ordained priests to several

places where there are bodies of poor Catholic laborers, and in some of these places there is not the semblance of a church. How happy would I be to be able to assist each of these with a few hundred dollars to begin small churches and abodes for themselves; and what encouragement would it not give the poor people among whom they go and upon whom they must depend for everything![13]

By the time of Bishop Tyler's death in 1849, the Diocese of Hartford was staffed by fourteen priests, who served 20,000 Catholics in twelve churches throughout Rhode Island and Connecticut. The Catholics of Fairfield County were served by two priests: the Rev. Michael Lynch at St. James in Bridgeport, and the Rev. John C. Brady at St. Mary's in Norwalk.[14] The Catholics in the Greenwich–Stamford area were occasionally visited by priests of the Diocese of New York and by Jesuits and faculty members from St. John's College, Fordham.[15] Among these early visiting priests was the Rev. Francis McFarland, the future third Bishop of Hartford.

Bishop Bernard O'Reilly

With the coming of the Rev. Bernard O'Reilly in late 1850 as the second Bishop of Hartford, the organization of the Church in Connecticut and Rhode Island began in earnest. He was born in Ireland and educated in Canada and the United States. Upon his arrival, the Bishop set out on a program intended to increase the number of priests and seminarians, to employ the Sisters of Mercy from Ireland, and to establish a number of schools, academies, orphanages, and churches.

Not two months after his installation as the Ordinary of Hartford, Bishop O'Reilly wrote to the officials of the Propagation of the Faith at Paris reporting on the poor state of his diocese. As the result of Irish immigration, the Catholic population had increased from 20,000 in 1849 to 45,000. Such a rapid increase required at least thirty–five priests instead of the staff of thirteen then present. His thirteen churches proved inadequate to the numbers of arriving immigrant Catholics; he required thirty, along with funds for schools. The Bishop related his most pressing needs in a letter dated January 11, 1851:

We can do little without sufficient number of priests, and we cannot save the children, without a Catholic education. All the influences which are here are against our religion's, and, . . . it is only by great zeal, purely Catholic education and sufficient number of priests, that we can save our own and make progress against heresy.[16]

Bishop O'Reilly immediately set out in search of good priests. By the end of his first year he had increased the number of priests to twenty, boasting that it was ". . . the largest increase thus far, found in some dioceses of this country."[17] In order to insure the supply of good priests for his diocese, he established a seminary at his own residence in Providence. By the end of 1851, he counted nineteen students. He also granted the rector of All Hallows College in Dublin the authority to select worthy students for service in Hartford and to act as his vicar general,

". . . in all matters appertaining to my subjects in your House, such as the receiving, promoting them to Holy Orders, and dismissing them, if their conduct should call for the latter."[18]

Strapped for funds as well as priests, Bishop O'Reilly required any seminarian studying for Hartford to pay half the costs of his education, the balance to be carried either by the diocese or by one of the European missionary societies. Since the diocese already was bound by heavy debt from the construction of churches and the training of seminarians, the Bishop preferred to dismiss any student who was unwilling or unable to carry his own financial burden, rather than enlarge the diocesan debt by preparing a man for the priesthood who displayed no spirit of self–sacrifice.[19]

The Bishop visited Europe in search of priests willing to serve in Hartford. At first, he had been wary of employing older Irish priests who presented themselves for service within his diocese. Pressed by the desperate need for priests to work among his growing immigrant congregations, he grudgingly employed them. His clerical staff increased. But, by 1853, the wisdom of employing some of the older Irish priests who had served in churches in Ireland was questioned, and the Bishop determined not to accept any others except those trained especially for his diocese:

I do not, I must confess, wish to receive priests who have been on the *Irish missions* and for reasons doubtless well known to you. The love of the Irish missions is one, the *reverse* of *disinterestedness*. Consequently the Spirit of self-gain . . . has been the case in but too many instances, and has proved to be greatly injurious to religion. There are exceptions no doubt, marked and sure, and such, if any, I would wish to receive, if I could get them.[20]

In a number of letters to the rector of All Hallow's, he insisted that those men who were destined for service in the Diocese of Hartford should be ready and willing to work in the missions immediately after their ordination and not expect vacation. He wrote:

> I would however prefer to have them [the seminarians] come at the termination of their studies, and ordain them here, if this would not be contrary to the rules of your house. When ordained in Ireland, they will try to remain a time amongst their friends, whilst their services are much needed here.[21]

Bishop O'Reilly was interested in priests who would work and who placed the salvation of souls above any desire for personal gain or comfort. He showed little patience with those who placed any claims ahead of their ministerial responsibilities within the missions. His fiery temper, combined with his insistence upon a clergy willing to work as strenuously as he, led to some discontent among his priests. Bishop O'Reilly desired only one type of priest: "We want here true priests, pious and disinterested. Others can do no good."[22] He found, however, that not all priests coming to his diocese were of the same mind. By April, 1854, the Bishop had dismissed a number of foreign–born priests from his service:

> I can rely (confidently) but on my own priests [American–born], this I am convinced by sad, painful experiences. Of all the others I received [foreign–born] I was able to retain but three; the balance I had to dismiss after giving some scandal by their unpriestly conduct.[23]

The Church in Fairfield County

The unexpected flood of Irish immigrants into Connecticut proved an almost insurmountable obstacle to the newly established Church in the state. The largest settlements in Connecticut during the decade of 1850 to 1860 were found in Hartford, New Haven, and Fairfield Counties. Fairfield County's population grew by 15,000 during that decade. The largest Irish settlements were located in Bridgeport, Norwalk, Danbury, Stamford, and Greenwich.[24] Such an increase in the number of Catholics exacerbated the effects of the priest shortage in the county.

Prior to Bishop O'Reilly's administration, two missions had been established in Fairfield County, each with a resident priest: St. James in Bridgeport, established in 1842, and St. Mary's in Norwalk, established in 1848. These were the original centers of Catholicism for all of Fairfield County. Bishop O'Reilly divided the jurisdiction of the county between these two original missions and two newly established ones: St. Peter's, established in Danbury in 1851, and St. John's in Stamford, established in 1854. The care of the Catholics within the county was divided among these churches, whose priests rode the circuit during the year, periodically visiting the larger towns along with the small hamlets and settlements in order to celebrate Mass, administer the sacraments, preach, and instruct the young. It was from these four towns—Bridgeport, Norwalk, Stamford, and Danbury—that outlying missions would be established and the firm foundation of Catholic life in the county begun.

These provisions, however, proved to be insufficient to the needs of the Catholic communities scattered throughout the county. As a result of the drastic shortage of priests, the faithful had been encouraged by the American Bishops to meet on their own on Sundays for prayer, scripture reading, and catechetical instruction of the young. Only in this way could they maintain some rudimentary Catholic spiritual life and identity.[25] The form of Catholic life that developed was based upon traditional Catholic piety, albeit extra–sacramental. However, the seeds of an "Americanized" Catholicism were taking root. Having organized and sustained their rudimentary Catholic communities themselves, without the presence and work of a priest, certain practices, beliefs, and forms of administration unique to their missionary situation developed, which were often more Congregational than Catholic. The influence of a strongly democratic society, and the example of the successful congregational government in the various Protestant churches, proved very powerful when combined with the absence of dedicated priests. Having lived and worshiped without the aid of a priest or bishop, some began to question the necessity of the clergy for worship, as well as the absolute authority of the hierarchy in ecclesiastical administration. Catholic practices combined with democratic principles produced a form of Catholicism unique to the isolated towns.

Many Americans believed that Catholics, undoubtedly, would lose their faith and be absorbed into mainstream Protestant American life by the second generation. This would occur because there were so few priests in Connecticut to bolster their ancient faith. The Rev. James Lynch, the Catholic rector in Birmingham, Connecticut, wrote to the rector of All Hallow's College in 1854.

This assumption was to a great extent founded on experience. The Catholics who came here for the last two centuries were thinly scattered through the country, where in nine cases out of ten they never had an opportunity of seeing a priest, of assisting at the Holy Sacrifice, or of receiving the Holy Sacrament of the Church. Though they adhered to the faith, their children grew up in ignorance of it—they associated, intermarried, and gradually identified themselves in every respect with their Protestant neighbors.[26]

The opposite, however, proved to be true. Despite the numerous and erroneous reports concerning the loss of millions of Catholics in America during the last century, few actually lost their Catholic faith. The bulk of the Irish immigrants who arrived in this country until 1840 were composed of non–Catholics. Those who followed in the subsequent decades arrived with a Catholicism freshly enlivened by the Catholic Emancipation in England, the preaching of the temperance leader Father Theobald Mathew, and the political preaching of Daniel O'Connell that united Catholicism with Irish nationalism.

As sentiments towards the Church became less friendly with the advent of the Know–Nothing Party in the 1850's, the press capitalized on the false impression that great numbers of Catholics had fled the Church in America. Following the inauguration of Stamford's Know–Nothing candidate William T. Minor as Governor of Connecticut, in May, 1855, the editor of the *Norwalk Gazette* dubbed a lecture recently delivered in Ireland as "encouraging," since the speaker reported that the Church in America ". . . loses sixty percent of the children of Roman Catholic parents.' "[27]

Some of the Protestant Churches within Fairfield County also used the false reports of an Irish exodus from the Church as the basis for their own proselytizing among the Irish Catholic community. Traveling preachers, ready to denounce the Roman Church, existed in abundance. One such preacher was the Rev. Dr. Welch who traveled through southern Connecticut during the autumn of 1855. Reportedly a one–time Catholic priest, Welch traveled throughout Fairfield County preaching at the First Congregational Church in Norwalk and Protestant churches in Bridgeport, Stamford, and Danbury. In order to enhance his message and further entice potentially interested Irish Catholics, the good doctor preached a portion of his sermon in "the Irish language for the benefit of such of that nation as may choose to attend."[28]

With only a small number of Catholics in the state, the greater portion of Connecticut society had nary a clue as to the real teachings of the Church, the nature of the allegiance owed the pope by the local Church, or the actual relationship of the priest to his people. As the Know–Nothing Party grew in influence, the anti–Catholic rhetoric increased correspondingly. The alleged evil effects of the priest upon the poor Catholic immigrants was one of the favorite topics pursued in the pulpits and press throughout the county.

The editor of the *Norwalk Gazette* voiced the Know–Nothing views concerning the Catholic priest in an editorial entitled, "Can a Romish Priest be a True American Citizen?"[29] The priests of the Catholic Church, wrote the editor, owed total allegiance—temporal and spiritual—to the pope. The priest exercised full control over every aspect of the life of his congregation, including their right of suffrage and selection of political candidates. Since such activity and control was unconstitutional, the *Gazette* questioned the capacity of any Catholic priest to be an American citizen.

The effectiveness of this un–American enslavement of American citizens by the Catholic priests was insured by the oath that the editor falsely claimed to be taken by every Catholic bishop in America. For the convenience of his readers the editor provided an English translation:

I, . . . [name of the newly appointed Catholic bishop], from this time forward, will be faithful and obedient to my Lord, the Pope, and his successors. The councils with which they trust me, I will not discover to any man, to the injury of the Pope and his successors. I will assist them to retain and defend the Popedom and the ROYALTIES OF PETER against all men. I will carefully conserve, defend, and promote the rights, honors, privileges, and authority of the Pope. I will not be in any council, fact or treaty, in which anything prejudicial to the person, rights, or power of the Pope is contrived and if I shall know any such things I will hinder them to the utmost of my power, and with all possible speed, I will signify them to the Pope. To the utmost of my power I will observe the Pope's commands, and will make others observe them. I will impugn, and persecute all heretics, and rebels to my Lord, the Pope.

The means by which each bishop carried out his promise were the ministrations of his priests, and especially of the Jesuits who, the editor claimed, were also bound by similar oaths. They, in turn, held their congregations captive by means of the confessional. The entire purpose of the Church in America, and of the priesthood in particular, was ". . . to control the free elections of our country, . . ." an objective to which all Catholic ecclesiastics in America reportedly had sworn allegiance.

The Roman Catholic Church was the perfect institution for the overthrow of the American Republic, so the argument continued. The key to such treachery was the ministration and loyalty of the Roman priest to his superiors. The editor concluded:

> The individual votes as the priest dictates; the priest follows the decree of the prelate, and he so controls the election as shall best serve the interests of the Pope, the establishment of the Church and its subsequent complete rule over the country. The final extinction of the heresy of Protestantism in free America, by management of the ballot box, is the object of all ranks from the Pope downward.

Despite the invective launched against the Roman priesthood from Protestant pulpits and the local press, the resident priests found themselves esteemed as valued citizens by the local communities in which they lived. It was the work and example of those early resident priests within Fairfield County that affected the lives and sentiments of the Protestant majority in regards the Church in a much more profound, long lasting, and positive manner than did any accusations or reports to the contrary, no matter how sensational. The people of the larger towns possessing a Catholic church saw for themselves that their neighbors, although Catholics, were not enemies of liberty, and that their priests were not thirsty for the blood of heretics or the subjection of America to papal rule.

A case in point, as was mentioned in Chapter I, involved the death of the Rev. John Brady in 1854, who had been identified by the *Norwalk Gazette* as the first rector of St. Mary's Church in Norwalk. A controversy arose over his burial in Hartford, that provided the occasion for attacks against the Church as the enemy of American liberty. The incident also provoked praise for Fr. Brady as a faithful pastor of his people, a one-time neighbor, and valued citizen of Norwalk who had gained ". . . the very general respect of our citizens."[30] The institution of the Catholic Church was seen as un–American. Yet, the priests who served within the county were seen to be good men. They were attentive to their people and loyal citizens, despite the fact that they subscribed to a Church whose theological doctrines and practices were deemed to be unenlightened and un–American by the vast majority.

One such priest was the Rev. Thomas J. Synnott who served as the Rector of St. James and St. Augustine Churches in Bridgeport from 1852 until his death in 1884. He first showed his colors on the occasion of the gubernatorial inauguration of William T. Minor in May, 1855. Rabidly anti–Catholic and anti–immigrant, Minor's address for the occasion was a classic example of Know—Nothing invective that laid before the public a plan for Connecticut's future in which the foreign—born and the Catholic had little place. While praised in all areas of the county as a forceful exposé of America's Anglo—Saxon heritage and liberty, only in Bridgeport did Minor's words draw fire as being traitorous to America's true spirit of liberty. The editorial response of William S. Pomeroy, the Protestant editor of Bridgeport's *Republican Farmer,* objected vehemently to Minor's charges against the Catholic immigrants. Pomeroy's thesis was that ". . . in the matter of religion, the immigrants of this day are not very different from what they uniformly have been." He then proceeded with a detailed history of the Catholic Church in the United States, reminding his readers of several facts: it was Catholic Maryland that provided America with the first exercise in freedom of religion, that Catholic foreign—born patriots ". . . un—naturalized, and directly from foreign vessels, . . ." had played an important part in America's Revolution, and a Catholic had affixed his signature to the Declaration of Independence.

Pomeroy's source of information was the Rev. Thomas Synnott, who capitalized upon the editor's native love of freedom in order to sound the only defense of his Catholic congregation in the entire county. Pomeroy continued,

> . . . with nothing in the history of Catholics in this country to show even a doubt of their devotion to its institutions, civil and religious, that wonderful gentleman from Stamford, the distinguished Wm. T. Minor, the illustrious third—rate lawyer of the place, and redoubtable Captain of the 'Light Guard,' undertakes to impeach their character, their principles and their patriotism.[31]

The conclusion of the editorial was that America need fear nothing from the naturalized Catholic immigrant, nor from the Catholic Church. Rather, the enemy of the Republic was any man who professed sentiments such as Governor Minor's, who, while touting the benefits of American liberty, at the same time undermined it by his own discrimination and prejudice.

Although the Know—Nothing administration was shortlived, it had a long—lasting affect upon Catholic life in Connecticut. The General Assembly passed an act in June, 1855, prohibiting the Catholic Church from corporate ownership of property. It required that all Church land be held by the respective congregations instead of the individual bishops, as was common Catholic practice. The immigration and naturalization laws were also changed to require a longer residency period for the foreign—

born prior to his being enfranchised. Since the largest arriving immigrant group was Irish and Catholic, the new requirements were seen as direct attacks upon the Church. Condemned as un–American by the local press and public leaders, Catholics formed a closed society of their own, and entered into a ghetto–like existence that colored all aspects of their lives—spiritual, familial, political and social—far into the next century.

The most evident sign of this reaction to the Nativist rule and the general anti–Catholic atmosphere in Connecticut was the beginning of Catholic schools. By the time of Bishop O'Reilly's death in 1856, Catholic schools had opened in Catholicism's two centers within Fairfield County. Bridgeport's Catholics had two free schools, one for boys, the other for girls, and Norwalk opened a school in the rear of its small church in 1855. Catholic schools were to become a central part of this new, self–sufficient, ghetto Catholicism as the Church developed over the coming years.

The clergy themselves were affected by the accusations that their Church was indeed the enemy of democracy. The question of the nomination of bishops was an especially sensitive issue. The process for the appointment of candidates for vacant sees was usually carried on by the local metropolitan and his suffragan bishops, with the final decision being made in Rome. A desire for a more democratic process, involving the local clergy, began to surface in some parts of the country, including Connecticut.

Following Bishop O'Reilly's death in 1856, three priests of the Diocese of Hartford wrote to the authorities at Propaganda Fide in Rome to inform them of the state of affairs of the Church in the diocese, and to put forth their own candidate as the late Bishop's successor.[32] The priests also reported that the late Bishop, although popular among some of his priests and the faithful, was not well respected because of ". . . his ignorance of theology and ecclesiastical discipline." They observed that a lack of cooperation between priests and Bishop O'Reilly had existed in the diocese, especially since the priests regarded themselves as possessing piety and zeal equal to that of their Bishop. The result was that the priests had paid little attention to Bishop O'Reilly.

The priests contended that the method of nominating bishops for America was a problem. Since the local priests were usually excluded from the process, the associates and favorites of the bishops were always named, usually with little regard or consideration of their actual talents or abilities. The result was that older priests found themselves governed by younger and less experienced men than themselves. Too often, these bishops were neither respected nor obeyed, a situation that gave rise to discord, scandal, and damage to the Church. As priests of the Diocese, they believed that they should have a say in the naming of their next bishop.

They informed Rome that the diocesan missions were isolated and separated from each other. This made priestly visits infrequent, since travel around the state was difficult. The bishop who would succeed Bishop O'Reilly, therefore, had to be a man of great ability. A man who could give to his priests an example of a splendid priestly life that would inspire them even in their isolated missions. The priests hoped for a bishop who would love prayer and meditation; a true leader who could give a strong example to the people, especially since the Church was ". . . surrounded by public opposition and battling sectarianism." They demanded ". . . a strong bishop able to stand up to the enemies of the Church and able to convince those who are victims of doubt." Their candidate was a classmate from the seminary, the Rev. Jeremia Cummings, the rector of St. Stephen's Church in New York City and an outspoken supporter of the abolitionist movement.

Since the Nativists in America had succeeded in discrediting everything foreign in the minds of the American–born citizen, the Roman authorities acknowledged the necessity of naming American–born bishops to American sees. The whole question of the participation of the local clergy in episcopal nominations was tabled, however, since it appeared to be neither expedient nor prudent at that time.[33] The nomination as the third Bishop of Hartford fell to the Rev. Francis McFarland, who was appointed by Pope Pius IX on January 9, 1858.

Bishop Francis McFarland

Bishop McFarland was born in Pennsylvania in 1819 and educated at Mount St. Mary's College and Seminary at Emmitsburg, Maryland. He had been a member of the faculty of St. John's College, Fordham, and had done missionary work within Fairfield County during his teaching years. American–born, well educated, and dedicated to the Church, he appeared to be the perfect choice to whom Rome could entrust the Church of Hartford before a hostile, Nativist society. Bishop McFarland had been chosen earlier for the episcopal dignity when, in 1857, he was named Vicar Apostolic of the newly established Vicariate of Florida. He declined the nomination,[34] as well as those to the diocese of St. Paul and to the newly opened Nebraska Territory.[35] He was highly regarded by Archbishop John Hughes of New York, who requested that Bishop McFarland be named his coadjutor and successor in 1858. Archbishop Hughes saw the young Bishop as a man whose talents merited greater responsibility than that offered in Hartford, ". . . which is of small importance compared to this, [that] could easily be provided for by another appointment."[36] Rome, aware of Bishop McFarland's abilities, felt otherwise, and he remained in Hartford to stabilize the Church in Connecticut and Rhode Island until his death in 1874.

Upon his arrival in the Diocese, Bishop McFarland found himself in a dilemma. He desperately needed priests, but was unable to finance their seminary education. Hartford was saddled with a debt of $25,000 to various seminaries for the education of its priests. The Bishop was tempted to recall his thirteen seminarians from their studies until the financial situation of the diocese improved.[37] In an impassioned letter to the Paris missionary authorities, he described the obstacles to the Church's development in his diocese. The entire diocesan debt totalled $250,000. There was an additional debt of $50,000 for the construction of four churches, along with $3,000 interest, and another debt of $9,000 for an orphanage begun by his predecessor. The problem was compounded by the impoverished state of the Catholic populace. The majority were factory workers, who, as a result of the closure of many factories, ". . . were reduced almost to a state of beggardom."[38] The Church could expect little financial support from the Catholics within the two states.

The majority of his clergy was Irish—born: only six of his fifty—one priests were born in America by 1862, while forty—three were born in Ireland.[39] Since the majority of the Catholics in the diocese was Irish, it was a logical consequence that the clergy would be of the same ethnic background. Yet, it was during Bishop McFarland's years in the Diocese that the number of American—born vocations increased, while missionaries from Canada and European countries other than Ireland began to arrive in large numbers along with European and French—Canadian Catholics.

Connecticut's Irish Clergy

Following the Civil War, the number of non—English speaking Catholics within Fairfield County grew. Nonetheless, the majority of the Catholics and the clergy continued to be of Irish

131

lineage, if not birth.[40] By 1868, Bishop McFarland could boast that Hartford's was the largest ordination class in the entire country for that year, the majority being of Irish extraction or birth.[41] It was under his guidance that the ethnic background of the clergy in the diocese began to change in order to meet the needs of the arriving non–English speaking immigrants. He also continued his predecessor's policy of educating his seminarians overseas and extended the diocese's patronage beyond All Hallows College in Dublin to include the seminaries in Rome, Louvain, and Montreal, so that his future priests might be fluent in the languages of the arriving immigrant Catholics.[42]

The diocese supported a goodly number of seminarians during Bishop McFarland's years.[43] Their education was funded by means of parish collections and by subsidies received from the various European missionary societies. Strapped for funds, the Bishop often requested his newly ordained priests to begin repaying the diocese for their seminary education. He sometimes required them to forfeit their vacations and forward the money to the diocese.[44] The system of free education for the diocese's ecclesiastical students came to a quick end in 1864 with the establishment of financial quotas to be paid by each suffragan diocese of New York for the support of the provincial seminary at Troy, New York. Hartford, already deeply in debt, was assessed an annual contribution of $5,000.[45] In order to defray the seminary expenses, Bp. McFarland decided that the cost of the seminary education would fall upon the seminary students themselves who would be liable for the costs after their ordination. Another reason for the change in policy was that,

> . . . some of our people complain of the expense of educating seminarians. Our constant collections are an embarrassment to us. . . . As they [priests] are generously supported they never have any real difficulty in doing this.[46]

Even though very much in need of priests, Bishop McFarland proved himself a discriminating man, who demanded zealous, dedicated men. In a letter written to the rector of All Hallow's College in Dublin, he described the type of individuals he demanded as his priests:

> There is much room here for zealous missionaries, and such can do great good. But most of our young men are anxious for rich livings, and here it is really difficult to provide support for the requisite number of priests. Besides, a love of luxury lends to intemperance and other

vices, and unfits the young priest both for study and labor. Disinterestedness is even more needful here than zeal—but it is not common. Our people require *instruction* and therefore every priest who could labor with fruit among them, should be able to speak English fluently and correctly. We often find priests who know theology well, fail from the awkwardness with which they express themselves in the pulpit and elsewhere. We are just now going through a season of some trial in the United States. Vice and immorality have been developed fearfully by the present war. It requires a brave heart to stand up against the tide of wickedness now spreading over the land. We will continue to look to our seminaries to form the Missionary Spirit for this work.[47]

Poorly Trained Priests

Upon his arrival in the diocese, Bishop McFarland characterized his clergy as ". . . full of zeal and quick to make sacrifices, . . ." for their people in order that the Church might become solidly established.[48] Zealous they may have been, yet the affect of their zeal and good will was often offset by the lack of administrative and financial skills of many, by the occasional cases of outright dishonesty, and by the internal squabbles concerning parochial jurisdiction that arose among the priests themselves. The enormous financial debts that the newly established churches incurred during Bishop McFarland's years were due in part to the poverty of the people. They were also the result of the financial and administrative ineptitude of many a rector. This financial fumbling was often disruptive to the normal Catholic life of the local church communities.

Norwalk's Catholics revolted in 1858, following the financial malpractice of the rector. Scandalized by the priest's poor administration, members of St. Mary's succeeded in convincing the Bishop of the necessity of removing him from office. The removal and suspension of the Rev. Richard O'Gorman, however, did little to assuage the irate congregation, who barred the temporary replacements sent by Bishop McFarland from entering their church. Public meetings were held that denounced the Bishop and his priests during the early summer of 1858, until the arrival of the Rev. John Mulligan in July.[49] Fr. Mulligan, the first priest in Connecticut to receive a doctorate in Rome, succeeded in calming the congregation. He rectified the financial situation of the church and began the work of organizing the Catholic missions in Westport and New Canaan, which were dependents of Norwalk.[50] Danbury's Catholics found their church to be deeply in debt after the transfer of their rector, the Rev. Thomas Drea, in late 1861. His replacement, the Rev.

Ambrose Manahan, further discovered that parochial funds were unaccounted for and that the mission itself was in a state of total disrepair. He wrote Bishop McFarland in January, 1862, revealing the true situation of St. Peter's:

> When I arrived here [Danbury] on November 9th, . . . I found the house in a great measure stripped of the little furniture it ever had. There was not a drop of wine nor a candle for mass—and everything appears as if no priest had been here for years: The altar linens soiled and ragged; vestments in deplorable state and the little church presenting the look of a second or third rate station, only visited from afar at long intervals. He [Drea] sold everything in the Barn and Stable: Horse, Carriage, harness, hay and yet everybody here says they gave the money he collected for their purchase with the understanding that they were for the congregation. . . .[51]

Fr. Manahan's administration, which lasted until late 1864, although honest, was far from effective in remedying the financial problems of the mission. Unaccustomed to financial affairs, the priest combined personal and parochial funds, thus entangling St. Peter's in legal and financial problems concerning personal and parochial debts for years following his departure from Danbury.[52] The rector of Newtown, the Rev. James Daly, was found to be in the same predicament as his confrere in Danbury. Fr. Daly had combined both personal and private funds and, despite the large debts already incurred and the small income garnered from his tiny congregation, he had continued to purchase land in Newtown and the surrounding areas.[53] By June, 1868, the financial situation and the priest's health both necessitated a change of administration. Bishop McFarland received reports of financial mismanagement from Newtown. After warning the priest numerous times, the Bishop decided that the only solution was the removal of Newtown's rector.[54] Fr. Daly wrote Bishop McFarland pleading for more time in order to pay his debts and clear his name. Dedicated to his people, yet clearly inexperienced in administration, he wrote,

> If you take me away before the first of August my name will not be favorably remembered in New Milford and Newtown. Your will, dear Bishop, be done.[55]

The problems of the Catholics of Stamford and Greenwich, then a mission of Stamford, centered around the ministrations of the Rev. Edward O'Neill. He served as the assistant priest at St. John's in Stamford from 1860 until his death in the summer of 1862.[56] The priest appeared at the rectory door one day asking for assistance from the rector, the Rev. James O'Neill. The rector of the church took him in and gave him room and board as an act of charity for a destitute brother priest. Since the rector of St. John's was in great need of priestly assistance, he hired Fr. O'Neill on a temporary basis, even though he had no knowledge of the priest's background. The rector offered him room and board along with the pew rentals from the small chapel in Greenwich in return for his ministrations to the Catholics of that town.

Such an arrangement proved unsatisfactory to the newly arrived priest. In order to augment his income, he sold cemetery plots in the Catholic cemetery for prices far above the usual fee, without the knowledge of the rector.[57] Upon the death of the Rev. Edward O'Neill in 1862, his brother claimed that unpaid salary was due the deceased's estate from St. John's, and threatened legal action and publicity if his claims were not honored. The rector, the Rev. James O'Neill, wrote the Bishop and expressed his frustration with the entire affair that had caused scandal in the mission and contributed in bringing about the weakening of the church's already ailing finances:

> I thought that the last days of poor Fr. O'Neill's life would have put an end to the scandals of which he was the occasion but it appears that it remains for a graceless covetous Brother and his respectable attorney to threaten to add one more as climax to the events of a life which cannot be too quickly forgotten.[58]

St. Mary's in East Bridgeport also had its problems and proved a source of ill sentiment among the local priests and people of Bridgeport and Norwalk during Bishop McFarland's years. The Rev. Francis Lenihan, the second rector of St. Mary's in Bridgeport, felt compelled to prohibit the Rev. Peter Smith from entering the city during the summer of 1862. Fr. Smith, the founding rector of the church, was then the rector of St. Mary's in Norwalk. He had been a popular and effective priest in Bridgeport and continued many of the friendships he had made there even after his departure to Norwalk. Fr. Smith organized a parish outing and picnic for his Norwalk congregation to be held in Bridgeport. This proved unsatisfactory to the rector of East Bridgeport, who complained to the Bishop. Since Fr. Lenihan had neither the authority to prohibit the priest's entry into the city, nor any right to condemn the actions of another congregation, his orders were simply ignored by Fr. Smith.[59]

Fr. Lenihan's bruised ego was dealt a further blow when his predecessor performed the wedding of two one–time residents of East Bridgeport. Regardless of the fact that the couple no longer lived in Bridgeport and that the ceremony took place in Norwalk, Fr. Lenihan felt that his rights as rector had been violated. He felt that anyone born in East Bridgeport was subject perpetually to his jurisdiction, regardless of their present residence in the state. He, therefore, demanded that Fr. Smith be censured by the bishop for his act of interference in the affairs of East Bridgeport, and that the stipend for the marriage be sent to him, since the couple were his subjects. Fr. Lenihan wrote Bishop McFarland expressing his outrage, stating:

> The parish [St. Mary's in East Bridgeport] is publickly [sic] scandalized by the act, and I need not tell you that I feel my position to be that of *Assistant* to Father Smith of Norwalk, rather than *Pastor* of East Bridgeport, from the control which he really exercises in matters of the parish.[60]

Fr. Lenihan's continued complaints succeeded in producing a division between the clergy in Bridgeport and Norwalk. Such conflict was not limited to the ill disposition of one man, but was continued by Fr. Lenihnan's successor at St. Mary's, the Rev. Richard O'Gorman.

Fr. O'Gorman was reinstated into active service by the Bishop due to the shortage of priests. He was sent to St. Mary's where he served as the rector of East Bridgeport during 1866 and 1867. While there, he turned his sights on the rector St. James in Bridgeport, the Rev. Thomas J. Synnott. The occasion for one of Fr. O'Gorman's attacks was the parish picnic held in the summer of 1867 by the Catholics of St. James. Fr. O'Gorman felt that his authority was being compromised since some members of his church had planned to attend this activity of the "rival" Catholic church of Bridgeport. To show his displeasure, Fr. O'Gorman mounted his pulpit on Sunday, June 30, 1867, and condemned any from St. Mary's who might attend the St. James picnic on July 4th, stating that they would be cursed and that he, as rector, " '. . . would stand at the gate and shoot any of my people who go. . . .' "[61]

Such internal squabbles and jealousies among the clergy weakened the effectiveness of the Church's work by dividing the efforts of the priests and straining the relations between church communities. The already uncertain financial stability of the local churches was weakened further by the dishonesty or administrative ineptitude of many of the rectors, as seen in the above examples.

An attempt was made by the Bishop to regulate the affairs of his diocese by means of priests' meetings. His clergy regularly gathered for theological conferences and discussions at district meetings,[62] a practice begun by Bishop O'Reilly in 1854. These meetings took the place of formal synods during the formative years of the Diocese of Hartford, at which time the state of the diocese was reviewed and discussion conducted between the priests and their bishop concerning common pastoral problems and concerns.[63]

Rome was not enthralled with this apparently democratic practice[64] and reminded the Bishop that the canons of the Council of Trent required the periodic convocation of solemn diocesan synods.[65] The apparent failure of such meetings to rectify the poor work of the clergy did little to alter Rome's judgement of their uselessness. Bishop McFarland continued his yearly meetings and discussions with his clergy, nonetheless. They provided a forum for the open exchange of ideas without the fear of adverse reactions from the Bishop, which practice proved to be a rare commodity in other ecclesiastical circles of the day.

One example of the open nature of these meetings was expressed in 1870 in reaction to an announcement made by Bp. McFarland concerning the establishment of canonical parishes in the diocese. The Bishop wanted his priests' reactions and thoughts and so invited them to write to him in early March of that year. The priests preferred to communicate their reactions and ideas to their Bishop in person, and requested the Rev. Thomas Hendricken, the future founding Bishop of Providence, to communicate their preference to Bishop McFarland. Fr. Hendricken wrote that the priests of the diocese, ". . . were more than thankful that they might give you their opinions without restraint or hindrance." The real reason for the meeting, continued Fr. Hendricken, would concern the fears of the priests about their future,

> . . . for although contented with the more than Justice [sic] with which you govern, a time may come, said they [the priests], when matters could be entirely altered.[66]

More than a close personal relationship between the bishop and his priests was required for the success of the missions in Fairfield County. The affect on normative Catholic life of the poor training, administrative ineptitude, and personal problems of the local clergy were exacerbated by the poor communications and distance between Fairfield County and its bishop, then living in Providence, Rhode Island. The work of the Rev. Thomas J. Synnott in Bridgeport as a representative of the Bishop to Fairfield County was a temporary measure until a greater number of better trained clergy could be had. Fr. Synnott's mission, St. James in Bridgeport, was the only church in the county that was free from any financial or internal problems. This was the result of the strong leadership of its rector who exercised an authority within the county that was second only to the Bishop of Hartford.

Rev. Thomas J. Synnott

Fr. Synnott was born in County Kilkenny, Ireland, in 1818. He came to America with his family in 1850 and settled in Philadelphia. It was there that Bishop O'Reilly succeeded in acquiring his services for the Hartford Diocese. Following his ordination, Fr. Synnott was assigned to Providence, Rhode Island, where he remained until August, 1852, when he was named the Rector of St. James in Bridgeport. Three other priests were then resident within Fairfield County, serving in Norwalk, Danbury, and Stamford. Bridgeport had the largest and oldest Catholic community in the county, and its rector enjoyed a type of patriarchal honor within Catholic circles. Fr. Synnott was to prove himself a dynamic and influential priest not only among his people and fellow clerics but also among the larger population, exercising an authority that was far from simply honorific. He could be called the unofficial "chorbishop" of Fairfield County.

Fr. Synnott already had made his influence felt in Bridgeport and the county during the election of Governor William T. Minor in 1855. He had served three years as the rector of St. James Church at that time and would continue there until his death in 1884. One of the most important projects involving Fr. Synnott was the passage of the resolution amending the anti–Catholic laws of incorporation that appeared in 1855 under Governor Minor's Nativist regime. Anti–Catholic sentiment had diminished greatly following the Civil War as the result of the strong support of the Union expressed by the Catholic clergy and faithful both at home and on the battlefield. The Connecticut laws of 1855 that prohibited the Catholic Church from incorporating property in accord with canon law, however, remained in effect even after the Connecticut troops returned

Old St. Mary Church, Norwalk, (c. 1858). This, the second Catholic mission in Fairfield County, was founded in 1848. This first church was completed in 1851. Courtesy the Norwalk Historical Reference Library, Lockwood House, Norwalk.

St. Peter Church, Danbury, (c. 1870). Courtesy the Danbury Scott-Fanton Museum and Historical Society.

"Church and State"
America, although solidly, if unofficially Protestant, boasted that no
link existed between any religion and the state.

"The American River Ganges"

The need for Catholic schools was insisted upon by American bishops by the middle of the last century to protect the faith of Catholic children against anti-Catholic teachings. Many Protestants were aghast at such a demand, and feared such sectarian schools would be Catholic tools designed to undermine American liberties.

"Grab All"

American nativists used Protestant pulpits and press to instruct Americans concerning the true nature of the Catholic Church. Behind a facade of piety and religion, according to the nativists, was a papal plot to conquer the world.

"The Promised Land"
   With the fall of Rome and the Papal States in September, 1870, the
fears and groundless warnings of the nativists that Pope sought to conquer
America, aided by the hordes of Catholic immigrants, received new force,
as seen in Thomas Nast's cartoon of 1871: Pope Pius IX and advisers,
atop St. Peter's Basilica in Rome, cast their sights on the American Republic
and prepare to attack.

Bishop Shehan and Pope John XXIII. Courtesy Bridgeport Diocesan Archives.

The Apostolic Delegate in the United States, Archbishop Amleto Cicognani, Bishop Shehan and his secretary, the Rev. George Curtiss prior to the groundbreaking ceremony for Notre Dame High School, Bridgeport. Courtesy, Bridgeport Diocesan Archives.

Mother Sacred Heart, CSJ, the foundress of St. Joseph Hospital. Stamford, Courtesy Bridgeport Diocesan Archives.

Bishop Shehan and Mother M. Bernadete De Lourdes, O.F.M. of St. Joseph Manor, Trumbull. Courtesy Bridgeport Diocesan Archives.

Bishop Shehan and Archbishop Francis Keough of Baltimore, on the occasion of Archbishop Shehan's return to Baltimore, 1961. Courtesy Bridgeport Diocesan Archives.

home. Since the public sentiment toward the Church had improved markedly, Bishop McFarland decided to work for the passage of a new bill to free the Church in regard to the incorporation of its property.

The Rev. Matthew Hart, Rector of St. Patrick Church in New Haven, was called upon to head the work. He early discovered that opposition to the Church in Connecticut did indeed exist, and that a strong lobby would be needed if the state legislators were to be convinced of the necessity of passing a new bill.[67] The 1855 law required all church property to be invested in the individual congregations, which was the common practice of the Protestant Churches. The Catholic Church wanted to change the law in order to reestablish its normative practice, whereby the bishop or the diocese would hold the deed to all Church property. On June 14, 1866, the bill on corporations was referred by the Connecticut House of Representatives to the Judiciary Committee for review. It was reported against and soundly rejected on the following day.[68]

In order to rouse support for the amendment, Fr. Hart called upon the priests in Connecticut to speak with their local representatives who could then mount a lobby in favor of the proposed bill.[69] The major support for Fr. Hart came from the Rev. Bernard Tully, then Rector of St. Mary's Star of the Sea in New London; Rev. Peter A. Smith, Rector of St. Mary's in Norwalk; Rev. James O'Neill, Rector of St. John's in Stamford; and the Rev. Thomas J. Synnott, Rector of St. James in Bridgeport.[70] Under the leadership of Fr. Synnott, the Fairfield County priests followed the instructions of Fr. Hart to contact their local state representatives and to appear in New Haven for the proceedings in the House of Representatives on June 22, 1866.[71]

The opposition to the bill was led by the former state governor, Chauncey Fitch Cleveland. He opposed the Church's proposed amendment because he felt that it would legally incorporate the bishop himself.[72] As many of the representatives began to change their votes to favor the Church as a result of the lobbying of the local rectors and those legislators in favor of the bill, Cleveland explained his real reasons for opposition and conceded defeat. Fr. Hart related his meeting with Cleveland to his Bishop:

Governor Cleveland came to me today and volunteered an explanation for his conduct, on the grounds of consistency. He has voted all his life against particular acts for particular denominations and *He knows,*

139

he says, *that we will carry the bill in spite of him,* but he feels bound to oppose it.[73]

Later the same day, Cleveland met again with Fr. Hart and told him that he would be absent from the capitol the following week. If a vote were called during his absence, it would be assured to pass. Fr. Hart wrote the Bishop, "We literally *flanked* him out of the field without a blow being struck."[74]

The opposition to the bill was limited once Cleveland had given way. On June 26, 1866, the day of the final vote, support was so nearly universal that the only two speakers against the bill were ignored. One, a Mr. Grigg, began a tirade against the pope and the danger of papal interference in American affairs. Fr. Hart related that "He soon worked the House into a fit of laughter in the midst of which he subsided." The other speaker, a Protestant minister, was roundly told that the affair was none of his business since it did not deal with his denomination.[75] There were only five negative votes cast, the majority of the opposition coming from Windham County. It was discovered, however, that the bill had not received the full support of Catholic clergy in Connecticut, nor from all the Democrats who,

> . . . would just as soon see the bill refused as granted. And so convinced was I of this that I hinted it to some Republican friends, who said that if any Democrats would oppose the bill, they [the Republicans] would make a party question of it, and carry it in spite of them.[76]

The bill allowed for the incorporation of parish property whereby the Bishop, Vicar General, and two elected lay trustees of each church would form individual parish corporations within the Diocese. Such corporations would be governed by the statutes of the Diocese of Hartford. Even though the proceedings received little notice from the press in Fairfield County, the outcome was important for the normal development of the Church.

On the local Bridgeport scene, Fr. Synnott proved himself to be a prodigious builder during his years in Bridgeport. He succeeded in building the original St. Mary's Church on the East Side; the first frame church of St. Thomas in Fairfield; the new St. Augustine's Church in Bridgeport, which replaced the old St. James; and began St. Agnes Convent. He showed himself to be a shrewd land speculator by securing land for the Church that would later prove valuable as the city expanded. A quarry in Black Rock was purchased by St. James and brought the church added revenue. The quarry was also an effective means of cutting construction costs for the mission, since it provided the stone required for the new St. Augustine Church and the new St. Agnes Convent.[77]

Fr. Synnott also employed his native ingenuity and his church's resources for the enhancement of the Church's influence in the local Bridgeport community and throughout Fairfield County. He established friendly relations with the clergy of the various Protestant Churches in the city by simple courtesies, financial assistance given to various charities, and the donation of building materials from his mission's quarry. One such example was the donation of the building stone required for the construction of St. Paul's Episcopal Church on Washington Park in 1870.[78] He did the same with local city officials. By improving relations between the city and the Church, he successfully weakened the belief that priests and the Catholic Church were neither tolerant of, nor in harmony with, the principles of democracy.[79]

His major contribution to the local community was his two terms of service on the Bridgeport Board of Education from 1878 until his death in 1884. His work helped to provide a strong public school system within the city, while at the same time lessening the use of often anti–Catholic, sectarian textbooks and methods of education employed in other public schools throughout the country. In its Memorial to Fr. Synnott, the Board of Education characterized the Rector of St. Augustine's as

". . . a man of education, tact and ability, and although a clergyman, still a man without prejudice or bigotry, his was a happy and tolerant disposition."[80]

Fr. Synnot's pastoral sense, sharp business acumen, and personal attractiveness combined to make him the most influential priest in Fairfield County during his thirty–two year rectorate in Bridgeport. In the words of the historian of Bridgeport, Fr. Synnott did ". . . more than any other man to promote the cause of Catholicity in this part of the Country."[81] The Rector of St. James, which became St. Augustine's, served as the Bishop's "envoy" to far–off Fairfield County, that was light years away from the See City of Providence in many respects. He influenced most aspects of Church life within Fairfield County and exercised an authority that touched the finances, administration, and work of every mission in the county, as well as the appointment of priests and the establishment of new missions.[82]

The Church in Connecticut Changes

The remoteness of the bishop from his Connecticut Catholics was lessened by Rome on April 28, 1872, when the Diocese of Providence was created, reducing the Diocese of Hartford to the confines of the State of Connecticut. Bp. McFarland's return to Hartford in May of that year marked the beginning of a new period of the Church in Connecticut. By this time the Church was firmly established in every part of the state. The nearly 140,000 Catholics of the state worshiped in 76 churches, served by 77 priests.

By the time of the division of the diocese in 1872, the Catholics of Fairfield County were served by eleven priests resident at six churches, and responsible for nine mission chapels and numerous mission stations. Sunday schools were established at every church and mission, and Catholic schools were in operation in Bridgeport, Stamford and Danbury.[83] Bishop McFarland wrote in 1873 that,

> Nearly every town and village in the State has a Catholic priest living within its limits, or is frequently visited by him. Christian instruction is therefore secured, and for this reason our people are content to build up homes for themselves and their children in any portion of the diocese. . . .[84]

As the ethnic complexion of the diocese continued to change during the years subsequent to Bishop McFarland's rule, the provisions made by him would prove inadequate to insure the pastoral care required by congregations composed of non–English speaking men and women. No longer primarily from Ireland, or of Irish descent, each immigrant group began to clamor for its own church staffed by a priest of the same nationality. Unconcerned with the limitations of the diocese's funds and manpower, the arriving European immigrants too often demanded immediate responses to their requests for priests and specialized care. The bishop's refusal or inability to comply with the wishes of many immigrant groups, because of an insufficient number of immigrant priests or those fluent in the required languages, was often taken as an act of prejudice, insulting to the national pride of the various immigrant groups.

Bishop Lawrence McMahon: "New" Immigrants and the "Irish" Clergy

Bishop Lawrence Stephen McMahon was named the fifth Bishop of Hartford as the mass immigration from Europe began. Serving as Bishop during the years 1879–1893, McMahon pursued his predecessors' policy of training his Irish and American–born priests in European and Canadian seminaries as a means of supplying the growing need for priests to minister to immigrant communities. The employment of foreign–born priests of religious orders was also a part of his program to minister to the foreign–born Catholics in Connecticut. During his years in Hartford, Bishop McMahon introduced into the diocese the La Salette Fathers and the Missionaries of the Congregation of St. Charles Borromeo, who ministered respectively to the French–Canadian and Italian communities in the state.

It was during Bp. McMahon's years that the first national churches were organized in Fairfield County. St. Joseph's Church was formed in 1886 principally for the German Catholics of Bridgeport, and St. John Nepomucene Church was formed in 1891 in response to the petitions of the Catholic Slovak community, also in Bridgeport. Even though the Catholic image in Connecticut was decidedly an immigrant one prior to Bishop McMahon's years, it was only during his time that that image began to become much more multinational. So rapid was the growth of the Church in Connecticut during his years, that it was suggested that Hartford might be raised to the archiepiscopal dignity, and Connecticut formed into a new ecclesiastical province.[85]

The concern of the Bishop for the welfare of the Catholic immigrants was in no way diminished by his overwhelmingly Irish clergy, who generally cooperated with generosity and zeal. The Bishop responded to the needs of his people as they arose. Yet the problem of employing dedicated and honest immigrant priests would prove to be one of the major obstacles to the bishop's immediate accedence to the requests for national parishes for the individual national groups. The problem of vagrant foreign priests, or those who had immigrated to America without the permissions of their European superiors, was a real one in America. Desperate for priests able to speak the required languages, many American bishops found themselves compelled to employ such immigrant priests, oftentimes with disastrous and scandalous results.

Bogus priests also appeared in greater numbers as the Catholic immigrant population in Fairfield County grew. Catholics of South Norwalk, Westport, Fairfield, and Stratford were visited in 1878 by a man dressed as a priest who relieved the unsuspecting faithful of some of their funds. He claimed to be a priest of the diocese and explained that he was collecting for a new church to be built for the growing Catholic population within the county.[86] By 1880 the problem had become rather worse, especially in Bridgeport, as the *Connecticut Catholic* observed,

> Bridgeport, . . . is often infested by bogus characters of both sexes collecting money under various guises and pious pretenses. On more than one occasion, we have heard our pastors cautioning Catholics against holy vagrants of this sort. . . . The marauders who bore down on this city, had not even 'letters of marque' to exhibit in their favor.[87]

Despite the rapid ethnic diversification within the Church's ranks in Connecticut, the bulk of the clergy remained of Irish birth or descent. Of the sixteen priests resident within Fairfield County in 1880, only one, the Rev. Joseph Schaele at Bridgeport's St. Joseph Church, was not of Irish extraction.[88] The heightened pro–Irish sentiment in the Church that appeared during the latter part of the century was the natural result of the overwhelmingly Irish background of the Church's faithful and clergy.

The church societies founded by priests during Bishop McMahon's years, although open to all Catholics, were composed mainly of those of Irish descent. An example of this, the Knights of Columbus, was founded in New Haven in 1882, establishing its first council in Fairfield County in Bridgeport in 1885. A fraternal, charitable religious organization, originally for Catholic men, the Knights would develop into a very important and influential organization in the Church.[89] The Catholic Benevolent Legion, established in Stamford under the guidance of the rector of St. John's Church in 1883, although offering charitable assistance to all Catholics regardless of ethnic origin or birth, was composed primarily of Irish Catholics.

"Home Rule" for Connecticut Catholics

Besides his attempts to secure adequate priestly ministry for the growing immigrant Catholic population in his diocese, Bishop McMahon also showed his concern for the protection of the rights of Connecticut Catholics as citizens to participate in public life. The Catholic clergy were now called upon by their Bishop to exert a greater influence upon their local communities by defending the right of Catholics to attain leadership positions in business and government, regardless of their ethnic background or religious affiliation. It was during Bishop McMahon's years that the clergy and official Catholic press of the state began to manifest more openly their pro–Irish penchant, especially in the areas of local politics, labor and reform, all of which were artfully linked with the cause of Irish nationalism, comparing the English oppression of the Irish to the Protestant political control of Connecticut's government.

The Irish nationalist leaders, such as Charles Stewart Parnell, were responsible also for garnering the support of the Irish, American, and English clergy in support of Irish home rule. Parnell founded the National Land League in Ireland in 1879 following a disastrous economic crisis and crop failure. Backed by assistance from Irish–Americans and members of the Irish and American Church hierarchies, Parnell embarked upon a program of legal land reform that would remove ownership of Irish land from the hands of the English aristocracy, in favor of the tenant farmers.

The Church's support for the Irish cause was expressed clearly in Bishop McMahon's call for a special parish collection ". . . to rescue from hunger, sickness and death the unfortunate people of our own native land [Ireland], or the land of our fathers and mothers. . . ."[90] But stronger support came from the churches themselves that had established local Land Leagues throughout the entire diocese.[91] The local Land Leagues united all other Irish societies in their support of land reform and home rule in Ireland. They also offered the Church a public forum in which to demonstrate the loyalty of Irish–Catholic citizens to America; the strength of Irish virtue, through support of Catholic temperance societies; and the potential political clout of Irish Catholics, through the membership of the Ancient Order of Hibernians.

The oppression of the tenant farmers in Ireland by their English landlords was quickly likened to the political control exercised by the Protestant majority in Connecticut, that kept Irish–American Catholics from public office. The festivities of St. Patrick's Day in 1881 provided the occasion for expressions of Irish nationalism by local Irish–Catholics. These were transformed by the *Connecticut Catholic* into gems of political demagoguery in preparation for the upcoming Bridgeport elections.

Both St. Augustine's and St. Mary's Churches celebrated high Masses for packed churches, followed immediately by lectures on Ireland and the Land League. Fr. John Rogers delivered his impassioned diatribe, entitled "English Oppression in Ireland during the past Three Centuries," to his congregation at St. Mary's. The Rector of St. Augustine's did likewise, linking the nostalgia of his Irish congregation to the specter of English–Protestant terror and injustice that stalked the Emerald Isle.[92]

Following these festivities, the *Connecticut Catholic* likened Ireland's fight for independence from the English Protestant ruling class to that battle then being fought by the Irish–Catholic candidates in the local Bridgeport political contests. Both in Ireland and in Bridgeport the Irish–Catholic did battle against the tyranny of the Protestant ruling class that was perceived by the Church as keeping Irish–Catholics from their rightful place in government and society. As the local campaigns began in Bridgeport, the *Connecticut Catholic* offered its support for Irish Catholic citizens such as ". . . City Clerk Keating, Selectman Driscoll, Lawyer Phalon [*sic*]," and called for a united Catholic vote against the Republican foe:

> Too long have the unscrupulous ones been in the majority, and it should be the job of every citizen to commence the work of political restoration, by placing at the head of the ticket a man worthy of the respect and confidence of the entire party, . . . Already have our Irishmen received from the republican organ the usual fling, and it remains to be seen whether the Catholic democrats will unite. . . .[93]

On the eve of the elections in November, the Bridgeport Catholic churches and the Land League organized a mass meeting at the Bridgeport Opera House. The main attraction was an address by Thomas P. O'Connor, a member of the British Parliament and supporter of Parnell and the land reform. After an introduction by the Republican Mayor Wessels, O'Connor spoke out against the injustices of British rule in Ireland, called for land reform, and for united efforts on the part of all to sustain and support the rights and dignity inherent in all men.[94] The Democrats were far from victorious in any of the contests. Yet the Bridgeport elections of 1881 were the first in any large city within Fairfield County in which the Church attempted to exercise its influence by enlisting Irish nationalistic fervor and Catholic loyalty in order to secure the election of one of its own.

As Bridgeport's Catholic population continued to grow due to immigration during Bishop McMahon's years, the Church's attempts to influence local elections in the third largest city in the state also grew in intensity. Support from local churches was never foreign to Connecticut politics. Never before, however, had any individual church counted such a large number of voters within its ranks or possessed such potential influence upon the political thought of its constituents as had the Catholic Church, especially as its immigrant population steadily increased.

Since the number of votes cast in Bridgeport had an effect upon the state representation in the capitol, the outcome of the elections drew attention greater than expected in local politics. As the Church became more forceful in its support of various Democratic candidates during the years, the Republicans began to fight back, as in the 1892 mayoral and state elections. The Republicans ran the 1892 Bridgeport mayoral campaign on two issues: a call for the strict enforcement of the Sunday liquor laws, and a call for honesty in city government that would protect the rights of American citizens.

The Democrats were portrayed as depraved, power–hungry individuals who held the citizens of Bridgeport in their thrall for personal gain. The "ring," as the Democrat's "machine" was dubbed by the Republicans, was alleged to have entered into a relationship with the saloon owners of the city, promising to weaken the stringent application by the police of the Sunday liquor laws in return for their vote.[95] Since the saloon keepers were involved, so the accusation ran, the immigrant vote could easily be handed over to the Democrats, since the influence of barkeepers over the intemperate immigrant was so great.[96] Even though intemperance had been condemned by the Third Plenary Council of Baltimore in 1884, and temperance societies existed in every Catholic church in the county, the false image of the Catholic immigrant as the cause of social ills and the slave of liquor and vice proved hard to kill.

The Republican campaign received the hearty support of every Protestant church in the city. Two days prior to the elections, the *Bridgeport Daily Standard* published an appeal for support of the Republican ticket that was signed by 28 Protestant pastors. The Sunday sermons delivered in nearly all the Protestant churches prior to the election gave further support to the Republicans since they dealt with temperance, the Sunday liquor laws, or Christian government. Bridgeport's Catholic rectors refrained from entering into the fray. Only the *Connecticut Catholic* voiced its opinion. It warned that the Republican candidates were interested more in the preservation of their own political machine, the maintenance of the power held by the Anglo–Saxon Protestant establishment, and the defeat of the Irish–Catholics, than they were with the welfare of Bridgeport.[97]

The Republicans were victorious in Bridgeport, but elsewhere in the county the Democrats held sway. Regardless of party victory or defeat, the Church took pains to question why no Catholic was privy to election to high office, except in those areas of the country where the majority was Catholic. Holding that a candidate should be elected because of his ability and integrity, not because of his religious beliefs or church membership, the paper editorialized,

> Surely, Catholics, neither as individuals nor as adherents of a religious institution, can be accused of lacking loyalty to the genius of American citizenship. Why, then, should this ostracism from high civic places prevail on account of religious preference?[98]

Catholics Are Loyal Americans

As anti–immigrant and anti–Catholic feelings grew with the rise of immigration, the Catholic clergy did their utmost to portray the American Catholic as loyal to America, regardless of the land of his birth. During the quatercentenary celebration of the discovery of America in 1892, the *Connecticut Catholic* asked why no prominent Catholic, lay or ecclesiastic, had been invited to participate in the opening ceremonies of the Columbian Exhibition in Chicago, since Columbus and his patroness Queen had both been communicants of the Roman Church.[99] Indignant that Catholics should be banned from high–level participation in what was seen by the Church as an American and a Catholic event, Church authorities in Connecticut protested loudly.

Cities throughout Connecticut celebrated the event, and none was larger than that held in Bridgeport. The Church leaders of the city made sure that Catholic representation was dominant, with phalanxes of the Knights of Columbus, various Catholic societies from Bridgeport and other cities, priests, religious and Catholic school children marching in the city parade carrying banners and outfitted in full uniform and insignia, lest their identity as Catholic Americans go unnoticed. More than 20,000 people witnessed this overwhelmingly Catholic civic event, and cheered with wild enthusiasm while city representatives greeted a replica of the Santa Maria as it docked in Bridgeport Harbor.

The *Connecticut Catholic* contributed to the exaggerated patriotic fervor of the moment when it commented,

> If Columbus could have foreseen the ovation that greeted the landing of his representative Friday, he surely would have postponed his voyage 400 years and chosen Bridgeport instead of San Salvador as his landing place.[100]

Church officials felt compelled to come to the defense of one of their own because of nativist sentiment expressed in the Park City not one week after the tumultuous Columbian celebrations.

The occasion was the attack by Bridgeport's Judge Perry, a Republican, upon John J. Phelan, the Irish–born, Catholic Democratic candidate for the position of Connecticut's Secretary of State. In a last ditch effort to undermine the election prospects of the Democrats, Perry addressed a Southport rally stating that,

> For thirty–one years we have run this country without the help of the Democratic party, and we don't want your votes now. My ancestors came over with the early settlers, and it made my blood boil to hear a recent importation in this hall claim to have been elected secretary of state and kept out of office by the Republican Party.[101]

The *Connecticut Catholic* defended Phelan as a respected Bridgeport lawyer, leader of the Democratic side of the House of Representatives in 1885 and the Supreme Knight of the Knights of Columbus. The paper held that neither Phelan's religion nor his Irish birth should be used as a barrier to his election. The defense added,

> He [Perry] falls back on the American Constitution, the real meaning of which Perry seems to be ignorant of as he is of the ordinary rules of gentlemanly courtesy.[102]

The belief that much of the practice, discipline and doctrine of the Catholic Church was as foreign to America as was most of the Church's constituency was held by many inside as well as outside the Church. Members of the American hierarchy such as James Cardinal Gibbons of Baltimore and John Ireland, Archbishop of St. Paul, worked to prove that the Church and America were indeed compatible. They desired to build a new, American, and Catholic civilization in the United States, with an American Catholic Church as its centerpiece.[103]

"Home Rule" for Connecticut Priests

The death of Bishop McMahon in 1893 provided the occasion for the clergy of the Diocese of Hartford to express their similar opinion that the Church in America should be more in tune with American principles. Their support for Irish Home Rule was easily translated into the cause of Home Rule for the American Church in Connecticut. At an informal meeting of members of the clergy following the month–mind Mass for the late Bishop, a committee of priests was formed. A circular was drafted and sent to all Connecticut priests ". . . to secure an expression of the sentiment from the clergy, . . . relative to the election of a new Bishop."[104] Rome already had heard rumors of such a desire on the part of members of the clergy to elect their own bishops in America. Needless to say, Rome roundly condemned the practice earlier that year.[105] Ignoring the condemnation, the self–appointed committee of twenty–five Connecticut priests decided that the next bishop should be a member of the Hartford diocesan clergy. They were distressed that the previous Bishops of Hartford had all been chosen from outside the diocese, even though qualified diocesan priests had been available. The consensus ". . . in favor of home rule" led to the drafting of the circular. The priests of the diocese were asked to prepare a *terna* of three names that would be sent to members of the American hierarchy, the Apostolic Delegate and to Rome.

The clergy's choice fell to the Rev. Michael Tierney, then rector of St. Mary's Church in New Britain. Fr. Tierney also had been chosen by the diocesan consultors and permanent rectors earlier that September. The second choice fell to the Rev. William Harty, and the third to the Rev. Thomas Broderick. The nomination was hailed by the local press as a welcome democratic innovation within the Church. It proved to be the source of embarrassment to some Church leaders, especially the Apostolic Delegate, since the press suggested that he had sanctioned the election.[106]

The three men whose names appeared on the terna were not universally popular among the Connecticut clergy. Fr. Tierney was referred to by some of the clergy as "Sly Mike," Fr. Harty as "Pious Bill," and Fr. Broderick as "Lazy Tom."[107] Others among the clergy thought themselves to be more suitable than those nominated. The Rev. Denis J. Cremin, Rector of St. Augustine's in Bridgeport, was one such self–proclaimed worthy. After writing to the Propaganda on numerous occasions—once with a suitable gift of $5,200—he felt himself justified in expecting to receive the nomination.[108] When his name did not appear, he wrote a scathing letter to Rome, attacking the Archbishop of Boston, his coadjutor, and the three Hartford priests nominated for the Hartford See.[109]

Inquiries by Rome into the administration of the late Bishop McMahon also proved to be embarrassing. In testimony given to the Propaganda by the Rev. Thomas Shahan, a Hartford priest who had been a close friend of the late prelate, Bishop McMahon was accused of relaxing clerical discipline in the diocese during his later years, and of giving bad example himself by occasionally indulging in drink and playing cards with his priestly associates. The alleged result of such an example by the Bishop was the intemperance of the clergy, that sometimes led to the scandal of the faithful. Another result of the Bishop's lax discipline was negligence of many priests regarding the recitation of the breviary and the daily celebration of Mass, or the pursuance of studies or writing following ordination.[110]

Rome's choice was in accord with the wishes of the majority of the clergy of Hartford, and the Rev. Michael Tierney was named to the See of Hartford on December 2, 1893, consecrated Bishop and installed on February 22, 1894. In a letter from the Cardinal Secretary of State, Bishop Tierney was instructed that the most pressing need in his diocese was the spiritual perfection of his diocesan clergy by a restoration of clerical discipline. This would be effective only if the Bishop's constant exhortations to his priests concerning perfection and faithfulness to their priestly vocation were fortified by his own example of piety and pastoral dedication. The younger clergy, especially, were to be well–formed spiritually and encouraged to continue studying after ordination, in order to serve their people better.[111]

Bishop Tierney became renowned for his building projects throughout the diocese, for his generous accommodation of Catholic immigrants that helped to create for them a welcoming atmosphere, and for his strong temperance work.[112] The bishop from Norwalk also must be credited with having contributed more to the creation of a Catholic identity and culture for his people than any of his predecessors. By the time of the bishop's death on October 3, 1908, the Catholics in Fairfield County worshiped in 31 churches, supported 14 parish schools, and received the ministrations of 51 diocesan priests.

Bishop Michael Tierney from Norwalk

Bishop Tierney was born in Ireland in 1839. He and his family came to America when he was eight years old, and settled in Norwalk. He attended St. Mary's Church, where he served as an altar boy and received his early catechism instructions and sacraments that nurtured his priestly vocation. His early studies were completed in the Norwalk public schools, followed by seminary studies in Kentucky, Montreal, and Troy, New York.[113]

At the beginning of Bishop Tierney's administration, the Catholic population of his diocese was estimated to be 250,000, served by 195 diocesan priests in 178 churches. Fairfield County was estimated to contain 33,000 Catholics, who worshiped in seventeen churches, served by twenty–nine priests.[114]

In his first diocesan report, Bishop Tierney stated that the moral and spiritual condition of his clergy was in no way as bleak as had been suggested by the respondents to the Vatican's questions at the time of his predecessor's death. The Bishop assured the Roman authorities that the diocese was flourishing, both morally and materially, and that his priests had shown themselves to be generally hard–working and cooperative.[115]

The Bishop's favorable report to Rome concerning the condition of his clergy was followed by action. He required his clergy to make an annual two–week retreat at the Jesuit retreat house on Keyser Island in South Norwalk. None was excused, except for emergencies. The clergy of the Diocese had been required to make annual retreats for years. Bishop Tierney's program, however, separated the clergy into "younger" and "senior" groups, determined by the years of ordination of each priest. These groups retreated from their parochial duties on separate occasions. The "younger" clergy were required to take an annual examination in dogmatic and moral theology, canon law, liturgical and pastoral practice, and scripture. The examinations were taken by the younger priests through their first five years of ordination, as an attempt to encourage post–ordination studies. The examinations also revealed the thoughts of the younger clergy concerning pastoral work and afforded the Bishop an opportunity to impress his policies upon his younger men. The retreats fostered a camaraderie among the priests and allowed for the dissemination of the Bishop's ideas and policies, as well as offering spiritual benefits to the retreatants through prayer and meditation in a tranquil atmosphere.

Priests for Connecticut

The two most pressing needs of his diocese, however, involved the provision of an adequate number of vocations, especially to minister to the growing number of immigrants within Connecticut, and a diocesan seminary in which the Bishop could come to know his future priests and be assured of their proper training. By 1894, the diocese was supporting 60 ecclesiastical students, 28 of whom were pursuing their philosophical studies, while the remaining 32 studied theology in preparation for ordination. Twenty–one of his theologians attended St. John's Seminary in Brighton, the provincial seminary for the Boston Province. The remainder studied in seminaries in Washington, D.C., London, Genoa, and Rome.[116]

Bishop Tierney decided to initiate his own program of seminary preparation that would maintain a high number of vocations while assuring a solid academic and spiritual foundation upon which the major seminaries might build. The seminary program also would include the study of foreign languages. This would prepare many for studies abroad and, thus, provide the diocese with priests capable of speaking the languages required in the ministry to the immigrant Catholics within the state. St. Thomas Seminary opened its doors on September 7, 1897, with a student body of 37 young men. The faculty was composed of priests from the diocese, and included the Rev. Hubert Dahme of St. Joseph Church in Bridgeport, who taught German, and the Rev. Thomas Ryan of St. Peter Church, Danbury, who instructed the students in Greek. St. Thomas Seminary exercised an immense influence upon the priests of the state. It eventually provided a four–year high school preparatory program, as well as the first two years of college education and seminary preparation for the majority of Connecticut's clergy until the early 1970's.

Bishop Tierney's interest in the immigrant communities of his diocese led him to expand his predecessors' program of foreign studies for his seminarians. Convinced of the absolute need for clergy capable of speaking foreign languages and familiar with the cultures of his immigrant Catholics, the Bishop assigned many of his seminarians to study in Italy, France, Poland, and Belgium. The important results of these studies for the spiritual development of the immigrant communities in the dioceses was commented upon by the *Catholic Transcript,* which wrote that Tierney,

. . . has scoured the Continent of Europe to secure places in the seminaries where candidates for the priesthood might make themselves proficient in the language of these strangers. . . . The Bishop of Hartford has the honor of being the forerunner in this direction, and we venture the prediction that he will not be long without followers. Perhaps time will prove that his policy is the solution to the vexed problems of national parishes.[117]

Bishop Tierney favored the establishment of national churches, established for the individual language groups and independent of the local territorial churches. During his fourteen–year administration, he established eighteen new missions within Fairfield County, nine of which were national churches for immigrant congregations. He encountered difficulty, however, in acquiring a sufficient number of zealous, foreign–born priests to staff the newly established churches, especially for the arriving Catholics from eastern and southern Europe. Those he did find usually proved very effective. But his program of linguistic and foreign theological studies for American–born seminarians proved to be the one, practical long–term solution.

The Bishop's view of the priesthood and high regard for the work of the priest provided the strong impetus for the solid development of Catholic life within the state. Commenting upon the priesthood, he addressed his clergy in 1899, stating that,

There is no body of men who have in their hands the power to secure the future well–being of this great country equal to the priesthood of the Catholic Church.

Since all American institutions depended upon a ". . . deep–seated spirit of religion," for their permanency, and since the Catholic Church was the Church of the "plain people," the priest's influence was immense for the safe–guarding of the nation and the salvation of souls.[118] The evil that he most wished to protect his people from was the abuse of alcohol.

Temperance Work

The Church's strong stand against the abuse of the Sunday liquor laws stemmed from the evil effects of alcoholism upon the working man who made up the bulk of the Catholic population.

One of the worst foes labor has is the viley–conducted saloon. Whether as consumer or retailer the laborer is undermining his cause by tying up to the debasing influence of the wretched barroom.[119]

154

The Bishop saw the source of all moral problems among the faithful to be intemperance, and he called upon his clergy to work to stamp out this source of spiritual evil. Total Abstinence Societies, already extant in most of the churches of the diocese, received added support during Bishop Tierney's years. He was the President of the Catholic Total Abstinence Union of America and heartily supported the efforts of his clergy on behalf of temperance among Catholics. The faithful were encouraged to take the pledge while the clergy were urged to double their efforts for the cause of temperance. During the 1899 meeting of the Catholic Total Abstinence Union of America, the Bishop stated,

> Now, as the dawn of another century is brightening the sky we appeal to the priesthood of our land to make a still more vigorous onslaught against the hydra–headed evil of drunkenness.[120]

In late October, 1898, the priests of St. Peter's Church in Danbury began a public campaign against Sunday liquor sales in their city. They roused the faithful at all the Sunday Masses on October 24 by preaching against the flagrant violation of the law, and continued their assault at a mass meeting on October 27 in the church basement, attended by Protestant and Catholic citizens alike. They were united in their resolve to protest the violation of the Sunday liquor law and issued an ultimatum to all public officials that they would find themselves bereft of supporters at the ballot boxes unless they assisted the temperance protest.[121] The Father Mathew's Temperance Society Committee was formed by the protesters to impress upon the minds of the public officials the seriousness of the matter and the need to enforce the law.[122] So effective was the protest and the organizational work of the Rev. Henry Lynch, Rector of St. Peter's, that all but one saloon owner obeyed the closure laws after only three weeks of protest.[123]

The Stamford Catholic clergy began their protest in late 1899. To mark the twentieth anniversary of the St. Joseph Total Abstinence Society of St. John's Church, the Catholic leaders stated,

> We feel, as we look at what is being wrought in Stamford by her gilded palaces and lower dives, that we must be up and doing. . . . Help us to welcome the day of deliverance to the enslaved of Stamford, many of whom desire to leave behind the wretched demon [alcohol] who seeks their souls as well as their body.[124]

The priests of Bridgeport united their efforts in 1902 and declared war on the saloon owners who broke the Sunday closure laws and on the police force for their lax enforcement of the law. The Rev. William Lynch, then serving as the temporary administrator of St. Mary's, spoke out against the saloonists. A number of them were Catholics who were willing to make ". . . their brothels the Sunday rendezvous of no inconsiderable element of our population."[125] A war similar to that launched by the Danbury priests was begun by the priests of Bridgeport that year. The Rev. James O'Donnell, Rector of St. Mary's, Norwalk, joined his voice to the temperance movement in July, 1902, rigorously attacking the vices of Norwalk, which he named as immorality and drunkenness, thus beginning his crusade for stronger enforcement of the Sunday laws.[126]

With the bulk of its members arriving from countries where the temperate use of wine and spirits was a part of their cultural life, the Church never supported any prohibition legislation. It did continue, however, to encourage temperance movements as a remedy to the intemperate habits of many of its members, especially those of the laboring class. Temperance was not the only issue concerning the worker that occupied the Church's attention during Bishop Tierney's years. The city priests of the diocese also concerned themselves with labor relations, decent and safe working conditions, and fair wages and hours for the working man, so many of whom were Catholics.

The Clergy and the Working Man

On May 15, 1891, Pope Leo XIII issued his encyclical letter, *Rerum Novarum,* dealing with the relationship between capital and labor. It put forth the social principles that would determine the Church's actions in support of labor. The encyclical condemned socialism, then attractive to many in the working class in Europe, and supported the right of the individual to private property. The Pope taught that the responsibilities of the state included protecting private property, regulating working conditions, assuring fair wages and encouraging a fair distribution of property. Even though the Church's primary duty was to remind mankind that his ultimate destiny and happiness was not of this world or in its possessions, the Church, nonetheless, bore the responsibility of promoting justice and charity among people, reminding those in civil authority of their responsibilities.

Hartford's Bishops employed their Catholic paper to mold public and Catholic opinion concerning labor, while the efforts of the local rectors reinforced the pro—labor stance of the administration by supporting the cause of the workers. The efforts of the Church in favor of labor were especially clear in the Danbury Hatters Strike of 1893 and the Bridgeport Trolley Strike of 1903, the two most publicized strikes in the history of Fairfield County.

The Danbury Hatters Strike began in 1893 and continued through a series of legal battles that were not concluded until January, 1915. Following a breakdown in negotiations in 1893, the D.E. Loewe and Company of Danbury announced an end of the closed shop that had been adopted by the union and management in 1885. The result was a lockout of over 4,000 employees on November 25, 1893, with the projected effect of stagnating all business and subjecting thousands more to destitution.[127]

The lockout, which continued until the following January, did little to dissuade the union that the re–establishment of a closed shop policy was essential to the well–being of the workers. The union continued to work for a closed shop, instituting a boycott of all Loewe's hats. This caused the company to bring suit for damages against members of the Hatters Union. The real estate and bank holdings of more than two hundred union members in Danbury, Bethel, and South Norwalk were attached as a result.

In the midst of the legal wranglings, a settlement was reached between the United Hatters and the National Hat Manufacturers Association in June, 1909. Through the agency of the Rev. H. C. Meserve of the First Congregational Church and the Rev. John D. Kennedy, Pastor of St. Joseph's Church in Danbury, an agreement was arrived at which allowed fifteen of the city's hat factories to re–open. The agreement had been devised by Fr. Kennedy, and became known as the "Kennedy Agreement." It was a compromise between the two sides concerning the use of union labels in non–union work and the continued membership of the manufacturers of Danbury in the National Association.[128] The effect of the agreement was the end of the strike in Danbury, Bethel, and New Milford. While the representatives of the United Hatters hoped that the local Danbury decision would serve as the basis for a nation-wide settlement,[129] the Associated Hat Manufacturers filed suit against the manufacturing firms that had settled with the union.[130]

The work of the Rev. John Kennedy, Rev. Walter Shanley and the Rev. H. C. Meserve was important in the labor dispute. So strong was their pro–labor influence that one of the representatives of the National Manufacturers Association, Martin M. Mulhall, attempted to weaken their united efforts. He offered bribes and favors to the Rev. Meserve, which he refused, and unsuccessfully attempted to divide the united pro–labor position of the city's two Catholic pastors.[131]

The decision of the lower courts favored the company over the American Federation of Labor and the United Hatters of North America, which had been named as defendants. Finally, after being tried in the Supreme Court and retried in lower courts, the company was declared the winner of the lengthy legal contest. The United Hatters of North America were judged to have been guilty of restraining interstate commerce by its boycott of Loewe products, thus violating the Sherman Anti–Trust Act. The decision was not a total defeat for the unions, however. As a result of the actions of the A.F. of L., Congress passed the Clayton Act of 1914 that exempted labor organizations from the provisions of the Sherman Act and made boycotts by unions legal weapons against big business.

The Bridgeport clergy also played an important role in the settlement of the Bridgeport Trolley Strike of 1903. Employees of the Connecticut Railway and Light Company had attempted to unionize for some time. Their efforts were unsuccessful since the company's management and owners opposed the move. By May, 1903, 250 employees went on strike in Bridgeport, demanding a pay raise of 22½ cents instead of the proposed raise of 20½ cents per hour. On Sunday, May 18, the company brought in 130 strikebreakers who manned and operated the trolleys through a tense Bridgeport. By early afternoon, rioting had broken out, with bottles, brickbats, stones, and other debris being used by the striking workers against scabs and policemen alike. Fearful that more serious rioting might break out, 70 deputies were sworn in to beef up the city police force of only 58 officers, and the state militia was put on alert.[132]

As the two-month-long strike progressed, protests of the railway company were called for by the striking workmen. On the evening of June 26, a mass rally was held in Washington Park in support of the trolley company employees. Estimates of 7,000 people by the *Bridgeport Evening Post*, to between 10,000 and 15,000 by the very pro-labor *Bridgeport Sunday Herald*, showed the strength of support given the striking workers, who called upon the citizens of Bridgeport to walk rather than ride as a protest against the company's opposition to unionization.[133] The rally, which received the support of Bridgeport's pro–labor Mayor, Denis Mulvihill, selected a committee to deal with the company authorities and negotiate a settlement. The committee was composed of the Rev. B. L. York, a Protestant clergyman, E. B. Peck and the Rev. William Lynch, Rector of the newly established St. Charles Church.[134] The committee proved to be very effective in representing the workers' grievances and bringing about a final settlement to the strike.[135]

The problems encountered by the clergy in labor relations further encouraged them to enlist the assistance of the Catholic layperson in actively exercising his Catholic faith in order to affect American society.

Catholic Parish Life: the "Lay Apostolate"

Since the parish remained the center of the spiritual and social life of many Catholics, it was seen by the clergy as influencing all aspects of the lives of its members. It was the local parish that was to prepare its members spiritually, intellectually, and morally that they might become the leaven for society, exercising Catholic principles and demonstrating Catholic faith and morality in the areas of government, business and academia. The Church was to be defended by living testimonies to its truth through lives of Catholic virtue that manifested the true apostolic and evangelic basis of Catholic doctrine and practice. American Catholics were being prepared by their clergy for an active lay apostolate that would promote virtue and true religion, bring about the salvation of many, and reinforce the foundations of American society.

Annual missions were offered in every parish, given by the Fathers of the Connecticut Apostolate. This was a group of diocesan priests, organized by Bishop Tierney, whose work was to offer week–long missions as a means of spiritual renewal in all the parishes throughout Connecticut. They visited each parish in the state once every three years. Fairfield County was first offered these missions during the early part of 1900.

Brookfield was one of the first towns in the county to receive the newly organized mission band. Then only a small village of strong Yankee sentiment and few Catholics, Brookfield was visited in January, 1900. The results were remarkable, not only for the Catholic population, but also for the local Protestant community. The *Catholic Transcript* commented that,

> . . . in this retired spot we were witnesses to the liveliest kind of religious excitement called up by the unheard of temerity of Catholic priests

coming to enlighten men who considered all our co–religionists as benighted children of paganism. There is one section of New England where Puritanism still thrives, where priests are abhorred, where our doctrines are Satanic tenets, where the confessional is a money–making scheme, where we are still offspring of the Scarlet Woman.[136]

The missionaries were well-received by Protestants and Catholics alike. The faith of the small Catholic community was confirmed, the misconceptions concerning the Church held by many Protestants were dispelled, and a number of converts were made.

As the Catholic population in the state continued to grow through increased immigration, the Church became aware of the potential influence of the Catholic vote. The Church desired that the Catholic portion of the electorate be well–formed by its priests in Catholic doctrine and principles in order to affect the entire life of the state. Referring to the fact that the Catholic population of the state had reached nearly 350,000, or more than one–third the estimated total population by 1906, the *Catholic Transcript* alluded to the growing Catholic vote and influence, stating that,

> . . . we are growing morally as well as numerically. It were wisdom on the part of those who create our legislatures not to treat us as a body apart. We do not want favors, we do not look for that which belongs to others. We look for and we expect a square deal, nothing more.[137]

In many ways, this concept was a Catholic version of much of the Protestant revivalist spirit of the previous century. The Catholic clergy now saw the Church as the only institution capable of insuring the stability of the American Republic, since it was Catholicism alone that was the true faith. Catholics, well–versed in Catholic truth and possessed of a lively Catholic faith, were to renew the American spirit. These sentiments were echoed by some of America's greatest prelates, among them, James Cardinal Gibbons, Archbishop John Ireland, and Bishop Thomas J. Conaty. They were printed in the *Catholic Transcript*, and echoed in local sermons throughout the state.[138]

To prepare the people of God for their apostolate, local parishes provided various programs, services, and resources. Disconcerted by the lack of works by Catholic authors in local public libraries, many churches in Fairfield County opened their own libraries, the largest of which was St. Peter's in Danbury.[139] Catholic clubs and debating societies, which had become popular by the end of the previous century, received support from local pastors. The young Catholic men and women of St. Mary's Church in Norwalk were encouraged to form and defend their opinions in open debates with leading citizens on topics of current interest, such as the morality of capital punishment, restricted immigration,[140] or the Catholic roots of American liberty.[141] Most parishes also had their own athletic programs. Having experienced unfriendly sentiments in some local Y.M.C.A. organizations, Catholics organized their own Young Men's Catholic Associations in most churches by the turn of the century. These supported friendly athletic competition between parishes and various Catholic associations. Bonds between Catholics from different areas of the state were strengthened, a Catholic identity, a strong character and sense of success independent of the Protestant establishment were fostered in this way.[142]

Catholic Schools

Catholic schools also played an important part in Catholic life, offering good primary education and religious formation to Catholic children throughout Connecticut. Bishop Tierney's years saw an increase in parish schools in the state from forty–eight to eighty, fourteen of which were in Fairfield County. His years also saw the first effort to standardize the curriculum of the Catholic schools within the state. This was undertaken by the Rev. Patrick J. McCormick, who was appointed as the first Diocesan Supervisor of Schools in 1906. Fr. McCormick, then an assistant priest at St. Augustine Church in Bridgeport, recognized the need to improve and centralize the diocesan schools. This was to be done by improving the teacher training of the religious women who served as teachers and by standardizing the curriculum in the schools. Teaching sisters were to receive more in–depth training during their novitiate that would be extended to two years. This was to be followed by teaching examinations and required teaching certificates for all diocesan teachers.

Prior to Fr. McCormick's term as school's supervisor, the curricula of most Catholic schools in the state had been determined by the course of studies in the local public schools and were geared to the preparation of students for the passing of the public high school entrance examinations.[143] The basic courses of reading, writing, and arithmetic were offered in all schools, but other subjects and activities varied from parish school to parish school. The work of standardization was to

161

be left to Fr. McCormick's successor, the Rev. William J. Fitzgerald. The death of Bishop Tierney in 1908 and the nearly two year delay before the appointment of Bishop Nilan compounded the difficulties already extant within the school system itself.[144] Yet, the efforts of Fr. McCormick laid the foundations for further developments in the state's Catholic schools as one of the key instruments for the formation of dedicated Catholics.

Bishop Tierney also patronized the work of religious congregations of men and women that affected Catholic life in the county positively during the coming decades. It was during these years that the Holy Ghost Fathers entered Fairfield County. The missionary priests and lay brothers opened a senior scholasticate for their seminarians at Ferndale in Norwalk in December, 1906. These priests and brothers made the Catholics of the county aware of the Church's worldwide missionary work. They assisted in parish work and opened their seminary to the young men of the area in an effort to encourage vocations to the priesthood and religious life. Not ten years after the opening of Ferndale, the *Catholic Transcript* opined that "before many years Ferndale will be one of the show places in Southern Connecticut."[145] The Holy Ghost priests and brothers at Ferndale did, indeed, develop a Catholic showplace in Norwalk that continued to affect the Church in Southern Connecticut until its closure in the late 1970's.

Bishop Tierney also began St. Vincent's Hospital in Bridgeport. The hospital was staffed by the Sisters of St. Vincent de Paul, and opened as the first Catholic hospital in the county on June 28, 1905. It offered a Catholic atmosphere and the ready services of priests and religious to those Catholics of Bridgeport who were sick or dying.

Bishop John Nilan

Bishop John J. Nilan, a native of the Archidocese of Boston, was named by Pope Pius X to succeed Bishop Tierney on February 14, 1910. Bishop Nilan had spent the entirety of his nearly thirty–two–year priestly career engaged in pastoral ministry. Upon his arrival in Connecticut, the Bishop discovered that the state was no longer a Yankee enclave. The American–born population was only 35.5% of the total population in the year of his appointment to Hartford. Bishop Tierney's ambitious building programs had provided the "material fabric of religion."[146] Bishop Nilan saw his task to be the continuance and reinforcement of those programs, policies, and institutions.

162

He continued the pastoral care of immigrant Catholics. Seminarians were encouraged to study the languages of the Catholic immigrants. Since the opening of St. Thomas Seminary in Hartford in 1897, the sons of immigrants had been enrolled as candidates for the priesthood. Although predominantly of Irish heritage, the enrollment included representatives of all of the major Catholic immigrant groups.[147] By the time of Bishop Nilan's arrival, the majority of his priests were still of immigrant stock, but were Connecticut—born. They were the sons of immigrants who were taking their rightful place in the Church of their forefathers.[148] The *Catholic Transcript* commented on the large number of vocations in 1912,

> Providence has a method of its own for meeting the needs of the hour. The foreign population of the diocese no less than the native is disposed to yield up its sons for the priesthood and to secure for them the advantage of training on American soil.[149]

Such priests were needed, especially with the outbreak of World War I and the resulting flood of immigrant workers into Fairfield County.

Bridgeport's Priests and Social Problems

The population was also on the move from the rural areas to the cities, with New Haven and Bridgeport the largest in the state, claiming inhabitants exceeding the 100,000 mark.[150] The areas surrounding the industrial cities in Fairfield County rapidly developed.[151]

The outbreak of World War I in 1914 transformed Bridgeport, making it a center of munitions production in the country. In the words of the *The New York Times*, ". . . regardless of how the war is affecting others, it is demonstrating itself good business for Bridgeport and Bridgeport people."[152] Large munitions contracts from the warring foreign powers inundated Bridgeport with workers and attendant social problems on a scale previously unknown. By 1914, the city's population was 104,000; by 1918, it totalled 183,000. Housing shortages, poor sanitary conditions, juvenile delinquency, and overcrowding resulted from the rapid influx of workers. Since over 75 percent of those arrivals were Catholic immigrants, the local pastors saw a need for action.

The war and the resultant manufacturing boom in Bridgeport provided the occasion for the first joint venture on the part of the Catholic clergy and laity to organize the Church's efforts in the area of social work, while publicly expressing Catholic civic principles. Occasions such as the dedication of new schools and the laying of corner stones for churches, offered the forum for Church officials to publicly address the topics of the day, such as labor questions, housing, and the relationship of the Catholic Church to the nation.

The laying of the cornerstone for St. James Church in Stratford on July 13, 1913, was one such occasion. The Rev. John H. O'Rourke, SJ, addressed Bishop Nilan and the large congregation gathered for the event. He spoke on the affect of the Church upon the nation, Bridgeport, and Stratford. He stated,

> The Catholic Church, and the Catholic churches which dot the land in the thousands are the very bulwark of the nation, the strength of our country. For these churches by their teaching stand for that which makes for our permanent growth, for our enduring stability. If the teachings that shall be heard under this roof be carried out in men's lives then we shall be a safe and free people.[153]

Fr. O'Rourke continued that only the teaching of the Catholic Church, as taught in Stratford's new church, could preserve American justice and virtue by destroying the spirit of class hatred, insuring just wages for the laborer, safeguarding the family against divorce, uprooting political corruption, and promoting honest government. The construction of St. James Church had a special meaning for the Catholics of Stratford:

> Make men see and live up to these doctrines and you have done more for the permanency and growth of the nation than if you have strengthened the police force, increased the army or built battleships. There is what this church in Stratford means for Stratford.[154]

The first real call for city protection of the immigrant laborer in Bridgeport during the war came from the Rev. Andrew E. Komara, Pastor of St. John Nepomucene Church. He called for the establishment of a new building code, capable of bringing about a solution to Bridgeport's housing problem by imposing restrictions and requirements on the construction of new homes. He argued that industrialization brought about problems that manufacturing interests were incapable of solving alone. The quality of housing and living conditions had a powerful influence upon workers' quality of life and labor, the priest continued. This, in turn, affected the quality of the contribution and participation of the workers in society, either for the well–being of the community or for its destruction. The Pastor of St. John's concluded that the government had a moral obligation to assist and protect the poor. He continued that the unsanitary and dilapidated conditions of old wooden and brick buildings in Bridgeport, overcrowded, and possessed of a wretched water supply, " '. . . is a libel on our vaunted civilization. The working-man is entitled to consideration at the hands of the building promoter.' "[155]

According to Fr. Komara, the heart of the problem was the poverty of the immigrant laborer that compelled him to have recourse to the rents such as were offered in Bridgeport. Since the foreign–born were becoming the backbone of New England, the need for immediate aid to them was the moral obligation of all in authority. Especially important were the areas of reme-dial and preventative laws in housing, more stringent temper-ance and labor laws, and improved housing and working condi-tions in Bridgeport.

The influence and contribution of Bridgeport's priests in regard to labor and housing during the war were impressive. The City of Bridgeport attempted to administer assistance to the poor by means of its Board of Charities. Among its members were the Rev. Charles J. McElroy of St. Augustine Church, and the Rev. Matthew J. Judge of Sacred Heart Church since 1911.[156] The Rev. James B. Nihill of St. Patrick Church served on the executive committee of the State Board of Charities and Correction.[157]

The efforts of the State Board were limited, especially since it served only in an advisory capacity. Bridgeport's Mayor Clif-ford B. Wilson developed the first city plan with a view of housing and recreational facilities for the large number of work-ers. The Bridgeport Chamber of Commerce, organized in 1915, established the Bridgeport Housing Company that built war workers' housing projects throughout Bridgeport and the Black Rock area of the city.

Since so many of the workers in the city were Catholic, it was felt by many of the local clergy that the Church should assist them as much as possible. Local pastors had made previous attempts to enter into social work among the poorer Catholic families of Bridgeport. The Rev. Richard Moore, Pastor of Sa-cred Heart Church, and the Rev. Thomas P. Mulcahey, chaplain of the state's Holy Name Society, both attempted to widen the field of labor of the Holy Name Society of Bridgeport to include cooperation with city officials to end the social evils brought about by poor housing and poverty.[158]

Through the efforts of the clergy the Holy Name Society had become popular among Catholic men during Bishop Nilan's first years in Hartford. Having staged mass parades in Bridgeport of over 4,000 Catholic men, and in Stamford of over 3,000 participants, it was hoped by many Church officials that such a large resource of laymen could be harnessed in order to put into action Catholic social and charitable principles.[159] Local parish societies and groups performed charitable works, but with no central organization to coordinate the efforts, the effects were minimal.

The Catholic Charitable Bureau of Bridgeport

In late 1915, the priests of Bridgeport petitioned Bishop Nilan to establish a Catholic Charitable Bureau to assist them. The work of Fathers Komara and Judge paved the way for the establishment of the Bureau. Encouraged by a letter from the Pastor of Sacred Heart Church, the Rev. Richard Moore, and a visit from the Rev. James Nihill, recently named Pastor of St. Augustine's, Bishop Nilan met with the city priests in December, 1915, and placed before them a plan for a Bridgeport Bureau of Catholic Charities. The organization would coordinate the work of the area's Catholic charitable organizations and serve as a clearing house for all the area's philanthropic societies in order to assist the Catholic families in Bridgeport. Bridgeport's five territorial parishes were to be taxed one percent of their gross receipts annually to support the project. The Bridgeport Bureau was the forerunner of the diocesan agency that was formed in 1920.

Miss Marguerite T. Boylan, the first trained Catholic social worker in the state, was appointed Executive Secretary to take charge of the Bridgeport Bureau.[160] The Rev. Richard Moore was appointed its treasurer, and the presidents of the five area conferences of the newly organized Society of St. Vincent de Paul constituted the Bureau's first advisory committee.[161] The Bureau received assistance and support from public officials and private societies. It expanded its work to include the assistance to the poor, the care of dependent children, the securing of temporary and permanent homes for orphans and the assuming of guardianship in some cases, and the organization of clubs for young men and women.

Through the efforts of Marguerite Boylan and Mrs. Catherine Cullinan Sullivan, the Bureau established the first private program in the city to assist children brought into court. Since the majority of the population was Catholic, the largest number of delinquents were also Catholic, thus providing a need for assistance and representation by the Church in the local courts. These women, and later volunteers, visited the courts daily. They spoke with children who were in legal trouble, along with their families, legal representatives and judges, in an effort to secure remedial assistance for the offenders. During the first four years of the Bureau's existence, nearly five hundred children were assisted and received counseling, education, and spiritual instruction, while their families were given financial and moral aid from the Church.[162]

During its first year, the Bureau also organized a series of lectures by prominent Catholic priests and laymen who addressed the social problems of an industrial society. Outlining broad Catholic social principles as the foundation for effective reform, the speakers led the participants to apply these principles to the local situation. They called for the charitable work of an active Catholic laity as essential to the formulation of any effective solution that would strike at the causes of Bridgeport's social evils, and not merely their effects.[163]

The Bureau expanded its work during the war. In order to assist mothers involved in wartime factory work, St. Vincent's Day Nursery opened under the management of the Sisters of Charity. Assisted by local factories, especially the Remington Arms Company, and by dedicated laywomen, the Bureau's nursery performed a great service throughout the war.

The Bureau also served as the local service office for the National Catholic War Council, organized by the American bishops. It began the Red Cross Auxiliary at St. Augustine's and elsewhere in the city and coordinated Catholic volunteers for service in war activities, such as the War Savings Stamps, Liberty Loans, War Risk Insurance, Knights of Columbus, Fatherless Children of France, and the United War Work Campaign.[164]

The Clergy and World War I

The Catholic clergy in Connecticut gave strong support to the war effort. Led by Bishop Nilan and the chancellor of the diocese, the Rev. John Murray, the priests of the diocese supported much of the wartime charitable works, and called upon the men of their congregations to enlist, as they themselves did as chaplains.[165] The work of the Knights of Columbus in favor of the American fighting men during and after the War stands out as one of the most impressive efforts of any Catholic organization of the period.

The Knights provided a powerful example of the blending

of Catholicism and patriotic fervor. Immediately following America's entrance into the War in April, 1917, the Knights petitioned Washington to be allowed to erect recreation centers for the American soldiers in the United States and Europe. Since 35 percent of the American forces were Catholic, the Knights felt that the Catholic fighting men would benefit from a Catholic presence, instead of relying solely upon the services provided by the Evangelical Protestant Y.M.C.A. that had proved itself rather unsympathetic to the Catholic Church on numerous occasions.[166]

To this end, the Knights began a war fund to raise $1 million to provide for the planned recreation centers. Each local council of the Knights was assessed a given quota to be raised by local War Fund Drives. Bridgeport's Catholic community, composed of more immigrant groups than any other in the state, strove to prove its loyalty to the American cause. It sponsored draft rallies and supported all Church efforts and programs in favor of the American cause, including that of the Knights.

On September 4, 1917, the Park City Council of the Knights held a banquet in honor of its sixty drafted members. The speaker of the evening was the Rev. Joseph A. Mulry, SJ, the President of Fordham University. Giving voice to the pro–American sentiments of his audience, he encouraged Bridgeport's young, Catholic draftees that they were fighting God's battle as well as America's:

'When you go over the top, remember that you are fighting for God, your flag and country, and may God help the Germans.'[167]

The same spirit was manifested when the Bridgeport Council began its fund drive in January, 1918. Striving to reach a $50,000 goal, the Knights collected $13,000 before the drive began.[168] Within one week the goal was surpassed by nearly $19,000, with contributions coming from private citizens, businesses, and political organizations.[169]

Even though Catholic support and organization for the Knights' project was strong in this country, many organizational problems in Europe existed concerning the establishment of the proposed centers. The Rev. Patrick McGivney, brother of the founder of the Knights, Supreme Chaplain, and Pastor of St. Charles Church in Bridgeport, accompanied the national director of the order, William Mulligan, in the spring of 1918 to investigate the problems in France and to begin the construction of some of the centers.[170] Their visit and report led to the sending of additional war–field secretaries to speed up the establishment of centers in France. Among those sent as secretaries were five Bridgeport Knights: Michael J. Keyes, James A. Buckley, Leo M. Whelan, Albert Sullivan, and Michael McKiernan.[171]

The local parishes played their part in the American effort. Enlistment rallies were held throughout the county supported by parish societies in order to encourage American Catholic young men to defend their country. Service flags were proudly displayed in all Catholic churches and society halls in the county, attesting to the number of enlisted men from each congregation by the number of stars on the flags. St. Augustine's in Bridgeport sent 200 men; St. Charles, 300—the largest number from any one parish in Fairfield County.[172] Parish societies banded together to sew and knit for the boys overseas. They provided medical supplies and encouraged all parish members to do their part to assure an American victory.

The Church and the Post–War Era

The Catholic clergy encouraged their people to play a prominent part in the preliminary work of reconstruction after the War. The American bishops, through the National Catholic War Council and, later, the National Catholic Welfare Council, established agencies and programs to meet the immediate post–war problems. They established vocational training for disabled soldiers and former servicemen, began settlement work on an extensive scale, and provided material assistance to France, Belgium, and Italy. The establishment of employment agencies for servicemen returning to America proved to be one of the most effective of all the Church's programs. A chain of employment agencies was established in all the major industrial centers in the country by the National Catholic War Council to provide or find employment for the returning soldiers. Besides securing employment, the agencies also informed the returning soldiers of government benefits, insurance, or compensation to which they were entitled, but often unaware.[173]

Responding to the bishops's plan, the Knights of Columbus played an especially important role in the establishment and operation of these agencies. Each council formed small groups of their men to visit factories, trade schools, and businesses presenting the case of the unemployed soldier to employers.[174] By September, 1919, the Bridgeport Knights had opened their own employment bureau at the Knights of Columbus Clubhouse on Washington Avenue. There they offered vocational and occupational courses for business and industry and free social services to the all returning servicemen, in addition to employment services.[175]

Many of the charitable and social activities and programs of the Church continued to be offered during the economic difficulties of the 1920's and 1930's by several organizations: the Knights, the Bridgeport Bureau in conjunction with various city agencies, parish organizations, and by the Bridgeport Council of Catholic Women, established in Bridgeport in January, 1921.[176] These organized efforts, combined with the generosity provided by individual priests, religious, and parish organizations in the larger territorial parishes throughout the county, succeeded in alleviating much suffering during those years.

Americans became isolationist following the War, distrusting all things foreign, fiercely attacking every movement or thought that slightly resembled socialism or Bolshevism. The Knights of Columbus vowed shortly after the War to ". . . speed the effort to stamp out Bolshevism and radicalism," since both were deemed destructive to the Catholic and American way of life.[177]

The administrative committee of the National Catholic War Council issued a "Program of Social Reconstruction" on February 12, 1919, that was followed by a pastoral letter from the American hierarchy the following September. Based upon *"Rerum Novarum"* of Pope Leo XIII, the letter was the American bishops's labor code applying Catholic social teaching to the American post-war condition and addressing questions that were then of burning importance. The bishops emphasized the supremacy of the moral law in labor relations and promoted the rights of the community in industrial disputes. They condemned the notion that the working class and the wealthy were enemies by nature. The letter continued,

> The moral value of man and the dignity of human labor are cardinal points in this whole question. . . . treating the laborer first of all as a man, the employer will make him a better workingman; by respecting his own moral dignity as a man, the laborer will compel the respect of his employer and of the community.[178]

The bishops affirmed labor's right to organize and management's right to enforce agreed–upon contracts. They called for a fair wage and urged arbitration over violence or strikes in the settlement of labor disputes. Quoting Leo XIII, the bishops rejected the division of modern society into castes—the wealthy, holding power only because of their wealth, and the needy multitude, powerless because they lacked wealth.[179]

When first released, the bishops' pastoral letter, and their program for reconstruction, met with stiff opposition.[180] They were condemned as socialist and un–American by Stephen C. Mason, President of the National Association of Manufacturers.[181] Nonetheless, the bishops' pastoral was simply another attempt by the clergy to extend the Church's influence into the mainstream of American life.

Catholics as Americans

The construction of the National Shrine of the Immaculate Conception on the campus of the Catholic University of America in the nation's capital was another solid statement by the clergy that Catholicism was an integral and irremovable part of American life. The project was the idea of a Connecticut priest, Bishop Thomas J. Shahan, Rector of the University, who received papal approbation for the Shrine in 1914. Following the War, nationwide collections and subscription campaigns were carried on in order to finance the project. On September 23, 1920, Cardinal Gibbons laid the cornerstone and inaugurated the construction. Since the project was the work of a Connecticut priest, it was only fitting that the cornerstone be provided by a Connecticut Catholic layman. James Sexton of Bridgeport was the donor of the New Hampshire granite block. The cornerstone, a symbol of Bridgeport's American Catholics and their pride and participation in a national American Catholic project, was greeted by over 100,000 Catholics on its way from Bridgeport to Washington, D.C., and was hailed, at least by Catholics, as "one of the finest stones ever placed in an American building."[182] The Catholic Shrine in the heart of the United States capital was to symbolize the central place of Church in the life of America.

The meaning of the symbol was to be secured by the combined work of the clergy and laity. In order to exercise such influence, American Catholics first needed the assurance of a sound education and a solid foundation in Catholic moral principles. This would be accomplished through the efforts of parishes and Catholic schools. Improvements continued to be made in the diocesan school system after the war. The curricula of the Catholic schools in Connecticut had been standardized by the 1914 "Syllabus" prepared by the Rev. William J. Fitzgerald and representatives from the three branches of the Sisters of Mercy in

Connecticut. The "Syllabus" was revised in 1926 under the Rev. Edward Flynn and again in 1935 under the Rev. Austin Munich.

The Catholic clergy recognized the need for religious education of the majority of Catholic children within the state who attended public schools. The Rev. Matthew Traynor, Pastor of St. Mary Church in Bridgeport, tackled the problem. After his appointment to St. Mary's in 1924, Fr. Traynor saw the need for improved religious education programs in the local parishes. Realizing the ineffectiveness of Sunday school classes, he sought to establish a program of religious education in conjunction with the local public schools. With the help of William I. McAndrew, the Catholic Principal of Walterville School in Bridgeport, Fr. Traynor discovered that the majority of the Catholic children in the public schools rarely went to Mass and knew little concerning the basics of their faith.[183] Mr. McAndrews suggested the program by which every child would be released from public schools early once a week in order to attend religious classes at their respective churches.[184] Fr. Traynor took McAndrew's idea and presented it to the local Protestant ministers. With their support secured, Fr. Traynor approached the Board of Education and won their unanimous approval. The Bridgeport system was later adopted throughout the state.

The Catholic students were instructed by the priests and religious sisters within the city. Under Fr. Traynor's successor, the Rev. M. Ernest Wilson, a course of studies was developed by the Rev. Patrick Quinlan, then at Holy Rosary Church in Bridgeport. The course was developed primarily for the Catholic children in the Bridgeport religious education classes, but was later adopted throughout the country.[185]

The active formation of American life, government and society by American Catholics who were well–informed intellectually and spiritually, was a constant theme throughout the Church in America, despite the suspicions of some that the Church might be the supporter of social unrest in America. To emphasize the belief that American Catholics and their Church had the right and obligation to speak out on public issues, the Holy Name Societies held parades in each of the major cities of the state, such as those in Fairfield County on October 10, 1920. Over 2,000 representatives from the surrounding towns marched through Danbury. Bridgeport mustered over 13,000 Catholic men, marching from St. Augustine Church to Seaside Park, where Benediction was celebrated accompanied by religious and patriotic airs. Stamford's Holy Name Society marched with over 4,000 Catholic men from the surrounding area.

At each demonstration in the state one of the local pastors delivered an address on the Church's mission in America, and the obligation of clergy and laity alike to make their beliefs felt in society. The Rev. Nicholas Coleman, pastor of St. Catherine of Siena Church in Riverside, addressed the Stamford gathering, with words similar to those of his brother priests throughout the state. He declared that the Church had the right to participate in all negotiations for peace, whether at Versailles or at home in labor and social disputes. God, through His Church, must be admitted to all of the nation's councils.[186] Despite such demonstrations, the pundits' view prevailed that the Church, while composed of American and naturalized members loyal to the country, nevertheless followed a creed and practice that was still foreign to America. The most dramatic example of this was the defeat of Al Smith in the presidential campaign of 1928. Smith's campaign was undermined by vicious anti–Catholic bias that questioned his ability as a Catholic to serve as President of the United States.

The idea that a Catholic President of the United States would be subject to the rule of the pope was expressed by the Methodist Episcopal Bishop of Western New York, Bishop Leonard. Outraged that Smith, an elected American official, should have publicly kissed the ring of the pope's representative in New York City Hall, the Protestant bishop stated,

> In my opinion, therefore, and I am sure it is held by millions of American citizens, no governor who kisses the Papal ring can be elected President. The expression I used was that 'he cannot come within gunshot of the White House as president.' This I firmly hold. . . . Any public official surrenders the American heritage and admits inferiority by kissing the ring of the foreign Papal legate in the City Hall of New York City, a building primarily devoted to civil, not religious uses. By such an act I believe there is an acknowledgement of the supremacy of the Church over the State. . . . This is a Protestant Country and will ever remain so.[187]

Despite the assertions of the Methodist cleric, the Catholic clergy in Connecticut continued to insist upon the important role of the Church in American life. The year 1930 marked the centennial celebration of the first Mass celebrated in Bridgeport. Pontifical Mass was celebrated at St. Augustine Church on Sunday, November 23, 1930, by the auxiliary Bishop of Hartford, Maurice McAuliffe, with a sermon by the rector emeritus of the Catholic University of America, Bishop Thomas J.

Shahan. Solemn benediction followed in the evening, celebrated by William J. Hafey, Bishop of Raleigh, North Carolina, with a sermon by the Rev. Dermott McArdle, CP, of St. Michael Monastery in Union City, New Jersey. The sermons and celebrations recalled the determination and dedicated work of the Catholics through the century, in union with their priests and religious women, to establish the Church within Fairfield County. The celebration clearly stated that, although the Church had arrived with men and women of foreign birth, it was no stranger to America, and, indeed, had become an integral part of life in southern Connecticut and an essential safeguard of American society and ideals.[188]

The Church and the Great Depression

The Great Depression provided the clergy with another opportunity to emphasize the Church's mission to affect society by its social and moral teachings by means of an active Catholic lay apostolate. The local pastors and clergy were known for their charitable assistance to the poor of their parishes during the depression years. The Rev. John McGivney, pastor of St. Charles in Bridgeport, was known to have paid the rent for a number of poor families and widows as well as supply coal, food, and clothing to those who were in need.[189] The usual place to request assistance was in the confessional, where both monetary and spiritual assistance could be had without notoriety or loss of self–respect before neighbors and friends.[190] This was not uncommon in the other parishes of the county. Various parish societies organized during the depression years to assist needy families. St. Peter's in Danbury, for instance, began a program of milk distribution among its needy parishioners, while its Guild opened a dental clinic in the parish school to serve the parish poor.[191] The clergy and the Bridgeport Charitable Bureau continued to work in conjunction with city programs to relieve the poor and unemployed, while supporting the efforts of the federal government.

The *Catholic Transcript* proudly began posting the NRA eagle on its front page on September 22, 1933, and continued to support the reconstruction programs until the end of the depression. Local offices of the Catholic Charitable Bureau in Bridgeport, Norwalk, Danbury, and Stamford, organized the efforts of all the local parochial charitable organizations to assist the poor of their towns. The *Catholic Transcript* constantly ran front–page stories concerning the successful work of the Catholic laity, active in local Councils of Catholic Men and Women and other Catholic organizations. The Catholic heroes and heroines were not the athletes, businessmen, or students who had succeeded, but those Catholics who had contributed to the solution of social problems in their home towns through charitable action and dedicated work.[192]

Such united action between Catholic laity and clergy in social programs provided the topic for many an address given to various Catholic lay groups. The Rev. Lawrence Doucette of St. Anthony Church in Bridgeport addressed the Bridgeport Council of Catholic Men in November, 1933, and called them to support both the Catholic Bishops' social teachings and the programs of the NRA.[193] A similar message was conveyed to the New Haven Council of Catholic Women in an address by Catherine L. Fitzpatrick, Principal of Maplewood Junior High School in Bridgeport and the President of that city's Teacher's Association. In her address, entitled "The Part of Womanhood in Catholic Action," delivered in December, 1933, Fitzpatrick defined Catholic Action as,

". . . a concerted effort on the part of the laity to carry out the social recommendations of their pastors and the Bishop of the diocese."[194]

The number of priests during the 1930's had dramatically increased. By the middle of the decade, with the arrival of Bishop Maurice F. McAuliffe in the spring of 1934, there were 631 diocesan and religious priests within the Diocese of Hartford. The 51 parishes of Fairfield County were staffed by 107 priests. The diocese supported a total of 214 students in its preparatory seminary and 175 in various American and European major seminaries. Those who were newly ordained during these years were not assigned to summer work immediately following ordination, since no place could be found for them in the parishes. They simply remained at their family homes and were notified by mail each week concerning their weekend assignments, where they would relieve a priest who was either ill or on summer vacation.[195]

In November, 1933, the American Bishops called for all Catholics to unite their efforts with those of the President and Congress in an attempt to rectify the evils of American society that had produced the sufferings of the depression years. They enumerated the causes of the Great Depression as corruption in government, unjust business practices that gave free rein to greed, pornographic literature, and the growing film industry. These forces, when united, brought ". . . starvation to the bodies of men and poison to their souls. . . ." The bishops continued,

> Before there can be any hope for a return to political liberty, social peace, or economic justice, the spiritual life of the nation must be renewed, there must be an awakening of faith in God and a renewal of trust in His providence.[196]

Connecticut's Bishop believed this and set about to awaken a spiritual renewal in his people with the help of his clergy.

Bishop Maurice McAuliffe

Bishop McAuliffe began his program of spiritual and economic renewal within the Diocese the following July, 1934, with the institution of the Legion of Decency. In a pastoral letter of July 11, the Bishop addressed his people, calling their attention to the ill effects of many modern–day films upon the family and society:

> The films are an outrage to decency, morals and religion. The themes of these motion pictures is [sic] usually divorce, illicit love, marital infidelity and gangster crimes. They attack the personal purity of life and the sanctity of the home and ridicule the religious sanction of the moral law and obedience to lawful authority. When they are not totally bad they are suggestive and pander insidiously to the lowest passions of human nature. They are a menace to home and society.[197]

Catholics received wide support from many Protestant and Jewish congregations throughout the state and were urged to enroll in the Legion on the following Sunday. Their task was to accept pledge cards with which to enlist the support of their non–Catholic neighbors and to protest the productions of the movie industry by boycotting local theaters.[198]

Youth work was also seen as an important tool for the spiritual formation of Catholic youth who would later contribute to the renewal of American society, business and government. The first organized work among the young Catholics of the diocese began at Bridgeport's St. Charles Borromeo Church in 1928 under the direction of the Rev. Francis Morrissey. He began his program, which was a forerunner of the diocesan C.Y.O. programs, in the basement church at St. Charles. The evening meetings began with brief catechetical instructions, followed by socials or sports activities.[199]

The Rev. John Loughlin, professor of Greek at St. Thomas Seminary at the opening of Bishop McAuliffe's administration, saw the need for more organized efforts in favor of Catholic youth. He took it upon himself to call on the pastors in the larger cities, asking for their support and assistance in the organization of a "High School Club" in 1936. Since Bridgeport was the largest city in Fairfield County, the local pastors of the territorial parishes were called upon to assist. The Rev. Peter McClean of St. Augustine, Rev. John McGivney of St. Charles, and Rev. John Moore of Sacred Heart Church, all organized youth groups to care for the Catholic young men and women attending Harding High School on the East Side, Central High School on Golden Hill, and Bassick High School on the West Side.

Fr. Loughlin's C.Y.O. programs, which received support from several sources, including the public recreations departments throughout the state, the National Youth Administration, and the local councils of Catholic Women, counted nearly 10,000 members in its ranks by 1938.[200] These and other parish–sponsored societies were for young men and women of high–school age and single Catholics already beginning their careers and were begun in the larger parishes in Bridgeport and in the other larger cities within Fairfield County. Offering religious instructions, social and sports events, as well as opportunities for community service, these parish groups flourished until the beginning of America's involvement in World War II.[201]

The Rev. Thomas Henahan, a young curate at St. Augustine's, was given the direction of the C.Y.O. and the McClean Club for the Catholic students from Central High School. Fr. Henahan gathered the largest youth group in the city for classes, social events, and talent shows offered by the members at the local city theaters.[202] He also worked to coordinate the efforts of all of the parish youth groups to bolster the spiritual life of the city's youth. Working in cooperation with the officials of the city's high schools, many of whom were Catholics, Fr. Henahan began city high school retreats in the 1940's. He secured the assistance of three priests of the Congregation of the Holy Ghost and of the Immaculate Heart of Mary, then operating a seminary at Ferndale and a novitiate at Ridgefield. Their task was to give the students retreats consisting of three evening and three daytime sessions. The schools cooperated by releasing all Catholic students from classes on the retreat days. The program continued to grow under Fr. Henahan's tutelage to include national parishes like St. Raphael and Saints Cyril and Methodius, which hosted social events for the other youth groups from the territorial parishes as well as the high school retreats.[203]

The Bishop's interest in Catholic education and formation of the state's young Catholics was displayed clearly in his working with the Jesuits of the New England Province and the establishment of Fairfield College Preparatory School and Fairfield University. The Bishop wanted a Catholic boys' high school in the Diocese, and the Jesuits were anxious to open a college in Connecticut. They had been invited into the Diocese as early as 1861 when Bishop McFarland had sought the establishment of a Jesuit house and school within the state, but without success.[204] Their first foothold in the Diocese did not come until 1889, when they purchased the John H. Keyser Estate in South Norwalk. There they established the Manresa Institute and converted the estate into a retreat center that served the priests of the Diocese as well as the Jesuits of the East Coast until the property was sold in 1954.[205]

Both the Bishop and the Jesuit Provincial, the Very Rev. James H. Dolan, SJ, considered the time to be right for the establishment of a Jesuit secondary school in the state, despite the war.[206] The first item of business was the procuring of land for the school within the state. The Fairfield estates of the late Oliver Gould Jennings and of the financially straitened Walter B. Lasher were purchased by March, 1942. The Fairfield College Preparatory School was placed under the direction of its first Rector, the Rev. John J. McEleney, SJ, and was slated to open its doors on September 9, 1942.[207]

By the Spring, some basic decisions had been reached concerning the campus, curriculum, tuition, and faculty of the new high school. The school would be restricted to boys and offer traditional liberal arts and humanities programs. The original estate buildings were to be remodeled to serve as school and administrative buildings. The Jennings house was to be renamed the Bishop McAuliffe Hall and serve as the main school building, housing classrooms, laboratories, cafeteria, library, and a chapel. The former Lasher estate would become the Cardinal Robert Bellarmine Hall and serve as the residence for the Jesuit faculty as well as provide additional classrooms and other student facilities.[208] Officers for the new school had also been chosen. The Principal was to be the Rev. Leo A. Reilly, SJ; the Administrator was the Rev. Edward J. Whelan, SJ; and the Treasurer was the Rev. John W. Doherty, SJ. The remainder of the faculty was chosen by midsummer, 1942.[209] With limited funds, the Jesuit Fathers assigned to begin the school found themselves employed in various activities other than education. The priests were called upon to plant trees, tend gardens, drive tractors, and be responsible for the general maintenance and janitorial duties required on the grounds and in the buildings.[210]

On August 5, 1942, Bishop McAuliffe blessed Bellarmine Hall. Representatives from every parish within the county were present as a show of support for the new school.[211] The school year began with ceremonies at McAuliffe Hall, presided over by the Bishop who called the opening of the new school, "the happiest day in the history of the Hartford Diocese." He continued in his address to the first class that,

> It seems the school is being founded in response to the challenge of the postwar period. What education will be most important should be guided by the things of God.[212]

June 16, 1943 was the first graduation exercises to be held at "Fairfield Prep." The nine graduates were addressed by Governor Baldwin; the President of the school, the Very Rev. John McEleney, SJ; and by Bishop Henry J. O'Brien, auxiliary to the Bishop of Hartford.[213] In his address to the graduates, Governor Baldwin told the boys that the Christian teachings they had received would be the best guide to solve any problems confronting them in the world they were going to enter. He reminded them that American democracy was different from the democracies of other nations,

> . . . because we believe that individual freedom and liberty are a God–given gift to man. It is for this ideal that men have been willing to sacrifice their lives.

The Governor continued that the duty of these nine Catholic graduates

> . . . should be to continue to spread that ideal and after the war has been won, to extend the American concept of democracy throughout the world.[214]

The Jesuits' desire to open a college in Connecticut was not put off by the war or lessened by the opening of a preparatory school. The Fairfield University of St. Robert Bellarmine was chartered by the state as a college on May 29, 1945. The curriculum was very similar to those offered at Holy Cross College in Worcester and Boston College in Boston. The college Dean, the Rev. Laurence Langguth, SJ, wrote of the curriculum and the theory of education followed at Fairfield University:

> The school stands four square in the conviction that the best medium of learning is the liberal arts, that the best mental discipline is still to be gained from those subjects which teach a young man nothing more useful than how to live a full Christian life, richly dowered with the experience of the past, acutely alive to the present, and working with burning hope for the future.[215]

The first college class was composed of graduates of "Fairfield Prep" and young men returning from military service. The Jesuit schools at Fairfield filled a need for Catholic secondary education that was felt strongly in Fairfield County. The schools proved fine Catholic resources for the county, since they provided excellent educational and spiritual formation for young Catholic men, and instilled and nurtured vocations to the priesthood and religious life in not a few of their graduates. The priests of the faculties also exercised an influence upon Catholic life in the county, since they generously assisted in the work of the local parishes and served as spiritual directors for priests and laity alike.

Mothers' Circles, or Parent–Educator Groups, were other means designed to raise the moral and religious character of young Catholics within the diocese. St. Augustine's in Bridgeport was the first parish in Fairfield County to organize a Circle in the summer of 1941, under the leadership of Mrs. Lawrence Keith. Their task was to work for the purchasing of books written by Catholic authors by local public libraries that would be offered in active, general circulation. They also provided religious education books and texts dealing with child–care and psychology to Catholic mothers, in order ". . . to help educate and rear children healthy and Catholic."[216]

Throughout the 1930's and early 1940's, the American bishops issued a number of pastoral letters dealing with social problems in the world and in the country. The proper relationship with God, the sanctity of the family, the right to ownership of private property, the workers' right to a fair wage, and the government's responsibility "to abolish conflicts between classes with divergent interests," were major themes.[217]

In their "Statement on the Church and Social Order," issued on February 7, 1940, the American bishops iterated their belief that social renewal and justice could come about only by a spiritual renewal in American society:

Our economic life then must be reorganized not on the disintegrating principles of individualism but on the constructive principle of social and moral unity among the members of human society. In conformity with Christian principles, economic power must be subordinated to human welfare, both individual and social; social incoherence and class conflict must be replaced by corporate unity and organic function; ruthless competition must give way to just and reasonable state regulations; sordid selfishness must be superseded by social justice and charity. Then only can there be a true and rational social order; then only can we eliminate the twin evils of insufficiency and insecurity, and establish the divine plan of a brotherhood of man under the fatherhood of God.[218]

Catholics and World War II

Catholics prepared for war along with other Americans; they preferred peace, but were willing to support their nation if peace were impossible to maintain. Unity among Americans and the sacrificing of private interest for the national good were constant themes. In September, 1941, the cornerstone for the new St. Joseph Hospital in Stamford was blessed by Bishop McAuliffe. The speaker for the occasion was Governor Robert Hurley, who pointed out that the hospital was not simply an institution for Catholics, but was a work for the welfare of all American citizens of Stamford. The hospital was a symbol of Catholic Americans affecting their community as well as a symbol of the united efforts and generosity of all, regardless of creed:

'They [citizens of Stamford] joined together, they pulled together, not in the interest of any special group or class, but in the interest of all. That spirit made America great. That is the kind of spirit we need today in this hour of national crisis.'[219]

The same sentiments were expressed by the Rev. Francis J. Sugrue on September 4, 1941, as seventeen young men left Greenwich for the army induction center in Hartford. He called upon all citizens of Greenwich to join their hands to the work of national security, and told the young men, "Whether we enter this war or whether we shall have the blessings of peace, you will have done your own duty magnificently." He continued,

We must all remember that there is not one man or woman in this country who would be better off any other place in the world. There was a time, even when smart people would smile indulgently when anybody said anything patriotic. But in the last two years we have learned the tremendous gifts we have here.[220]

The Japanese attack on Pearl Harbor in December, 1941, shocked the nation. On December 11, Bishop McAuliffe pledged the loyalty of the Catholics of the diocese to the American war effort. While deploring war, he called for unity of action among all Catholics for victory that would bring "to a speedy end this unprovoked and unjust war."[221] On December 22, Archbishop Edward Mooney, Chairman of the Administrative Board of the National Catholic Welfare Conference, conveyed to President Roosevelt the united support of the Church in America in securing victory and peace for the United States. The President responded assuring the bishops,

> We shall win this war and in victory we shall seek not vengeance but the establishment of an international order in which the spirit of Christ shall rule the hearts of men and of nations.[222]

The war, and the resulting government policies and programs, affected every aspect of American life and, to some degree, the social and religious mission of the Church.[223] Religious practice was adapted to accommodate the schedule of defense work, especially in the larger industrial cities like Bridgeport. Dispensations from the eucharistic fast were granted for those engaged in the night shift in defense plants, and permission was granted by Bishop McAuliffe to celebrate Mass in the factories for the workers.[224] Special prayers, novenas, and services were held in every church in the state. December 8, 1942, the Feast of the Immaculate Conception, was designated by the American Bishops as a national day of prayer for victory, "asking divine guidance and protection of our soldiers and sailors."[225]

At the same time the clergy and faithful were praying for victory and peace, and supporting the American war effort, the Church continued to manifest its concern for the maintaining of certain values, such as the proper education and formation of Catholic youth, integrity of the family, and the rights of laborers.[226]

In order to further the Church's work for social justice during the war, especially in the area of labor relations, the Diocese of Hartford established the Diocesan Labor Institute in Hartford with the Rev. Joseph Donnelly as its director. By January, 1942, the *Catholic Transcript* began carrying a weekly column by Fr. Donnelly, dealing with Catholics and their participation in the war and their trust in God's providence in their lives and in the life of the nation.[227]

Labor schools were established in Waterbury and, in March, 1943, in Bridgeport, with the purpose of improving labor–management relations and maintaining America's industrial development.[228] Bridgeport's director was the Rev. James F. Murphy who organized an eight–week evening course on the Church's social teachings concerning unions and labor movements for all union members of Bridgeport, regardless of their faith. The courses included were "Catholic Social Philosophy," taught by Murphy; "Public Speaking," taught by Attorney James J. O'Connell, a graduate of the Yale Law School; "Parliamentary Law," taught by Attorney Margaret E. Connors, also a graduate of Yale.[229]

The clergy's work in support of the War was led in Connecticut by Bishop McAuliffe. He was appointed to the State Committee of the 1942 War Fund Campaign of the USO, and leant his efforts to the establishment of USO clubhouses in Windsor Locks, New London, Hartford, and Bridgeport. He urged his priests to buy war bonds and to instruct their congregations to cooperate fully with all government efforts. The *Catholic Transcript* was filled with stories of the heroics of Catholic soldiers and volunteers. The most renowned Catholic hero from Fairfield County was Colonel Henry A. Mucci of Bridgeport, who received a hero's welcome from the city's populace in July, 1945, in recognition of his bravery in the Philippines.[230] The paper clearly pointed out that the sons and daughters of Catholic immigrants were doing their duty well. The paper carried recipes designed to support wartime rationing, and helpful hints to Catholic mothers touching upon aspects of wartime family life, such as guiding children through blackouts.

Catholic organizations, such as the Knights of Columbus, offered their services and support throughout the diocese. The Knights from the St. Augustine Council in Stamford did their part for the war effort by offering their facilities for use by the sailors of the U.S. Naval Training School in Noroton Heights for the duration.[231]

Convinced of the "mystical implications" of their war work by the Rev. Eugene A. Moriarity of St. Patrick Church, the Bridgeport Council of Catholic Women doubled their efforts for America's fighting men and women.[232] The Council began its membership drive in 1943 under the direction of the Rev. Thomas Gloster. His message, similar to that expressed by priests throughout the county and the diocese during the war, was that theirs was a twofold work: "Religion and charity at home, and the spiritual and temporal welfare of the men in the armed forces."[233]

Bishop Henry J. O'Brien

Bishop McAuliffe died on December 15, 1944, only a few months prior to the end of the War. To his successor, Bishop Henry J. O'Brien, fell the task of carrying out the postwar rehabilitation programs of the American bishops within the Diocese. Immediately after the end of hostilities in Europe, Bishop O'Brien began his appeals to the faithful for assistance to the refugees and persecuted peoples of Europe, asking for funds and donations of clothes.[234] He also sought Catholic families willing to adopt children orphaned by the war and established a diocesan resettlement committee that found homes for thousands of refugees.[235]

The American bishops issued their pastoral letter entitled "Between War and Peace" on November 18, 1945. The prelates observed that "war is over but there is no peace in the world." They called upon the great powers to work for true peace based upon the protection of the rights of all individuals. They asked if the United States were keeping the pledges made to Poland at Yalta and condemned the government's silence over the atrocities and repressive actions reported from the Baltic countries, then absorbed by the Soviet Union. They wrote,

What is happening behind the blackout of eastern and southern Europe is a stark contradiction to the high ideals which inspired our fighting to save the world from totalitarian oppression.

The bishops concluded their letter calling for mercy on the part of the Allies in their treatment of the vanquished nations, and demanded that America be concerned with the future of Italy, Germany, Austria, and Hungary. Calling for punishment of those individuals guilty of war crimes, instead of punishment of entire peoples, the bishops instructed resource–rich America of its moral obligation to come to the material assistance of the war–torn nations in order to stem the suffering of millions.[236]

The bishops continued their call for a just and lasting peace in their pastoral letter of the following year, entitled "Man and the Peace!" The basis of all problems in the peace negotiations, according to the bishops, was the question of man's nature. It was a question concerning the disposition of the world powers to protect or hinder the individual in the exercise of his God–given rights. The Soviet Union was seen as the primary menace to the free exercise of man's God–given rights and, as such, was a threat to any hope for a just peace.[237]

The Church Against Communism

The United States responded to the economic needs of the European nations with the Marshall Plan that invested nearly $12 billion dollars in European recovery programs. The threat of Communist aggression was dealt with by the so–called "Truman Doctrine," that justified the sending of financial aid and military advisors to any nation threatened by Communism.

Condemnation of Communist aggression, the oppression of the rights of individuals and the religious persecution wrought by the Communist regimes following the War were recurrent themes of the Church on the national and local levels. Joined with this was a condemnation of secularism within American society, which threatened the stability of the family and the nation itself, since the growing secularism elevated the satisfaction of the individual over the welfare of society.[238]

Catholics from Fairfield County gathered in Bridgeport in the spring of 1949 to demonstrate their solidarity in the fight against atheistic Communism and secularism. Led by the Revs. Thomas F. Henahan, Joseph W. Reynolds, and Thomas P. Mooney, 10,000 Catholics gathered at Bridgeport's Seaside Park on May 15, 1949, to pray for all peoples oppressed by Communism, for the conversion of Russia, and for peace in the world. The demonstration was sponsored by the local parishes, the Catholic War Veterans and the Bridgeport and Fairfield Knights of Columbus. Gathering for Benediction and prayer, the faithful listened to the words of the celebrant, who coupled Communist aggression to the growing secularism in America as allied threats to the security of the family and the nation. Faithfulness to God, a return to strong American ideals, and the ministrations of the Catholic Church alone could safeguard America.[239]

Conclusion

The work of the bishops and priests of Connecticut successfully met the spiritual needs of the Catholic faithful through the establishment of churches, the celebration of Mass and the sacraments, the preaching of the Gospel, and the teaching of the faith. During the latter part of the last century, once these needs were being met regularly, the clergy began to push their faithful in a new direction, encouraging American Catholics to affect America by their active Catholicism. They who had been nourished spiritually with the sacraments and instructed in the Gospel and the Church's teachings were to go and make their mark upon American life. A change had occurred: no longer was a Catholic to be timid because his faith was condemned as un–American. He was to be loud in his profession of that faith, since Catholicism was touted by its clergy as the sole safeguard of America's liberty.

Following the Korean War—America's first armed resistance to Communist aggression—Connecticut once again began to feel the effects of radical social and economic change. Since most of its industry had been defense related, the end of hostilities once again signaled an economic slump in the cities. Fairfield County experienced a shift in population during the late 1940's and 1950's greater than any other county in the state. As the heavy industries of the larger cities slowed down, many moved into the developing suburbs and were replaced in the cities by native–born Americans from other states searching for work and by immigrants from Europe, the Caribbean, and Latin American countries.

Along with such radical shifts in population came serious social problems, especially in Fairfield County. One such problem was juvenile delinquency. The children of many "better families" within Fairfield County were providing problems for the authorities in the cities. By 1953, Stamford had established an evening curfew for all children under 15 years of age "as a direct result of gang warfare between teenagers following block parties."[240] Housing shortages, racial tensions, and the need for schools were all problems to be addressed during the next decade.

The Church had grown over the previous years along with the general population. The Diocese of Hartford had the largest Catholic population of any American diocese after Brooklyn by 1953.[241] In the 279 parishes within the Diocese of Hartford, over sixty percent of all the children born in Connecticut in 1952 were baptized, and over forty-nine percent of all the marriages within the state were performed.[242] By 1950, Fairfield County counted 504,342 residents, a rapid increase since 1940, when the population numbered 418,384. Nearly one–half of the 1952 population—216,562 individuals—professed to be Catholic. The portion of the population that was of foreign–

birth was also high, totalling 78,592 persons, or 15.6 percent of the total population of the county. This was reflected by the number of national parishes. Of the sixty-one parishes in the county in 1953, twenty were established for immigrant congregations. Bridgeport counted nineteen parishes, of which ten were national churches, the largest number in any Connecticut city.[243] By 1953, the Church in Fairfield County had grown sufficiently to require a local bishop.

CHAPTER V

BRIDGEPORT'S FIRST BISHOP: LAWRENCE JOSEPH SHEHAN
(1953–1961)

Bridgeport was a city of great energy. It was the largest city in Fairfield County, third largest in the state, by the commencement of this century's fifth decade. It had achieved prominence over the years because of its various manufactures, especially its armaments industry, and because of the inventions of Elias Howe, R. Buckminster Fuller, E.P. Bullard, and others. Phineas T. Barnum made Bridgeport his home and served as its mayor, bringing the Park City renown through his circus, his political antics, and the lionizing of its most famous native son, Tom Thumb. Bridgeport was also the home of the largest number of immigrant communities in the state by the turn of the century. One of its residents, the German immigrant Gustave Whitehead, successfully flew the first motor–powered airplane in 1901, predating that of the Wright Brothers by nearly two years. This capital of industry and city of immigrants became a religious capital on December 2, 1953.

Two New Dioceses: Bridgeport and Norwich

The division of the Diocese of Hartford into three separate dioceses and the formation of a new ecclesiastical province in 1953 was dictated by necessity. The decision to divide Hartford was made by the Roman authorities. Yet the details of the division itself, and those concerning the formation of the Dioceses of Bridgeport and Norwich, were made in Hartford, and to some extent with the assistance of Francis Patrick Keough, then Archbishop of Baltimore.

Archbishop Keough, a native of New Britain, was ordained a priest for the Diocese of Hartford in 1916 and served in pastoral and chancery posts until 1934 when he was appointed the fourth Bishop of Providence. He remained there until his promotion to the See of Baltimore thirteen years later. Throughout his years in Providence and Baltimore, the Archbishop maintained contact with his family and friends within the Diocese of Hartford, keeping abreast of the ecclesiastical affairs of his home state. Such firsthand knowledge of the Church in Connecticut served as an invaluable source of information for Archbishop Keough's close friend Archbishop Amleto Cicognani, then Apostolic Delegate in the United States. Although of assistance to the Delegate in the division of the Diocese of Hartford, Archbishop Keough did not have the deciding word concerning the final plan; that was left by Rome to the Hartford authorities.[1]

Apparently preferring not to exercise any clear control or direction of the details involved in the division of the diocese, the *stylus curiae* of the Roman Consistorial Congregation was simply to refer to the appropriate canons of the 1917 *Code of Canon Law,* and leave the local ecclesiastical authorities to interpret them as they deemed expedient, in accord with local conditions and needs.[2] The final decisions concerning the division of the Diocese of Hartford, therefore, were formulated in Hartford itself, based upon the population of each county within the state.[3]

The Catholic population of Hartford, New Haven, and Litchfield Counties, which ultimately comprised the Archdiocese of Hartford, totaled 587,415, with 168 parishes, 378 diocesan priests, and 31 priests of religious orders. The proposed Diocese of Bridgeport was to be coterminous with Fairfield County, which was heralded as one of the wealthiest in the nation, with 216,562 Catholics, 58 parishes, 136 diocesan priests and 10 religious priests. The *Bridgeport Sunday Herald* prematurely opined that Litchfield County was slated for inclusion into the diocese to be established in the western portion of the state.[4] The rumor, although false, was widely accepted by the Catholic clergy and was given to the paper by the Rev. Raymond H. Stephenson as such, but interpreted by the *Herald* as Gospel truth.[5] The Diocese of Norwich was to include Middlesex, New London, Tolland, and Windham Counties, with an estimated Catholic population of 120,969, 53 parishes, 104 diocesan priests, and 4 religious priests. With such a low Catholic population within its predominantly rural area, Norwich originally was to be granted Litchfield County as well.[6]

Each of the new dioceses received a patrimony, or a contribution from the archdiocese with which to establish new administrations. The amount of this patrimony was determined by the archdiocese according to the *cathedraticum,* the annual tax

190

paid by each parish to the diocese, along with the debts payable to Hartford by the priests for their education and those debts of institutions in each county. Such debts were to be remitted by the archdiocese and made payable to Bridgeport and Norwich, in order to supplement the cathedraticum and the cash donation of Hartford to each new diocese.

The cathedraticum of the Counties of Hartford and New Haven amounted to the largest in the state, totaling $156,115, as were the debts of those counties, totaling $848,300. The cathedraticum of Litchfield, Middlesex, New London, Tolland, and Windham Counties totaled only $50,420, with a debt to the archdiocese of only $82,600. The cathedraticum of Fairfield County was $69,733, and its debts amounted to $183,000.[7] Along with the remission of their counties' debts, the Diocese of Norwich received $150,000 with which to establish itself,[8] while the Diocese of Bridgeport received $250,000.[9] Following the division of Hartford, the wags of the diocese put forth their own commentary on the division of the state, the assignment of clergy, and the patrimonies granted each new diocese by Hartford: "Hartford got the priests, Bridgeport got the money, and Norwich got the faith." The Dioceses of Bridgeport and Norwich were canonically established on August 6, 1953. Until bishops were named and took possession of their sees, Archbishop–elect Henry J. O'Brien of Hartford was to serve as the Apostolic Administrator and exercise the faculties of a residential bishop in each diocese.[10]

The First Bishop of Bridgeport: Lawrence Joseph Shehan

The nomination of bishops for the two new Connecticut dioceses was not left to the competency of Hartford. It was here that Archbishop Keough exercised his knowledge of Connecticut and his influence upon the Apostolic Delegate, a respected and intimate friend. At the time of the division of Hartford, no younger bishop existed in the American hierarchy for whom Archbishop Keough had higher esteem or more warm and deep personal friendship than his auxiliary bishop, Lawrence Joseph Shehan.

Lawrence Shehan was a native Baltimorean, born on March 18, 1898. The third of six children born to Thomas Patrick Shehan and Anastasia Dames Schofield, Lawrence enjoyed the love of parents whose delight was their children and whose strength was their Catholic faith. The Shehan clan received their early sacraments and religious training at St. Ann's Church, and their early education at the hands of the School Sisters of Notre Dame, then teaching in the parish school. By the end of his eighth grade, Lawrence seriously began to entertain thoughts of the priesthood, which had previously been only vague and fleeting. Through the influence of his pastor, Lawrence overcame the objections of his father and completed the entrance examinations for St. Charles College, then the preparatory seminary for Baltimore. He pursued his studies for the priesthood there, at St. Mary's Seminary, and at the North American College in Rome, where he was ordained a priest on December 22, 1923. During his years of priestly ministry in Baltimore and Washington, Father Shehan manifested his devotion to the Church along with his great talents and abilities. After serving in various pastoral and chancery posts, Father Shehan was named to the titular See of Lydda and appointed auxiliary Bishop of Baltimore and Washington on November 17, 1945. He remained in that post until his transfer to Bridgeport in 1953.

A strong friendship developed between Archbishop Keough and his auxiliary during the years and continued after Bishop Shehan's transfer to Bridgeport, as seen in the correspondence between the two prelates. An ease and familiarity of expression was the hallmark of their correspondence that allowed a blending of serious content with light, friendly humor. Archbishop Keough euphemistically addressed Bishop Shehan as "Your Eminence" very frequently in his letters; both correspondents showed their mutual respect and a deep friendship born of a shared dedication to and love for the Church.[11]

Bishop Shehan himself expressed the depth of his friendship with the archbishop in his memoirs. It had been Archbishop Keough who had worked for the appointment of Bishop Shehan as his coadjutor with right of succession, and upon the archbishop's death in 1961, Archbishop–elect Shehan not only felt the weight of his office, but the depth of his sorrow at the death of his friend. Cardinal Shehan recalled his feelings as he prepared the sermon for the funeral of his superior:

> . . . as I set about the task of writing it, I had a deep sense of sorrow and personal loss at the death of one who in so many ways—but always in his own unique way—had shown me so many signs of friendship. My sorrow was all the more poignant because on my return to Baltimore, I had looked forward to working with him for some—hopefully, many—years and to a growing personal friendship.[12]

Archbishop Keough's detailed knowledge of Connecticut, his familiarity with the talent and abilities of his auxiliary bishop, and his desire for the effective furthering of the Church's work, led him to recommend Bishop Shehan as the founding bishop of the newly created Diocese of Bridgeport. The Apostolic Delegate too had for many years been associated with Bishop Shehan and thought very highly of him. Accordingly, the Holy See announced the appointment of Lawrence Joseph Shchan as the first Bishop of Bridgeport on September 1, 1953.[13]

The bishop–elect planned to meet with Msgr. John Hayes of Stamford and the priests of the designated cathedral in Bridgeport to organize the chancery and cathedral staff of his new diocese. On the morning of October 4, 1953, precisely at 10:00, the rectory door bell rang, and the slight, grey–haired and bespectacled figure of the bishop–elect of Bridgeport awaited entry into his new home. Punctuality, a soft–spoken, unassuming manner, respect for his priests, and a love of the Church would be the best remembered virtues of Bishop Shehan.

During the cathedral meeting, the bishop discussed the needs of the new diocese, especially that of Catholic secondary education. He also decided upon the necessary appointments of his new chancery and cathedral staff. Monsignor John Kennedy would serve as the vicar general; Rev. George Curtiss as chancellor; Rev. James McLaughlin as the Bishop's secretary; Rev. James Murphy as the director of Catholic Charities, cemeteries, and rector of the cathedral.[14] The cathedral rectory, a stately mansion of the previous century, was to serve as the chancery offices and the residence for the bishop and cathedral staff. Since its tower was listing precariously, and the general fabric of the plant was in need of repair, the bishop instructed that the necessary renovations be made immediately in time for his installation.

The name of Lawrence Shehan had become a household word among the Catholics within Fairfield County by the time he arrived on December 1, 1953. The secular and religious press revealed every known public fact about the man, from the events of his life and ecclesiastical career to the details of his five–foot six–inch frame. He was a slight man with strong facial features, greying hair, and engaging, merry eyes. His slight 130–pound frame found exercise and relaxation in tennis, swimming, golf, and sailing. The Bishop was renowned for his scholarly work, public speaking, and his love of the works of John Cardinal Newman. Building upon this foundational information, the sermons by parish priests and the instructions of the religious sisters completed the county's preparation for the Bishop's arrival.

Brian Hariskevich was a student at Blessed Sacrament School when Bishop Shehan arrived. As one of their more reliable altar boys, he was chosen to serve as an acolyte in the procession welcoming the Bishop at the Bridgeport Railroad Station. Short for his age, Brian was captivated by the fact that a man of such an unimpressive stature could capture the imagination of the thousands of people who stood outside the station and lined the streets of Bridgeport on the dreary December day of the Bishop's arrival.[15]

Just as every other Catholic child in Fairfield County, Brian had been informed about the importance of the arrival of a bishop in Bridgeport. Lawrence Shehan was no ordinary man, according to the sisters. He was a successor to Christ's chosen apostles who was to exercise Christ's own authority in union with the pope and the other Catholic bishops. With the arrival of the bishop the city's significance and dignity would be amplified, meriting a more notable place in the Church's work and history of salvation. The editor of the *Bridgeport Post* echoed this sentiment that Bridgeport was now

. . . a religious capital, and December 2, 1953, will be noted in municipal history as the date of the elevation of Bridgeport to an episcopal See in the spiritual network which embraces the world.[16]

As he now remembers, Brian was resentful that Bishop Shehan was not a native son. Nonetheless, he and his classmates were as captivated by the imminent arrival of this holy man as was any other Catholic in the county. Brian expressed his pride by boasting to his cousins in Ansonia that he would be confirmed by Bridgeport's own resident apostle, while they would be constrained to await the pleasure of their bishop, resident in Hartford, in order to receive the sacrament.

Bishop Shehan's arrival into his diocese was marked by tumultuous receptions along the railroad line in Riverside, Stamford, and Norwalk. Phalanxes of flag–waving school children had been ferried to the stations by their teachers where they joined with thousands of parishioners to cheer the arrival of their new Bishop. Words of welcome by local officials were mixed with improving sentiments from the local clergy designed to impress the importance of the moment upon the minds of the already impressed crowds. At each of the three stops Bishop Shehan expressed his thanks to all gathered and imparted his blessing to the crowds of the faithful who fell to their knees, providing the ubiquitous press with icons of Catholic piety for the benefit of their readers. Between stations, the Bishop met with clergy and friends who had come with him from Baltimore, or who boarded the train in New York to accompany him to Bridgeport. Members of the clergy of the new diocese furnished the Bishop with a running commentary on the affairs of the Church in Fairfield County as they sped towards Bridgeport. Despite their informative narrative, they were unable to adequately prepare the bishop for the reception he would receive in the Park City.

The day was dreary, cold and grey, yet those who awaited the arrival of Bishop Shehan at the Bridgeport station numbered nearly 3,000. The route from the station to the cathedral was lined with an equal number of school children, and the cathedral itself was jammed with over 1,200 people.

Brian Hariskevich and the other altar servers were to lead the bishop in procession from the station to the cathedral. As they waited for the train, the weather worsened, rendering the prospects for a successful execution of the planned ceremonies poor at best. The surplice that Brian had meticulously starched and ironed that morning was not holding up well under the light drizzle, while his mother periodically offered him his yellow slicker. Mortified, and assured of the fact that a short altar boy in a dripping surplice followed by a pestering mother could never succeed in impressing the Bishop, Brian could do little more than lose himself in the anticipation of the crowd and hope for the best.

The arrival of the train renewed the excitement of the crowd below on the street, as well as the city and church officials on the overhead platform. Mayor Jasper McLevy and the Rev. Thomas Mooney, Pastor of St. Ambrose Church, both welcomed the Bishop on behalf of the city and its Catholic population. Bishop Shehan thanked the officials and joked that he hoped the inclement weather would not bode ill for the beginning of the new diocese. He continued,

I am now with all my heart and soul a citizen of Connecticut, an inhabitant of Fairfield County, and a resident of Bridgeport. It is my earnest hope that I shall spend the rest of my days among you; it is my fervent wish that my coming may bring to you an added blessing from Almighty God.[17]

The Bishop had dispelled the ill effects of the cold and inclement weather with his gentle humor and heartfelt sentiments. The diminutive altar boy in his dripping surplice was mightily impressed by his new Bishop. So important a man that his arrival could muster local officials and such a vast number of the citizenry, yet he was gentle and earnest, possessing a sense of humor—and of unremarkable height! The rain and cold could not dampen Brian's pride or the excitement of those gathered, for they had received their Bishop, and he had assured them of his loyalty and devotion.

The installation ceremonies the following day attracted crowds larger than those that had welcomed the Bishop to Bridgeport. Present among the 4,000 people in attendance were Governor John Lodge, Bridgeport's Mayor Jasper McLevy, Supreme Court Justice James C. Shannon, two nuns from every convent in the diocese, 400 priests, 50 monsignori, 34 seminarians, 24 bishops, and three archbishops. The well–known auxiliary bishop from New York, Bishop Fulton Sheen, was among the prelates present at the ceremonies. Already renowned for his oratory and television appearances, he found himself nearly ignored by the crowds who preferred the autograph of the Bishop of Bridgeport.[18]

Bishop John L. Russell of Charleston, South Carolina, delivered the homily at the installation ceremonies. He reflected that the Church in Connecticut had grown with remarkable rapidity during the previous 110 years since the foundation of the Diocese of Hartford. Now, continued the bishop, there are as many dioceses in the state as there were priests in 1843. With the appointment of a bishop in Fairfield County, Bridgeport became a new link in

the divinely welded chain binding the historic past of Catholicity . . . to the living present with its new born questions clamoring for attention and solution.[19]

One such problem, according to the bishop, was the threat of atheistic Communism. The Church had survived persecutions during its 2,000–year history and would survive the assaults of hostile governments in the present age. The installation of Bishop Shehan, the speaker concluded, was a sign to the world of the glories of the Church in America: even while the Church was being humiliated and destroyed in countries behind the Iron Curtain, here in America she flourished. Bishop Shehan addressed those gathered in the cathedral church immediately following his installation. Two things augur well for the new diocese, he said: the special blessing sent to the diocese by Pope Pius XII, and the forthcoming inauguration of the Marian

Year on December 8, 1953, commemorating the centenary of the definition of the Dogma of the Immaculate Conception. The bishop's first official act as the Ordinary of Bridgeport was to dedicate his episcopate to the Blessed Virgin Mary. His second act was to reaffirm his loyalty to the Pope as the successor of St. Peter and Vicar of Christ. He continued, "Mary then will be our heavenly protectress; the Supreme Pontiff will be our earthly father and guide."[20] Since the Church had placed St. Augustine as the patron of the cathedral, so too was he to be the patron of the new diocese and the model for its bishop. Bishop Shehan promised to give to his people in Bridgeport that which St. Augustine gave to his people of Hippo—the gift of devotion and love. "With you—as did Augustine with the people of Hippo—I hope to live and die."

The Promotion of Catholic Life

As wildly excited and impressed as the populace of the new diocese may have been at the arrival of their bishop, Fairfield County was far from being the Heavenly Jerusalem. Lest anyone think for a moment that Fairfield County was fully under the sway of Rome, the Beverly and Highway Theaters offered the film "Martin Luther: the Man who Changed the World" on the two days marking the commencement of the new bishop's rule. In order to remove any thought harbored by Bishop Shehan that pornography played no part in the cultural life of the diocesan capital, Bridgeport's Art Cinema, near the cathedral, featured Lili St. Cyr in "Striporama" and Georgia Southern and Rocita Royce in "Cinderella's Love Lesson" at the time of the bishop's arrival. City officials denounced the growing delinquency of the youth in the cities within Fairfield County, while the readership of the *Bridgeport Telegram* was informed that atheistic Communism in this country had been unmasked by the undercover work of Marlane MacLane Kowall. The 27–year–old daughter of the movie "tough guy" Barton MacLane, told her story of being an undercover agent for the government and how her dealings with a Communist party member was "the most nauseating experience I have ever known," but worthwhile since it saved her country from the clutches of the Russians.[21]

Despite their faults, Catholics and non-Catholics alike manifested a euphoria and excitement that pointed to the fact that something important had begun within their area of the state with the founding of a Catholic diocese. The new Bishop easily sensed this and employed that euphoria and sense of united purpose to accomplish the projects of his new diocese during the ensuing years.

The promotion of Catholic life was the primary goal of the bishop during these years. Catholic life was not merely characterized by religious observance or devotion. It was a way of life in which every facet, interest, relationship, and activity was grounded in Catholic belief and principle. Catholic life was a way of life centered on God and guided by charity and formed by the Church. Prior to his arrival in Bridgeport, the Bishop elaborated that,

> . . . if there is to be any depth of our religious life, that life must be the integrating force of our whole existence. It must determine not only the manner in which our religious duties and exercises of devotion are performed but also the character of recreation we take, the kind of books we read, the type of persons we choose for our friends and associates. In reality there can be no feature of our life which remains untouched or unaffected.[22]

This work of promoting a truly Catholic life among the faithful of the diocese was not to be his alone. The Bishop early recognized his limitations and expressed his need for sound advice and dedicated assistance on the part of the clergy and faithful. He expressed this in his remarks delivered at the banquet following his installation. He said,

> Today you, the priests and people of Bridgeport, and I, your bishop, undertake together a most serious work. It is a work which we can do only together. As for myself, I am fully aware of my weakness and of the handicaps under which I labor. I have never had occasion to lose sight of my dependence, first indeed on almighty God, but also on my fellow priests and lay helpers. I have always seemed so small, so inadequate to the heavier burdens, that others could never quite resist the temptation to pitch in and help with whatever task was at hand. . . . That, too, I hope will be my experience here in the Diocese of Bridgeport.[23]

In the same address, the Bishop called to mind the nature of the episcopal office, quoting the patron of the diocese, St. Augustine, who wrote,

> 'The Bishop rules not for the sake of the honor but for the sake of the service. . . . The Bishop must rule the faithful in such a manner as to be mindful that he is their servant.' It will be my endeavor to labor constantly with all my strength for you and for the best interests of the church in this diocese.[24]

Spiritual Needs

The Bishop's pastoral concern for the spiritual welfare of his people was evident in his first pastoral letter calling for the celebration of the Marian Year. As part of the Marian observances, the Bishop also announced that he would inaugurate the Family Rosary Hour on the evening before the feast of the Immaculate Conception. The rosary would be recited each night of the week and broadcast over local television station WICC until the close of the Marian Year the following December.

Besides the normal sacramental ministry of the Bishop—confirming young Catholics in the faith and ordaining men to the priesthood—the bishop exercised an active ministry for the provision of the spiritual needs of his people. Aware of the needs of factory workers unable to attend daily Mass during Lent, the Bishop inaugurated a program of daily Mass and a sermon for Catholic workers on their lunch hour, celebrated in the local factories. The General Electric Institute was the site of the first Lenten Mass offered by the Bishop in 1954. The same program was extended to other factories in the subsequent years.[25]

For the spiritual benefit of the Diocese, the Bishop gave permission to the Sisters of the Order of Our Most Holy Saviour to enter the diocese in 1955 in order to establish a retreat house in Tokeneke. The order is a contemplative, semi–cloistered one whose members live a life of prayer, conducting retreats for laymen and women. They became interested in Fairfield County through the agency of Mrs. Marguerite Tjader Harris who donated her property to the order for the establishment of such a religious house.[26]

Only two other retreat facilities existed within the diocese at the time of Bishop Shehan's arrival. The Villa Maria Retreat House in Stamford, owned by the Bernardine Sisters, had been in operation since 1947. The retreat house operated by the Holy Ghost Fathers in New Canaan had served the Catholic community for years. Even though providing a great resource for the diocese, these two facilities were not sufficient for the needs of the Catholics within the county. Accordingly, Bishop Shehan gave permission to the Swedish Sisters in 1957 to begin their work in Tokeneke at "Vikingsborg."

Threats to Catholic Life: Communism and Materialism

Bishop Shehan worked to transmit the Catholic spiritual message to as many people within the county as possible. He worked to solidify a Catholic identity among his people that was more than a mere membership in an institution. The spiritual nature of the Church and the role of the faithful in the salvation of American society were key themes of the bishop's writing and frequent addresses. In order to convey these themes as effectively as possible, Bishop Shehan developed a strong relationship with the local media. This proved an effective means of publicizing diocesan events and providing spiritual and catechetical instruction to thousands of people within the diocese. Every movement of the diocese during the Bishop's years received maximum, detailed coverage. In 1955 the Bishop provided a seven–part series of Lenten reflections on Christ's passion and death entitled "The Drama of Life" that appeared in the *Bridgeport Post*. The series proved a great success, since it provided practicing Catholics with material for their spiritual reflection, non–practicing Catholics with an attractive appeal to return to the Church, and non–Catholics with an inside look at Catholic faith and teaching.[27] Bishop Shehan delivered numerous addresses and homilies during his years in Bridgeport in order to combat any threat to Catholic life among his people. Regardless of the occasion or location of his talks, the Bishop was aware that his words and ideas affected Catholic life within the country, and especially within his own diocese, where he iterated his sentiments and ideas with frequency and conviction. Those threats that he deemed most destructive to Catholic life were Communism and materialism. Since both ultimately denied God as the center of one's life, both were equally repugnant to and destructive of Catholic life.

The arrest of Jozsef Cardinal Mindszenty in 1954 by the Communist government in Hungary provided Bishop Shehan with his first occasion for attacking Communism. During the "Cardinal Mindszenty Holy Hour" on February 14, 1954, the Bishop narrated the evils of atheistic Communism to those assembled in the cathedral. The audience already had been informed of such deprivations of liberty through the anti–Communist excesses of their co–religionist, Senator Joseph McCarthy. Now the claims by the government that Communism was Godless were confirmed by the Bishop himself, who accused Moscow of being the enemy of all religious beliefs and of God himself. The bishop stated,

The Cardinal's tragedy has served, as perhaps no other event could, to bring home to our people the true nature of the enemy with which our civilization is faced.[28]

In an address to members of the local Bridgeport labor unions, delivered at a communion breakfast in October, 1954, Bishop Shehan continued his theme that both Communism and materialism were destructive of Catholic life. Commenting upon the Encyclical *Rerum Novarum* of Pope Leo XIII, the Bishop emphasized that the principles of natural law and morality must be applied to modern–day problems and employed in maintaining the proper relationship between capital and labor in the workplace. Natural law, he continued, and religious truths are closely linked. Since there is a tendency to reject and deny religious truths, there is also a tendency to reject and deny the natural law. He continued,

Of this we can be sure, if both labor and capital look with reverence to God and God's law, not only will there be no unsolvable problems between them but there will also be a strong and loyal partnership which in time will bring this country the type of unity and strength which will make the United States invincible in the face of even the greatest foe.[29]

The essential necessity of the love of God as the source of all personal, economic and social stability was again emphasized by Bishop Shehan in a sermon entitled, "Unity in Charity— Freedom in Justice," delivered in St. Matthew's Cathedral in Washington, D.C., on February 6, 1955, before high–ranking government officials. The bishop stated that the country was in need of a moral unity. This unity springs from the will of the people and will lead the country to save itself and the world from impending disaster and war, he said. It could be achieved only through "a national atmosphere of charity," which is the bond of unity. Modern times, the Bishop continued, have tended to ignore or deny the connection between moral and civil law, "substituting the good of the state, i.e., the advantage of the government, for the common good." The good of the government must coincide with the common good, since the only reason for government's existence is the promotion of the common good. Often, as seen in Communist nations, the common good is secondary to the good of the government, the political party or the legislators themselves.

It is to be hoped that by increasing emphasis on moral law as the foundation of all law, and on the concept of the common good as the sole object of government, our country will preserve its noblest traditions which are the basis of our patriotic love.

That which has done most to undermine the sense of brotherhood and a love of country

. . . has been man's worship of material progress—particularly his worship of the science which was so largely responsible for that progress.

Throughout all of mankind's history, the Bishop continued, his plans for Utopia have failed, since they were based upon his knowledge and abilities alone. Man's only salvation from the prospect of total destruction lies in his "controlling the arm of Western science by the mind of Western philosophy, guided by the eternal truths of God." He concluded,

To God then modern man must turn for his salvation. That salvation will come not merely from a knowledge of the truths of God, but from the love of God which is the essence of true religion. From God comes the Brotherhood of Man, and from God comes all the blessings this country has brought to us. Only through love of God can man overcome that selfishness which seeks to destroy both love of fellow-man and love of country.[30]

The safeguarding of the common good against the insurgencies of a totalitarian government was emphasized in 1959. In response to a call by Pope John XXIII to all Catholics in that year, Bishop Shehan called for a day of prayer for the persecuted Catholic Church in Communist China. Placards requesting prayers for the persecuted Chinese Church appeared in all of the churches and Catholic schools of the diocese. All Catholics within the diocese were asked to pray at home with their families, in school, and in their parish for the conversion of the Chinese. An address by the Bishop was broadcast over five Fairfield County radio stations in Bridgeport, Norwalk, Danbury, and Stamford on February 13, 14, and 15, 1959, outlining the horrors endured by faithful Catholics at the hands of the Chinese Communists. A diocesan–wide poster contest was sponsored by the Propagation of the Faith office of the Diocese, with the purpose of fixing in the minds of Catholic school children the threat of atheistic Communism to the Church and the country.

Bishop Shehan expressed his ideas concerning the affects of materialism on the individual in an address to the National Association of Manufacturers in 1960. Commenting on the then–recent pastoral letter of the American Bishops entitled the "Need of Personal Responsibility," the Bishop told his audience that there was need for personal responsibility in the world. Modern man has shown too great a willingness to relinquish his rights and obligations to various organizations. The American Bishops, he continued, feel that it is time to restore personal responsibility through ". . . commitment of the individual to do what he is able to do through the initiative of self–reliance."[31]

The new age would be one of bigness and power, reducing the ordinary man to the insignificance of a number. He would become totally dependent upon his employer for his financial and social security. Since he is not consulted or encouraged by management to exercise any initiative or responsibility on the job, the individual would lose the pride of craftsmanship and his sense of self–worth. The duty of management extends further than the mere supplying of employment opportunities while being concerned only with its own profits, affluence, and security. Management's responsibilities extend to the concern for the rights and welfare of the workers, fair prices, and the public good.

The fundamental explanation for the present situation in the country is the devolution of American society into a sensate culture. Bishop Shehan continued,

> Modern man has become so engrossed in the pursuit of material plea-sure, material wealth, material power, material security that he has in large measure lost sight of the spiritual aspects, the higher goals of his life. He has become unaware of any responsibility higher than that of satisfying his physical and worldly cravings.

Parallel to the growth of this sensate culture is the decline of religious belief in the modern world:

> In spite of all the talk about increasing interest in religion and growth in church membership there is little doubt that religious conviction, which is essential to all real religion, has steadily weakened in the modern world and has ceased to exercise any considerable influence on the larger part of modern society.

The Bishop elaborated that the false belief that material science offers the only path to truth and knowledge, aligned with the idea that evolution and not God is the ultimate explanation of all that exists, have produced a totally materialistic society in which the ultimate moral good is ownership, while the identity of any individual is defined only by the marketable talents and resources of which he is possessed by nature.

The ultimate answer is God. A return to God is not simply a renewed interest in the phenomenon of religion or in the latest religious books of the day. Neither is it the assumption of church membership. Rather, to return to God intimates a return to prayer, in the sense of pondering the fundamental truths of one's existence, one's origin, and one's end. It involves communing with God and depending upon Him alone for spiritual enlightenment and help.

Such a return to God entails the conscientious study of moral law and the fulfillment of one's duties to God. The practice of self–control, justice, fraternal charity, fortitude,

> . . . not as optional ideals developed by man, but as sacred duties imposed by God. It means the practice of these virtues not merely in private life, but also in business, in all social and civic activities.

Since the vast quantities of products created by industry make a critical contribution to society, shaping the lives of men and women, it is the leaders who have the responsibility to establish the quality of life. Only the application of such principles can stem the destructive forces of materialism in the world. The bishop concluded,

> It should be your determination, therefore, that your products and policies will never lower the moral and spiritual tone of society, rather that they will always promote responsible living; that they will serve human needs rather than gratifying human desires.

These were the ideas behind the pastoral program of Bridgeport's first Bishop. It was a program designed primarily to strengthen Catholic life, making it an all–pervasive influence of society, while destroying all that was threatening to it.

Catholic Schools: Tools of Catholic Life

The most pressing need within the new Diocese was an overall program designed to strengthen the family as the primary influence in the spiritual and intellectual development of the youth of America. It was the positive influence of a solid Catholic family life, linked with the solid intellectual and doctrinal regimen of Catholic education that alone could produce a Catholic laity possessed of a strong Christian character and morality, and a clergy devoted to the Church and willing to make any sacrifice necessary for the furtherance of the Gospel.[32] A by-product of this strong Catholic family influence would be a strong America, freed from the polluting influences of pornography, materialism, and atheistic Communism.

In Bishop Shehan's plan the immediate tool for such a revivification of the Catholic family would be the Catholic high school.

The high schools would be the instruments capable of producing educated, mature Catholic laymen and women who would shape society along Catholic principles. Such schools would also nourish vocations to the priesthood and religious life, thus producing new generations of dedicated Church leaders who could guide a well–educated Catholic laity in its reforming endeavors.

The Bishop's concept of Catholic education and the influence of Catholic high schools for the benefit of the Church can be seen in two addresses that he delivered on those topics. The first was presented in Atlantic City, New Jersey, to the National Catholic Educational Association meeting there in April, 1959. The second was delivered on the occasion of the dedication of Northwest Catholic High School in the Archdiocese of Hartford—the first Catholic high school in the archdiocese—on September 24, 1961.

The overall commitment of Catholic education, the Bishop began in his 1959 address, was stated in the general legislation of the Church:

Catholic education, free from doctrinal error and from moral danger, is to be provided for all the faithful from the days of their childhood.[33]

The Church was committed, insofar as possible, to provide total Catholic education to her members.

The Bishop observed that practical, financial problems had always plagued the Church's attempts to provide such a school system in America. However, the problem of personnel was even greater than that of financing. Both are related since the American system of Catholic education presupposes an adequate supply of priests, religious brothers, and sisters to serve as teachers in its schools. The heart of this problem, the Bishop continued, is in the recruitment of religious vocations. The hope for increased vocations lies in the development of Catholic high schools.

The Catholic lay teacher, while slowly becoming the main stay of Catholic education, should not be considered as a temporary substitute for the religious sisters, brothers or priests. They should expect to make sacrifices for the furtherance of Catholic education, while at the same time receiving just wages, security, and continued training. Only then could Catholic schools hope to maintain the highest levels of instruction.

Bishop Shehan listed four resources upon which the Church

could depend regarding its Catholic schools. The first two are the dedication of the Catholic laity and that of the religious. The bishop continued:

> . . . we must never forget that our real endowment is the consecrated lives of our religious—an endowment which steadily grows and in the long run may prove the more secure and the more fruitful. Nor should we overlook the asset of so many able and devoted laymen, whose dedication to the cause and whose willingness to sacrifice is not less than that of the religious.

The third resource is the Church's possession of a philosophy of life that is ancient, tested by time, "standing squarely on demonstrable truth," that supplies a philosophy of education. The fourth resource is the certainty of divine truth and the consciousness of a divine mission which produces a "clear and irrevocable commitment."

In his address at the dedication of Hartford's first Catholic high school in 1961, Bishop Shehan answered the question, "Why Catholic high schools?" Catholic high schools, he said, offered three priceless advantages: a sound program of intellectual training, the essential instrument for the formation of character, and an invaluable opportunity for religious instruction and spiritual growth.

The primary purpose of a high school, the Bishop continued, is the intellectual development of its students. It is not, however, the sole purpose of such institutions. High schools cannot ignore the formation of character ". . . without which the misguided intellect can easily become destructive of society."[34]

The basic interest of those parents who send their children to Catholic schools is the intellectual development of their children. A well–rounded education in the sciences, history, mathematics, literature, and languages is essential. However, the development of the moral character is also essential. Public high schools have failed to provide their students those elements of conduct essential to formation of a strong moral character. Catholic high schools have the edge over their public counterparts in this area, since Catholic schools have fixed, universally binding moral principles. Therefore, the ultimate justification for Catholic high schools is the religious atmosphere and instruction provided, resulting in the development and formation of a religious life and strong Christian character. "The eternal truth of the Christian religion must serve as the ultimate justification of the Catholic High School." Since God exists, and we are destined to eternal life, redeemed by Christ, then it is clear that the religious truths of the Catholic Church are the ones truly worth knowing.[35]

Catholic Schools for the Diocese

Possibly apprised of the general situation of the Church within Connecticut by Archbishop Keough prior to his departure from Baltimore, Bishop Shehan noted the need for Catholic high schools within the county during his first visit to the diocese in October, 1953.

In an address delivered to teachers at the Bridgeport Teachers' Association meeting in June, 1954, the Bishop expressed his opinion that the then—present trend toward secularism in public education posed a threat to the students and to the country. Since the principle of the separation of Church and State had been pushed to the limit, the Bishop continued, religion had been successfully removed from the developing character of many children in the public school system of Bridgeport. "Religious education," he continued, "is an essential part of all education."[36] The need for Catholic education was real, especially on the high school level.

Catholic schools were seen as the instruments necessary for the dissemination of the Church's social and moral teaching to the younger generations of Catholics who would take their place in the world in order to shape and mold society according to the Gospel.[37] Such schools would provide the Catholic youth of the diocese with sound principles in both the intellectual and moral order, fostering true Christian maturity as well as vocations to the priesthood and religious life.[38] It was Bishop Shehan's contention that

> . . . the whole future of our Church and our country depends upon our youth. To provide them with sound religious and moral training at the time when it can be most effective is a major concern of us all.[39]

The most effective means to achieve that end would be to provide Catholic education for all Catholic children throughout the diocese, from kindergarten through high school. This became the Bishop's first goal.[40]

Diocesan High Schools

Fairfield County possessed only a handful of Catholic high schools that were primarily accessible to the children of the wealthier members of the Catholic community. Fairfield College Preparatory School in Fairfield and St. Basil's Preparatory School in Stamford were open to boys. Sacred Heart Academy in Stamford, under the auspices of the Sisters of St. Joseph, and two Academies of the Sacred Heart operated by the Madames of the Sacred Heart at Noroton and Greenwich were open to Catholic girls. Bishop Shehan was determined "to overcome the imbalance of Catholic high school education in the diocese" and make such education a possibility for "those families on the lower–income scale."[41]

Prior to Bishop Shehan's arrival in Bridgeport, plans for a parish high school in Greenwich had been approved by the Bishop of Hartford. The project would prove to be a model for the diocesan high school programs of Bishop Shehan. The support of the Catholic community was immediate and positive, since the idea was generally favored and popular and was actively promoted by Msgr. Michael J. Guerin, a man of no little ability and personal charm. But the completion of the project was hindered by objections of the larger Protestant community and by the local zoning board, since the proposed site of the school was of sizeable acreage in a residential area of prime value.[42] Hearings were held during the later part of March, 1954, at which Msgr. Guerin did battle with the town's planning and zoning board, ultimately winning their approval, albeit with certain restrictions.

The Greenwich project provided a focus for the efforts of the Bishop in favor of regional, diocesan high schools. So convinced was Bishop Shehan of the support for such schools within the county that he boasted to Cardinal Spellman of neighboring New York, ". . . every section of Fairfield County will want to emulate Greenwich in getting high schools under way."[43]

After consultation with the local pastors, it was decided that the first diocesan high school would be located in Bridgeport, where the largest Catholic population within the county was located.[44] The success of the fund–raising drive for the Bridgeport school would determine the furthering of the high school project throughout the diocese, particularly in Stamford, Norwalk, and Danbury.

The diocesan high school project was to become the primary focus of all diocesan and parochial energy within Fairfield County. All requests by religious orders to lead special collections in the parishes for their missionary or educational work were denied by the Bishop while the high school fund–raising drives were underway.[45] With the battles concerning St. Mary's

High School fresh in his memory, the bishop was aware of the tender sensibilities of non–Catholics concerning the Church's tax–exempt status. Accordingly, he refused the requests of numerous religious orders to establish religious houses or other institutions within the diocese, lest such a proliferation of tax–exempt properties of the Catholic type undermine the willingness of town officials to approve his high school plans.[46] Even the proposed diocesan Confraternity of Christian Doctrine Conference, scheduled to be held in Bridgeport in 1955, was cancelled for fear that any distraction might weaken the prospects of success for the diocesan high school campaign.[47]

The *Bridgeport Sunday Post* of March 6, 1955, announced the beginning of the first high school drive with the front–page banner headline, "Bishop Launches $1,500,000 High School Building Fund Drive," accompanied by the architect's rendering of the proposed Catholic high school. The forty–room school was to open in September, 1956, and serve the thirty–two area parishes included in the fund drive. Except for the Bridgeport high school, all other Catholic high schools were initially planned by the Bishop to be coeducational, since "our centers of population are too small to support separate high schools for boys and girls, at least at the beginning."[48]

The *Bridgeport Post* continued its coverage of Bishop Shehan's school drive in a generous editorial the following week. The editor, George C. Waldo, commented that the call for Catholic high schools in the county was the natural outcome of the flourishing parish school system. Catholics, while satisfied with the education offered in the public schools and willing to pay taxes for the support of those schools, nonetheless, wanted their children to receive religious as well as academic instruction, especially in their teenage years. The editor reminded his readers that the savings to the local school boards would be substantial, since the opening of a Catholic high school would lessen the outlay of funds for educational improvements and the erection of additional public schools.[49]

The fund–raising campaign was under the direction of the Community Counselling Service. It had made its mark in the Diocese already by successfully carrying on a number of drives, most notably, that for St. Mary's High School in Greenwich. Committees were organized and led by prominent clergy and laity, with J. William Hope serving as general chairman of the Bridgeport drive and Msgr. William Kearney as his clerical counterpart.

The parishes of the greater Bridgeport area were assigned

a minimum goal and grouped into four divisions according to location. The campaign was to be carried out from March until mid–June and was divided into two phases: the memorial gifts phase and the general phase.

The memorial gifts phase of the campaign was under the direction of Lewis A. Shea, President of the Connecticut National Bank. The idea of a Catholic high school was so popular in the Bridgeport area that the campaign's minimum goal of $1,500,000 was exceeded by the end of the first phase by nearly $400,000. From the close of the first phase of the drive on April 12, the goal was no longer simply to garner enough support to begin a new school, but rather to build the school without a debt.[50]

The general fund drive was solemnly opened by Bishop Fulton J. Sheen, the well–known television preacher and director of the Propagation of the Faith in the United States. Since Bishop Sheen's usual activity was geared to the raising of funds for the foreign missions, he found it humorous that he should be called upon in order to elicit the support of the faithful for Catholic education in what he called "the foreign mission field of Connecticut."[51] Commenting to Bishop Shehan upon his visit to Bridgeport, the auxiliary bishop of New York joked that "I eagerly look forward to the day when not only Nigeria, but Bridgeport, will boast of a great Catholic High School."[52]

Thousands of lay men and women volunteered their services to reach the Catholics of the Bridgeport area during the following month of the campaign. The local clergy were pressed into service to oversee the efforts of each parish, as well as to answer the fifteen telephones set up in the cathedral rectory during the twenty–one-day effort. The rectory–chancery, already bustling with parish and diocesan activity, became even more crowded with hordes of clerics and lay people involved in the drive. One of the priests on the cathedral staff at the time recalled that the rectory was so hectic during the drive that no parish work could be done other than the celebration of daily Mass and funerals. The remainder of the days were occupied with the answering of phones for the drive. The entire chancery–cathedral schedule was altered to accommodate the school project. Even the schedule of meals provided for the chancery and rectory staff was adapted to coincide with the change of shifts of priests working the telephones.[53]

The drive ended in mid–June with a total of nearly $4,000,000 pledged for the new school project. So impressed by the outcome of the campaign, the success of which was greatly due to the personal dedication of the Bishop, the 4,000 volunteers recommended that the school be dedicated to the Bishop himself.

Bishop Shehan, totally satisfied with the results, was fearful that the money pledged would not be collected, as was the problem during the campaign for the addition to St. Joseph Hospital in Stamford. All was to be done as carefully as possible but with considerable rapidity, lest the momentum of the drive and fervor of the people be lost, resulting in a mountain of pledges but no real cash with which to carry the project to a successful completion. He felt it to be imperative that the rough grading of the site on Park Avenue begin at least by June 12, the date of the first installment of the pledges. All was to be prepared, construction bids announced, ground broken, and plans readied, no later than August 1.[54]

Accordingly, ground was solemnly broken on the second sweltering day of July. Despite the heat, nearly 5,000 people flocked to the site of the planned high school to watch as the Apostolic Delegate, Archbishop Amleto Cicognani, turned the first spadeful of dirt. In his address, the Pope's representative congratulated the Catholics of the new diocese for their signal accomplishment and generosity. He continued,

> Indeed, you are its founders, and by your ready and most generous response to the appeal of your zealous bishop, you have shown yourselves anxious and almost impatient to provide this center of education.[55]

By supplying the means with which to make this school a reality, the Catholics of the diocese were continuing the work of the Church as Christ's instrument to teach Catholic truth to the nations. This school, he continued, was also a sign of their patriotism as Americans. Religious and civil leaders always had worked hand in hand in America to provide a program of education,

> . . . inspired with the thought of God and thus cooperating in the formation of a God–centered democracy.[56]

As work progressed on the building, a type of high school fever swept through the Diocese, inspiring petitions and plans for Catholic high schools in other cities within the county. By November, the Bishop called a meeting of Stamford pastors to discuss the prospects of a Catholic high school in that city; by February, 1956, he succeeded in engaging the Dominican Sisters of Newburgh, New York, to staff the proposed Danbury high school; and by May the architect, Anthony DePace, was discussing construction costs for the proposed Norwalk school.[57]

Bishop Shehan High School was to serve as an instrument for the preaching of the Gospel and for the safeguarding of American liberties: for God and for Country. This dual purpose was preached throughout the fund–raising campaign and during the months of construction. During the July 4th Barnum Festival Parade through Bridgeport in 1957, D'Andrea's religious supply store sponsored the prize–winning float, which symbolized the school's dual purpose. A mountain of carnations supported a large cross, in back of which a celestial vision of the Bishop Shehan High School broke through a dawn of yellow, red, and white blossoms, floating upon billowy, white cumulus clouds. Peggy O'Neill and Carmen Luciano had been chosen to stand on either side of this vision of triumphant Catholic education as representatives of all Catholic youth of freshman age in the Bridgeport area. They stood ready, albeit somewhat stage–shy, to be formed and molded according to the Bishop's plan in the Diocese's first Catholic high school, as the float nobly proclaimed, "For God and Country."

The decorations of the school also betrayed the dual purpose of the new school proposed by the Diocese. Four sculpted panels on the corner pylon of the gymnasium bearing the coat of arms of Pope Pius XII and that of Bishop Shehan, the seals of the City of Bridgeport and that of the Town of Fairfield, attested to the belief that Catholic education was the only instrument able to animate America in an age of growing secularism and materialism.

Bridgeport's first Catholic High School was completed and ready for dedication by late September, 1957. Its name was changed by the Bishop to Notre Dame High School in accord with his promise to dedicate his episcopate and his work to the Blessed Mother. The school was designed with a girls' classroom unit with a capacity for 1,100 girls, and a boys' classroom unit with a capacity equal to that of the girls', along with auditorium, gymnasium, cafeteria, and chapel. Notre Dame was hailed as the largest secondary school in the county and the largest Catholic high school in New England.

September 24, 1957 was the day of the dedication of the new school. An estimated 10,000 people clogged the roads of the city and its surrounding area on their way to witness the dedication ceremonies at the hands of the prelate who was the embodiment of all that it meant to be American and Catholic—Francis Cardinal Spellman of New York.

The dais in front of the school was a field of red, occupied by the prelates from nearby dioceses, attended by chaplains vested in their monsignorial robes, and local pastors in black. The Apostolic Eparch of Stamford, Bishop Ambrose Senyshyn, OSBM, was evident in his long cape of apostolic purple, as he represented his fellow Catholics of the Byzantine Ukranian Rite. Directly in front of the dais sat the representatives of the religious sisters of the diocese in the habits of their respective congregations. Next to them sat the members of the local clergy in white surplices and black cassocks, some with black birettas, others sporting fedoras or homburgs, presenting a slightly less ordered image than did the religious sisters. Hundreds of altar boys stood in front of the diocesan clergy, presenting a well-groomed, if fidgety, appearance in their cassocks and surplices. Battalions of Sisters of Notre Dame de Namur and habited Brothers and Fathers of the Holy Cross occupied the front row in ordered file in the afternoon sun, watching the final actions preparing the school that they would soon administer. To the sides and in back of the clergy and religious were unordered crowds of the faithful and the curious, along the sides of which were positioned members of the incoming freshman class—girls on the right, boys on the left—all uniformed and proud. Bishop Shehan's diminutive, yet erect and dignified figure, and Cardinal Spellman, resplendent in cardinalatial crimson were easily recognizable as the stars of the day.

After less than four years as the Ordinary, the founding Bishop of Bridgeport could count this accomplishment as his most splendid and the day as the most important after the establishment of the Diocese itself. Not only were the Catholics within Fairfield County united juridically within the boundaries of the Diocese of Bridgeport, they were also united in their identity as Catholics through the personality, charisma, and devotion of their Bishop, which encouraged them to unite in a sense of common purpose. Theirs was the duty to strengthen their Church, their nation, and their community by propagating their apostolic faith and developing the moral and intellectual character of their children. The dedication of Notre Dame High School in Bridgeport supplied them with the model for the realization of that purpose, as well as the taste of success necessary to spur the local efforts of other communities toward the completion of similar projects.

Stamford was the site of the next diocesan high school. The campaign was launched by the Bishop on February 26, 1956. The opening of the school was scheduled for September of the subsequent year. The drive, directed by Alphonsus J. Donahue, Jr., set a minimum goal of $1,000,000 to begin the $2,500,000 project. Only nine parishes participated in the drive, as compared with Bridgeport's thirty–two. Despite the few parishes in the area, the campaign resulted in nearly $2,000,000 pledged.

The forty–room school, which was to be administered by the Sisters of the Congregation of Notre Dame, was dedicated by the Apostolic Delegate on October 23, 1958.[58] In his address to the crowd of 4,500 people, Archbishop Cicognani spoke once again of the Church's mandate to teach the nations as being in line with the intentions of America's founding fathers to establish a "nation under God."[59] He continued,

> It is wrong to think that it is enough for the school to provide for subjects of knowledge and learning and maintain an attitude of neutrality toward religion. Such neutrality is not possible.[60]

The Archbishop paraphrased St. Augustine, the patron of the diocese, stating that,

> earthly society must collaborate with and put into effect the providential plan of God for the increase of the heavenly city, helping that part of it 'which is traveling on this earth.' You parents, teachers and benefactors have helped toward the proper intellectual and spiritual formation of the cherished youth who are preparing themselves for the society of tomorrow.[61]

Norwalk's Central Catholic High School was the third and last of the Bishop's planned diocesan high schools to be completed during his years as Bridgeport's Ordinary.

The Catholics resident in the county's second center of Catholicism had hoped for years to be able to establish a Catholic high school in their city. Members of the Holy Name Society of St. Joseph Church in South Norwalk wrote the bishop in March, 1955, expressing the "great interest" among Catholics in the city for a Catholic high school.[62] The Bishop already had determined that a school should be located in Norwalk, but was then occupied with the Bridgeport campaign.

A meeting of the local clergy was called for January 10, 1957, to discuss the proposed high school and to organize the fund–raising campaign.[63] The campaign was chaired by a prominent Catholic, Judge Alfred Santaniello, who, with a work force of 1,000 volunteers, raised a total of $1,750,000 for the proposed school. The success of Norwalk's campaign was the result of a combination of the two ingredients already proved to be winning in the school campaigns in Bridgeport and Stamford: "The Bishop's support along with the work and dedication of the many volunteers made the drive in Norwalk more than a success."[64]

The ground–breaking ceremony took place in 1957, and the school was dedicated in September, 1959, by the Apostolic Delegate, Archbishop Egidio Vagnozzi.[65] The school was to be staffed by the Sisters of Notre Dame de Namur, already teaching at Notre Dame High School in Bridgeport, and would offer facilities for over 1,000 students from Norwalk and the surrounding towns.

In view of the rising costs of Catholic education, the whole problem of federal aid to private schools came to the fore following the election of John Kennedy as the nation's president. Federal legislation was proposed in Congress providing aid for public schools, to be used for school construction, special projects, and the payment of teachers' salaries. Even though the money for such aid would come from the taxes levied upon the personal wealth, property, and income of all of the nation's citizens—for the purpose of promoting and preserving the general welfare of all—the federal aid was to be limited to public schools.

As Bishop of Bridgeport, President General of the National Catholic Education Association, and Chairman of the Education Department of the National Catholic Welfare Conference, Bishop Shehan was obliged to comment upon the proposed legislation. He felt that such a bill would deprive the parents of Catholic school children of those benefits guaranteed by the Constitution. Without such federal aid, Catholic education ". . . ultimately will become impossible for a great number of our Catholic children—those who need it the most."[66] Unless Catholic and private schools were included in the aid bill, the Bishop felt that the Catholic Church would be pushed out of education by the rising costs resulting from the aid to public schools.

Personally, Bishop Shehan felt that an injustice to American Catholics was being perpetrated by the bill. Yet, he felt that a defeat of all federal aid to schools would be

> a victory since I am convinced our schools would be better off if there were no federal aid at all either to public or private schools. I believe the vast majority of Bishops feel this way too.[67]

The only defense against the proposed legislation would be the united action of the Catholic laity:

> I am convinced that parents of children attending Catholic schools
> will obtain a measure of justice only when our Catholic laity generally
> become convinced about this matter and make themselves heard.[68]

It was their duty, the Bishop contended, to convince Congress of the justice and constitutionality of the Catholic cause and to awaken all Catholics to the injustice of their exclusion from the benefits of a bill intended for the benefit and welfare of all.[69]

Despite the problems facing the Church, the Bishop was determined that the school system should continue to develop. Besides the high school projects throughout the diocese, he also supported the efforts of local pastors to begin parish schools, and worked to secure the assistance of communities of religious sisters in order to further the educational system of the diocese. Fifteen new parochial schools were built and additions completed on ten previously existing schools during Bishop Shehan's years in Bridgeport.

Religious men and women were needed to staff the new parish schools as well as the new diocesan high schools. Six new religious communities of women were introduced into the diocese, five of which were involved in education. Four established provincial houses within its boundaries. One community of men located its provincial house within the diocese also during the Bishop's tenure. There were numerous requests from various religious congregations of sisters to enter the diocese, establish provincial headquarters or academies and institutions of their own. Only those were admitted by the Bishop whose work could fit into his schema for the diocese, the realization of which was begun with the opening of these various schools.[70]

Catholic Youth Work

Bishop Shehan was concerned that all Catholic youth come into contact with the Church's teaching and activities. Those Catholic students attending public schools received their religious education through the catechetical programs of their local parishes, as had been the case prior to the establishment of the diocese in 1953. One year after the installation of the Bishop in the diocese, Bridgeport played host to the first diocesan Confraternity of Christian Doctrine Congress. The ideal situation, reported Bishop Shehan, would be the construction of enough Catholic schools within the diocese to accommodate all of the Catholic children within the county. Since this could not be effected in the near future, the 15,789 Catholic children then attending public schools would continue to receive their religious instructions in their local parishes.

The main speaker of the congress was Bishop John J. Wright of Worcester, Massachusetts. Not only did he emphasize the need for the religious instruction of Catholic youth, but he also underlined the responsibility of the laity to educate their own children. He said,

> Only the laity penetrate the areas of individual, family, professional, social and public life to which the principles of Jesus Christ must be brought.

> Accordingly, only the laity can reduce these saving principles to terms which will be intelligible to those in the areas where Christ's truth must make itself felt. This means teaching, for what is teaching if not the communication of the truth, its reduction to terms intelligible to those who are taught?[71]

Bishop Shehan also recognized the Church's responsibility to help form the character of the Catholic public high school students within the diocese. To this end the Bishop encouraged the continuation of many of the parish programs for high school youth. He also emphasized the need for the development of local Catholic Youth Organizations, dedicated to ". . . the up-building and preservation of Christian character in Catholic young men and women."[72] These organizations would guide Catholic youth along the "proper paths of education and . . . supplement formal education insofar as character formation is concerned."[73]

The importance of parish participation in the CYO programs was emphasized by Bishop Shehan in an address delivered in Buffalo, New York, to delegates of the Catholic Youth Organization Convention, convened in September, 1961. The time when parish complexes were devoted to elementary school education is now past, the Bishop told his audience. Parishes must now plan and be planned with CYO organizations in mind. The absolute necessity of extending the Church's influence to the minds and lives of young Catholics prompted such measures. He continued,

> In the long run, until we are prepared to offer Catholic high school education to all Catholic youth, our work for Catholic students in public high schools are likely to prove the most vitally important part of the Church's program for young people.[74]

Such programs offered by the Church must include good educational, athletic, and cultural events that would prove attractive and stimulating to young people. "But every phase of our whole program must be aimed at our central purpose— to develop and preserve solid Christian character in those who participate." The Bishop continued,

> the substance of character is moral habits; the essence of character is moral principles. Christian character is nothing else than a group of moral habits built upon the principles of the natural law and Christian teaching and molded into one organic whole under the influence of the Christian ideal.

According to the Bishop, these principles derive their validity and binding force from the fundamental truths of religion. The central task of Catholic youth work and its essential instruments, therefore, are derived from the very nature of the Christian character. Since most public high school students are exposed to secularist concepts, such as the supremacy of science, the development of man as a product of natural, material forces, ". . . the end result is a rejection not only of religious truths but also of moral law as fixed and unchanging principles, universally binding." The more effective a secular high school is, therefore, ". . . the more likely it is to be destructive of the very foundations of moral character."

The heart of CYO work, therefore, is the program of religious instruction and activity; it is not merely social. The Catholic student must know the truth of religion. He must realize the essential point concerning human nature: man is different from all other creatures and is not merely another part of the material world. He is set apart and superior to every form of material substance and animal life. Mankind is set apart, the Bishop continued, by his spiritual activities and faculties: free will and intellect; thought and volition, which proclaim the existence of a spiritual soul "which is the crown of material creation, whose existence depends upon God."

Bishop Shehan saw the CYO programs as more than mere religious education and moral instruction. The ultimate aim of the program must be the building of Christian character, based on religious and moral truths. Any religious instruction must be completed by a program of spiritual activities and practice along with a complete program of cultural, social, and athletic activities that will furnish the "opportunities to develop moral habits which are the substance of the Christian character." In essence, the Bishop's concept of the Church's program for Catholic public high school students was that it should be a course in Christian living, with each instructor giving his personal example of a lived faith, and not merely teaching facts.

With the view of expanding the diocese's CYO efforts, Bishop Shehan signed a five-year lease for the former state armory from the Bridgeport Brass Foundation for $300,000 with an option to buy the property. The diocese planned to complete a capital improvement program for expanding and developing the center for the use of Catholic high school students in the Bridgeport area. The renovation of the gymnasium was to be completed as well as the addition of an indoor pool, library, and reading and conference rooms. The renovations of the facility were completed under Bishop Walter W. Curtis, and it was named the Archbishop Shehan Center.

Priestly Vocations

Not only would the various Catholic educational programs of Bishop Shehan assist in the formation of a strong Catholic laity, it was also hoped that they would nurture the seed of religious vocations to the priesthood and religious life among the Catholic youth of the diocese.

One of the first actions of the new Bishop was the establishment of a vocations program under the direction of Msgr. Michael Guerin on January 14, 1954. Since there were very few native vocations, it was decided to appoint district vocation directors. They were to organize the vocation efforts within their own areas of the diocese and to meet each month with Msgr. Guerin, in order to coordinate their efforts. Among those involved were the Revs. William Fletcher, Thomas Keeney, William Nagle, Alfred Carmody, and James McGrath.[75] A large number of vocations were found in the graduating classes of the Fairfield College Preparatory School, but many of them continued to come from outside the boundaries of the diocese.

To strengthen the program for vocations on the parish level, Bishop Shehan approved the establishment of a chapter of the Serra International Club, an organization of laymen devoted to the development of vocations. The first Bridgeport chapter was inaugurated in late 1956, with the Rev. William Nagle as its chaplain.[76]

In June, 1955, the Bishop spoke to members of the Serra Club, emphasizing that,

> the single most important task with which the Church is faced at the present time is that of fostering vocations to the Priesthood and to the Religious Life.[77]

It was the development of vocations, the Bishop believed, that "holds the key to all other major problems."[78] His words were not mere rhetoric delivered for the benefit of an audience interested in vocations. The Diocese was, indeed, experiencing a shortage of priests, so much so that by 1954 the Bishop had begun visiting seminaries in search of recruits for the diocese.[79] In 1956, as the priest shortage continued, Bishop Shehan requested the loan of some priests from the Archdiocese of Hartford. Bridgeport had ordained 17 new priests since the diocese was established. But the gains were quickly equaled by the number of priests lost through death, retirement, relinquishment, or disability. Most other east–coast dioceses appeared to be developing in this area. Since Bridgeport was not, the Bishop was led to admit that "for the present I do very badly need priests."[80] In 1954 there were 158 diocesan priests ministering to an estimated 243,668 Catholics within the diocese. By 1956 the number of priests had risen to 174, as had the Catholic population, which then totalled 267,300 persons. There were 83 religious–order priests working within the Diocese also, but theirs was primarily extra–parochial work, such as teaching.[81]

Rome's response to the first diocesan report glowed with praise for the increase within the priestly ranks of the Diocese, and contained the suggestion that any possible vocations crisis might be addressed by the establishment of a diocesan minor seminary.[82] With the resources and energy of the Diocese dedicated to the establishment of diocesan high schools, such a suggestion could not then be implemented. The prudence of such an establishment was also a factor, since the lack of clerical students, coupled with a general shortage of priestly manpower, did not bode well for the establishment of a new seminary in a country then so filled with small seminaries of questionable quality.[83]

By 1959, the work of the diocesan vocation department had grown. All of the students attending the four diocesan high schools along with the seventh and eighth grade students in thirty–nine parish schools had been included in vocation programs. Forty parish adult groups had been addressed on the need for vocations. Altarboy programs, parish vocation clubs, and CYO groups had all emphasized vocations as essential to Catholic life. These efforts, combined with the natural effect of the diocesan high schools, Fairfield College Preparatory School, Fairfield University and the local parishes, resulted in a slight rise in the number of vocations to the priesthood and religious life.

In a report to the Vatican, Bishop Shehan opined that the primary obstacle to the development of vocations within the diocese was the "worldly spirit found in many families." The bishop felt that the key to vocations was the influence of the Catholic family itself. The Bishop continued,

> The problem as I see it is to foster strong Catholic family life and to instruct parents concerning the necessity of vocations, the meaning of vocations, the blessing of a vocation to the family, and the means by which vocations can be recognized and fostered.[84]

In 1959 Pope John XXIII expressed his interest and his fear that priestly vocations were not being fostered in proportion to the growing need for priests throughout the world.[85] In response to the Pontiff's concern, the Congregation for Seminaries and Universities invited all dioceses to inscribe their respective diocesan efforts for vocations in the "Pontifical Work of Priestly Vocations" established in 1941 by Pope Pius XII.

Bridgeport's vocation program became affiliated with the Pontifical society and was formally known as the "Apostolate for Priestly and Religious Vocations" under the direction of Msgr. James McLaughlin and twelve associate priests.[86]

The results of these efforts would not be seen until after Bishop Shehan had left the diocese. There had been a visible increase, however, in the number of seminarians by the time of his departure in 1961. By the end of that year, the diocese reported twenty–five high school seminarians; fifteen studying philosophy, and forty–nine completing their theological studies in preparation for ordination.[87]

New Parishes: Centers of Catholic Life

The need for priests also reflected the need for new parishes within the diocese resulting from shifting populations and the influx of new immigrants. Fairfield County experienced greater shifts of its population following World War II than did any other county in the state. Large numbers of people began moving from the cities into the newly developing suburbs within Fairfield County. The large city parishes, once the showcases of Catholic life, found their security threatened as their constituency moved away, leaving the enormous parish plants to the newly arriving immigrant and minority groups.

All of the parishes established by Bishop Shehan were begun in areas then considered to be more woodlands than suburbs, as part of a farsighted pastoral plan that recognized the long–range implications of the developing suburbs. Today these parishes are all part of thriving suburban communities, with congregations numbering in the thousands. The first of these new parishes was St. Lawrence in Huntington, established in 1955, followed by Notre Dame of Easton the next year. In all, a total of 15 new parishes were established in anticipation of the larger, continued exodus of Catholics to the suburbs during the subsequent decades.

In the bishop's mind, the parishes, whether in the cities or in the growing suburbs, were to be centers of Catholic life. They were to provide spiritual nourishment to their members, who would then influence the larger communities by their lives formed by Christian principles, morality, and Church social teachings. The parishes also would serve as vehicles by which the Bishop could teach his people and encourage them to an active Catholic life.

In a letter to all the parishes of the diocese in February, 1955, the Bishop announced the observance of Social Action Sunday and encouraged the faithful and clergy to become more aware of the Church's social teachings in order to affect the greater community. The Bishop observed that Fairfield County was the perfect location for the Church in Connecticut. The county was attractive to diversified industry because of its location; it held great promise for all races and classes of people; and it was possessed of a great natural beauty and resources. By the dissemination and practice of the Church's principles of social teaching and morality, Fairfield County could be the showcase of the Church in America. The Church's teaching, the Bishop reasoned,

> should be brought home to owners and managers of industry, to leaders of labor, and to the ranks of people, who, involved in social problems, should profit most by the wisdom of the Church's doctrine.[88]

The local parishes, then, were to assist in the dissemination of these teachings. They should form their members by means of parish organizations and the effective preaching of the clergy, in order that Catholic teaching might affect all areas of life within the county.[89]

Hispanic and Portuguese Catholics

Not all of those arriving within Fairfield County settled in the suburbs during Bishop Shehan's years. Catholic immigrants continued to enter the county during the 1950's. Those arriving from Europe following World War II, the Korean War, and the Hungarian uprising found the problems of resettlement somewhat lessened by the presence of already established immigrant communities, even in the suburbs. Others were not so fortunate and found it necessary to begin the process of organizing communities and churches. They desired to worship according to their own native customs and to employ their own language, as had the Catholic immigrants who arrived before them.

The pastoral care of Catholic immigrants throughout the world was of particular interest to the Church in the years following World War II. Pope Pius XII expressed his concern on numerous occasions for those victims of the war forced to flee their homes as political refugees and immigrants. He approved the efforts of the American hierarchy to secure the relaxation of the country's restrictionist policies in regard to immigration,[90] and personally appealed for the easing of American immigration restrictions to groups of American legislators who visited him after the war.[91]

In a letter to the American Bishops in December, 1948, the Pope voiced the Church's teaching on the right of individuals to migrate in order to find a better life and called upon the Church in the United States to do all in its power to assist them.[92] On August 1, 1952, the Pope issued his apostolic constitution, "On the Spiritual Care of Migrants" (*Exsul Familia*), in which he restated the Church's teaching concerning immigration and laid down the norms to be followed by the Church throughout the world in its pastoral care of the immigrants.[93] Despite the fact that some of the norms proposed by the papal constitution were inapplicable to the United States, *Exsul Familia* clearly expressed the Church's continued interest in the well—being of the immigrants, while reaffirming much of the pastoral program already employed in the United States.[94]

Since many of the refugees of the war sought asylum in the United States, the Church's revised program in favor of the immigrants found a ready testing ground. Connecticut provided an attractive home for many of the immigrants who entered the country by way of New York and settled within the large cities nearby, which offered job opportunities and the comfort of already established immigrant communities and churches.

The Holy See instructed the American bishops to reevaluate their respective pastoral programs in favor of the Catholic immigrants in light of the norms proposed by *Exsul Familia*.[95] After gathering information from all the national parishes within the diocese, Bishop Shehan began to formulate his own program for the care of the newly arrived non–English speaking Catholics within Fairfield County.[96]

Two groups emerged as those most in need of specialized pastoral programs: the Hispanics and the Portuguese. With the existence of so many national city churches in the diocese with shrinking congregations, however, the wisdom of establishing new national churches was questioned.[97] Bridgeport, with more national parishes than any other city in Connecticut, was the subject of much discussion concerning the future of national parishes.[98] At the time, the primary need of the Catholic immigrants was seen by Bishop Shehan and his priests only from a linguistic point of view with little thought for the cultural needs or background of the immigrants. The supplying of priests and religious capable of speaking the necessary languages would suffice, while the Church's specialized programs would serve as a temporary buffer between the immigrants and the larger English–speaking community. This would be a temporary solution, supplying the religious needs of the immigrants until English could be mastered, leading to membership in the local territorial churches as the ultimate goal.[99]

Catholic Puerto Ricans formed the bulk of the Hispanic population within the northeast following World War II. They settled primarily in New York. As a result of Connecticut's boom economy during the Korean War, the Puerto Rican population began to grow, most settling in the larger cities of the state. The flight from Connecticut's cities was hastened by the arrival of the Hispanics and Blacks who arrived in search of jobs. Color and race were important in the identity of all Americans at that time. The majority of the immigrants of the previous generation had been white. Now, for the first time, the Church was faced with the arrival of non–white immigrants in large numbers. The sons and daughters of the Catholic immigrants of previous generations quickly forgot the prejudices that their parents and grandparents had endured upon their arrival, and were all too quick to exercise the same prejudice and hatred against the arriving Hispanic. As Jay Dolan pointed out in his recent work,

> racial discrimination would have a major influence in shaping the attitude of people and priests toward Hispanic Catholics.[100]

The Church had attempted to assist the growing Puerto Rican community in Bridgeport in 1953, prior to the establishment of the Diocese of Bridgeport. The Rev. James Murphy, Director of the Catholic Charities Bureau, took a strong interest in the needs of the Hispanics and initiated special services for them in conjunction with Sacred Heart Church on Myrtle Avenue in August of that year.[101] The following year, Fr. Murphy opened a Puerto Rican Center on State Street under the guidance of Catholic Charities to provide social services and counseling by a staff of Puerto Rican social workers, under the direction of a Holy Ghost Father, the Rev. Albert J. Bullion, CSSp.[102]

By 1956, Bishop Shehan appointed the Rev. Francis Campagnone to head the Diocese's work among Bridgeport's Catholic Hispanics. At first intending to establish a national parish, the Bishop was dissuaded by Father Campagnone and convinced that the more effective means would be the establishment of temporary mission chapels, administered by a Spanish–speaking priest under the care of the local territorial parishes.[103] Father Campagnone was given charge of the pastoral work among the Catholic Hispanics in the West End of the city, working from Sacred Heart Church, while the Rev. Victor Torres–Frias was assigned to care for those on the East Side from St. Mary's Church.[104]

In the fall of 1957, the first of two chapels was opened in Bridgeport for the Hispanic community. The former Holy Trinity Greek Catholic Church on Boswick Avenue was purchased by the Diocese in September of that year and renamed under the patronage of Nuestra Señora de Providencia. It was established as a succursal chapel of Sacred Heart Church and administered by Father Campagnone who served as its chaplain while retaining his position as an assistant pastor at Sacred Heart.[105]

The second chapel, Nuestra Señora de Guadalupe, was opened on the East Side of the city in April, 1958. The old Christian and Missionary Alliance Protestant Church on East Main Street was purchased by the Diocese, along with its residence and auditorium. This was made a mission chapel of St. Mary's and placed under the care of Father Torres–Frias, who continued as the assistant pastor at St. Mary's.[106]

By 1958, the Catholic Hispanic population within the diocese numbered 15,000 persons. Bridgeport claimed about 12,000, Norwalk 1,800, and Stamford 1,200.[107] The diocesan plan to integrate the Hispanic Catholics into existing parish structures, and to assist in their acculturation to their new homeland was ambitious for so small and so new a diocese.[108] Despite opposition from many of the laity and some of the clergy, Bishop Shehan pushed ahead. He solicited funds for the project and secured Spanish–speaking religious sisters in order to meet the needs of the growing Catholic Hispanic population.

The Missionary Sisters of the Most Blessed Sacrament and

Mary Immaculate from Madrid responded to the Bishop's invitation to work among the Hispanic community of Bridgeport and arrived from Madrid in the fall of 1960.[109] They entered into an apostolate that included catechetical work, home visitation, parish census, and charitable projects among the Hispanic community within the city.[110]

The response of the Hispanic communities of Bridgeport was enthusiastic, with Mass attendance generally high, contributions substantial enough to support the chapels, and a freedom from internal squabbles that had marred the development of the national churches in the county during the previous seventy–five years.[111] By the summer of 1961, Bishop Shehan decided that the Hispanics should be given their own parish. Since the larger Catholic Hispanic community was on the East Side, St. Mary Church appeared to be the better choice as an Hispanic parish. Bishop Shehan was transferred to Baltimore, however, before he could implement his plan.[112]

The diocese extended its Hispanic apostolate to Norwalk and Stamford in the spring of 1960. Mass was to be celebrated in the basement churches of St. Mary's in Norwalk and St. John's in Stamford for the Hispanic congregations. This pastoral plan, similar to that already established in Bridgeport, also called for the future establishment of Hispanic pastoral centers in each city.[113] The programs begun in Norwalk and Stamford by Fathers Campagnone and Torres–Frias were in response to the petitions of the Hispanic communities of those cities. Prior to this, those Hispanic Catholics desirous of receiving the sacraments or counselling in their native tongue, were obliged to travel to Bridgeport—as had the early Catholic Irish immigrants 120 years earlier, when St. James was the only Catholic Church in the county.

The Catholic Portuguese of Bridgeport received the attention of Bishop Shehan soon after the founding of the Diocese. In 1954, the Vatican took special interest in the Catholic Portuguese in the United States and wrote to the American bishops requesting information about the pastoral programs in their respective dioceses for the Portuguese.[114]

Portuguese Catholics had resided in Bridgeport since the 1920's. Most arrived from Massachusetts and Rhode Island after the closure of many of the textile mills in those states. Their numbers remained small, however, and by 1930 there were only an estimated 235 Portuguese in the entire city.[115] The largest community formed in the area of Bridgeport known as "the Hollow," around St. Augustine's Church, and established the Club Portugues Vasco da Gama in 1931 as a mutual aid society. The club flourished for a short while, but was soon abandoned.

Bishop McAuliffe of Hartford enlisted the help of the Rev. James Murphy in 1944 to assist the Portuguese community in Bridgeport by purchasing the former Knights of Columbus Hall, which would be outfitted as a new Portuguese center where a priest might celebrate Mass for the community. This was, however, rejected by the Portuguese community, which preferred to re–establish the Vasco da Gama Club in connection with St. Augustine's. The services of a Portuguese priest at Fairfield College Preparatory School were secured in 1949 to celebrate Mass and the sacraments during the Christmas and Easter holiday for his co–nationals at both St. Augustine's and St. Mary's Churches. The majority of the Portuguese did not avail themselves of his services, since most returned to Massachusetts and Rhode Island to celebrate the holidays with their families. After five years, therefore, the services of the priest were no longer offered.

By 1954, the Portuguese community within Fairfield County had increased significantly in number. The Diocese of Bridgeport counted 7,500 Portuguese Catholics within its borders in that year. A serious obstacle to the pastoral work of the Diocese for the Portuguese was posed by the division within the Portuguese community between those from the mainland country and those from the one–time colony of the Cape Verde Islands. The majority of the county's Portuguese residents were Cape Verdeans. Those settling in the Bridgeport–Stratford area numbered about 5,000 persons and attended the Churches of St. Augustine, St. Patrick, St. Mary, Blessed Sacrament, and St. James. Those who settled in areas centering around Danbury, with 2,500 inhabitants, attended St. Peter's Church.[116] The division within the Portuguese community was demonstrated in Bridgeport by the formation of separate, often rival, social clubs, and Holy Name Societies, by Cape Verdeans and by mainland Portuguese.[117]

The Diocese then counted 243,000 Catholics served by 140 active priests. The greatest obstacle to the establishment of a Portuguese ministry was the lack of any Portuguese priest in the diocese. The problem was not merely one of language, but rather of ethnic origin, since the people preferred the ministrations of one of their own countrymen to those of an American priest able to speak the language. In April, 1956, the diocese arranged for the arrival of a young priest from Portugal to work among his fellow countrymen within Fairfield County. The Rev. Constantino Caldas was assigned to Bridgeport, since it was home to the larger Portuguese community. He was to establish a chapel for the Portuguese at St. Augustine's Cathedral and also attend to the needs of his fellow countrymen in the Danbury area.

The Danbury community was not pleased with the arrangement, and its members expressed their displeasure to the Bishop, demanding their own Portuguese priest. Besides the fact that the Portuguese bishops were not willing to export their few priests to America, Bishop Shehan also was anxious that the Portuguese community first respond well to the efforts of Father Caldas before further committing the diocese to a more extensive immigrant apostolate.[118]

The response of the Bridgeport community was not as strong as had been expected. Of the estimated 2,500 Catholic Portuguese in Bridgeport in 1960, an average of only 250 people attended the two Sunday Masses celebrated each week since Father Caldas began his work at St. Augustine's in 1958.[119] One of the reasons for the poor response on the part of the Portuguese community was that many felt slighted by the Church, since they saw themselves as the only national group in the diocese not granted their own church.[120]

A committee of Portuguese Catholics from Bridgeport wrote to the Bishop in June, 1960, petitioning for their own national parish.[121] Since 1958, and unbeknown to this self–appointed committee, Bishop Shehan and Father Caldas had been looking for property in Bridgeport suitable for a Portuguese chapel. Despite the suggestions of his advisers, Bishop Shehan felt it necessary that the Catholic Portuguese community have their own church.[122] It was the Bishop's intention to follow the program already employed for the Hispanic Catholics of Bridgeport, by establishing a mission chapel for the Portuguese to allow them the use of their language and customs until they could more easily join the local territorial parishes.

None of the property or church buildings proposed by the bishop was acceptable to Father Caldas and the committee, since they preferred land in the North End of the city. In accord with their desires, Bishop Shehan approached the Pastor and congregation of Bridgeport's German national Church of St. Joseph. The Church's congregation was shrinking as its older immigrant members died and its American–born members moved to the suburbs. The Bishop saw St. Joseph as a logical choice to serve the growing Portuguese community. The parish location was perfect, and it already had a church, school, and rectory. An unexpected resurgence of German nationalism and nostalgia squelched the Bishop's plans, however, and he was forced to look elsewhere.[123]

The Bishop wrote the Portuguese committee in July, 1960, explaining the financial limitations of the Diocese due to the expansive school–construction projects then going on, and elaborated upon his policy concerning the national churches. He wrote,

> We are guided [in the choice of property] by available money. In the case of other national groups we have limited ourselves to the expenditure of the amount of cash on hand plus a debt for which the Diocese feels it can safely assume responsibility. . . .

The Bishop continued that the purchase must be approached in a practical and realistic manner in order to gain Rome's permission for the establishment of a national church. He continued, "I must, however, have a perfectly feasible plan to lay before the Holy See when I seek such permission."[124]

A parcel of land was finally found on Huntington Road on the East Side of Bridgeport that became the site of the present Church of Our Lady of Fatima. It was originally intended to be a chapel, subject to the St. Charles parish, and administered by Father Caldas as its chaplain. One of Bishop Shehan's last official acts as the Ordinary of the diocese was the approval of the construction plans for the new church.[125]

St. Joseph Manor

Along with education and tending to the needs of immigrants, another area of need within the Diocese was that of care for the elderly. Early in 1951, the Sisters of St. Thomas of Villanova expressed their desire to open a Catholic convalescent home in Norwalk to Bishop Henry J. O'Brien. The sisters had been in Norwalk since 1948, serving on the domestic staff at the seminary owned by the Holy Ghost Fathers. Preferring the work for which their congregation was founded, the local superior of the sisters wrote of her convalescent–home project to the Bishop of Hartford asking his permission.

The proposed site in Norwalk was a former children's hospital once operated by the Episcopal Church. Since the order would be more than able to supply the number of sisters required to staff a convalescent home, the only minor problem would be the securing of adequate funds for the purchase of the property. The sisters saw no great obstacles to the project and informed the Bishop that once the project had received his permission and the former Episcopal hospital renovated, ". . . it would only need the blessing of Your Excellency to replace the shadows of Henry VIII" to insure success.[126]

Bishop O'Brien was loath to give his permission to a project that appeared to be rather unstable financially. It was only after the direct intervention of Eugene Cardinal Tisserant, the Cardinal–Protector of the Order, and Archbishop Amleto Cicognani, the Apostolic Delegate, that permission finally was granted the sisters in 1952.[127] Accordingly, the facility was purchased, renovated, and opened that spring.[128]

Bishop Shehan was interested in the establishment of convalescent homes for the aged within the diocese. He gave permission to the Sisters of St. Thomas to open a novitiate in Norwalk, to assure an adequate number of sisters for their work at Notre Dame Convalescent Home.[129]

The need for a diocesan home for the aged and infirm was still real. Bishop Shehan, therefore, began plans for such a facility in 1957. St. Joseph's Manor was to be located on the property of the former Hubbell Estate in Trumbull, which was purchased by the Diocese in January, 1958. The facility was to be staffed by the Carmelite Sisters for the Aged and Infirm who entered the Diocese in May, 1956, when they purchased a summer house for the Order outside Danbury. The sisters came to the attention of the Bishop at that time as being of possible assistance to him in the establishment of a diocesan home for the aged.[130]

Having secured the needed property and a capable staff, the final element necessary for the realization of the project was funds. Bequests totalling $200,000 had been left to the Diocese for the express purpose of establishing such a facility. With these funds serving as an unofficial indication of the support for the work, Bishop Shehan announced the opening of a diocesan building fund for the aged in February, 1958, under the auspices of the Council of Catholic Women.[131] The goal of the drive was $1,000,000 to be pledged by the seventy–one parishes within the diocese.

By late February, 1958, months before the formal opening of the campaign, Bishop Shehan reported to local pastors and members of the pre–campaign committee that $180,000 had been pledged by fifteen persons.[132] By March, another gift of $50,000 was made to the fund, prior to the official opening of the campaign.[133] The enthusiasm for St. Joseph Manor was so great within the Diocese that the total $1,000,000 goal was nearly met by the pledges from the memorial gifts phase of the drive, which totalled $922,662.[134] The general phase of the campaign was directed by the Diocesan Council of Catholic Women, led by the Council's chairwoman, Mrs. John K. Murphy, in conjunction with the efforts of the six regional presidents throughout the diocese, moderated by the Rev. Thomas Henahan. A program of house–to–house visitation of all wage–earning Catholics within the diocese was organized by the Council, employing 6,000 women volunteers. The *Catholic Transcript* commented on the drive and the work of the Council:

> The Diocesan Council of Catholic Women will play the chief role in the general canvassing. This fact alone is an infallible earnest of success. The enthusiasm, dedication, and hard work of the council are famous far beyond the bounds of the diocese. When they put their hearts and hands to a task, it is done to perfection.[135]

The total of the general campaign more than doubled the original goal, reaching $2,185,649 by the close of the drive in late May.

St. Joseph Manor was completed and formally dedicated on Sunday, October 2, 1960, by Archbishop Henry J. O'Brien of Hartford. The Manor was able to accommodate 300 residents within its five floors and was hailed as the largest and most modern facility of its kind in the state.[136] With the completion of this work, Bishop Shehan was now free to devote his efforts to the further organization of the diocese.

The First Synod of Bridgeport

On October 17, 1960, Bishop Shehan announced that the First Synod of Bridgeport would be celebrated during the coming year in order to put the Diocese on a sound canonical foundation. A rash of diocesan synods had been celebrated in the northeast during the 1950's. Since the Diocese had existed for seven years, the Bishop felt it expedient to call upon the experience of the clergy regarding the practice of the faith within the county. The clergy of the Diocese were invited by the Bishop to submit suggestions to the twelve commissions of priests named to study various areas for legislation and to propose necessary statutes. The blueprint for the synod was taken from the practice of other synods recently held in the United States, especially that of the Archdiocese of Hartford.

The areas for discussion and legislation concerned the clergy, deans and pastors, assistant priests and chaplains, religious women, the sacraments, sacred times and places, divine worship and sacramentals, the teaching authority of the Church, and the Church's temporal responsibilities.

In accordance with universal Church practice, the laity were considered in the legislation only insofar as they were members of parishes and Catholic societies. The laity, in fact, had no say in the preparations of the synod at all. At first glance this might seem odd, considering that the Second Vatican Council was to be convened in only a few years. The operating principle at the time, however, was that the laity had no place in the legislative process of the Church itself, whether on a diocesan or a parish level. The entire nature of the synod, in fact, was clerical, having for its primary purpose the simple codification of the practice within the diocese. It was viewed merely as an internal process, having little effect upon the greater community or on members of the Church other than the clergy. The solemn session of the synod mirrored this clerical, internal orientation of the legislation itself. The solemn session was scheduled for a weekday, June 14, 1961, when most of the laity were working or attending to their families. Any of the faithful who might have been free to attend were ceremoniously ushered forth from the closed–door proceedings, as was the practice elsewhere in the Catholic world. So internal was the nature of the synod that the local papers did not even report on the proceedings, a remarkable fact since the press usually responded with in–depth coverage of every Catholic event or pronouncement within the county, as the result of Bishop Shehan's good relations with the media.

The Bishop's own address opening the solemn session expressed the aim of the synod. The Bishop said that the principle guiding the Church universal guided his actions as he opened the synod:

the care and salvation of souls, must now be the highest law guiding us in the application of our statutes to the religious life of our diocese.[137]

The holiness of the people, the Bishop continued, depended upon the holiness of their priests. The statutes of the synod, therefore,

are meant to help you, the priests of this Diocese, in safeguarding and in developing your own priestly character and in the more effective performance of your priestly work.

232

In order to facilitate the work and communication between the Bishop, the commissions, and the clergy during the preparatory stages of the synod, the Rev. Bartholomew Skelly was appointed as the Procurator of the Clergy. He presented the thoughts of the priests upon proposed legislation before the Bishop and the diocesan consultors.

This arrangement proved effective, as exemplified by the consideration of legislation concerning the Christmas collection in each parish. The practice of giving the Christmas collection to the pastor had developed during the previous century as a means of covering the operating costs of the rectory. Since the Catholic congregations were originally small, the collections often proved barely sufficient to cover the church's regular expenses. Accordingly, the Christmas collection was given over to the pastor of each church and served to cover those ordinary expenses for the room and board of the clergy. Later, under the Diocese of Hartford, parishes were asked to give a small subsidy toward the rectory expenses. When Bishop Shehan came to the diocese he immediately changed the practice, mandating that all the expenses of the local rectory be subsumed into the general parish expenses. Presupposing that the logical outcome would be the end of the Christmas collection practice, he said nothing about it.[138] But the practice of giving the Christmas collection to the pastor continued, which by then was viewed as his personal property. Not a few pastors had come to find their financial circumstances much improved because of the Christmas largess of the faithful, so much so that the collection had come to be viewed as the pastor's right.

The threatened removal by legislation of such a boon to the clerical estate provoked a torrent of protest from the pastors of the diocese. The synodal procurator conveyed these protests to the Bishop. Respecting the overwhelming will of his pastors, Bishop Shehan tabled the proposed legislation and left the question of the collection to his successor.

While the synodal decrees came in part from the reflections and suggestions of the clergy, it was the Bishop along with Fathers John Toomey, William Genuario, and George B. Curtiss who actually gave the final form to the decisions and statutes. The Bishop urgently wanted to complete the work of the synod, which led him to push himself and his staff to conclude the synodal preparations as soon as possible.[139]

The First Synod of Bridgeport, while far from being earth–shattering, confirmed the identity and maturity of the Church within Fairfield County. It provided some legislation needed for normative Catholic life and ministry, thereby completing the foundation for a more effective Catholic presence within the county.

Bishop Shehan Returns to Baltimore

The Synod proved to be the final project that Bishop Shehan brought to completion within the Diocese. Shortly after its completion, in mid–July, 1961, the Bishop received his appointment as the coadjutor archbishop of Baltimore with right of succession to Archbishop Francis Keough. Bishop Shehan had been rumored to be destined for things greater than Bridgeport for years. Whenever any see larger than Bridgeport fell vacant during the 1950's, Bishop Shehan usually was rumored to be Rome's immediate choice.

The Bishop's great friend, Archbishop Keough, himself often joked concerning the future of the Bishop of Bridgeport. During Bishop Shehan's first *ad limina* visit to Rome in the fall of 1959, Archbishop Keough jokingly introduced Bishop Shehan to his secretary, Father John Toomey, as ". . . the next Cardinal Archbishop of Baltimore."[140]

Whether half joking or prophetic, by October of the following year Archbishop Keough invited Bishop Shehan to consider accepting the position as his coadjutor. Bishop Shehan responded to the Archbishop on January 5, 1961, writing:

> I have given considerable thought to your suggestion about the future. I have always tried to make it my practice to seek nothing, but to accept what is assigned to me and then to do the best I can. I do not want it thought that I am asking for a change. Nor would I want it thought that I have been unhappy up here. On the contrary, I have been very happy, particularly in the things I have been able to accomplish with the cooperation of the priests and people. I am confident that I would go on being happy, for there is still plenty to do. The point is that I shall be content with whatever the Holy See wants me to do.[141]

The official announcement of the Bishop's transfer to Baltimore appeared in the headlines of the Bridgeport papers on September 11, 1961. In his remarks to the press, the Archbishop–elect thanked the Holy Father for the appointment and continued that,

> It is, however, with deepest regret that I leave the Diocese of Bridgeport. From its priests and people I have received the greatest kindness and most loyal and helpful cooperation. Among them I spent more than seven of the happiest years of my life. It is my sincere hope that they will continue to keep me in their prayers.[142]

234

September 27 was the day of the Archbishop's departure from Bridgeport. At St. Augustine's, he addressed the assembled crowds recalling the successful drives for the Catholic high schools, St. Joseph Manor, for the new churches and parish schools throughout the diocese. He then called upon those present to work for the development of the Catholic faith of the youth of the Diocese, and especially the development of vocations,

> . . . since the whole future of the Church of this jurisdiction depends on the number of vocations to the priesthood and the religious life that this diocese produces.[143]

Recalling the warmth and support he had received from his clergy and people he continued,

> Almost eight years ago I came to you as a complete stranger. The warm and sincere welcome you accorded me immediately won my whole-hearted affection. The encouragement and support you gave every diocesan endeavor has strengthened that bond of affection by which I felt from the beginning I was united with you.

Leaving a filled cathedral, the Archbishop was accompanied by Mayor Tedesco of Bridgeport and members of the local clergy to the railroad station, which was jammed with over 5,000 people. There he bade farewell to members of the clergy and the laity who had supported his projects during the past years. Before boarding the train, Ray Flicker the President of the Post Publishing Company, handed the archbishop early editions of *The Bridgeport Post* with the announcement of the appointment of Bishop Walter W. Curtis as the second Bishop of Bridgeport.

Conclusion

During his years as Bishop of Bridgeport, Bishop Shehan had completed a large number of projects. Fifteen new parishes were established and seventeen new church buildings completed, with four others near completion; four regional Catholic high schools built and the site for the fifth purchased; fifteen new parochial elementary schools had been opened, five more were under construction while others had been renovated; the total elementary and secondary Catholic school enrollment had risen substantially during his years; six new religious communities of women and three of men had entered the diocese; three new provincial houses, a new seminary and novitiate were opened for the various religious orders within the diocese; St. Joseph's Manor was completed and new wings were added to St. Vincent Hospital in Bridgeport and St. Joseph Hospital in Stamford; an episcopal residence had been purchased as had a new home for the chancery offices and the Catholic Charitable Bureau; a diocesan synod had been celebrated; and a diocesan youth recreation center was established in Bridgeport.

The work of the first Bishop of Bridgeport was of heroic proportions, materially speaking. But of even greater import was the prestige that he gave to the Church, the priesthood, and Catholic life in Fairfield County during his administration. His years in Bridgeport have been called an "era of good feeling" by one of the priests of the diocese, to describe the atmosphere within the diocese among priests, religious, and lay people. The people sensed the devotion and love their bishop felt for them. The priests felt a fraternity among themselves and with their Bishop that was fostered by the Bishop's solicitude for them, for he was "a father to younger priests; a companion and support to the older priests."[144] It was a good time to be a priest, a religious sister or brother, because the already existing identity of priests and religious was enhanced and bolstered by the prestige given by the Bishop. Bishop Shehan strengthened the belief that Catholic ministry and Catholic life were important, and the responses of his people and clergy alike were astounding.

Bishop Shehan's major contribution as the founding Bishop of Bridgeport was his leadership of the Catholic Church in Fairfield County, which had come of age upon his accession to the newly established see. Important as his building projects were, it was his ministry as a bishop, characterized by a dedication to his people, his fraternity with his priests and religious, and his deep love for the Church, that formed the hallmark of his years in Bridgeport.

NOTES

ABBREVIATIONS

AAS	*Actae Apostolicae Sedis*
ABALT	*Archives of the Archdiocese of Baltimore*
ABOST	*Archives of the Archdiocese of Boston*
ABPT	*Archives of the Diocese of Bridgeport*
ACMS	*Archives of the Center for Migration Studies, Staten Island*
AFHS	*Archives of the Fairfield Historical Society*
AGS	*Roman Archives of the Generalate of the Congregation of the Missionaries of St. Charles Borromeo*
AHTFD	*Archives of the Archdiocese of Hartford*
ALOCK	*Archives of the Lockwood Matthews Mansion Museum, Norwalk, Connecticut*
AMERCY	*Archives of the Convent of Mercy, West Hartford, Connecticut*
ANYC	*Archives of the Archdiocese of New York*
APF	*Archives of the Sacred Congregation for the Evangelization of Peoples, or "de Propaganda Fide":*
	ACTA *The "Acta" of the General and Particular Congregations*
	APNS *The "New Series," 1893–1922*
	S.C.AMER.CENT. *Scritture Riferite nei Congressi America Centrale dal Canada all'Istmo di Panama*
	S.C.ANTILLE *Scritture Riferite nei Congressi Missionari Antille*
	S.O.C.G. *Scritture Originali Riferite nelle Congregazioni Generali, 1622–1892*
ASV	*Secret Vatican Archives*
	SDIS *Archives of the Secretariat of State*
	DELAPUSA *Archives of the Apostolic Delegation in the United States*
AUND	*Archives of the University of Notre Dame*
ASSND	*Archives of the School Sisters of Notre Dame Provincial House, Wilton, Connecticut*
n.d.	*No date given in a specific document*
n.p.	*No place of origin given in a specific document*

INTRODUCTION

[1] J. Hammond Trumbull, *The Public Records of the Colony of Connecticut Prior to the Union with New Haven Colony* (Hartford, 1859), vol. II, p. 35.

[2] Charles J. Hoadly, *Records of the Colony or Jurisdiction of New Haven, from May, 1653, to the Union. Together with the New Haven Code of 1656* (Hartford, 1858), p. 562.

[3] J. Hammond Trumbull, *The Public Records of The Colony of Connecticut Prior to the Union with New Haven Colony* (Hartford, 1850), vol. I, p. 545. Henceforth this collection will be referred to as the *Connecticut Records*.

[4] The Roman authorities were aware of the anti–Catholic sentiments of the English colonists. Nonetheless, the Church early on had shown interest in the British and French colonies as fertile fields for Catholic missionary activities in North America, assigning to the Jesuits and the Capuchins the task of investigating such missionary prospects early in the 17th century. For complete studies of the early work of the Jesuits and Capuchins in regard to the North American missions, cf. Lucien Campeau, *Monumenta Historica Societatis Iesu*, vol. I (Rome, 1967); vol. II (Rome, 1979); John Lenhart, "The Capuchin Prefecture of New England," in *Franciscan Studies*, March, 1943, (New Series, vol. 3), no. 1: pp. 21–46, 180–195, 306–313.

[5] Toleration for various Protestant churches was granted grudgingly by the Connecticut authorities in 1708 and 1743. Charles J. Hoadly, *Connecticut Records* (Hartford, 1870), vol. V, p. 50; (Hartford, 1875), vol. VIII, p. 522.

[6] Hammond J. Trumbull, ed., *The True Blue Laws of Connecticut and the False Blue Laws Forged by Peters* (Hartford, 1876), p. 184: The New Haven Code of 1656 describes the General Court as "the ministers of God, for the good of the people; And have power to declare, publish, and establish, for the plantations within their jurisdictions, the lawes [sic] He hath made, and to make and repeale [sic] orders for smaller matters, not particularly determined in Scripture. . . ."

[7] *Connecticut Records* (Hartford, 1873), vol. VII, p. 211.

[8] *Connecticut Records* (Hartford, 1875), vol. VIII, pp. 454–457. Francis I. Hawks, William Perry Stevens, *Documentary History of the Protestant Episcopal Church in the United States of America* (New York, 1863), vol. I, p. 40: No minister or church community was allowed to function or practice their faith within Connecticut without the permission of the local authorities. In 1706 an Anglican minister, the Rev. Mr. George Muirson of Rye, was prohibited from practicing his ministry to the small number of Anglicans then resident there.

[9] Arthur J. Riley, *Catholicism in New England to 1788* (Washington, D.C., 1936), p. 231: Anglicans were granted privileges in 1727; Baptists and Quakers in 1729.

[10] Daniel Barber, "The History of My Own Time," Part I, in *Boston Monthly Magazine*, vol. 1826–1828, pp. 3–10.

[11] *Connecticut Records* (Hartford, 1859), vol. III, p. 299.

[12] James H. O'Donnell, *History of the Diocese of Hartford* (Boston, 1900), p. 46.

[13] *Connecticut Records* (Hartford, 1877), vol. X, pp. 452–453.

[14] *Ibid.*, p. 453: Fairfield received 17 Acadians; Stratford, 14; Norwalk, 12; Stamford, 9; Danbury, 6; Greenwich, 6; Newtown, 4.

[15] Newtown Town Hall: Town Records, April, 1756.

[16] Francis I. Hawks, William Stevens Perry, *Documentary History of the Protestant Episcopal Church in the United States of America* (New York, 1863), p. 31. James A. O'Donnell, *History of the Diocese of Hartford* (Boston, 1900), p. 75.

[17] APF, S.C. Anglia Amer. Antille, vol. I, f462r–465v: Rev. Pietro Arcedeckne to Pope Clement XII, Rome, 1736: Arcedeckne petitioned the pope to send missionaries to the Catholic English, Scots, and Irish who had been sent to the various British colonies, including those of New England.

[18] *Connecticut Gazette*, January 5, 1764, quoted in O'Donnell, p. 40.

[19] APF, S.C.Amer. Cent., 1763, f290r–291v, Ricardus Deboren (Challoner) to Propaganda Fide, n.p., July 2, 1763: The English colonies were apparently under the ecclesiastical jurisdiction of the Vicar Apostolic of London, until 1784. Reporting to Rome on the condition of the Church in the colonies, he reported that the open exercise of Catholicism was prohibited by law, except in the colonies of Pennsylvania and Maryland.

[20] So strong was the abhorrence of all things Catholic by the authorities in the English colonies that the Gregorian calendar, computed by Jesuit scientists and mathematicians under the auspices of Pope Gregory XIII and approved in 1582, was not employed in the English colonies until 1752.

[21] AFHS, File, 1974, 135, Baptismal record from the Archives Municipales de Toulouse (copy).

[22] The doctor's son was to establish the first printing press and newspaper in Fairfield, the "Fairfield or Independent Gazette—the Intelligencer."

[23] Charles Hoadly, *Connecticut Records* (Hartford, 1887), vol. XIV, p. 309.

[24] *Connecticut Records* (Hartford, 1881), vol. XII, p. 495.

[25] Cornelia Penfield Lathrop, *Black Rock, Seaport of Old Fairfield, 1644–1870* (New Haven, 1930), p. 166.

[26] *New England Primer Enlarged. For the More easy attaining the True Reading of English; To which is added, The Assembly of Divines Catechism* (Boston, 1727), p. 32.

[27] Mother Mary Peter Carthy, *English Influences on Early American Catholicism* (Washington, D.C., 1959), p. 20.

[28] Worthington Chauncey Ford, ed., *Journals of the Continental Congress, 1774–1789* (Washington D.C., 1904), vol. I, p. 34.

[29] Quoted in "Catholics and the American Revolution," in *The American Catholic Historical Researches*, N.S., vol. II, January, 1906, no. 1, p. 10.

[30] *Ibid.*, p. 88.

[31] In February, 1776, Congress once again attempted to solicit Canada's assistance. This time by means of a commission composed of Benjamin Franklin, Samuel Chase, Charles Carroll of Carrollton, a Catholic, and his brother, the Rev. John Carroll, later the first bishop in the United States. The mission failed to impress the French Canadians.

[32] Daniel Barber, "The History of My Own Times," in *Boston Monthly Magazine*, vol. 1826–1828, part I, p. 17.

[33] Thomas Paine, "Crisis, No. 5," quoted in "Catholics and the American Revolution," in *The American Catholic Historical Researches*, N.S. vol. II, January, 1906, no. 1, p. 11.

[34] Benedict Joseph Fenwick, *Memoirs to Serve for the Future Ecclesiastical History of the Diocese of Boston* (Yonkers, 1970), p. 7.

[35] In his "Address to Officers and Soldiers of the Continental Army," Benedict Arnold claimed that the colonial alliance with Catholic France had prompted his treason during the revolution.

[36] Barber, *op. cit.,* p. 17.

[37] Bp. John Carroll to Matthew Carey, January 30, 1789, in Thomas O'Brien Hanley, *The Carroll Papers,* (Notre Dame, 1976), vol. I, p. 482: Carroll, the first Catholic bishop in the United States, observed that the revolutionary forces "swarmed with Catholic soldiers."

[38] *Newtown Bee*, August 10, 1900: Since the French Catholic forces were in Connecticut on two Sundays—June 24th at Hartford, and July 1st at Newtown—Mass must have been celebrated for the troops. The Mass in Hartford would have been the first celebrated in Connecticut; The Mass in Newtown, the first in Fairfield County. Cf. also "Centennial Celebration of the First Mass in Connecticut (June, 1781), Sunday, June 26, 1881, in St. Peter's Church, Hartford" (Hartford, 1881).

[39] Quoted in Peter Guilday, *The Life and Times of John Carroll* (New York, 1922), vol. I, p. 365.

[40] ABALT, n. d., George Washington to "The Roman Catholics in the United States."

[41] These laws did little for Catholics within the state. Regardless of their few numbers and lack of priests, Catholics would have found it very difficult to establish legally their own churches, since such establishment depended upon the approval of the local Congregational government.

[42] Timothy Dwight, "The Duty of Americans, at the Present Crisis, Illustrated in a Discourse, Preached on the Fourth of July, 1798" (New Haven, 1798), pp. 6–28.

[43] Richard J. Purcell, *Connecticut in Transition: 1775–1818* (Middletown, 1963), pp. 3–5.

[44] APF, S.C. Amer. Cent. 1814, "Missions of North America," f5r–8r; 9r–10v.

[45] APF, S.C. Amer. Cent. 1825, Bishop Ludovico DuBourg to Propaganda Fide, Natchitoches, October 6, 1825.

[46] The local Hartford newspaper, the *Connecticut Observer*, noted the growing number of Catholics in the city in its number of July 29, 1829: "The religion which imposed a yoke on our fathers . . . is pressing its way into our land."

[47] ABOST, "Journal of the Diocese of Boston, 1829–1849," vol. I, p. 317; II, p. 16.

[48] ABOST, "Journal of the Diocese of Boston, 1825–1849," vol. III, p. 12: Bishop Fenwick mentions only the missions of Bridgeport, Derby, and Norwalk as coming under the care of the Rev. Michael Lynch upon his appointment to the Bridgeport church.

[49] APF, ACTA 1853, vol. 215, f 241v, Bishop Thomas Heyden to Propaganda Fide, Bedford, Pennsylvania, November 12, 1852: The Bishop of Natchez reflected that the multiplication of dioceses in the United States was of little value. Among those recently erected dioceses which he deemed superfluous

was Hartford, the territory of which he believed could be ruled more effectively from New York.
[50] ABOST, Society for the Propagation of the Faith, 1835–1846, 3.11, Boston, n.d., Bishop Fenwick to the Propagation of Paris (draft).

Chapter I: An Immigrant Church: Irish Catholic Foundations

[1] John England "The Republic in Danger," Letter V, August 16, 1831, in Hugh P. McElrone, ed., *The Works of the Right Rev. John England* (Baltimore, 1884), vol. II, p. 445.
[2] Gerald Shaughnessy, *Has the Immigrant Kept the Faith?* (New York, 1969), p. 92: the actual total immigration for that period was 33,803,274. However, Shaughnessy's number represents the net immigration, taking into account the number of immigrants who returned to their native country after arrival.
[3] Clive Day, *The Rise of Manufacturing in Connecticut, 1820–1850*, Tercentenary Commission of the State of Connecticut (New Haven, 1935), vol. XLIV, p. 2.
[4] Fairfield County had always outstripped all other Connecticut counties in grain production, with Fairfield, Norwalk, Wilton, Weston, Redding the most productive towns. Stamford had the largest grain mills in the state, producing flour solely for export.
[5] Hamilton D. Hurd, *History of Fairfield County, Connecticut, with Illustrations and Biographical Sketches of Its Prominent Men and Pioneers*, (Philadelphia, 1881), pp. 95–100, 617, 654, 817–818, 866: Prior to 1850, some of the principal manufactured goods were produced in Bridgeport, such as saddles and carriages; Redding produced iron and wire products along with sieves; Ridgefield manufactured leather goods, hats, boots, and shoes (over 5,000 pairs in 1800), and ducking (about 3,000 yards annually); Westport had the first carding machine in the country by 1805, and developed a thriving cotton manufacturing business as a result of the War of 1812; Bethel was renowned for its combs and hats; Danbury primarily for its hatting industry, which by 1800 employed nearly 3,000 people and produced over 20,000 hats.
[6] AUND, F66–3895, Bp. Bernard O'Reilly to Paris Propagation of the Faith, Providence, January 11, 1851.
[7] James H. O'Donnell, *History of the Diocese of Hartford* (Boston, 1900), pp. 257–258. Those Catholics then in Bridgeport were: Mrs. McLoughlin, Mrs. McConnell, Bernard Kennedy, Peter Carey, John Carey, Michael Sullivan, Joseph Delaney, James McCullough, John Reilly, James Gillick, James Ward, Thomas Garey, Edward Lutz, and John Coyle. Fr. Fitton maintained the tradition that priests from New York and Providence had ministered to the Catholics of Bridgeport during the late 1820's.
[8] *Ibid.*, pp. 276–277.
[9] W. Chapin, *A Complete Reference Gazeteer of the United States of America* (New York, 1839), pp. 41, 77, 94, 226.
[10] James Montgomery Bailey, *History of Danbury, Conn., 1684–1896* (New York, 1896), p. 212. Danbury boasted only one Irishman in 1828, Peter O'Brien, who lived in a "genuine shanty made of stone, clay, and turf, with a barrel for a chimney." He was considered quite a novelty by the local populace who would "frequently drive that way to get a sight of his small retreat." *Centennial Anniversary of Saint Rose Church, Newtown, Connecticut, A Pictorial History, 1859–1959*, p. 22: Daniel Quinlivan was the first Irishman to settle in Newtown, arriving in 1830. Even though Ridgefield had a number of factories

and mills, Quinlivan worked as a hired hand on the farm of Captain Joseph Nichols, whose wife was a convert to Catholicism.

[11] *The Republican Farmer,* July 19, 1842.

[12] AABO, Journal of the Diocese of Boston, vol. II, September 11, 1836–August 31, 1842, pp. 55, 69, 248.

[13] *Ibid.,* p. 279.

[14] Samuel Koenig, *Immigrant Settlements in Connecticut: Their Growth and Characteristics,* Works Progress Administration Federal Writers' Project for the State of Connecticut (Hartford, 1938), p. 180.

[15] John L. Andriot, ed., *Population Abstract of the United States* (McLean, Virginia, 1983), vol. 1, pp. 101–102.

[16] AUND, F66 3894, Bishop William Tyler to Propagation of Paris December 30, 1847. In his 1846 report, Bishop Tyler reported a Catholic population of 9,000 for his diocese, which included both Rhode Island and Connecticut. In his 1847 report he stated that the Catholic population had risen to 20,000.

[17] *Norwalk after Two Hundred & Fifty Years* (South Norwalk, 1901), 36c.

[18] Charles M. Selleck, *Norwalk After Two Hundred and Fifty Years, an Account of the Celebration of the 250th Anniversary of the Charter of the Town,* (South Norwalk, 1901), p. 61.

[19] *Norwalk Gazette,* February 4, 1851.

[20] *Stamford Advocate,* January 18, 1851: "This very neat edifice which has been recently finished, on Meadow Street, in this village, was dedicated on Sunday last by appropriate ceremonies. Mass in Stamford has first been celebrated in 1842 by the Rev. James Smyth of New Haven, in the house of Patrick Drew."

[21] *Connecticut Observer,* November 2, 1829. *The Catholic Press,* July 11, 1829: This, the first Catholic paper in Connecticut, was founded in 1829, the same year that an Episcopal church was purchased for Catholic use, and the first resident rector assigned in Hartford. Of these events, the *Connecticut Observer,* a Congregational weekly in Hartford, observed: "We understand that a Roman Catholic press has arrived in this city. . . . How ill it will read in history, that, in 1829, Hartford, in the State of Connecticut, was made the center of a Roman Catholic mission."

[22] Thomas Brigden, "A Brief Sketch of the True Religion, Written in the Form of Letters by a Native of Connecticut formerly a Member of the Presbyterian Church, and Since a Catholic Convert. Together with the Motives that conducted His Choice, and the Invincible Reasons that now Hold Him in the Catholic Communion" (Hartford, 1831), p. 82.

[23] ABOST, Journal of the Diocese of Boston, vol. I, Nov. 1, 1825–Sept. 10, 1835, December 4; 6, 1830, f. 133.

[24] Jarvis Morse, *A Neglected Period in Connecticut's History, 1818–1850* (New Haven, 1935), p. 135.

[25] Horace Bushnell (1802–1876) was born in Bantam, Connecticut, and exercised a strong influence in the state as pastor of the North Street Congregational Church in Hartford for over forty years. Lymann Beecher (1775–1863) was born in New Haven, Connecticut, served as pastor in various Congregational churches in Boston, Connecticut, and New York, and pursued a successful career as a writer and lecturer.

[26] Lymann Beecher, "Plea for the West," 2nd edition (Cincinnati, 1835), pp. 54–55, 59.

[27] Horace Bushnell, "Crisis in the Church" (Hartford, 1835), p. 24.

[28] Throughout this period a series of anti–Catholic books and periodicals appeared which played upon the ignorance and isolation of many Americans. Pornographic scenes of priests seducing unsuspecting maidens in convents and confessionals were common fare, and eagerly consumed the attention of many Americans who had little if any knowledge of anything Catholic. The first of these, published in 1835, was entitled, *Six Months in a Convent* and claimed to be the confessions of Rebecca Reed. It was lauded by the Protestant press, as was another work, *Awful Disclosures of the Hotel Dieu Nunnery of Montreal,* released in 1836, and credited to one Maria Monk, purportedly another escaped nun. Although engaging in its detail of sexual liberalities between priests and nuns, of secret passages linking convent and priest's house, and of a hidden cemetary for the burial of the offspring of illegal clerical liasons, the book was actually written by a group of Protestant ministers and laity, among whom was Connecticut's own Theodore Dwight, editor of the *Hartford Courant*. The tale of Maria Monk, even though proven false, continued to enjoy an unparalleled popularity, selling over 300,000 copies by the opening of the Civil War; it was reprinted in 1960.

[29] Horace Bushnell, *Building Eras in Religion* (New York, 1881), pp. 357–358. While lecturing in England in 1846, representing the anti–Catholic society known as the "Christian Alliance," Bushnell penned his "Letter to Pope Gregory XVI," in which he flippantly explained to the pontiff that the purpose of the Alliance was to preach true religion in Italy. He continued, "It [the society] works no secret plots against your peace. Its object is openly professed, namely to prepare the way for a reformation of your church by rendering it accessible to truth." In a marginal note in the 1881 edition, Bushnell delightedly added that his letter had been condemned by the Roman Church and placed upon the Index of Forbidden Books.

[30] Horace Bushnell, "Barbarism the First Danger" (New York, 1847), p. 5. *Concilium Plenarium Totius Americae Septentrionalis Foederatae, Baltimori Habitum Anno 1852* (Baltimori, MDCCCLIII), p. 49 (Decree XXI); p. 59: Bushnell's fears concerning the insidious efforts of the Church in America appeared to receive a boost in 1852 when the The First Plenary Council of Baltimore petitioned, and received from the pope, the authority to grant a plenary indulgence to those who joined the Sodality for the conversion of non–Catholics in North America.

[31] Hamilton D. Hurd, *History of Fairfield County, Connecticut* (Philadelphia, 1881), p. 262. *Danbury Times,* May 28, 1851; June 25, 1851: The three bankers were William H. Clark, Aaron Seeley, and Samuel Stebbins. *Danbury Times,* March 19, 1851: Despite Danbury's distaste for all things Catholic, it did approve the work of the Irish temperance leader, the Rev. Theobald Mathew. The *Times* reported that the priest had sent a gold watch to P.T. Barnum in appreciation for his advocacy of the temperance movement.

[32] *Norwalk Gazette,* September 26, 1854: "It was ascertained that some rascally incendiary had bored a hole in each of the rear corners [of the church], and pouring in some liquid combustible, had set it on fire."

[33] John L. Andriot, ed., *Population Abstract of the United States* (McLean, Va., 1983), vol. 1, p. 100.

[34] Samuel Koenig, *Immigrant Settlements in Connecticut* (Hartford, 1930), p. 17.

[35] John Andriot, *op. cit.,* pp. 101–102.

[36] *John Carroll Noonan, Nativism in Connecticut, 1829–1860* (unpub. dissert., Catholic University of America, Washington, D.C., 1938), p. 255. Towns in

Fairfield County with populations of 5,000 inhabitants dramatically increased between 1850 and 1860:

	1850 Population	1860 Population
Bridgeport	7,560	13,299
Norwalk	4,651	7,582
Danbury	5,964	7,234
Stamford	5,000	7,185
Greenwich	5,036	6,522

[37] AUND, F66–3903, Bishop Bernard O'Reilly to Council of the Propagation of the Faith, Paris, July 27, 1851.

[38] John Carroll Noonan, *Nativism in Connecticut, 1829–1860* (Washington, D.C., 1938), p. 267. The total seating capacity of these eight chapels was 4,520, while the total property value of Church holdings in Fairfield County by 1860 was $68,000.

[39] Since the United States was considered mission territory until 1908, there were no canonical parishes or pastors within the country, only missions administered by rectors.

[40] APF, ACTA (1855), vol. 219, f500r–502r, "Ristretto con Sommario Sopra gli Atti e Decreti del primo Concilio Provinciale di Nuova York, 30 Aprile, 1855."

[41] AUND, F66–3905, Bp. O'Reilly to Paris Propagation of the Faith, Paris, January 17, 1856. (Emphasis original).

[42] Horace Bushnell, "Discourses on Christian Nurture" (Boston, 1847), pp. 6–7.

[43] Horace Bushnell, "Common Schools," in *Connecticut Pamphlets*, (Hartford, 1853), vol. 28, p. 2.

[44] AUND, All Hallow's Missionary Correspondence, 1843–1877, Providence, n.d., Sr. Mary Francis Halpin to "Dear Rev. Father."

[45] *The Metropolitan Catholic Almanac, 1850* (Baltimore, 1849), p. 103.

[46] *Metropolitan Catholic Almanac, 1854* (Baltimore, 1853), p. 134.

[47] *Norwalk Gazette*, August 7, 1855.

[48] Arthur J. Heffernan, *A History of Catholic Education in Connecticut* (Washington, D.C., 1937), The Catholic University of America Educational Research Monographs, vol. X, no. I, p.20.

[49] *Ibid.*, pp. 19–21. Bridgeport's Catholic school opened in the house of John Coyle and was taught by Mary Quigley. Norwalk's Catholic school was conducted by a Mr. and Mrs. Hession. Danbury's teachers were John Flood and Mrs. Frank Reardon.

[50] *Norwalk Gazette*, February 6, 1855.

[51] *Ibid.*, April 3, 1856.

[52] AUND, Leopoldine Society, Reel 10, O'Reilly to Abp. V. Edward Milde, Providence, October 6, 1852.

[53] APF, S.C.Amer. Cent., vol. 19, f719v, "Relazione dello stato della Diocesi di Hartford fino al giorno 16 Maggio 1862."

[54] AHTFD, Episcopal Correspondence, Rev. Francis Lenihan to Bp. McFarland, Bridgeport, March 20, 1865.

[55] *Ibid.*

[56] AUND, F66–3918, Bp. McFarland to Paris Propagation of the Faith, Providence, June 12, 1865.

[57] *Sadlier's Catholic Almanac and Ordo for 1866* (New York, 1866), p. 173:

School		Boys	Girls
Bridgeport	St. James	120	130
Norwalk	St. Mary	75	80
Danbury	St. Peter	90	115
Stamford	St. John	125	130

[58] APF, Lettere, 1870, vol. 364, f937v, Rome Abp. Giovanni Simeoni to Bp. McFarland, Rome, November 30, 1870 (draft).

[59] APF, S.C. Amer. Cent., vol. 364, f1007r, Bp. McFarland to Simeoni, Providence, March 10, 1871.

[60] Quoted in Albert E. Van Dusen, *Connecticut* (New York, 1961), p. 221.

[61] *Norwalk Gazette*, April 24, 1855. "Can a Romish Priest be a True American Citizen?" The answer given by the paper was "no," since his total allegiance was to a temporal power—the pope. The paper furnished an oath which it claimed, falsely, that every priest in America was bound to take: "I, from this time forward, will be faithful and obedient to my Lord, the Pope, and his successors. The councils with which they trust me, I will not discover to any man, to the injury of the Pope, and his successors. I will assist them to *retain and defend the Popedom* against all men. I will carefully conserve, defend, and promote the rights, honors, privileges, and authority of the Pope. I will not be in any council, fact, or treaty, in which anything prejudicial to the person, rights, or power of the Pope is contrived and if I shall know any such things I will hinder them to the utmost of my power, and with all possible speed, I will signify them to the Pope. To the utmost of my power I will observe the Pope's commands, and *make others observe them*. I will impugn, and persecute all heretics, and rebels to my Lord, the Pope." Bishops and Jesuits were bound to use the confessional as a means of coercing the faithful to obedience and to the destruction of the enemies of the Church. The article concludes, "The individual votes as the priest dictates; the priest follows the decree of the prelate, and so he controls the election as shall best serve the interest of the Pope, the establishment of the Church and its subsequent complete rule over the country. The final extinction of the heresy of Protestantism in free America, by management of the ballot box, is the object of all ranks from the Pope downward."

[62] *Norwalk Gazette*, May 30, 1854. A jewelry advertisement poked fun at the party's secrecy: "Be sure to purchase all your Jewelry at Clark's and you will cease to KNOW NOTHING, for you will know you have got a bargain, if nothing else." October 3, 1854: "The man who could see through a mill–stone was hired to penetrate a certain granite building, with his eyes, to find out the secrets of the Know–Nothings." Throughout 1854, Bridgeport's *Republican Farmer* attacked the party in its editorials and reporting, as did the *Stamford Advocate*, but to a lesser extent.

[63] *Norwalk Gazette*, November 28, 1854.

[64] *Norwalk Gazette*, November 21, 1854; March 6, 1855; August 12, 1856: The Norwalk press continually protected its own against attack, whether Catholic priests or local Irish immigrants. The attacks against the Church and the hierarchy continued, describing various alleged attrocities perpetrated by Catholic hierarchs throughout the country. However, those priests and faithful in Norwalk were seen as "exceptions to the general rule," who had, despite their Roman faith, proved themselves loyal and productive fellow–citizens. Cf. an article entitled "Do the Irish give as well as receive?" in the March 6, 1855 number of the *Norwalk Gazette*.

[65] *Norwalk Gazette*, November 28, 1854.

[66] *Concilia Provincialia, Baltimori Habita Ab Anno 1829 usque ad Annum 1849* (Baltimori, MDCCCLI): The First Provincial Council of Baltimore (1829) urged bishops to secure the property deed prior to dedication of any church (Decree V). The council also denied that contributors of any congregation had the right of ownership or "jus patronatus" because of their donations (Decree VI). Clerics or laymen who disobeyed these decrees should be punished (Decrees VII; VIII). The subsequent four provincial councils (1837, 1840, 1843, 1847) reaffirmed these decrees, and the First Plenary Council of Baltimore (1852) extended them to the whole country (Decrees II, XV, XVI, XVII).

[67] "*Republican Farmer,*" May 8, 1855.

[68] *Republican Farmer,* May 8, 1855. *Stamford Advocate,* May 8, 1855: The *Advocate* praised the address of their native son as being without fault and very American since he employed a "preponderance of strong, honest Anglo–Saxon words, to the exclusion of those derived from the Latin + Greek." Stamford's paper, along with others in the county, condemned the *Farmer* for what they considered a personal attack upon the governor.

[69] APF, ACTA 1857, vol. 221, f98rv, Abp. John Hughes to Propaganda, New York, November 28, 1856.

[70] *Norwalk Gazette*, April 3, 1856.

[71] Hamilton D. Hurd, *History of Fairfield County, Connecticut* (Philadelphia, 1881), p. 101: The first Connecticut troops killed during the war were members of the German Rifle Company of Bridgeport, during a mishap at the Bridgeport train station on April 19, 1861.

[72] *Norwalk Gazette*, December 16, 1892.

[73] AUND, Bp. Francis McFarland to Paris Propagation of the Faith, Providence, December 20, 1862.

[74] APF, S.C. AMER. CENT., 1861–1862, vol. 19, f719r, Bishop Francis McFarland to Propaganda Fide, Hartford, May 16, 1862.

[75] AUND, F66–3912, Bp. Francis McFarland to Paris Propagation of the Faith, Providence, January 1, 1862.

[76] APF, S.C. AMER. CENT. 1864–1865, vol. 20, f911r–912r, Rev. Ambrose Manahan to Propaganda Fide, Danbury, July 20, 1864.

[77] APF, S.C. AMER. CENT. 1866–1867, vol. 21, f333v, Natalie Hannesley to Cardinal Barnabo, Norwalk, July 11, 1866.

[78] AUND, F66–3924, Bishop Francis McFarland to Paris Propagation of the Faith, Providence, July 6, 1867.

[79] ABPT, William F. Kearney, Parish notes: "Bridgeport, Old and Combined." Henceforth referred to as "Kearney notes."

[80] AHTFD, Annual Parochial Reports. Chapels were established in Fairfield (1854); Greenwich (1859); Westport (1860); New Canaan (1863); Ridgefield (1867), and were administered by the rectors of the canonical missions of the larger towns.

[81] AHTFD, Annual Parochial Reports.

[82] AUND, F66–3909, Bishop Francis P. McFarland to Paris Propagation of the Faith, Providence, January 16, 1860.

[83] APF, S.C. AMER. CENT., 1870, vol. 23, f548r–549v.

[84] AHTFD, Annual Parish Reports, 1872.

[85] James H. O'Donnell, *History of the Diocese of Hartford* (Boston, 1900), p. 461.

[86] *Danbury Times,* March 19, 1851.

[87] *Norwalk Gazette*, March 10, 1868. The editor appealed to the non–Catholic

citizens of Norwalk to support the Catholics in their fund drive for a new stone St. Mary's Church. He wrote, "At least let the money that is usually wasted in maddening the brain of poor Pat [with liquor] on electionday [sic], be given to build him instead a church. . . ."

[88] AUND, Paris Propagation of the Faith, F66–3919, McFarland to Propagation of the Faith, Providence, February 7, 1866.

[89] The baptismal records of the various early missions reveal the Irish majority among the Catholic population of Fairfield County until 1860:
Bridgeport: St. James (and missions): (1842–1860)—1,555 baptisms, of which 19 were Germans; 2 Puerto Ricans; 1 Dutch; 1 French, and the remainder Irish.
    St. Mary (and missions): (1857–1860)—276 baptisms, of which 21 were Germans and the remainder Irish.
Norwalk: St. Mary (and missions): (1854–1860)—575 baptisms of which 2 were Germans, and the remainder Irish.
Stamford: St. John (and missions): (1847–1860)—365 baptisms of which 2 were Germans, and the remainder Irish.
Danbury: St. Peter (and missions): (1847–1860)—850 baptisms of which 3 were Germans, and the remainder Irish.

[90] AHTFD, Annual Parochial Reports: In the year of the opening of the new church, the estimated total property value of St. Augustine's was $285,000, which included the church, rectory, land, a separate lot on Washington Ave., and two cemeteries. St. Mary's estimated value at the time of the opening of its new church on Pembroke St. was $120,000.

[91] *Catholic Transcript,* June 15, 1900. AHTFD., Annual Parochial Reports: St. Mary's estimated value was $110,000., which included the new church, rectory and land, four separate houses and cemetary.

[92] AHTFD, Annual Parochial Reports: Stamford's St. John's estimated property value in 1886 was $250,000., which included the church, rectory, convent, school, furniture, land, and cemetary. St. Peter's in Danbury reported an estimated value of $103,000., in 1875, including the new church, rectory, outhouse, land, and furniture. St. Rose in Newtown reported a value of $50,000 in 1883.

[93] Samuel Koenig, *Immigrant Settlements in Connecticut, Their Growth and Characteristics* (Hartford, 1938), p. 17.

[94] ALOCK, Florence Matthews Diary. "Lockwood—1870 Census." The Matthews employed ten servants: six were born in Ireland, three in France; one was Black, born in New York City.

[95] *Norwalk Gazette,* November 28, 1871.

[96] AHTFD, McFarland Papers, Episcopal Correspondence, 1872, Abp. John Hughes to Bp. McFarland, New York, July, 12, 1872.

[97] AUND, F66–3919, Bishop Francis McFarland to Paris Propagation of the Faith, Providence, February 7, 1866.

Chapter II: The 'New' Catholic Immigrants

[1] Gerald Shaugnessy, *Has the Immigrant Kept the Faith?* (New York, 1925), pp. 159; 165; 211.

[2] APF, Lettere 1883, vol. 379, f191v, Propaganda Fide to Bishop Lawrence McMahon, Rome, April 12, 1883 (draft): Besides the Bishop of Hartford, those of Boston, Springfield and Providence received a copy of this letter

requesting information on the German Catholics in New England, who were reportedly ". . . destitute of all religious assistance, with few of their own priests sent able to speak their language."

[3] APF, S.O.C.G. 1887, vol. 1026, f943r–944v, Bishop Kilian Flasch to Cardinal Simeoni, LaCrosse, April 7, 1885.

[4] APF, Acta 1887, vol. 257, f186r–217v, "Relazione con Sommario e Voto Intorno all 'elezione di quasi–parrocchie distinte per nazionalità negli Stati Uniti d'America."

[5] APF, S.O.C.G., 1887, vol. 1026, f1109r–1143v, Ireland and Keane to Simeoni, "Observations sur la question Des Allemandes Catholiques dans l'Eglise aux Etats-Units," Rome, December 9, 1886.

[6] APF, S.O.C.G., 1887, vol. 1026, f945r–948v, American Archbishops to Giovanni Cardinal Simeoni, New York, December 17, 1886.

[7] Acta Sanctae Sedis, Romae 1891–92, vol. 24, pp. 684–686.

[8] ASV, DelApUSA, DelAP, 3a, "Istruzioni speciali a Mgr. Delegato Francesco Satolli an. 1892."

[9] The entire correspondence may be found in APF, APNS, 1896, Rub. 153, vol. 98, f841–111r.

[10] APF, APNS (1897), vol. 119, R. 153, f360r, Card. Ledóchowski to Abp. Sebastiano Martinelli, Rome, April 26, 1897.

[11] APF, APNS (1897), vol. 119, R. 153, f361r, Abp. Sebastiano Martinelli to the United States Bishops, Washington, May 12, 1897.

[12] ASV, SdiS (1902), R. 280, Fasc., 10, "Rapporto sulle condizioni della Chiesa Cattolica negli Stati Uniti d'America, giugno–novembre 1886 da Monsignor Germano Straniero, pontificio ablegato presso Sua Ema Rvma il Sig. Card. Gibbons, Arcìves. di Baltimora." APF, APNS (1899), R. 153, vol. 169, f518r–524r, Rev. Peter Saurusaitis to Pope Leo XIII. Waterbury January 25, 1899.

[13] Connecticut Catholic, April 2, 1892; Catholic Transcript, October 14, 1893; March 3; April 7, 1894; December 13, 1906.

[14] Catholic Transcript, October 10, 1901.

[15] Haines built the Danbury and Bethel horse railway in 1887.

[16] Danbury Evening News, April 30, 1912.

[17] Danbury Evening News, April 29; 30; May 2, 1912. The Catholic Transcript, May 9, 1912.

[18] Danbury Evening News, May 2, 1912.

[19] Dolores Ann Liptak, European Immigrants and the Catholic Church in Connecticut, 1870–1920, (New York, 1987). This is the most indepth study of this subject to date.

[20] Catholic Transcript, January 18, 1901.

[21] Bridgeport Sunday Post, November 4, 1934.

[22] Bridgeport Sunday Post, October 21, 1934.

[23] Connecticut Catholic, July 3, 1880.

[24] AHTFD., Annual Parochial Reports: St. Joseph's reported the following statistics for the year 1886–1887:

Baptisms	65	Receipts	$ 2,500.00
Marriages	18	Debt	$ 4,117.45
1st Communion	27	Property Value	$16,000.00 (church, rectory, land, and adjacent lot, furniture)
Converts	2		

[25] AHTFD, Annual Parochial Reports: St. Joseph, 1890–1901. St. Joseph's property included the frame church, rectory, school, convent and land, valued in 1901 at nearly $30,000.

[26] *Catholic Transcript,* September 12, 1901.

[27] John Tracy Ellis, *American Catholicism* (Chicago, 1969), pp. 137–140.

[28] *Bridgeport Sunday Post,* October 14, 1934.

[29] *Bridgeport Sunday Post,* November 4, 1934.

[30] *Bridgeport Sunday Post,* January 15, 1978.

[31] ABPT, Parish Files, St. John Nepomucene, S. Loewith to Bp. McMahon, Bridgeport, April 6, 1889.

[32] AHTFD, Episcopal Papers, Bp. McMahon to S. Loewith, Hartford, April 9, 1889.

[33] AHTFD, Parrochial Correspondence, Michael Simko, Joseph Rosko, and Andrew Huyadi to Bp. McMahon, Bridgeport, September 13, 1890.

[34] Interview by the author of Dr. Michael Simko, Bridgeport, August 31, 1985. Dr. Simko is the son of Michael Simko, one of the founders of St. John Nepomucene Church.

[35] "Saint John Nepomucene Parish, 1891–1966, Diamond Jubilee."

[36] AHTFD, Annual Parochial Reports: St. John's first annual report was for the months April through December, 1891:

Baptisms	106	Receipts	$ 6,034.35
Marriages	36	Debt (Construction)	$ 5,000.00
Deaths	13	Property Value	$14,500.00
Catholics	about 1,400	Sunday School	36
Families	about 260		

[37] AHTFD, Annual Parochial Reports, 1896.

[38] ABPT, Parish files: St. John Nepomucene, Rev. Francis Pribyl to Bp. Tierney, Hazleton, Pa., April 25, 1897.

[39] AHTFD, Annual Parochial Reports, 1897.

[40] AHTFD, Episcopal Papers, 1899, Rev. Francis J. Pribyl to Bp. Tierney, Bridgeport, n.d.

[41] AHTFD, Episcopal Papers, 1899, Bp. Tierney to Rev. Francis J. Pribyl, Hartford, March 3, 1899.

[42] AHTFD, Annual Parochial Reports, 1898: Rev. J. Kossalko to Bp. Tierney, Bridgeport January 31, 1899.

[43] *The Catholic Transcript,* September 8; 29, 1899. The priests were sent, according to the *Transcript* to "harmonize all the heterogeneous elements of . . . the vast parish into one homogenitous corporation. . . ."

[44] ABPT, Parish Files, St. John Nepomucene, Rev. Joseph Kosslako to Bp. Tierney, Bridgeport, June 28, 1900. AHTFD, Episcopal Papers, 1900, Rev. Joseph Kossalko to Bp. Tierney, Bridgeport, July 9, 1900.

[45] "Golden Jubilee, 1891–1941, Church of St. John Nepomucene," p. 22.

[46] AHTFD, Episcopal Papers, Michael Quaka to Bp. Tierney, Bridgeport, May 18, 1907.

[47] ABPT, Parish files: St. John Nepomucene, Procurator of the Bishop of Hartford to Abp. Diomede Falconio, OFM, Hartford, December 7, 1907.

[48] AHTFD, Episcopal Papers, Abp. Falconio to Bp. Tierney, Washington, D.C., January 12, 1907.

[49] ABPT, Parish Files: St. John Nepomucene, Bp. Tierney to Abp. Falconio, Hartford, January 14, 1907.

[50] ABPT, Parish Files: St. John Nepomucene, Procurator of the Bp. of Hartford to Abp. Falconio, Hartford December 7, 1907.

[51] *Ibid.*

[52] ABPT, Parish Files: St. John Nepomucene, Abp. Falconio, to Bp. Tierney, Washington, D.C., January 17, 1908.

[53] AHTFD, Episcopal Papers, Abp. Falconio, to Bp. Tierney, Washington, D.C., October 21, 1911.

[54] *Bridgeport Post*, May 24; 25; 29, 1916: Only one other factional incident disrupted the parish life of the Slovak community in Bridgeport. On the morning of May 24, 1916, a large group of women parishioners of Sts. Cyril and Methodius stormed the rectory, destroyed the interior, and threatened the pastor in protest over his recent appointment and his recent removal from office of various parishioners. A petition for the removal of the Rev. Gaspar Panik was sent to the Bishop by 500 of the 4,000 parishioners. Thirteen of the organizers of the riot were found guilty in court, fined, and incarcerated for twenty–four hours. They were also excommunicated by Bishop Nilan, who came to Bridgeport to address the parish, confirm Panik's appointment, and assure the congregation that any further violent outbreaks would be met with further excommunications. There were none.

[55] *Catholic Transcript*, October 17, 1912.

[56] *Catholic Transcript*, February 20, 1913.

[57] *Catholic Transcript*, June 5, 1941.

[58] Interview by the author or Dr. Michael Simko, Bridgeport, August 31, 1985.

[59] *Catholic Transcript*, June 18, 1914.

[60] *Catholic Transcript*, September 30, 1915.

[61] Jubilé d'Or de la Paroisse St. Antoine de Padove de Bridgeport, Connecticut le 12 Novembre 1944," p. 5.

[62] *Ibid.* Other societies formed in conjunction with this original organization were the Naturalization or Citizenship Club, originally with 45 members, which began on October 13, 1892; the Dramatic Club, with 21 members, begun in May, 1893. *Bridgeport Sunday Post*, November 25, 1934: the Société de Saint Jean Baptiste later joined with the St. Jean Sick Benefit Society.

[63] *Ibid.* The 1892 census of the French population of Bridgeport revealed the professional diversity of the community. There were an estimated 600 French Canadians in Bridgeport at the time. There were 6 painters, 19 carpenters, 10 masons, 8 mechanics, 6 molders, 7 blacksmiths, 9 burnishers, 1 silversmith, 3 barbers, 7 clerks, 9 merchants, 3 brass–workers, 2 saddle and harness makers, 8 shoemakers, 4 musicians, 2 plumbers, 2 engineers. There were only 15 who owned their own property. Fifty-six had voting rights, and there was one French–Canadian selectman.

[64] APF, APNS (1896), Rub. 153, vol. 98, f124r–125v, Abp. John J. Williams to Card. Ledóchowski, Boston, September 30, 1896; Bishops of the Boston Province to Card. Ledóchowski, Boston, September 30, 1896.

[65] APF, S.C.Amer. Cent., 1892, vol. 58, f243r–254r, "Memoire sur La situation des Canadiens Francaises, bien Etats–Units de Amerique, Par Msgr. Antoine Racine, Eveque De Sherbrook," Sherbrook, Canada, February 26, 1892. For a complete study of the relationship of the French–Canadians and the Church in the United States, cf. Robert Rumilly, *Histoire Des Franco–Americains* (Lazard, Montreal, 1958).

[66] "La Travilleur," September 9, 1887, quoted in Dolores A. Liptak, *European Immigrants and the Catholic Church in Connecticut, 1870–1920*, p. 255.

[67] "Jubilé d'Or de La Paroisse St. Antoine de Padoue de Bridgeport, Connecticut le 12 Novembre 1944," p. 5. Those present at the March, 1892 meeting were the society's collectors: Edward Poisson, Joseph Bousquet, Philip Lariviere, Antoine Cadorette as well as the two elected as trustees.

[68] AHTFD, Annual Parochial Reports, St. Louis Church, New Haven, 1893.

[69] The other French churches in Connecticut in 1896 were St. James, Danielsonville (est. 1870); St. Laurent, Meriden (est. 1880); St. Louis, New Haven (est. 1886); St. Anne, Waterbury (est. 1886).

[70] AHTFD, Annual Parochial Reports, St. Anthony, 1896:

Receipts	$ 2,117.77	Baptisms	13
Debt	$10,297.70	Easter Communions	400
Property Value	$10,000.00	Marriages	2

Number of Catholics: 676 (50 are boarders)
Number of Families: 122

[71] AHTFD, Annual Parochial Reports: St. Anthony, 1898: There were 35 pupils who attended the Sunday school class during the year.

[72] AHTFD, Annual Parochial Reports: St. Anthony, 1902: The total number of French Catholics in 1902 was estimated to be 400.

[73] AHTFD, Annual Parochial Reports: St. Anthony, 1905. "Jubilé d'Or de La Paroisse St. Antoine de Padoue de Bridgeport, Connecticut le 12 Novembere 1944," p. 6: The school was closed in 1910 by the City Board of Health, since it was judged unhealthy for children to study in basement areas. The parish completed a school building in 1936.

[74] Herbert Geller, Bridgeport, "The Ethnic City" (Bridgeport, 1982), p. 56. This two–volume work is a reprinting of a series of articles written by Herbert Geller which appeared in the Bridgeport Sunday Post from 1977 through 1980. Henceforth it will be referred to as Geller's Bridgeport.

[75] Liptak, op. cit., p. 221.

[76] AHTFD, Annual Parochial Reports, 1900: St. Stephen's Church on Bostwick Avenue reported a membership of 1,000 Latin Rite Catholics. Holy Trinity Byzantine Catholic Church, also in the West End, reported 60 members, while the Hungarian Catholics of the Ruthenian Rite remaining on the East Side of Bridgeport were estimated to number 200.

[77] AHTFD, Episcopal Papers, 1897, Abp. Michael Corrigan to Bp. Michael Tierney, New York, November 27, 1897.

[78] AHTFD, Episcopal Papers, 1914 (copy), Bishop John Nilan to Abp. Henry Moeller, Hartford, November 3, 1914.

[79] Catholic Transcript, April 7, 1910.

[80] The Hungarian Catholics of the Latin and Eastern Rites originally met in the basement of St. Joseph Church, South Norwalk, until the second Hungarian Catholic mission of the Latin Rite was established there in 1907, under the patronage of St. Ladislaus. Chernitzsky's apostolic work extended also to his conationals in Stamford during his South Norwalk pastorate.

[81] Bridgeport Sunday Post, October 14, 1934.

[82] ASV, DelApUSA Stati Uniti 28, Card. Ledóchowski to Abp. Satolli, Rome June 20, 1896.

[83] ASV, DelApUSA, Stati Uniti 28, Abp. Satolli to Card. Ledóchowski, Washington, undated draft.

[84] ASV, DelApUSA, Stati Uniti 28, Decree of the Sacred Congregation of Propaganda Fide, Rome, May 1, 1897.

[85] APF, APNS (1903), Rub. 153, vol. 264, f313r–314r, Austro–Hungarian

Ambassador to the Holy See to Card. Ledóchowski, Rome, undated. (The Propaganda registered the communication on October 2, 1903.)

[86] AHTFD, Episcopal Correspondence, 1896, Abp. Michael Corrigan to Bp. Michael Tierney, New York, October 1, 1896.

[87] AHTFD, Episcopal Correspondence, 1900, A.A. Lings to Bp. Michael Tierney, Yonkers, N.Y., July 29, 1900.

[88] AHTFD, Episcopal Correspondence, 1900, Representatives of the Greek Church to Bp. Tierney, Bridgeport, July 5, 1900; Abp. Sebastiano Martinelli to Bp. Tierney, Washington, D.C., November 24, 1900.

[89] *Connecticut Supplement* (Bridgeport, 1944), vol. XII, p. 350.

[90] AHTFD, Annual Parochial Reports, 1900: The West End counted only 60 Eastern Rite Hungarian Catholics.

[91] *Geller's Bridgeport*, vol. II, p. 78.

[92] *The Connecticut Supplement*, vol. XII, pp. 359–360.

[93] AHTFD, Annual Parochial Reports, 1900; Episcopal Correspondence, 1901, Rev. Eugene Volkay to Bp. Tierney, Bridgeport, November 6, 1901. *Catholic Transcript*, April 7, 1910. By 1910, the Eastern Rite community of Hungarian Catholics in South Norwalk petitioned Hartford to have their own mission church which would be placed under the care of Holy Trinity Church in Bridgeport.

[94] *Ibid.*

[95] AHTFD, Episcopal Correspondence, 1906, Rt. Rev. Hodobay to Bp. Tierney, Philadelphia, February 15, 1906.

[96] *The Bridgeport Morning Telegram and Union*, December 26, 1904. AHTFD, Episcopal Correspondence, 1905, Rt. Rev. Hodobay to Bp. Tierney, Philadelphia, January 3, 1905; Bp. Ortynski to Bp. Tierney, Philadelphia, September 16, 1908.

[97] AHTFD, Annual Parochial Reports, St. Joseph; St. Ladislaus, South Norwalk.

[98] *Catholic Transcript*, May 16, 1912.

[99] Two Eastern Rite Catholic churches in Bridgeport were led into schism from the Catholic Church by their priests. St. Mary The Virgin Ruthenian Catholic Church on Beach Street broke with Rome in 1929. St. John the Baptist Church broke with Rome in 1931, led by their pastor the Rev. Orestes Chornock.

[100] *Catholic Transcript*, June 27, 1912.

[101] Daniel S. Buczek, *Immigrant Pastor; The Life of the Right Rev. Lucyan Bojnowski of New Britain, Connecticut* (Waterbury, 1974), p. 153, ft. nt. 8. The first Polish priest assigned to St. John's was the Rev. Lucyan Bojnowski who served the Catholic Poles of Bridgeport during 1895.

[102] AHTFD, Annual Parochial Reports, St. Michael the Archangel, 1899.

[103] Paul Fox, *The Polish National Catholic Church* (Scranton, n.d.), p. 30. "St. Joseph's Polish National Catholic Church Diamond Jubilee Booklet," (Bridgeport, 1982).

[104] AHTFD, Episcopal Correspondence, Msgr. Bojnowski to Bp. Tierney, New Britain, October 4, 1899.

[105] AHTFD, Episcopal Correspondence, Bp. Tierney to Pastors of the Diocese of Hartford, Hartford, October 6, 1899.

[106] APF, APNS (1899), vol. 168, rub. 153, f644r, Rev. John Synnott to Card. Ledóchwoski, Hartford, September 21, 1899.

[107] AHTFD, Annual Financial Reports, St. Michael the Archangel, 1899.

[108] *Bridgeport Evening Post*, July 2, 1906.

[109] *Catholic Transcript*, September 24; December 31, 1903; October 8, 1908.

[110] AHTFD, Episcopal Papers, Rev. James Donovan to the Very Rev. Hyacinth Fudzinski, D.D., O.M.C. (copy), Hartford, June 30, 1906; July 18, 1908.

[111] *Catholic Transcript,* April 7, 1910. Interview by the author of Msgr. John Horgan, Bridgeport, August 25, 1986.

[112] ABPT, Parish Files, St. Michael the Archangel, #1: William Redden to the Rev. John G. Murray, Bridgeport, August 21, 1906.

[113] ABPT, Parish Files, St. Michael the Archangel, #1, Abp. Falconio to Bp. Tierney, Washington, D.C. December 15; 20, 1906.

[114] ABPT, Roman Correspondence, Card. Ledóchowski, "Instructio S. Congregationis de Propaganda Fide ad Rmos. ordinarios locorum, in quibus Polonarum Congregationis existunt," Romae, May 2, 1898.

[115] ABPT, Parish Files, St. Michael the Archangel, #1: Abp. Falconio to John Kuszaj (copy), Washington, D.C., December 20, 1906.

[116] "St. Joseph's Polish National Catholic Church Diamond Jubilee Booklet," (Bridgeport, 1982). AHTFD, Annual Parish Reports, St. Michael the Archangel, 1906, 1907. There was a decrease in the number of Catholics at the time of the split from 3,000 in 1906, to 2,150 in 1907. The number of deaths in that year was only 27, mostly children.

[117] *Bridgeport Telegram,* February 19, 1907.

[118] *Geller's Bridgeport,* vol. 2: John Kuszaj, Francis Sniadecki, Ksawery Januszkiewicz, Peter Kubus, John Tatarzycki, Anthony Wolski, Vincent Czerwonka, Martin Buczer, Joseph Dymkowski, Anthony Dabrowski, Francis Paul.

[119] ABPT, Parish Files, St. Michael the Archangel, #1: William Redden to the Rev. John G. Murray, Bridgeport, n.d.; same to same, Bridgeport, August 21, 1906.

[120] *Bridgeport Sunday Post,* October 28, 1934. Sterling Street was renamed Pulaski Street in honor of the Poles, through the influence of Louis Abriola, the Italian alderman from Bridgeport.

[121] *Catholic Transcript,* August 22, 1907.

[122] AHTFD, Annual Parochial Reports, St. Michael the Archangel, 1908: The statistics for the first year of Fr. Baran's administration are as follows:

Baptisms	135	Receipts	$ 59,096.37
Confirmations	274	Debt	$ 61,274.96
1st Communions	30	Property Value	$111,855.19
Marriages	27	Sunday School	127 (3 teachers)
Deaths	28		

[123] Robert F. Foerster, *The Italian Emigration of Our Times* (Cambridge, 1919), p. 390 ff.

[124] John Tracy Ellis, *Documents of American Church History* (Milwaukee, 1962), p. 463.

[125] APF, ACTA 1883, vol. 252, f1099r–1241r, "Relazione con Sommario e nota di Archivio circa la presente condizione della Chiesa Cattolica negli Stati Uniti di America," Rome, October 1, 6, 8, 1883.

[126] APF, S.O.C.G., 1885, vol. 1023, f848r–850r, Archbishop James Gibbons and Bishop Thomas Becker to Giovanni Card. Simeoni, Wilmington, "Idibus Ianuariis [*sic*]," 1885.

[127] APF, ACTA 1887, vol. 257, f507r–529r, "Rapporto sull 'Emigrazione Italiana con Sommario," Rome, November, 1887.

[128] Edward C. Stibilli, *The St. Raphael Society for the Protection of The Italian Immigrants, 1887–1923* (unpub. PhD. dissert., South Bend, 1977). This is one of the most complete works on the subject to date.

[129] AGS, 625/1b, Rev. Francesco Zaboglio to Bp. Scalabrini, New Orleans, December 21, 1891.

[130] AHTFD, Episcopal Papers, Bp. McMahon to Card. Simeoni (copy), Hartford, February 10, 1888.

[131] AGS, 550/1, Rev. Francesco Zaboglio to Bp. Scalabrini, New York, March 20, 1891.

[132] AGS, 648, Rev. Carlo Bertorelli to the Rev. Francesco Zaboglio, New York, n.d.

[133] AGS, 648, Rev. Carlo Bertorelli to Rev. Francesco Zaboglio, Pittsburgh, August 26, 1892.

[134] APF, APNS (1895), vol. 74, Rub. 153, f840r, Annual Diocesan Report of Hartford, 1894.

[135] AGS, 648, Rev. Beniamino Bertò to Bp. Scalabrini, Bridgeport, n.d.

[136] *The Bridgeport Morning Telegram and Union*, December 23, 1904.

[137] *Ibid.*

[138] Anthony J. Tomanio and Lucille N. LaMacchia, "The Italian-American Community in Bridgeport," (Bridgeport, June, 1953), University of Bridgeport Student Monograph, #5, p. 15. Other Protestant missions for the Italians in the Bridgeport area were those of the Pentecostal Church on Green Street; Trinity Episcopal Church on Courtland Street; and St. Michael the Archangel Episcopal Church in Tunxis Hill.

[139] *Catholic Transcript,* October 10, 1901.

[140] *Catholic Transcript,* January 18, 1901.

[141] "Golden Jubilee 1903–1953, Holy Rosary Church, Bridgeport, Connecticut"; "Re–dedication Booklet of the Church of the Sacred Heart, Stamford, Sunday, May 12, 1968." According to local folklore, Ceruti came to Bridgeport by mistake. Thinking he was in Stamford, so the story goes, Ceruti alighted from his train in Bridgeport. When informed that the Italian community of Bridgeport was larger than that of Stamford, he decided to stay and begin work. Unfortunately, there is no shred of truth to this tale, since all of the documentation points to his having been assigned directly to Bridgeport.

[142] AGS, 648, Rev. Gaetano Ceruti to Bp. Scalabrini, Bridgeport, April 25, 1903.

[143] AGS, 648, "Manifesto del Comitato Provvisorio," Bridgeport, January 23, 1903.

[144] *The Bridgeport Morning Telegram and Union*, March 21, 1904: The wood frame church, which was then the smallest in the city, was only 90 feet long, 35 feet wide and 25 feet high, with a seating capacity of 200 persons.

[145] *Catholic Transcript,* January 11, 1901. The Churches of St. Stephen and St. Michael opened in 1900 to serve the respective Hungarian and Polish communities of Bridgeport. St. Peter's territorial parish also was founded in that year.

[146] AHTFD, Annual Parish Reports, "Our Lady of Pompeii; Holy Rosary," 1904, 1905. In 1905 the total property value of Holy Rosary was $19,000. including church, house and land. The total number of parishioners was 3,000 persons.

| Baptisms | 181 | First Communions | 100 |
| Marriages | 40 | Easter Communions | 300 |

[147] AHTFD, Episcopal Correspondence, Bp. Tierney to Abp. Falconio (copy), Hartford, December 21, 1904.

[148] *Bridgeport Morning Telegram and Union,* January 10, 1905.

[149] AGS, 648, Bp. Tierney to Bp. Scalabrini, Hartford, March 28, 1905.

[150] AGS, 554/6, Rev. Pietro Novati to Rev. Domenico Vicentini, Boston, December 6, 1906.

[151] AGS, 554/8, Rev. Domenico Vicentini to the Rev. Antonio Demo, Piacenza, September 13, 1908.

[152] *Bridgeport Sunday Post,* October 7, 1934.

[153] "Golden Jubilee 1903–1953, Holy Rosary Church, Bridgeport, Connecticut," (Bridgeport, 1953), pp. 13–15.

[154] *Bridgeport Sunday Post,* December 30, 1934.

[155] AHTFD, Rev. William Wokovich Materials, William Wolkovich, "Lithuanian Origins in Connecticut and the Reverend Joseph Zebris," unpubl. paper (1976), pp. 44–49.

[156] AHFTD, Annual Parochial Reports, St. George, 1907.

[157] ABPT, Parish Files, St. George, Rev. Matthew Plavzinaitis to Bp. Tierney, Bridgeport, May 26, 1907.

[158] *Bridgeport Evening Post,* October 14, 1907. *Catholic Transcript,* October 17, 1907.

[159] ABPT, Kearney notes.

[160] William Wolkovich, *Lithuanian Pioneer Priest of New England* (Franciscan Press, 1980), p. 160.

[161] ABPT, Parish Files, St. George, Bp. Tierney to the Rev. Victor Paukszto, Hartford, September 18, 1907.

[162] *Bridgeport Sunday Post,* December 30, 1934.

[163] APF, APNS (1899), vol. 168, Rub. 153, f518r–524r, Rev. Peter Saurusaitis to Pope Leo XIII, Waterbury, January 25, 1899.

[164] AHTFD, Episcopal Papers, Rev. Victor Paukszto to Bp. Tierney, Bridgeport, September 20, 1907.

[165] AHTFD, Episcopal Papers, Rev. Felix Baran to Bp. Tierney, Bridgeport, September 22, 1907.

[166] AHTFD, Episcopal Papers, Rev. Felix Baran to Bp. Tierney, Bridgeport, September 25, 1907.

[167] Marge Fenick, "The American Lithuanians in the Bridgeport Community," (Univ. of Bridgeport, 1957), Student Monograph No. 10, p. 7.

[168] *Bridgeport Telegram,* June 30, 1924.

[169] *Catholic Transcript,* November 21, 1912.

[170] *Bridgeport Sunday Post,* May 26, 1963.

[171] Interview by the author of the Rev. Aloysius J. Hribsek, Fairfield, November 3, 1986.

[172] "Spomenica posvečenja slovenske pim. kat. cerkve sv. križa die 28. nov. 1915. Souvenir of the Dedication of the R.C. Sloven. Church of the Holy Cross, Bridgeport, Conn."

[173] John A. Arnez, *Slovenian Community in Bridgeport, Conn.* (New York, 1971), Studia Slovenica, Special Series, no. 2, pp. 11–12: Fr. Zakrajsek to Fr. Godina, New York, September 2, 1948.

[174] *Ave Maria,* September-October, 1930: The author is grateful to the Rev. Aloysius Hribsek, Pastor of Holy Cross Church, for translating this article and all other articles referred to from the Slovenian periodical, *Ave Maria.*

[175] *Ave Maria,* January, 1913, p. 17.

[176] Arnez, *op. cit.,* p. 12: Their were eight parishes from Slovenia represented in the church committee in Bridgeport:

PARISH	REPRESENTATIVES
Turnišče	Jožef Ceh; Frank Štefaner
Beltinci	Jurij Ferenčak; Štefan Virag
Bogojina	Štefan Pucko; Ivan Gjorek
Štrigova	Ivan Frass; Franc Nemec
Cankova	Leopold Zalman; Franc Benko
Selnica	Ivan Bakač; Pavel Cofek
Sobota	Štefan Škraban

Parishioners from the Styrian side of the Mura River: Martin Škrinjar.

[177] *Ibid.*, p. 13.

[178] *Ibid.*, p. 6.

[179] *Ibid.*, p. 17.

[180] *The Bridgeport Post*, February 7, 1950.

[181] Liptak, *op. cit.*, p. 7.

[182] *Catholic Transcript*, October 11, 1906.

[183] Ruth Andersen, *From Yankee to American; Connecticut 1865 to 1914* (Bridgeport, 1975), p. 38.

[184] U.S. Department of Commerce, *The Eighteenth Decennial Census of the United States; Census of Population, 1960* (Washington, D.C. 1963), Part 8: "Connecticut," pp. 8–7.

[185] Andersen, *op. cit.*, p. 65.

[186] Scott–Fanton Museum, Danbury, Moss Correspondence, J. Moss Ives to Rollin Woodruff, Danbury, April 4, 1908.

[187] For the best treatment of the Anglo–Saxon myth, cf. Barbara Miller Solomon, *Ancestors and Immigrants. A Changing New England Tradition* (Cambridge, 1956).

[188] Edward A. Freeman, a contemporary and associate of Fiske, supported the idea that Blacks, Jews and Irish Catholics should be eliminated. He expressed this in his private correspondence, wishing that every Irishman would kill a Black and be hanged for the offense. Quoted in William R. W. Stephens, *Life and Letters of Edward A. Freeman* (London, 1895), vol. II, p. 240.

[189] *Connecticut Catholic*, June 13, 1896.

[190] Edward George Hartmann, *The Movement to Americanize the Immigrant* (New York, 1967), pp. 19–20.

[191] *Catholic Transcript*, March 18, 1915. By 1910 the majority of immigrants arriving in Connecticut were from southern and eastern European countries, a change since 1900. Estimating the foreign–born population in the state to be nearly 200,000, the United State census reported that by 1910 over 45% were unnaturalized aliens. The highest percentages of unnaturalized immigrants in Connecticut were the Italians (70.2%), Hungarians (69.2%), Austrians (67%), Russians (65.3%), French Canadians (50.9%). The percentage of unnaturalized Irish immigrants in the state was only 19.4%, and the German only 16.2% of their total immigrant population.

[192] *Catholic Transcript*, May 2, 1907.

[193] ASV, DelApUSA, DelAp, 3a. Istruzioni speciali a Mgr. Delegato Francesco Satolli an. 1892.

[194] *Catholic Transcript*, October 7, 1915.

[195] *Christian Science Monitor*, December 22, 1917.

[196] *Catholic Transcript*, March 14, 1918.

[197] *Catholic Transcript*, March 8, 1917.

[198] *Bridgeport Telegram and Union*, March 5, 1917.

[199] ASSND, Bpt. St. John Nepomucene, 20.4.5.2.

[200] ASSND, Bpt. St. Joseph, 20.4.5.2, Sr. Mary Justus to V. Rev. Sr. Marty Willabalda, Bridgeport, October 23, 1927.

[201] *Hartford Courant*, May 12, 1918.

[202] Mary Paul Mason, *Church–State Relationships in Education in Connecticut, 1633–1953*, (Washington, D.C., 1953), Catholic University of America Educational Research Monograph, vol. xvii, October 1, 1953, no. 6, p. 239.

[203] Herbert F. Janick, Jr., *A Diverse People, Connecticut 1914 to the Present* (Chester, 1975), p. 15.

[204] *Bridgeport Times–Farmer*, January 20, 1919.

[205] *Bridgeport Times–Farmer*, January 20, 1919. *Catholic Transcript*, January 23; 30, 1919.

[206] *Catholic Transcript*, March 13, 1919.

[207] *Ibid.*

[208] *Catholic Transcript*, October 27, 1921.

[209] Kenneth T. Jackson, *The Ku Klux Klan in the City, 1915–1930* (New York, 1967), p. 239: Bridgeport's Klan membership during the years 1915–1944 was estimated to have been 1,500.

[210] David A. Chalmers, *Hooded Americanism, The History of the Ku Klux Klan* (New York, 1981), p. 268.

[211] ABPT, Parish Files, St. James, Stratford, Bp. John Nilan to Abp. Giovanni Bonzano (copy), Hartford August 17, 1912.

[212] ABPT, Parish Files, St. Michael, Rev. Charles B. Ratajczak, OMC to Msgr. George B. Curtiss, Bridgeport, January 21, 1954. Bishop Nilan had granted this permission in response to petitions by Polish Catholics living in outlying areas of the state's larger cities, fearful that they might join with the Polish National Church unless some specialized provisions were made for them.

[213] St. Joseph Church, South Norwalk: Italian Baptismal Records, 1903–1921.

[214] Interview by the author of Joseph Lagano, Norwalk, August 12, 1985; interview by the author of John Pinto, Norwalk, August 30, 1985.

[215] Interview by the author of the Rev. Ross Baxter, Fairfield, September 4, 1985.

[216] Kenneth Walter Cameron, *The Catholic Revival in Episcopal Connecticut (1850–1925)* (Hartford, 1965), p. 278.

[217] Interview by the author of the Rev. Joseph Racioppi, Fairfield, October 22, 1985.

[218] Interview with the Rev. Joseph Racioppi.

[219] *Catholic Transcript*, June 27, 1907.

[220] *Ibid.*

[221] Carmelo DiSano, "Brief History of the American Church," p. 62.

[222] Cameron, *op. cit.*, p. 278.

[223] *Ibid.*

[224] Interview with the Rev. Joseph Racioppi.

[225] Interview with the Rev. Joseph Racioppi.

[226] Gerald Shaugnessy, *Has the Immigrant Kept the Faith?* (New York, 1969 reprint), pp. 271–273.

[227] *Bridgeport Times-Star*, November 20, 1930.

Chapter III: Women Religious and Catholic Life

[1] ABPT, Parish Files, St. John, Stamford, Rev. James O'Neill to Bp. Francis P. McFarland, Stamford, July 19, 1864.

[2] ASSND, Bridgeport, St. John Nepomocene, 20.4.5.2: "School Chronicle, 1945–1970."

[3] *America,* July 10, 1909.

[4] Austin Francis Munich, "The Beginnings of Roman Catholicism in Connecticut," Tercentenary Commission of the State of Connecticut, Committee on Historical Publications, (New Haven, 1935), vol. XLI, p. 15.

[5] Charles Beecher, ed., *Autobiography, Correspondence, etc., of Lyman Beecher, D.D.* (New York, 1865), vol. II, pp. 334–335.

[6] *Ibid.,* II, p. 336.

[7] Quoted in John Carroll Noonan, *Nativism in Connecticut, 1829–1860* (PhD. dissert, C.U.A., Washington, D.C., 1938), p. 98.

[8] Horace Bushnell, "Crisis in the Church," (Hartford, 1835), p. 23.

[9] Lyman Beecher, "A Plea for the West," (Cincinnati, 1835), p. 105.

[10] AUND, F66–3882, Bp. Tyler to Paris Propagation of the Faith, Providence, February 24, 1845.

[11] AUND, F66–3888, same to same, Providence, January 20, 1847.

[12] AUND, F66–3894, same to same, Providence, December 30, 1847.

[13] Mother Teresa Austin Carroll, "Leaves from the Annals of the Sisters of Mercy," (New York, 1889), p. 389.

[14] *Hartford Courant,* May 24, 1852.

[15] *Norwalk Gazette,* June 12, 1855.

[16] *Norwalk Gazette,* June 19, 1855.

[17] Sister Mary Cecilia O'Reilly, *Sisters of Mercy in the Diocese of Hartford* (Hartford, 1931), p. 53.

[18] *Connecticut Catholic,* May 6, 1876.

[19] *Sadlier's Catholic Directory, 1881* (New York, 1881), p. 306. Stamford's Catholic school counted 310 students in 1881.

[20] Mother Teresa Austin Carroll, *Leaves from the Annals of the Sisters of Mercy* (New York, 1889), p. 501.

[21] APF, Lettere, 1877, vol. 373, f435r, Abp. Giovanni Battista Agnozzi to Bp. Galberry, Rome, September 14, 1877 (letterbook).

[22] James Donovan, ed., *Decreta Synodorum Hartfordiensium, in unum volumen Collecta* (Hartford, 1902), Caput XVII "De Scholis," nos. 116, 117, 118, 119, p. 65.

[23] *The Catholic Church in the United States of America* (New York, 1912), vol. II, pp. 350–351.

[24] *Norwalk Gazette,* March 4, 1879.

[25] *Sadlier's Catholic Directory, 1881* (New York, 1881), p. 306.

[26] *Connecticut Catholic,* April 13, 1880.

[27] *Connecticut Catholic,* May 15, 1880.

[28] "A Century of Faith—1876–1976," St. Thomas Parish Anniversary Commemorative Book, p. 27.

[29] ABP, Kearny notes, Danbury, St. Peter.

[30] *Greenwich Times,* June 6, 1984.

[31] Sr. Maria Eulalia Herron, *The Sisters of Mercy in the United States* (New York, 1929), p. 109.

[32] Heffernan, *Catholic Education,* p. 45.

[33] APF, Lettere 1885, vol. 381, f257rv, Abp. Domenico Maria Jacobini to Bp. McMahon, Rome, May 7, 1885 (letterbook).

[34] APF, ACTA 1883, vol. 252, f1238r, "Relazione con Sommario e Nota di Archivio circa la Presente Condizione della Chiesa Cattolica negli Stati Uniti di America, 1,6,8, Ottobre, 1883."

[35] *Connecticut Catholic,* March 29, 1884.

[36] James Donovan, ed., *Decreta Synodorum Hartfordiensium, in unum volumen Collecta* (Hartford, 1902), Caput XII, "De Catholica Juventutis Institutione," 130, p. 103.

[37] *Ibid.*, Caput XII, "De Catholica Juventutis Institutione," 232, p. 124.

[38] *Connecticut Catholic*, December 5, 1891. The school board was enlarged to 12 members in 1889, thus allowing the children of each Catholic school to be examined twice a year by the board.

[39] Heffernan, *Catholic Education*, p. 84. The Sisters of Mercy did not offer any systematic training program for their teaching sisters until after 1911.

[40] *Connecticut Catholic*, December 19, 1891; October 2, 1896.

[41] Heffernan, *Catholic Schools*, p. 90.

[42] AHTFD, Parochial Correspondence, 1890, School Report, 1890: Examination of Diocesan Parochial Schools: October 21, 1890. The comments of the board concerning the schools were as follows:

St. Augustine, Bridgeport	"Discipline very good—no remarks."
St. Peter, Danbury	"Discipline excellent—appointments first class."
St. Thomas, Fairfield	"Discipline good—poor school accommodation. Hard to judge correctly."
St. Mary, Greenwich	"Discipline very good—excellent school—girls department perfect."
St. Mary, Norwalk	"Discipline excellent, examiners highly pleased in all respects."
St. John, Stamford	"Discipline good—Apart from deficient primary grade, first class."

[43] APF, APNS (1895), Rub. 153, vol. 74, f831r, Hartford Diocesan Report, 1894.

[44] *Catholic Transcript*, January 18; April 11; July 11, 1901.

[45] AMERCY, Danbury Box, "St. Peter, Danbury."

[46] Heffernan, *Catholic Schools*, p. 108.

[47] *Catholic Transcript*, January 2, 1908. The Sisters of Mercy of Danbury allegedly endorsed an elixir called "Linonine." It was touted to be good for one's throat, lung troubles, and especially good for body–builders. It was composed of flax–seed oil emulsion, Irish moss, eucalyptus, glycerine, gultheria, and other ingredients.

[48] *Catholic Transcript*, February 27, 1908: An address by James Cardinal Gibbons on Catholic schools.

[49] ABPT, Parish Files: Sts. Cyril and Methodius, Slovaks of Bridgeport to Bp. Tierney, Bridgeport, September 14, 1907. Parish Files: St. John Nepomucene, Procurator of the Bishop of Hartford to Abp. Diomede Falconio, OFM, Hartford, December 7, 1907 (copy).

[50] *The Catholic Church in the United States of America* (New York, 1912), vol. II, pp. 281–282.

[51] ASSND, Bridgeport, St. Joseph, 20.4.5.2: "Chronicle 1915–1951."

[52] ASSND, Bridgeport, St. John Nepomucene, 20.4.5.2, doc. #6.

[53] *Catholic Transcript*, November 26, 1908.

[54] *Catholic Transcript*, July 4, 1912.

[55] *Catholic Transcript*, July 8, 1909.

[56] *Catholic Transcript*, January 4, 1912.

[57] Interview by the author of Sr. Mary Alexine McCollough, RSM, West Hart-

ford, July 27, 1985. Sr. Alexine was born on the East Side of Bridgeport in 1908 and attended St. Charles School.

[58] Interview with Sister Mary Alexine McCollough, RSM.

[59] Interview by the author of Mrs. Aida Curley, Bridgeport, July 26, 1985. Mrs. Curley was graduated from St. Charles School in 1915.

[60] "75th Anniversary: 1902–1977. The Parish of St. Charles Borromeo," p. 27.

[61] Interview by the author of Dr. Michael Simko, Bridgeport, August 31, 1985. Dr. Simko was a member of the class of 1908, the first of St. Charles.

[62] *Connecticut Catholic*, December 19, 1891. October 2, 1896.

[63] Interview with Sister Mary Alexine McCollough, RSM.

[64] Interview by the author of Mrs. Rosemary Marshall, Bridgeport, September 3, 1985. Mrs. Marshall, then Rosemary White, was member of St. Charles' graduating class of 1915.

[65] Interview with Sister Mary Alexine McCullough, RSM.

[66] *Ibid.*

[67] Interview with Mrs. Rosemary Marshall.

[68] Interview with Sister Mary Alexine McCollough, RSM.

[69] Interview with Mrs. Aida Curley.

[70] Interview by the author of Sister Ignatia Marie Federici, RSM, St. Philip Convent, Norwalk, July 2, 1986.

[71] *Ibid.*

[72] Interview with Sister Mary Alexine McCollough, RSM.

[73] Sister Mary Evelyn Greene, *From Vision to Action, the Sisters of Mercy of Connecticut, 1930–1982* (W. Hartford, 1983), p. 51.

[74] Sister Mary Valerian, *The Sisters of Mercy in the Diocese of Hartford* (Hartford, 1931), Introduction.

[75] Interview with Sr. Ignatia Marie Federici, RSM.

[76] Interview by the author of the Rev. Edward Rooney, Devon, Connecticut, August 27, 1985. Father Rooney was a graduate of St. Charles.

[77] Interview by the author of the Rev. Richard Toner, St. Charles, East Bridgeport, June 13, 1986.

[78] Interview by the author of Mrs. Jean Harding, Bridgeport, June 13, 1986.

[79] Interview with Sister Mary Alexine McCollough, RSM.

[80] Interview with Mrs. Aida Curley.

[81] Interview by the author of Mr. Salvatore Petriello, Bridgeport, August 13, 1985.

[82] *Bridgeport Post*, November 9, 1903.

[83] *Bridgeport Sunday Post*, July 2, 1905.

[84] *Catholic Transcript*, September 3, 1914.

[85] *Catholic Transcript*, July 23, 1914.

[86] *Catholic Transcript*, June 29, 1920.

[87] *Catholic Transcript*, November 15, 1917.

[88] *Catholic Transcript*, September 27, 1917.

[89] *Catholic Transcript*, June 29, 1920.

[90] *Bridgeport Post*, July 2, 1937. Such self–effacing service is one reason why no real records and documents of the sisters' work is available. Since all was to be done for God, little was to be in the public eye.

[91] St. Joseph Hospital, "Annals of St. Joseph's Hospital, Stamford, Connecticut," p. 18.

[92] Interview by the author of Sister Mary Assisium, CSJ, St. Francis Hospital,

Hartford, July 1, 1986. Sister Mary Assisum was one of the founding sisters of the hospital in 1942.

[93] Interview with Sister Mary Assisium, CSJ.

[94] *Ibid.*

[95] Interview by the author of Sister Daniel Marie, CSJ, St. Joseph Hospital, Stamford, June 27, 1986.

[96] ABPT, Sister Mary Assisium, CSJ to the author, Hartford, July 2, 1986.

[97] *Ibid.*

[98] *Ibid.*

[99] *Ibid.*

[100] *Ibid.*

[101] *Ibid.*

[102] "St. Joseph Hospital: First Annual Report, 1945. Covering the first three years from January 1, 1943 to December 31, 1945," p. 20.

[103] *Ibid.,* "Report to the Friends of Saint Joseph's Hospital, 1955," p. 5.

Chapter IV: Bishops, Priests and Catholic Life

[1] *Republican Farmer,* July 21, 1819.

[2] ALOCK, Florence Matthews Diary, Misc. Matthews: Sermon of the Rev. Justin Mitchell on Matthew 21: 44, Norwalk, January, 1802, original draft.

[3] ABALTO, Cheverus Correspond., Bp. Jean de Cheverus to Abp. John Carroll, New York May 11, 1815.

[4] ABOST, Journal of the Diocese of Boston, vol. I (Nov. 1, 1825–Sept. 10, 1835), Sept. 4, 1835, p. 317.

[5] St. Peter, Danbury, Baptismal Registers: 1844–1848.

[6] ABPT, Bp. William Tyler to the Rev. John Hand, Providence August 15, 1844 (copy).

[7] Richard J. Purcell, "Missionaries from All Hallows (Dublin) to the United States, 1842–1865," in the *Records of the American Catholic Historical Society of Philadelphia,* vol. LIII, Dec. 1942, no. 4.

[8] Hugh J. Nolan, ed., *Pastoral Letters of the United States Catholic Bishops* (Washington, D.C., 1984), vol. I, p. 38.

[9] ABPT, Bp. Tyler to the Rev. John Hand, Providence, November 26, 1844. (copy).

[10] ABPT, Bp. Tyler to the Rev. D. Moriarty, Providence, March 14, 1849 (copy). The oath for those clerical students for the Diocese of Hartford was, "Ego N.N. spondeo et juro me missionibus diocesis Hartfordiensis in perpetuum inservitum, sub obedientia ordinarii. Sic me deus adjuvet et haec sancta Dei evangelia."

[11] AUND, All Hallows Missionary Correspondence, 1843–1877, Bp. Tyler to the Rev. John Hand, Providence July 26, 1845.

[12] ABPT, Rev. Stephen Whelan to the Rev. Woodlock, Providence August 20, 1849 (copy).

[13] Bp. Tyler to the Propagation of the Faith, Paris, Providence, January, 1847, quoted in O'Connell, p. 129.

[14] *The United States Catholic Almanac, 1850* (Baltimore 1850), p. 103.

[15] AUND, Paris Propagation of the Faith, F66–3906, Bp. Francis McFarland to the Propagation, Providence, January 21, 1859.

[16] AUND, Council of the Propagation of the Faith, Paris, F66–3895, Bp. O'Reilly to the Council, Providence January 11, 1851.

[17] AUND, Council of the Propagation of the Faith, Paris, F66–3897, Bp. Bernard O'Reilly to the Council, Providence, December 28, 1851.

[18] AUND, All Hallow's Missionary Correspondence, 1843–1877, Bp. O'Reilly to the Rev. D. Moriarty, Providence, June 5, 1851.

[19] ABPT, Bp. O'Reilly to the Rev. D. Moriarty, Ballinagh, County Gavin, Ireland, February 5, 1853 (copy).

[20] ABPT, Bp. O'Reilly to the Rev. D. Moriarty, Ballinagh, County Cavan, Ireland, February 5, 1853 (copy).

[21] ABPT, Bp. O'Reilly to the Rev. John Hand, Providence, January 2, 1851 (copy).

[22] ABPT, Bp. O'Reilly to Rev. D. Moriarty, Providence, January 29, 1854 (copy).

[23] ABPT, Bp. O'Reilly to the Rev. D. Moriarty, Providence, April 21, 1854 (copy).

[24] John Carroll Noonan, *Nativism in Connecticut, 1829–1860* (unpub. dissert. Catholic Univ. of America, Washington, D.C., 1938) p. 255: Towns in Fairfield County with populations of 5,000 inhabitants dramatically increased between 1850 and 1860:

	1850 Population	1860 Population
Bridgeport	7,560	13,299
Norwalk	4,651	7,582
Danbury	5,964	7,234
Stamford	5,000	7,185
Greenwich	5,036	6,522

[25] Peter Guilday, *The National Pastorals of the American Hierarchy (1792–1919)*, (Westminster, Md., 1954), p. 72.

[26] Rev. James Lynch to the Rev. D. Woodlock, Birmingham, Ct., November 14, 1854, quoted in Richard J. Purcell, "Missionaries from All Hallows (Dublin) to the United States, 1842–1865," in *Records of the American Catholic Historical Society of Philadelphia*, vol. LIII, Dec., 1942, no. 4, p. 220.

[27] *Norwalk Gazette*, June 26, 1855.

[28] *Norwalk Gazette*, September 4, 1855.

[29] *Norwalk Gazette*, April 24, 1855.

[30] *Norwalk Gazette*, November 21, 1854.

[31] *Republican Farmer*, May 8, 1855.

[32] APF, ACTA 1857, vol. 221, f99r–100v, Revs. Edward J. O'Brien, Thomas Quinn, M.A. Wallan to Alessandro Card. Barnabò, Hartford, November 5, 1856.

[33] APF, ACTA 1857, vol. 221, f102rv, "Osservazioni comunicate alla Propaganda intorno alle elezioni dei vescovi per l'America Settentrionale in occasione della vacanza del Vescovo di Hartford."

[34] AUND, McFarland Papers, I–1a, fasc. 1850–1859, Abp. Patrick Kenrick to the Rt. Rev. Francis McFarland, Baltimore, March 30, 1857.

[35] AUND, Hartford Collection, Bp. Martin J. Spalding to Abp. John Purcell, Louisville, May 10, 1857.

[36] AUND, Abbot Bernard Smith Papers, PatI, Pos. 1, Abp. John Hughes to Abbot Bernard Smith, New York, April 8, 1858. Duggan claims that Hughes had supported McFarland's nomination for Hartford, the result of which

was to overturn the decision previously made to name the Rev. Matthew Hart of New Haven to the See. Hart, according to Duggan, had received the support and nomination of the Hartford clergy. Hughes' alleged support of McFarland for Hartford would seem improbable, especially since he worked to secure McFarland as his coadjutor.

[37] AUND, Paris Propagation of the Faith, F66–3904, Bp. McFarland to the Propagation, Providence, April 8, 1858.

[38] AUND, Paris Propagation of the Faith, F66–3906, Bp. McFarland to Propagation, Providence, January 21, 1859.

[39] APF, S.C. Amer. Cent., vol. 19, f714r–721v, Bp. Francis McFarland to Propaganda Fide, "Relazione dello stato della Diocesi di Hartford fino al giorno 16 Maggio 1862," Hartford, May 16, 1862.

[40] AUND, Paris Propagation of the Faith, F66–3924, Bp. McFarland to the Propagation of the Faith, Providence, July 6, 1867.

[41] James A. Rooney, "Early Times in the Diocese of Hartford, Conn., 1829–1874," in *Catholic Historical Review* 1 (June, 1915), pp. 148–163.

[42] AUND, Paris Propagation of the Faith, F66–3917, Bp. McFarland to the Propagation of the Faith, Providence, February 26, 1864.

[43] AHTFD, McFarland Papers, Parochial Correspondence, 1861, II, Rev. Peter A. Smith to Bp. McFarland, Bridgeport, August 31; September 29, 1861. The first "likely vocation" for the diocesan priesthood from Fairfield County was Patrick Murphy, from St. Mary's in East Bridgeport.

[44] AUND, All Hallow's Missionary Correspondence, 1843–1877, Bp. McFarland to Rev. Woodlock, Providence, July 17, 1860.

[45] AUND, McFarland Papers, I–1–b, fasc. 1864, Abp. John Hughes to Bp. McFarland, New York, September 28, 1864.

[46] AUND, All Hallows Missionary Correspondence, 1843–1877, Bp. McFarland to the Rev. Fortune(?), Providence, April 13, 1867.

[47] AUND, All Hallows Missionary Correspondence, 1843–1877, Bp. McFarland to Rev. D. Bennett, Providence, June 16, 1864.

[48] AUND, Paris Propagation of the Faith, F66–3906, Bp. McFarland to Propagation, Providence, January 21, 1859.

[49] APF, S.C. Amer. Cent. 1859–1860, vol. 18, f1622r–1629v, Rev. John Mulligan to Alessandro Card. Barnabò, Norwalk, November 6, 1860.

[50] AHTFD, McFarland Papers, Parochial Correspondence, 1861–II, Rev. John Mulligan to Bp. McFarland, Norwalk, September 10, 1861.

[51] AHTFD, McFarland Papers, Parochial Correspondence, 1862–II, Rev. Ambrose Manahan to Bp. McFarland, January 1, 1862.

[52] AHTFD, McFarland Papers, Parochial Correspondence, 1865–II, Rev. Philip Sheridan to Bp. McFarland, Danbury, January 6; February 7; March 3, 1865.

[53] AHTFD, McFarland Papers, Parochial Correspondence, 1867–II, Rev. James Daly to Bp. McFarland, Newtown, July 31, 1867.

[54] AHTFD, McFarland Papers, Parochial Correspondence, 1867–II, Bp. McFarland to the Rev. James Daly, Providence, n.d. Daly had not filed any parochial reports since his arrival in the parish in 1862.

[55] AHTFD, McFarland Papers, Parochial Correspondence, 1868–II, Rev. James Daly to Bp. McFarland, Newtown, July 14, 1868.

[56] AHTFD, McFarland Papers, Miscellaneous Correspondence, 1863–II, Mr. John O'Rourke to Bp. McFarland, New York City, January 19, 1863.

[57] AHTFD, McFarland Papers, Parochial Correspondence, 1863–II, Rev. James H. O'Neill to Bp. McFarland, Stamford, February 4, 1863.

[58] AHTFD, McFarland Papers, Parochial Correspondence, 1863–II, Rev. James H. O'Neill to Bp. McFarland, Stamford, February 4, 1863.

[59] AHTFD, McFarland Papers, Episcopal Correspondence, 1863, Rev. Francis Lenihan to Bp. McFarland, Providence, January 9, 1863.

[60] AHTFD, McFarland Papers, Episcopal Correspondence, 1863, Rev. Francis Lenhian to Bp. McFarland, Providence, January 9, 1863.

[61] AHTFD, McFarland Papers, Parochial Correspondence, 1867–II, Rev. Thomas J. Synnott to Bp. McFarland, Bridgeport, July 1, 1867.

[62] AUND, McFarland Papers, I–1–b, fasc. 1867, Rev. Thomas F. Hendricken to Bp. McFarland, Waterbury, January 28, 1867. Fairfield County was included in the New Haven Conference District of the diocesan clergy.

[63] APF, S.C. Amer. Cent., 1861–1862, vol. 19, f714r–721v, Hartford Diocesan Report, Bp. McFarland to Alessandro Card. Barnabò, Hartford, May 16, 1862.

[64] APF, Lettere 1877, vol. 373, f434v–435r, Alessandro Card. Franchi to Bp. Thomas J. Galberry, Rome, September 14, 1877 (draft): Galberry followed McFarland's practice and continued to disturb Rome. In response to the diocesan report of 1877, the Prefect of Propaganda Fide urged Galberry to call a synod soon, "lest discipline collapse and vice abound, such as might if you continue simply to meet with the clergy at luncheons."

[65] APF, Lettere, 1862, vol. 353, f501v–502r, Alessandro Card. Barnabò to Bp. McFarland, Rome, November 30, 1862 (copy); Lettere, 1870, vol. 364, f936v–937v, same to same (copy).

[66] AUND, McFarland Papers, I–1–c, fasc. 1870, Rev. Thomas F. Hendricken to Bp. McFarland, Waterbury, March 4, 1870.

[67] AHTFD, McFarland Papers, Parochial Correspondence, 1866–II, Rev. Matthew Hart to Bp. McFarland, New Haven, June 15, 1866.

[68] *Bridgeport Evening Standard*, June 15; 16, 1866.

[69] AHTFD, McFarland Papers, Parochial Correspondence, 1866–II, Rev. Matthew Hart to Bp. McFarland, New Haven, June 15, 1866.

[70] AHTFD, McFarland Papers, Parochial Correspondence, 1866–II, Rev. Matthew Hart to Bp. McFarland, New Haven, June 22, 1866.

[71] AHTFD, McFarland Papers, Parochial Correspondence, 1866–II, Rev. Matthew Hart to Bp. McFarland, New Haven, June 21, 1866.

[72] AHTFD, McFarland Papers, Parochial Correspondence, 1866–II, Rev. Matthew Hart to Bp. McFarland, New Haven, June 15, 1866.

[73] AHTFD, McFarland Papers, Parochial Correspondence, 1866–II, Rev. Matthew Hart to Bp. McFarland, New Haven, June 21, 1866. Emphasis is original.

[74] AHTFD, McFarland Papers, Parochial Correspondence, 1866–II, Rev. Matthew Hart to Bp. McFarland, New Haven, June 21, 1866.

[75] AHTFD, McFarland Papers, Parochial Correspondence, 1866–II, Rev. Matthew Hart to Bp. McFarland, New Haven, June 26, 1866.

[76] AHTFD, McFarland Papers, Parochial Correspondence, 1866–II, Rev. Matthew Hart to Bp. McFarland, New Haven, June 26, 1866.

[77] AHTFD, Annual Parochial Reports: Bridgeport, St. Augustine, 1876.

[78] *Connecticut Catholic,* May 29, 1880.

[79] AHTFD, McFarland Papers, Parochial Correspondence, 1865–II, Rev. Thomas J. Synnott to Bp. McFarland, Bridgeport, December 11, 1865.

[80] "Bridgeport Board of Education Reports, 1884–1890," vol. II, p. 9.

[81] Samuel Orcutt, *A History of the Old Town of Stratford and the City of Bridgeport, Connecticut* (W. Haven, 1886), Part II, p. 918.

[82] AHTFD, McFarland Papers, Parochial Correspondence, 1870, Rev. F. Rogers to Bp. McFarland, Newtown, December 23, 1870.

[83] *Sadlier's Catholic Directory* (New York, 1873), pp. 205–207.

[84] Stephen Byrne, *Irish Immigration to the United States: What It Has Been, and What It Is* (New York, 1873), p. 74.

[85] *Connecticut Catholic,* February 4, 1888.

[86] *Connecticut Catholic,* November 23, 1878.

[87] *Connecticut Catholic,* May 1, 1880.

[88] *Sadlier's Catholic Directory, 1880* (New York, 1880), pp. 280–282.

[89] Christopher J. Kauffman, *Faith and Fraternalism. The History of the Knights of Columbus, 1882–1982* (New York, 1982). This is the most comprehensive study of the Knights written so far.

[90] AHTFD, Circulars Journal I, 1850–1904, Bp. Lawrence S. McMahon to the rectors of the diocese, Hartford, January 19, 1880.

[91] *Connecticut Catholic,* February 5, 1881.

[92] *Connecticut Catholic,* March 26, 1881.

[93] *Connecticut Catholic,* March 26, 1881.

[94] *Bridgeport Daily Standard,* November 3, 1881.

[95] *Bridgeport Daily Standard,* March 28, 29, 30, 1892.

[96] *Bridgeport Daily Standard,* March 28, 1892.

[97] *Connecticut Catholic,* April 2, 1892.

[98] *Connecticut Catholic,* May 28, 1892.

[99] *Connecticut Catholic,* June 11, 1892.

[100] *Connecticut Catholic,* October 28, 1892.

[101] *Connecticut Catholic,* November 5, 1892.

[102] *Connecticut Catholic,* November 5, 1892.

[103] AUND, Soderini Manuscript, "Leo XIII and the United States of America."

[104] APF, APNS (1894), vol. 50, R. 153, f 253rv, "Htfd. Diocese, sede vacante," New Haven, September 26, 1893, Circular to Hartford Priests from the Priests' Committee.

[105] APF, APNS (1893), vol. 50, R. 153, f302r, "Hartford Diocese, sede vacante," Abp. Francesco Satolli to the editor of the "Meriden Record," Washington, D.C., October 23, 1893.

[106] APF, APNS (1893), vol. 50. R. 153, f302r, "Hartford Diocese, sede vacante," Abp. Satolli to the editor of the "Meriden Record," Washington, D.C., October 23, 1893.

[107] Interview by the author of the Rev. Msgr. John Horgan, Bridgeport Diocesan Archivist, May 3, 1985.

[108] APF, S.C. Amer. Cent., 1891, vol. 56, f611r–612v, Rev. Dennis Joseph Cremins to Giovanni Card. Simeoni, Bridgeport, June, 1891.

[109] APF, APNS (1894), vol. 50, r. 153, f252r–253v, Rev. Dennis Joseph Cremin to Mariano Card. Rampolla, Bridgeport, September 13, 1893.

[110] APF, APNS (1893), vol. 50, R. 153, f283r–287r, Rev. Thomas Shahan to Abp. Satolli, Washington, D.C., October 15, 1893.

[111] APF, APNS (1894), vol. 50, R. 153, "Hartford Diocese sede vacante," f 318r–320v, Miescyslaw Card. Ledóchowski to Bishop–elect Michael Tierney (draft), Rome, January 10, 1894.

[112] *Bridgeport Evening Post,* October 6, 1908; *Bridgeport Telegram,* October 8, 1908; *Catholic Transcript,* October 2, 1913.

[113] *Norwalk Gazette,* March 9, 1894.

[114] AHTFD, Annual Parochial Reports, 1894.

[115] APF, APNS (1895), vol. 74, R. 153, f853rv, Miescyslaw Card. Ledóchowski to Bp. Tierney (draft), Rome, November 13, 1895.

[116] APF, APNS (1895), vol. 74, R. 153, f817r–853r, Hartford Diocesan Report, 1894.
[117] *Catholic Transcript*, February 14, 1904.
[118] *Catholic Transcript*, February 3, 1899.
[119] *Catholic Transcript*, January 23, 1908.
[120] *Catholic Transcript*, February 3, 1899.
[121] *Catholic Transcript*, October 28, 1898.
[122] *Catholic Transcript*, November 4, 1898.
[123] *Catholic Transcript*, November 25, 1898.
[124] *Catholic Transcript*, December 29, 1899.
[125] *Catholic Transcript*, April 10, 1902.
[126] *Catholic Transcript*, July 17, 1902.
[127] *New York Times*, November 26, 1893.
[128] *Danbury News Times*, June 9, 1909.
[129] *Danbury News Times*, June 10, 1909.
[130] *New York Times*, June 17, 1909.
[131] *Danbury News*, July 2, 1913; *New York Times*, July 23, 1913; *Catholic Transcript*, August 21, 1913.
[132] *New York Times*, May 18; 19, 1903.
[133] *Bridgeport Evening Post*, June 27, 1903; *Bridgeport Sunday Herald*, June 28, 1903.
[134] *Bridgeport Evening Post*, June 27, 1903.
[135] *Catholic Transcript*, November 26, 1914. The Rev. Richard Moore, Pastor of Sacred Heart Church in Bridgeport, was also active in labor relations in the city. He was quite outspoken in support of the workers' rights on a number of occasions, most noticeably in 1914 when he supported the mail clerks and letter carriers during their strike.
[136] *Catholic Transcript*, January 19, 1900.
[137] *Catholic Transcript*, October 11, 1906.
[138] *Catholic Transcript*, March 14; April 4; May 2, July 4; September 5, 1907.
[139] *Catholic Transcript*, February 3, 1899.
[140] *Catholic Transcript*, March 1, 1901.
[141] *Catholic Transcript*, December 11, 1902.
[142] *Catholic Transcript*, August 9, 1906.
[143] *Connecticut Catholic*, December 19, 1891; October 2, 1896.
[144] Arthur J. Heffernan, *A History of Catholic Education in Connecticut*, The Catholic University of America Educational Research Monographs, (Washington, D.C., 1937), vol. X, Jan. 2, 1937, no. 1, p. 108.
[145] *Catholic Transcript*, August 10, 1911.
[146] *Catholic Transcript*, October 2, 1913.
[147] Dolores Ann Liptak, *European Immigrants and the Catholic Church in Connecticut, 1870–1920*, p. 178. Seminarians at St. Thomas Seminary, 1897–1921:

Ethnic Group	Number of Candidates	Number Ordained
Irish	647	152
French	42	9
German	23	11
Polish	42	14
Lithuanian	16	6
Slovak	21	9
Italian	11	3
Hungarian	3	2

[148] *Catholic Transcript*, February 9, 1911.

[149] *Catholic Transcript*, July 11, 1912.

[150] Ruth O. M. Andersen, *From Yankee to American: Connecticut 1865 to 1914* (Bridgeport, 1975), pp. 2–3.

[151] *Catholic Transcript*, August 21; November 20, 1913.

[152] *The New York Times*, August 15, 1915.

[153] *Catholic Transcript*, July 17, 1913.

[154] *Ibid.*

[155] *Catholic Transcript*, December 10, 1914.

[156] *Catholic Transcript*, November 30, 1911.

[157] *Catholic Transcript*, February 19, 1914.

[158] *Catholic Transcript*, October 15; November 19, 1914.

[159] *Catholic Transcript*, November 21; December 26, 1912.

[160] *Catholic Transcript*, January 13, 1916.

[161] ABPT, Parochial Files, Sacred Heart Church, Marguerite T. Boylan to Rev. James F. Murphy, Brooklyn, February 9, 1948. The board members were Thomas E. MacFarlan from St. Augustine's, Arthur J. Cummings from Sacred Heart, William A. Reddin from St. Mary's, John H. Coughlin from St. Patrick's, James E. Colgan from St. Charles.

[162] *Catholic Transcript*, August 12, 1920.

[163] *Catholic Transcript*, September 7, 1916. Dr. John A. Ryan of the Catholic University of America spoke on "The Church and Social Questions"; Dr. William J. Kerby, also of the University, spoke on "The Social Mission of Charity"; the Rev. Frederic Siedenburg, SJ, from Loyola, Chicago, spoke on "Health and Social Hygiene"; Dr. James Haggerty, from Ohio State University, spoke on "Juvenile Delinquency"; Edward F. McSweeney, former director of the Ports of New York and Boston, spoke on "Immigration."

[164] *Catholic Transcript*, October 25, 1917; January 31; February 7, 1918. At the beginning of America's participation in the war, there was much duplication and little organization of charitable works. The Catholic Charities Bureau greatly helped in eliminating duplication of efforts and co–ordinating the work of groups in the various parishes throughout the county.

[165] *Catholic Transcript*, September 27; October 11, 1917. March 14, 1918. The first three priests from Fairfield County to enlist as chaplains to the American forces were the Rev. Walter Casey from St. John's, Stamford, Rev. Edward A. Cotter from St. Peter's in Danbury, Rev. Philip Coholan from St. Rose in Newtown.

[166] Christopher J. Kauffman, *Faith and Fraternalism* (New York, 1982), pp. 197–207.

[167] *Catholic Transcript*, September 6, 1917.

[168] *Catholic Transcript*, January 17, 1918.

[169] *Catholic Transcript*, January 24, 1918: Bridgeport's Knights exceeded the amount collected by Hartford's council by $19,000. February 28, 1918: The Knights in Norwalk, Danbury, and Stamford also exceeded their goals with little difficulty.

[170] *Catholic Transcript*, March 21, 1918.

[171] *Catholic Transcript*, November 21, 1918.

[172] *Catholic Transcript*, January 17; November 22, 1917; April 18, 1918.

[173] *Catholic Transcript*, March 20, 1919.

[174] *Catholic Transcript*, May 29, 1919.

[175] *Catholic Transcript*, August 7, 1919; August 19, 1920.

[176] *Catholic Transcript*, January 20; May 5, 1921.

[177] *Catholic Transcript,* August 21, 1919.
[178] Hugh J. Nolan, ed., *Pastoral Letters of the United States Catholic Bishops* (Washington, D.C., 1984), 4 vols., vol. I, p. 317.
[179] *Ibid.,* p. 319.
[180] *Catholic Transcript,* March 3, 1920.
[181] John Tracy Ellis, *American Catholicism,* p. 135.
[182] *Catholic Transcript,* September 23, 1920.
[183] The Hartford Sisters of Mercy, *Tributes to Our Foundress for the Centennial of the Foundation of the Congregation of the Sisters of Mercy* (Hartford, 1931), p. 227.
[184] *Ibid.,* p. 228.
[185] *Ibid.,* p. 228.
[186] *Catholic Transcript,* October 14, 1920.
[187] *Catholic Transcript,* August 19, 1926.
[188] *Bridgeport Time–Star,* November 20, 1930.
[189] Interview by the author of the Rev. Edward Rooney, Devon, August 27, 1985.
[190] Interview by the author of Mrs. Aida Curley, East Bridgeport, August 26, 1985.
[191] *Catholic Transcript,* June 28, 1934.
[192] *Catholic Transcript,* December 14, 1933.
[193] *Catholic Transcript,* November 16, 1933.
[194] *Catholic Transcript,* December 7, 1933.
[195] Interview by the author of Msgr. Thomas F. Henahan, Fairfield, September 4, 1985.
[196] Hugh J. Nolan, ed., *Pastoral Letters* (Washington, D.C., 1984) vol. I, p. 106.
[197] *Catholic Transcript,* July 12, 1934.
[198] *Bridgeport Post,* July 16, 1934.
[199] Interview with the Rev. Edward Rooney, Devon, August 27, 1985.
[200] *Catholic Transcript,* July 3, 1941.
[201] Interview by the author of Mrs. Jean Harding, Bridgeport, May 11, 1986.
[202] Interview with Mrs. Jean Harding, Bridgeport, May 19, 1986.
[203] Interview with Msgr. Thomas Henahan, Fairfield, September 4, 1985.
[204] AUND, I–1–a, Rev. Augustine J. Thebaud, SJ, to Bp. McFarland, New York, July 30, 1861.
[205] Vincent A. Lapomarda, SJ, *The Jesuit Heritage in New England* (Worcester, 1970), pp. 196–197.
[206] *Bridgeport Post,* March 21, 1942.
[207] *The New York Times,* March 19, 1942.
[208] *Catholic Transcript,* May 14, 1942.
[209] *Bridgeport Post,* July 17, 1942.
[210] Robert William Turcotte, "A History of Fairfield University" (unpubl. M.A. thesis, Trinity College, Hartford, 1975), p. 9.
[211] *Bridgeport Telegram,* August 5, 1942.
[212] *Bridgeport Telegram,* September 10, 1942.
[213] *Bridgeport Post,* June 17, 1943.
[214] *Bridgeport Post,* June 17, 1943.
[215] Fairfield University, Nyselius Library Archives, Manuscript signed by the Rev. L. C. Langguth, SJ, January 23, 1949.
[216] *Catholic Transcript,* July 3, 1941.

[217] Hugh J. Nolan, *Pastorals* (Washington, D.C., 1984), I, p. 450, "Statement on the Church and Social Order," February 7, 1940.

[218] *Ibid.*, p. 452.

[219] *Catholic Transcript,* September 11, 1941.

[220] *Catholic Transcript,* September 11, 1941.

[221] *Catholic Transcript,* December 11, 1941.

[222] Hugh J. Nolan, ed., *Pastorals* (Washington, D.C., 1984), vol. II, p. 37.

[223] *Catholic Transcript,* November 19, 1942.

[224] *Catholic Transcript,* January 19, 1942.

[225] *Catholic Transcript,* November 19, 1942.

[226] "The Crisis of Christianity," November 14, 1941; "Catholic Support in World War II," December 22, 1941; "Victory and Peace," November 14, 1942; "The Essentials of a Good Peace," November 11, 1943, in Nolan, *Pastorals,* vol. II, pp. 28–49.

[227] *Catholic Transcript,* January 4, 1942.

[228] *Catholic Transcript,* March 9, 1943.

[229] *Catholic Transcript,* April 20, 1943.

[230] *Catholic Transcript,* July 19, 1945.

[231] *Catholic Transcript,* January 29; March 5, 1942.

[232] *Catholic Transcript,* December 17, 1942.

[233] *Catholic Transcript,* April 29, 1943.

[234] *Catholic Transcript,* July 5, 1945.

[235] *Catholic Transcript,* July 19, 1945.

[236] "Between War and Peace," November 18, 1945, in Nolan, *Pastorals,* vol. II, pp. 62–65.

[237] "Man and the Peace!" November 17, 1946, in *Ibid.,* vol. II, pp. 67–73.

[238] "Statement on Secularism," November 14, 1947; "The Christian in Action," November 21, 1948; "The Christian Family," November 21, 1949, in *Ibid.,* vol. II, pp. 74–96.

[239] *Bridgeport Post,* May 16, 1949.

[240] *Catholic Transcript,* August 6, 1953.

[241] *Catholic Transcript,* August 16, 1953.

[242] *Catholic Transcript,* May 28, 1953.

[243] *Catholic Transcript,* November 26, 1953.

Chapter V: Bishop Lawrence Shehan

[1] Lawrence J. Shehan, *A Blessing of Years: The Memoirs of Lawrence Cardinal Shehan* (Notre Dame, 1982), pp. 107–108.

[2] Interview by the author of Lawrence Cardinal Shehan, Baltimore, June 13, 1984.

[3] A case in point was the creation of the Diocese of Miami in 1958, in which Cardinal Shehan was involved as mediator. A controversy resulted concerning the patrimony granted the new created diocese by the mother diocese of St. Augustine, Florida. Such a problem could not have existed but for the lack of clear direction by the Consistorial Congregation at the time of the division of St. Augustine.

[4] *Bridgeport Sunday Herald,* August 16, 1953.

[5] Interview by the author of the Rev. Raymond H. Stephenson, Norwalk, May 19, 1986.

[6] AHTFD, Archdiocese: Erection File.

[7] *Ibid.*

[8] AHTFD, Erection File, Abp. Henry J. O'Brien to Bp. Bernard J. Flanagan (copy), Hartford, December 8, 1953.

[9] AHTFD, Erection file, Abp. Henry J. O'Brien to Bp. Lawrence J. Shehan (copy), Hartford, December 1, 1953.

[10] AHTFD, Erection file, "S. Congregatio Consistorialis Bridgeportensis–Novaricensis administrationem Apostolicae Decretum," Romae, September 2, 1953.

[11] ABALTO, Keough Correspondence, S–Z, Bp. Lawrence J. Shehan to Abp. Francis Keough, Bridgeport, December 30, 1954. Keough to Shehan (copy), Baltimore, January 5, 1955.

[12] Shehan, *A Blessing of Years,* p. 137.

[13] *Catholic Transcript,* September 3, 1953.

[14] Interview by the author of the Rev. Thomas Keeney, Bridgeport, September 4, 1986.

[15] Interview by the author of Brian Hariskevich, Fairfield, August 8, 1986.

[16] *Bridgeport Post,* December 2, 1953.

[17] *Bridgeport Telegram,* December 2, 1953.

[18] Interview by the author of Msgr. Patrick Donnelly, Bridgeport, August 13, 1986.

[19] *Bridgeport Post,* December 2, 1953.

[20] *Bridgeport Post,* December 2, 1953.

[21] *Bridgeport Telegram,* December 3, 1953.

[22] *Bridgeport Sunday Herald,* November 29, 1953.

[23] *Bridgeport Post,* December 4, 1953.

[24] *Bridgeport Post,* December 4, 1953.

[25] ABPT, Miscellaneous Documents, Bp. Shehan to Charles R. Weidman (copy), Bridgeport, February 1, 1956.

[26] ABPT, Religious Women, Robert M. Mcanerney to Msgr. George Curtiss, Bridgeport, June 20, 1955.

[27] *Bridgeport Post,* February 23, 1955–April 8, 1955.

[28] ABPT, Shehan sermons and speeches, Bridgeport, February 14, 1954.

[29] ABPT, Shehan, sermons and speeches, "Labor, Law and the Church," Bridgeport, October 5, 1954.

[30] ABPT, Shehan, sermons and speeches, "Unity in Charity—Freedom in Justice," Washington, D.C., February 6, 1955.

[31] ABPT, Shehan sermons and speeches, "The Spiritual Challenge of the New Age," New York, December 9, 1960.

[32] ABPT, Holy See: Congregation of Seminaries and Universities, Bp. Shehan to Joseph Card. Pizzardo (copy), Bridgeport, April 14, 1960.

[33] ABPT, Miscellaneous Documents: "Christian Education—Our Commitments and Our Resources," Bp. Shehan to the National Catholic Educational Association, Atlantic City, April, 1959.

[34] ABPT, Shehan sermons and speeches, "The Catholic High School—its Significance and Function." West Hartford, September 24, 1961.

[35] *Ibid.*

[36] *Catholic Transcript,* June 3, 1954.

[37] *Catholic Transcript,* June 17, 1954.

[38] ABPT, High Schools, Bp. Shehan to Francis Cardinal Spellman (copy), Bridgeport, August 10, 1955.

[39] *Bridgeport Sunday Post,* March 6, 1955.

[40] ABPT, High Schools, Msgr. James McLaughlin to Anthony J. D'Aprice (copy), Bridgeport, September 4, 1956.

[41] Shehan, *Blessing of Years*, p. 118.

[42] ABPT, Shehan: Miscellaneous Correspondence, Bp. Shehan to the Rt. Rev. Thomas Tobin (copy), Bridgeport, April 12, 1954.

[43] ABPT, New York Archdiocese File, Bp. Shehan to Card. Spellman (copy), Bridgeport, March 27, 1954.

[44] Interview by the author of Msgr. Thomas Henahan, Fairfield, September 18, 1985.

[45] ABPT, Shehan File, July–December, 1954, Bp. Shehan to Sr. M. Sebastiana (copy), Bridgeport, September 22, 1954. This file is filled with requests for special collections within the diocese that the bishop refused.

[46] ABPT, Miscellaneous Correspondence, Bp. Shehan to William Walsh, Jr. (copy), Bridgeport, June 2, 1954; Bp. Shehan to Very Rev. Serges Kafka, OFM (copy), Bridgeport, June 28, 1954.

[47] ABPT, Shehan Correspondence, Bp. Shehan to Bp. Matthew Brady (copy), Bridgeport, February 6, 1955.

[48] ABPT, High Schools, Bp. Shehan to Mother Cecile de la Providence, FSE (copy), Bridgeport, June 10, 1954.

[49] *Bridgeport Post*, March 9, 1955.

[50] *Bridgeport Post*, April 13, 1955.

[51] ABPT, High Schools, Bp. Shehan to Spellman (copy), Bridgeport, August 10, 1955.

[52] ABPT, High Schools, Bp. Fulton Sheen to Bp. Shehan (copy), New York, May 12, 1955.

[53] Interview by the author of the Rev. Thomas Keeney, Bridgeport, September 4, 1986.

[54] ABPT, High Schools, Bp. Shehan to Mr. Thomas Lyons (copy), Bridgeport, June 4, 1955.

[55] *Bridgeport Post*, July 3, 1955.

[56] *Ibid.*

[57] ABPT, High Schools, Bp. Shehan to Stamford Pastors, Bridgeport, November 25, 1955; Bp. Shehan to Mthr. Christina Marie (copy), Bridgeport, February 6, 1956; Bp. Shehan to Anthony DePace (copy), Bridgeport, May 16, 1956.

[58] *Bridgeport Sunday Post*, October 26, 1958.

[59] *Stamford Advocate*, October 24, 1958.

[60] *Catholic Transcript*, October 30, 1958.

[61] *Catholic Transcript*, October 30, 1958.

[62] ABPT, High Schools, Thomas V. O'Sullivan; Frank McBride; Raymond Dinnen to Bp. Shehan, South Norwalk, March 28, 1955.

[63] ABPT, High Schools, Bp. Shehan to Norwalk Priests, Bridgeport, December 26, 1956.

[64] Interview by the author of Judge Alfred Santaniello, Sr., Norwalk, July 24, 1985.

[65] *Norwalk Hour*, September 22, 1959.

[66] ABPT, Miscellaneous Correspondence, Religious Women: Bp. Shehan to Edward F. O'Donnell (copy), Bridgeport, May 24, 1961.

[67] ABPT, Shehan Papers, October–December, 1960, Bp. Shehan to Rev. Virgil C. Blum, SJ (copy), Bridgeport, November 29, 1960.

[68] *Ibid.*

[69] *Catholic Transcript*, March 16, 1961, Address by Bp. Shehan, "Federal Aid to Education."

[70] ABPT, Religious Women, Bp. Shehan to Mthr. Mary Chrysostom (copy), Bridgeport, July 6, 1956.

[71] *Catholic Transcript,* December 2, 1954.

[72] ABPT, Shehan speeches and sermons, "Personal Responsibility of those engaged in Catholic Youth Work," Buffalo, September 20, 1961.

[73] *Ibid.*

[74] *Ibid.*

[75] Interview by the author of the Rev. Thomas Keeney, Bridgeport, September 4, 1986. Father Keeney taught Latin each Saturday to those seminary candidates who had no classical training.

[76] ABPT, Holy See: Congregation of Seminaries and Universities, Msgr. James J. McLaughlin to Adrian Brenna (copy), Bridgeport, October 10, 1956.

[77] ABPT, Miscellaneous Documents, "Catholic Lay Organizations and the Promotion of Vocations," Bp. Shehan, Bridgeport, June 27, 1955.

[78] *Ibid.*

[79] ABPT, Misc. correspondence, Msgr. William Genuario, PA, to the author, Rome, October 22, 1986.

[80] ABPT, Holy See: Congregation of Seminaries and Universities, Bp. Shehan to Abp. Henry J. O'Brien (copy), Bridgeport, May 8, 1956. Hartford answered in the negative.

[81] ABPT, Holy See: Congregation of Seminaries and Universities, Diocesan quinquinial report, 1953–1958 (copy).

[82] ABPT, Holy See: Congregation of Seminaries and Universities, Joseph Card. Pizzardo to Bp. Shehan, Rome, October 19, 1959.

[83] "Statistical Report on Catholic Seminaries in the United States," Seminary Departments, National Catholic Educational Association (August, 1959), p. 3.

[84] ABPT, Holy See: Congregation of Seminaries and Universities, Bp. Shehan to Joseph Card. Pizzardo (copy), Bridgeport, April 14, 1960.

[85] AAS, vol. li, 1959, pp. 196, 313, 518, 577, 713.

[86] ABPT, Holy See: Congregation of Seminaries and Universities, Bp. Shehan to Pizzardo (copy), Bridgeport, May 10, 1960.

[87] ABPT, Holy See: Congregation of Seminaries and Universities, Report on Vocations of the Diocese of Bridgeport, 1962.

[88] *Catholic Transcript,* February 10, 1955.

[89] ABPT, Shehan papers, January–March, 1956, Bp. Shehan to Msgr. John O'Grady (copy), Bridgeport, March 14, 1956.

[90] The War Bride's Act of 1946 admitted 120,000 immigrants who were the wives and children of American servicemen during World War II. The Displaced Persons Acts of 1948 and 1950, and the Refugee Relief Act of 1953 allowed the entrance of another 600,000 immigrants, primarily from Germany, Hungary, Russia, Yugoslavia, Latvia, and Poland. In 1952 Congress passed the Immigration and Naturalization Act, better known as the McCarren–Walter Act, which, while maintaining the national–origins system, set up quotas for Asian nationalities previously excluded from entrance into the country. This allowed the additional entrance into the country of 158,361 immigrants, until the 1965 amendment to the law established new quotas.

[91] *L'Osservatore Romano,* March 14, 1946; October 3–4; 23, 1949.

[92] "Letter to His Excellency John T. McNicholas, Archbishop of Cincinnati and Chairman of the Administrative Board of the National Catholic Welfare Conference," (December 24, 1948), AAS, xxxxi, pp. 69–71.

[93] "Giulivo Tessarolo, ed., *Exsul Familia, The Church's Magna Charta for Migrants* (Staten Island, 1962).

[94] ABPT, Holy See: *Exsul Familia*, Administrative Board of the NCWC to Adeolato Giovanni Cardinal Piazza (copy), Washington, D.C., February 17, 1954.

[95] ABPT, Parish Files, Our Lady of Fatima, Bp. Shehan to Abp. Amleto Cicognani (copy), Bridgeport, May 25, 1954.

[96] ABPT, Parish Files. The pertinent correspondence between the bishop and the pastors within the county may be found in the files of the respective parishes.

[97] ABPT, Parish Files, St. Charles, Rev. Thomas Gloster to Bp. Shehan, Bridgeport, February 14, 1955.

[98] *Bridgeport Post,* December 2, 1953.

[99] Interview by the author of Msgr. Francis Campagnone, Bridgeport, February 10, 1986.

[100] Jay P. Dolan, *The American Catholic Experience, A History from Colonial Times to the Present* (Garden City, N.Y., 1985), p. 360.

[101] *Bridgeport Sunday Herald,* August 16, 1953.

[102] Interview with Msgr. Francis Campagnone.

[103] *Ibid.*

[104] ABPT, Parish Files, Our Lady of Providence. Msgr. Victor Torres–Frias to the author, San Juan, Puerto Rico, February 16, 1985.

[105] ABPT, Parish Files, Our Lady of Providence, Bp. Shehan to the Rev. Francis Campagnone (copy), Bridgeport, October 1, 1959.

[106] ABPT, Parish Files, Our Lady of Guadalupe, Bp. Shehan to Abp. Egidio Vagnozzi (copy), Bridgeport, November 13, 1959.

[107] ABPT, Parish Files, Shehan Papers, January–March, 1958, Bp. Shehan to Abp. Leo Binz (copy), Bridgeport, January 23, 1958.

[108] ABPT, Parish Files, Our Lady of Guadalupe, Rev. Torres–Frias to Bp. Walter W. Curtis, Bridgeport, January 31, 1962.

[109] ABPT, Miscellaneous Correspondence, Bp. Shehan to Rev. Mthr. General (copy), Bridgeport, July 6, 1960; Sr. Maria Inmaculada Aizcorbe Iriarte to Bp. Shehan, Madrid, July 16, 1960.

[110] *Bridgeport Post,* September 22, 1960.

[111] ABPT, Parish Files, Our Lady of Guadalupe. Rev. Torres–Frias to the author, San Juan, February 16, 1985.

[112] ABPT, Parish Files, St. Mary, Bpt., Bp. Shehan–Memorandum, Bridgeport, August 2, 1961.

[113] *Bridgeport Post,* April 6, 1960.

[114] ABPT, Parish Files, Our Lady of Fatima, Abp. Amleto Cicognani to Bp. Shehan, Washington, D.C., April 14, 1954.

[115] *Geller's Bridgeport,* vol. I, p. 52.

[116] ABPT, Parish Files, Our Lady of Fatima, Bp. Shehan to Abp. Amleto Cicognani (copy), Bridgeport, May 25, 1954.

[117] ABPT, Parish files, Our Lady of Fatima, Rev. James F. Murphy to Bp. Shehan, Bridgeport, May 21, 1954.

[118] ABPT, Parish Files, Our Lady of Fatima, Bp. Shehan to John Perry (copy), Bridgeport, July 11, 1956. Mr. Perry was the President of the Portuguese Civic League of Danbury.

[119] ABPT, Parish Files, Our Lady of Fatima, Rev. John Barney to Bp. Shehan, Bridgeport, July 5, 1960.

[120] ABPT, Parish Files, Our Lady of Fatima, John Perry to Bp. Shehan, Danbury, July 7, 1956.

[121] ABPT, Parish Files, Our Lady of Fatima, Mrs. Samuel Bandanza and Portuguese Catholics to Bp. Shehan, Bridgeport, June 27, 1960.

[122] Interview by the author of the Rev. Constantino Caldas, Bridgeport, December 4, 1986.

[123] Interview by the author of Msgr. Joseph Potter, Bridgeport, February 25, 1986.

[124] ABPT, Parish Files, Our Lady of Fatima, Bp. Shehan to Mrs. Samuel Bandanza (draft), Bridgeport, July 11, 1960.

[125] Interview by the author of Msgr. John Toomey, PA, Norwalk, February 10, 1986.

[126] ABPT, Miscellaneous Correspondence, Religious Women, Mthr. St. Kevin to Bp. O'Brien, Ferndale, November 12, 1951.

[127] ABPT, Miscellaneous Correspondence, Eugenio Cardinal Tisserant to Bp. O'Brien, Rome, February 5, 1952; Abp. Amleto Cicognani to Bp. O'Brien, Washington, D.C., February 12, 1952.

[128] *Bridgeport Post,* March 27, 1952.

[129] ABPT, Miscellaneous Correspondence, Religious Women, Sr. St. Gaston to Bp. Shehan, Neuilly–sur–Seine, August 18, 1954.

[130] ABPT, Miscellaneous Correspondence, Religious Women, Mthr. M. Bernadette de Lourdes, OCarm to Bp. Shehan, New York, May 26, 1956.

[131] *Bridgeport Post,* January 26, 1958.

[132] *Catholic Transcript,* March 6, 1958.

[133] *Bridgeport Sunday Post,* March 9, 1958.

[134] *Catholic Transcript,* May 1, 1958.

[135] *Catholic Transcript,* May 1, 1958.

[136] *Catholic Transcript,* September 29, 1960. *Bridgeport Sunday Herald,* October 2, 1960.

[137] ABPT, Shehan sermons and speeches, "Cura et Salus Animarum suprema lex," Bridgeport, June 14, 1961.

[138] Interview with Msgr. John Toomey.

[139] Interview with Msgr. John Toomey.

[140] Interview with Msgr. John Toomey.

[141] Lawrence Shehan, *A Blessing of Years* (Notre Dame, Indiana, 1982), p. 125.

[142] *Bridgeport Post,* September 11, 1961.

[143] *Bridgeport Post,* September 27, 1961.

[144] Interview with the Rev. Thomas Keeney.

IMPORTANT DATES

1622 Pope Gregory XV establishes the Congregation de Propaganda Fide. The Propaganda Fide guided the Church's growth in America until 1908.

1638/39 The "Fundamental Orders" of the Colonies of Quinnipiack and Connecticut.

1665 Quinnipiack and Connecticut merge to form the Colony of Connecticut. To be governed by royal charter.

1666 Fairfield County is established.

1708 Saybrook Platform.

1781 First Mass celebrated in Fairfield County at Newtown on Sunday, July 1, by Abbé Robin, chaplain of Rochambeau's French troops during the Revolutionary War.

1784 Rev. John Carroll appointed as the superior of the Church in America.

1789 The See of Baltimore is established by Pope Pius VI, and the Rev. John Carroll is named America's first bishop.

1790 The Rev. John Carroll is consecrated in England as the first Bishop of Baltimore with jurisdiction over all Catholics in the United States.

1796 Rev. Francis Matignon and Rev. John de Cheverus assigned to Boston by Bishop Carroll. The permanent establishment of the Church in New England begins.

1808 The Diocese of Boston is established. The Rev. John de Cheverus named the first bishop with jurisdiction over all of New England.

1810 The first meeting of the American bishops to establish common practice for Catholics in America.

1818 Connecticut Constitution: Catholics finally admitted to the full rights of citizenship and freedom of worship.

1820 Jerusha Booth Barber from Newtown enters the convent, becoming the first Connecticut born woman to enter into religious life.

1825 The Rev. Benedict Fenwick, SJ, named the second Bishop of Boston.

1829 The Rev. Bernard O'Cavanagh appointed to Hartford as the state's first resident priest: the beginning of the Church's organization in Connecticut.

The state's first Catholic paper, the *Connecticut Press* is begun by Bp. Fenwick in Hartford.

1830 Connecticut's first Catholic church is dedicated in Hartford by Bp. Fenwick.

277

The Rev. James Fitton celebrates the first Mass in Bridgeport in the house of James McCullough on Milne St. for the town's 17 Catholics.

1832 The state's second Catholic church established in New Haven. The Rev. James McDermott is given jurisdiction over the Catholics in Fairfield County: Catholics were found in Bridgeport and Norwalk, numbering 125 persons.

1833 The Rev. James McDermott celebrates the first Mass in Norwalk in the home of Michael Cooney with 25 persons.

1836 Bridgeport counts 100 Catholic adults. Plans are made to build a Catholic church. "Maria Monk" publishes *Awful Disclosures of the Hotel Dieu Nunnery of Montreal.*

1842 Connecticut's third Catholic church, St. James is dedicated in Bridgeport by Bishop Fenwick. The Rev. Michael Lynch is named the resident rector with the care of all Catholics within the county.

1843 The Diocese of Hartford is established as a suffragan of Baltimore, with jurisdiction over Connecticut and Rhode Island. The Rev. William Tyler is the first bishop.

1848 Bishop Tyler visits the Catholics of Norwalk in response to their petition for a resident priest. The Rev. John Brady is assigned to Norwalk. St. Mary's is the second Catholic mission within Fairfield County. Fr. Brady is to care for the Catholics in Danbury, Stamford, Greenwich, New Canaan, Westport, New Milford, Newtown and environs.

1850 Bishop Bernard O'Reilly named Hartford's second Bishop. The Diocese of New York is raised to an archdiocese with Hartford numbered among its suffragans.

1851 St. Mary's Church in Norwalk is consecrated by Bishop Bernard O'Reilly. A clapboard church is also dedicated in Stamford as a mission station of Norwalk. St. Peter Church is founded in Danbury as the county's third mission. The Sisters of Mercy arrive in the Diocese of Hartford, beginning their work in Providence. St. James Church in Bridgeport opens the first Catholic school in Fairfield County.

1852 The First Plenary Council of Baltimore. The Rev. Thomas J. Synnott named rector of St. James Church, Bridgeport.

1854 The First Synod of Hartford. The Rev. John C. Brady dies in Hartford. He is recognized as the first rector of St. Mary, Norwalk, by Fairfield County press, which leads to anti–Catholic campaign. St. John Church, Stamford, is established as the county's fourth mission.

1855 Know–Nothing candidate William T. Minor of Stamford is elected state governor. Anti–Catholic legislation begun. William S. Pomeroy, editor of the *Republican Farmer* in Bridgeport defends Catholics against Governor Minor's attacks. St. Mary in Norwalk opens the second Catholic school in the county.

1857 American College opened in Louvain, Belgium, to train American seminarians. St. Mary's Church is established in Bridgeport.

1858 The Rev. Francis McFarland named the third Bishop of Hartford.

1859 The North American College opened in Rome to train American seminarians. St. Rose of Lima Church is founded in Newtown.

1866 The Second Plenary Council of Baltimore. The Rev. Matthew Hart and other priests of Connecticut succeed in overturning anti–Catholic property and incorporation laws. The first Catholic temperance society in the county is organized at St. Peter Church, Danbury.

1869 New St. Augustine Church dedicated in Bridgeport to replace old St. James Church. Ancient Order of Hibernians organizes its first Connecticut division in Bridgeport.

1872 The Diocese of Providence is created. The Diocese of Hartford is rendered coterminous with Connecticut. Bishop McFarland moves to Hartford. The first Sisters of Mercy begin work in Connecticut, establishing motherhouses in Hartford and Middletown.

1875 The Rev. Thomas Galberry is named the fourth Bishop of Hartford. Propaganda Fide issues an instruction concerning the dangers to Catholic children in public schools.

1876 The Sisters of Mercy establish a motherhouse at Meriden. The Sisters begin a mission at St. John Church in Stamford. They are the first women religious to begin work in Fairfield County. St. Thomas Aquinas Church is founded in Fairfield. St. Mary Church is founded in Greenwich. Our Lady of the Assumption Church is founded in Westport.

1878 The Second Synod of Hartford.

1879 The Rev. Lawrence S. McMahon is named the fifth Bishop of Hartford. St. Mary Church is founded in Ridgefield.

1881 Bridgeport elections which occasioned the Church's first attempt to influence the Catholic vote in large city elections in Fairfield County.

1882 The Knights of Columbus is founded in New Haven.

1883 The Catholic Benevolent Legion is organized in Stamford at St. John Church. St. Mary's Church in Bethel is founded.

1884 The Third Plenary Council of Baltimore.

1886 The Third Synod of Hartford. St. Joseph Church is established for the Catholic Germans of Bridgeport. It is the first national church in Fairfield County.

1887 Decision of the Propaganda Fide concerning the pastoral care of Catholic immigrants in the United States.

1888 Pope Leo XIII issues his apostolic letter "Quam Aerumnosa" to the American bishops concerning pastoral care for Catholic Italian immigrants.

1889 The Jesuit Fathers purchase Keyser Estate in South Norwalk and open the Manresa Institute. St. Patrick Church is founded in Bridgeport.

1890 St. Joseph Church in Bridgeport begins the first school in the county for Catholic immigrants.

1891 Encyclical *Rerum Novarum* on the relationship of labor and capital by Pope Leo XIII. St. John Nepomucene Church is established for the Catholic Slovaks of Bridgeport. It is the first Catholic Slovak mission in New England and the second national church in Fairfield County. The Church of Our Lady of Pompeii, the forerunner of Holy Rosary Church, was established for Bridgeport's Catholic Italian community.

1893 The Apostolic Delegation is established in Washington. Priests of the Diocese of Hartford attempt to elect a new bishop in move for "home rule." The Rev. Michael Tierney from Norwalk is named the sixth Bishop of Hartford. Danbury Hatter's Strike begins. Sacred Heart Church is founded in Bridgeport.

1895 St. John Church is founded in Noroton (Darien). St. Joseph Church is founded in South Norwalk.

1896 St. Anthony Church is established for Bridgeport's Catholic French community. St. Stephen Church is established in Bridgeport for the

Catholic Hungarians of the Latin Rite. St. Aloysius Church is founded in New Canaan. St. Thomas Seminary is opened in Hartford.

1897 St. Stephen Church is founded for Bridgeport's Catholic Hungarian community.

1899 The Church of St. Michael the Archangel is established in Bridgeport for the Catholic Polish community.

1900 Holy Trinity Church is established as the first Byzantine Rite Church in Fairfield County. St. Peter Church is founded in Bridgeport. Sacred Heart Church is founded in Byram.

1902 Pope Leo XIII names the Right Rev. Andrew Hodobay as Apostolic Visitator to the Greek Catholics in the United States. St. Charles Parish is founded in Bridgeport.

1903 The Bridgeport Trolley Strike. Holy Name of Jesus Church is founded for Stamford's Catholic Polish community.

1905 St. Vincent Hospital opened under the administration of the Sisters of St. Vincent de Paul. The Greek Catholic Church of St. John the Baptist is founded in Bridgeport. St. Joseph Church is founded in Danbury.

1906 The Rev. Patrick J. McCormick, a curate at St. Augustine Church in Bridgeport, is named the first Diocesan Supervisor of Schools. The Holy Ghost Fathers open a seminary in Norwalk called Ferndale. St. Joseph Church in Shelton is founded. St. James Church is founded in Stratford.

1907 The Church of Sts. Cyril and Methodius is established in Bridgeport. Bishop Soter Ortynski is named as Bishop of the Greek Catholics in the United States. St. George Church established for Bridgeport's Catholic Lithuanian community. St. Ladislaus Church is founded for the Catholic Hungarians of South Norwalk. St. Mary Church is founded in Stamford. Francis Hodur, an excommunicated Roman Catholic priest, meets with dissatisfied Catholic Polish immigrants in Bridgeport who decide to break from the Catholic Church and form the schismatic Polish National Catholic Church.

1908 The Catholic Church in the United States is released from the jurisdiction of Propaganda Fide.

1910 The Rev. John J. Nilan is named the seventh Bishop of Hartford. St. Ann Church is founded in Danbury for the Melkite community. St. Paul Church is founded in Glenville.

1912 St. Ladislaus Church is dedicated for the Catholic Hungarians of South Norwalk. Danbury's Protestant ministers unanimously support the anti–Catholic "Guardians of Liberty."

1913 Holy Cross Parish is founded for Bridgeport's Catholic Slovenian community. St. Catherine of Siena Parish is founded in Riverside.

1914 Beginning of World War I: Bridgeport's armament industry booms as does its worker population. The Rev. Andrew Komara, Pastor of St. John Nepomucene Church, calls for housing and social reform. Project for the National Shrine of the Immaculate Conception receives papal approval. The project was the idea of Connecticut's Bishop Thomas J. Shahan, Rector of Catholic University. The Rev. William J. Fitzgerald develops the first "Syllabus" to guide the state's Catholic education.

1915 St. Vincent Hospital begins nursing residence under the direction of Sister Alice Cannon.

1916 Bishop Nilan and Bridgeport priests and laity establish the Catholic Charitable Bureau of Bridgeport under the direction of the Rev. Richard Moore and Marguerite T. Boylan. This was the forerunner of Catholic Charities.

1917 The American Bishops establish the National Catholic War Council to Catholic charitable and social efforts. Blessed Sacrament Parish is founded in Bridgeport.

1919 The American Bishops issue their "Bishops' Program of Social Reconstruction." The National Catholic Welfare Conference is founded. Connecticut establishes its Department of Americanization.

1920 James Cardinal Gibbons blesses the cornerstone for the National Shrine of the Immaculate Conception. The stone is the gift of a Bridgeport Catholic, James Sexton.

1921 Congress passes immigration restriction law.

1922 St. Ann's Parish in Black Rock is founded. Our Lady of the Assumption Parish is founded in Fairfield. St. Mary Ruthenian Catholic Church is founded in Bridgeport.

1923 Sacred Heart Parish is founded for Stamford's Catholic Italian community. Holy Name Parish is founded for Stratford's Catholic Slovak community.

1924 Congress passes further immigration restriction laws. William I. McAndrew, principal of Walterville School in Bridgeport, gains the assistance of the Rev. Matthew Traynor, Pastor of St. Mary Church, in program of early release time for public school children to attend religious education classes.

1925 Sacred Heart Parish is founded for Danbury's Catholic Polish community.

1926 St. Cecilia Parish is founded in Springdale.

1927 Congress passes immigration laws, setting an annual quota of 150,000 foreign arrivals into the country. St. Raphael Parish founded for Bridgeport's Catholic Italian community.

1928 The defeat of Alfred Smith, first Catholic presidential candidate of a major political party. The first organized youth work in the diocese is begun at St. Charles Church in Bridgeport by the Rev. Francis Morrissey. St. Ambrose Parish is founded in Bridgeport. St. Clement Parish is founded in Stamford.

1929 The congregation of St. Mary Ruthenian Catholic Church in Bridgeport breaks communion with the Roman Catholic Church.

1930 Centennial celebrations of the first Mass in Bridgeport. St. Benedict Parish is founded for Stamford's Catholic Slovak community.

1932 St. Anthony Parish is founded for Danbury's Maronite community. St. Emery Parish is founded for Fairfield's Catholic Hungarian community.

1934 Bishop Maurice McAuliffe is named the eighth Bishop of Hartford. The Legion of Decency is begun in the state. Sacred Heart Church is founded in Georgetown. St. Teresa Parish is founded in Trumbull.

1935 St. Maurice Parish is founded in Glenbrook. St. Thomas the Apostle Parish is founded in Norwalk.

1936 Catholic High School Clubs begun throughout the diocese by the Rev. John Loughlin. The Greek Catholic Church of St. John the Baptist in Bridgeport breaks communion with Rome, led by the excommunicated priest, Orestes Chornock.

1937   St. Roch Parish is founded in Greenwich.

1938   Holy Family Parish is founded in Fairfield.

1940   The American Bishops issue their "Statement on the Church and Social Order." Bridgeport city retreats for Catholic high school students begun by the Rev. Thomas Henahan.

1941   America enters World War II. Bridgeport's armaments industry booms. The Rev. Francis Haggerty, a curate at St. John Church in Stamford, begins the weekly radio program "Angelus Hour." St. Joseph Parish is founded in Brookfield.

1942   The Jesuit Fathers open Fairfield College Preparatory School. St. Joseph Hospital is opened in Stamford under the direction of the Sisters of St. Joseph of Chambery.

1943   The Rev. Joseph Donnelly, director of the Diocesan Labor Institute, establishes a labor school in Bridgeport to improve labor relations.

1945   Bishop Henry J. O'Brien is named the ninth Bishop of Hartford. The American Bishops issue their pastoral letter, "Between War and Peace."

1948   Our Lady of Peace Parish is founded in Stratford.

1949   Ten thousand Catholics from throughout the county gather at Bridgeport's Seaside Park to demonstrate against communist aggression.

1952   Pope Pius XII issues his apostolic constitution, *Exsul Familia* on the care of Catholic immigrants.

1953   The Diocese of Bridgeport is established by Pope Pius XII with Bishop Lawrence Shehan of Baltimore as its first Ordinary. The diocese is to include all of Fairfield County. St. Stephen Parish is founded in Trumbull (Stepney). Our Lady of Fatima Parish is founded in Wilton.

1954   Bishop Shehan begins the diocesan vocations program under the direction of Msgr. Michael J. Guerin. Our Lady of Good Counsel Parish is founded in Bridgeport. St. Edward the Confessor Parish is founded in New Fairfield. Our Lady of Grace Parish is founded in Stratford.

1955   St. Mary's High School opens in Greenwich. Shehan raises nearly $4,000,000 for the construction of Notre Dame High School in Bridgeport. St. Lawrence Parish is founded in Huntington. St. Catherine of Siena Parish is founded in Nichols. St. Francis of Assisi Parish is founded in Weston.

1956   The erection of the Exarchy of Stamford for Ukranian Rite Catholics. Fathers Francis Campagnone and Victor Torres–Frias are assigned by Bishop Shehan to begin an Hispanic apostolate in Bridgeport. Notre Dame Parish is founded in Easton.

1957   Notre Dame High School opens: the first of Bishop Shehan's diocesan high schools. It is the largest Catholic high school in New England; the largest secondary school in Fairfield County. The Chapel of Nuestra Señora de Providencia opens in the West End of Bridgeport for Catholic Hispanics. St. Matthew Parish is founded in Norwalk. St. Luke Parish is founded in Westport.

1958   The Eparchy of Stamford is established for the Ukrainian Rite Catholics in New York and New England, with Bishop Ambrose Senyshyn, OSBM, as the first Apostolic Eparch. Stamford Catholic High School opens. The Chapel of Nuestra Señora de Guadalupe opens on the East Side of Bridgeport for the Catholic Hispanics. The Rev. Constantino Caldas begins his work among the Catholic Portuguese in the diocese. St. Pius X Parish is founded in Fairfield.

1959 Norwalk's Central Catholic High School opens.
1960 The Hispanic Apostolate is expanded to assist Catholic Hispanics in Norwalk and Stamford. St. Joseph Manor is opened in Trumbull. St. Gregory the Great Parish is founded in Danbury. St. Jerome Parish is founded in Norwalk. St. Leo Parish is founded in Stamford. St. Mark Parish is founded in Stratford.
1961 The First Synod of Bridgeport. St. Anthony of Padua Parish is founded in Fairfield. Bishop Shehan leases the former state armory in Bridgeport as a C.Y.O. center. It was later dedicated as the Cardinal Shehan Center. St. Andrew Parish is founded in Bridgeport. Bishop Walter W. Curtis is named the second Bishop of Bridgeport.

ARCHIVES and
LIBRARY COLLECTIONS

Archives of the Apostolic Delegation in the United States, Vatican Secret Archives, Vatican City State.

Archives of the Archdiocese of Baltimore, 320 Cathedral St., Baltimore, Maryland 21201.

Archives of the Archdiocese of Boston, Lake St., Boston, Massachusetts 02135.

Archives of the Diocese of Bridgeport, 238 Jewett Ave., Bridgeport, Connecticut 06606.

Burroughs Library: Bishop's Room, 925 Broad St., Bridgeport, Connecticut 06604.

Archives of the Center for Migration Studies, 209 Flagg St., Staten Island, New York 10304.

Archives of the Fairfield Historical Society, 636 Old Post Rd., Fairfield, Connecticut 06432.

Archives of Fairfield University: Nyselius Library, North Benson Rd., Fairfield, Connecticut 06432.

Archives of the Generalate of the Congregation of the Missionaries of St. Charles Borromeo, Via Calandrelli 1, Rome 00153, Italy.

Archives of the Archdiocese of Hartford, 134 Farmington Ave., Hartford, Connecticut 16105.

Archives of the Lockwood House, 141 East Ave., Norwalk, Connecticut 06850.

Archives of the Lockwood Matthews Mansion Museum, 295 West Ave., Norwalk, Connecticut 06850.

Norwalk Public Library: Geneology Room, 1 Belden Ave., Norwalk, Connecticut 06850.

Pequot Library: Rare Book Collection, Southport, Connecticut.

Archives of the Sacred Congregation "de Propaganda Fide," Piazza di Spagna 48, Rome, Italy 00187.

Archives of the School Sisters of Notre Dame, 345 Belden Hill, Wilton, Connecticut 06892.

Scott Fanton Museum, Main St., Danbury, Connecticut 06810.

Archives of the Secretariat of State, Vatican Secret Archives, Vatican City State.

Archives of the Sisters of Mercy, 249 Steele Rd., West Hartford, Connecticut 06117.

Archives of the University of Notre Dame, 607 Memorial Library, Notre Dame, Indiana 46556.

BIBLIOGRAPHY

PRINTED SOURCES

A Confession of Faith, owned and consented to by the Elders and Messengers of the Churchs, in New–England, Assembled by Delegation at Saybrook, September 9th, 1708, Bridgeport 1810.

Acta et Decreta Concilii Plenarii Baltimorensis Tertii, A.D. mdccclxxxiv, Baltimorae mdccclxxxvi.

Annual Report of the Board of Education to the General Assembly, New Haven May, 1869.

BARBER, Daniel. "The History of My Own Times," in *Boston Monthly Magazine*, vol. 1826–1828.

BEECHER, Lyman. "A Plea for the West," Cincinnati 1835.

Bridgeport Board of Education Reports, 1877–1883, vol. I.

Bridgeport City Directory, 1895, Bridgeport 1895.

Bridgeport Directory and Annual Advertiser, For 1868–9, Bridgeport 1868.

Bridgeport and East Bridgeport Directory, Containing the Names of the Citizens, A Business Directory, and an Appendix of Useful Information, 1857–8, Bridgeport 1858.

BRIGDEN, Thomas. *A Brief Sketch of the True Religion, Written in the Form of Letters by a Native of Conn. Formerly a Member of the Presbyterian Church, and Since a Catholic Convert. Together with the Motives that Conducted His Choice, and the Invincible Reasons that now Hold Him in the Catholic Communion*, Hartford 1831.

Bureau of the Census. *Historical Statistics of the United States: Colonial Times to 1970*, Washington, D.C. 1975.

BUSHNELL, Horace. "Barbarism the First Danger," in *Connecticut Pamphlets*, vol. 72, New York 1847.

_____. "Building Eras in Religion," New York 1881.

_____. "Common Schools; A Discourse on the Modifications Demanded by the Roman Catholics," in *Connecticut Pamphlets*, vol. 28, Hartford 1853.

_____. "Crisis in the Church," in *Connecticut Pamphlets*, vol. 47, Hartford 1835.

_____. "Discourses on Christian Nurture," Boston 1847.

CARROLL, Teresa Austin. *Leaves from the Annals of the Sisters of Mercy*, New York 1889.

A Complete Reference Gazeteer of the United States of America, New York 1839.

Concilium Plenarium Totius Americae Septentrionalis Foederatae, Baltimori Habitum Anno 1852, Baltimori mdcccliii.

Concilia Provincialia, Baltimori Habita ab Anno 1829 usque ad Annum 1849, Baltimori mdcccli.

Connecticut Her Constitutions, Hartford 1935.

Course of Study and Syllabus for the Elementary Schools of the Diocese of Hartford, Hartford 1914.

DISANO, Carmelo. *Breve Storia Della Chiesa Americana ovvero L'Una, Santa, Cattolica ed Apostlica Chiesa di Cristo Gesu*, Hartford, 1924.

DONOVAN, James (ed.). *Decreta Synodorum Hartfordiensium, in Unum Volumen Collecta*, Hartford 1902.

DOUBERG, J. Huen. *Life of the Cardinal De Cheverus, Archbishop of Bordeaux*, Philadelphia 1839.

DWIGHT, Timothy. *The Duty of Americans, at the Present Crisis, Illustrated in a Discourse, Preached on the Fourth of July, 1798*, New Haven 1798.

FENWICK, Benedict (Joseph McCarthy, ed.). *Memoirs to Serve for the Future Ecclesiastical History of the Diocese of Boston*, Yonkers 1970.

Finning's Bridgeport Town and City Directory and Annual Advertiser, For 1855–6, Bridgeport 1855.

FITTON, James. *Sketches of the Establishment of the Church in New England*, Boston 1872.

FORD, Worthington Chauncey, ed. *Journals of the Continental Congress, 1774–1789*, Washington, D.C. 1904.

FREEMAN, Edward A. *Lectures to American Audiences*, Philadelphia 1882.

GRIGGS, W.N.; LOCKWOOD, D.B., compilers. *Bridgeport Directory for 1862 and 1863; Containing the Names, Residences, and Business of the Inhabitants of the City and Town of Bridgeport, Including East Bridgeport*. Bridgeport 1862.

HALE, Charles R. *Headstone Inscriptions, Town of Fairfield, Connecticut*, Hartford 1937.

HALL, Edwin. *An Exposition of the Laws of Baptism, As it Regards the Mode and the Subject*, Norwalk 1840.

HANLEY, Thomas O'Brien. *The Carroll Papers*, vols. I, II, III, Notre Dame 1976.

THE HARTFORD SISTERS OF MERCY. *Tributes to Our Foundress for the Centennial of the Foundation of the Congregation of the Sisters of Mercy*, Hartford 1931.

HASKEL, Daniel. *A Complete Descriptive and Statistical Gazeteer of the United States of America*, New York 1845.

HOADLY, Charles J. *Records of the Colony or Jurisdiction of New Haven, From May, 1653, to the Union. Together with New Haven Code of 1656*, Hartford 1858.

Hoffman's Catholic Directory, Almanac, and Clergy List Quarterly, Milwaukee 1890–1898.

LABAREE, Leonard Woods. *The Public Records of the State of Connecticut, From May 1789 through October 1792*, vol. 7, Hartford 1948.

MCELRONE, Hugh P., ed. *The Works of the Right Rev. John England*, vol. III, Baltimore 1884.

MATHER, Cotton, *Magnalia Christi Americana; The Ecclesiastical History of New England From Its First Planting in the Year 1620 Unto the Year of Our Lord 1698*, London 1702.

Metropolitan Catholic Almanac and Laity's Directory, Baltimore 1850; 1857; 1860.

New England Primer Enlarged. For the More Easy Attaining the True Reading of ENGLISH To Which is Added, The Assembly of Divines Catechism, Boston 1727.

NOLAN, Hugh J., ed. *Pastoral Letters of the United States Catholic Bishops*, 4 vols., Washington, D.C. 1984.

PERRY, Kate E. *The Old Burying Ground of Fairfield, Connecticut*, Hartford 1882.

ROONEY, James A. *The Connecticut Catholic Year Book, Being an Epitome of the History of the Church in the Diocese of Hartford from April, 1876 to May, 1877*, Hartford 1877.

Sadlier's Catholic Directory, Almanac, and Ordo, New York 1870; 1800 ff.

SHEHAN, Lawrence J. *A Blessing of Years. The Memoirs of Lawrence Cardinal Shehan*, Notre Dame 1982.

TESSAROLO, Giulivo, ed. *Exsul Familia, The Church's Magna Charta for Migrants*, Staten Island 1962.

TRUMBULL, Hammond J. *The Public Records of the Colony of Connecticut Prior to the Union with New Haven Colony*, vols. I, II, III, New York 1968.

The United States Catholic Almanac, 1834, New York 1834.

WEBB & FITZGERALD, compilers. *Bridgeport and East Bridgeport General and Business Directory, to Which is Prefixed an Appendix of Useful Information, 1867*, Bridgeport 1867.

SECONDARY SOURCES

AHLSTROM, Syndney E. *A Religious History of the American People*, New Haven 1972.

ANDERSEN, Ruth. *From Yankee to American; Connecticut 1865 to 1914*, Bridgeport 1975.

ANDRIOT, John L., ed. *Population Abstract of the United States*, vol. I, McLean, Virginia 1983.

ARNEZ, JOHN A. *Slovenian Community in Bridgeport, Connecticut*, "Studia Slovneica," Special Series, no. 2, New York 1971.

BAILEY, James Montgomery. *History of Danbury, Conn. 1684–1896*, New York 1896.

BARRETT, J.D. *A Comparative Study of the Councils of Baltimore and the Code of Canon Law*, Washington, D.C. 1932.

BEARDSLEY, E. EDWARDS. *The History of the Episcopal Church in Connecticut, From the Death of Bishop Seabury to the Present Time*, 2 vols., New York 1868.

BEECHER, Charles, ed. *Autobiography, Correspondence, Etc., of Lyman Beecher, D.D.*, 2 vols., New York 1865.

BILLINGTON, Ray Allen. *The Protestant Crusade, 1800–1860. A Study of the Origins of American Nativism*, Chicago 1964.

BUCZEK, Daniel S. *Immigrant Pastor; The Life of The Right Reverend Monsignor Lucyan Bojnowski of New Britain, Connecticut*, Waterbury 1974.

BYRNE, Stephen. *Irish Immigration to the United States: What it Has Been, and What it Is*, New York 1969.

CAMERON, Kenneth Walter. *The Catholic Revival in Episcopal Connecticut (1850–1925)*, Hartford 1965.

The Catholic Church in the United States of America, To Celebrate the Golden Jubilee of His Holiness Pope Pius X, 3 vols., New York 1908.

CARTHY, Mary Peter. *English Influences on Early American Catholicism*, Washington, D.C. 1959.

CHALMERS, David A. *Hooded Americanism; the History of the Ku Klux Klan*, New York 1981.

CURRAN, Francis X. *Catholics in Colonial Law*, Chicago 1963.

DAILY, Mary Renata. *The Connecticut Mind and Catholicism, 1823–1860*, New Haven 1939. (Unpublished dissertation.)

DANENBER, Elsie Nicholas. *The Romance of Norwalk*, New York 1929.

———. *The Story of Bridgeport*, Bridgeport 1936.

DAY, Clive. *The Rise of Manufacturing in Connecticut, 1820–1850*, in Tercentenary Commission of the State of Connecticut, XLIV, New Haven 1935.

DOLAN, Jay. *The American Catholic Experience*, Garden City 1985.

DUGGAN, Thomas S. *The Catholic Church in Connecticut*, New York 1930.

EAMES, Wilberforce. *Early New England Catechisms, A Bibliographical Account of Some Catechisms published before the Year 1800, for use in New England*, Worchester 1898.

ELLIS, John Tracy. *American Catholicism*, Garden City 1965.

———. *Documents of American Church History*, Milwaukee 1962.

FENICK, Marge. *The American Lithuanians in Bridgeport*, University of Bridgeport Student Monograph No. 10, 1957.

FERRIS, Ann. *The Anatomy of a Hospital: St. Vincent's Hospital Bridgeport, Connecticut*, Fairfield 1976. (Unpublished dissertation.)

FISKE, John. *American Political Ideas*. New York 1885.

———. *The Beginnings of New England or the Puritain Theocracy in its Relation to Civil and Religious Liberty*, Boston 1917.

FOERSTER, Robert F. *The Italian Emigration of Our Times*, Cambridge 1919.

FOX, Paul. *The Polish National Catholic Church*. Scranton n.d.

GAUSTED, Edwin S. *The Great Awakening in New England*, New York 1957.

GREENE, Mary Evelyn. *From Vision to Action, the Sisters of Mercy of Connecticut, 1930–1982*, West Hartford 1983.

GREENE, Mary L. *The Development of Religious Liberty in Connecticut*, Boston 1905.

GUILDAY, Peter. *The National Pastorals of the American Hierarchy (1792–1919)*, Westminster, Maryland 1954.

HALL, Verna M., compiler. *The Christian History of the Constitution of the United States of America*, San Francisco 1979.

HARTMAN, Edward George. *The Movement to Americanize the Immigrant*, New York 1967.

HAWKS, Francis I; PERRY, William Stevens. *Documentary History of the Protestant Episcopal Church in the United States of America*, 2 vols., New York 1863.

HEFFERNAN, Arthur J. *A History of Catholic Education in Connecticut*, in The Catholic University of America Educational Research Monographs, vol. X, Washington, D.C. January 2, 1937, No. I.

HENKEL, Willi, *The Final Stage of U.S.A. Church's Development under Propaganda Fide*, in Sacrae Congregationis de Propaganda Fide Memoria Rerum, III/1 1815–1972, Rome 1975, pp. 708–728.

HERRON, Maria Eulalia. *The Sisters of Mercy in the United States*, New York 1929.

HILL, S., ed. *History of Danbury*, New York 1896.

HURD, D. Hamilton. *History of Fairfield County, Connecticut, with Illustration and Biographical Sketches of Its Prominent Men and Pioneers*, Philadelphia 1881.

JACKSON, Kenneth T. *The Ku Klux Klan in the City, 1915–1930*, New York 1967.

JANIK, Herbert F. *A Diverse People, Connecticut 1914 to the Present*, Chester, Connecticut 1975.

KAUFFMAN, Christopher J. *Faith and Fraternalism: The History of the Knights of Columbus 1882–1982*, New York 1982.

KELLER, Charles Roy. *The Second Great Awakening in Connecticut*, New Haven 1942.

KOENIG, Samuel. *Immigrant Settlements in Connecticut: Their Growth and Characteristics*, Hartford 1938.

LAPOMARDA, Vincent A. *The Jesuit Heritage in New England,* Worchester 1977.

LATHROP, Cornelia Penfield. *Black Rock, Seaport of Old Fairfield, 1644–1870,* New Haven 1930.

LIPTAK, Dolores Ann. *European Immigrants and the Catholic Church, 1870–1920,* New York, 1987.

LORD, Robert, SEXTON, John E., HARRINGTON, Edward T. *The History of the Archdiocese of Boston, in the Various Stages of Its Development, 1604–1943,* 3 vols., Boston 1945.

LUCAS, Paul R. *Valley of Discord. Church and Society Along the Connecticut River, 1636–1725,* Hanover, New Hampshire 1976.

MASON, Mary Paul. *Church–State Relationships in Education in Connecticut, 1633–1953,* Catholic University of America Educational Research Monograph, vol. XVII, October 1, 1956, No. 6., Washington, D.C. 1953.

MCLAUGHLIN, William G. *New England Dissent, 1630–1833: The Baptists and the Separation of Church and State,* Cambridge 1971.

MORSE, Jarvis. *A Neglected Period in Connecticut's History, 1818–1850,* New Haven 1935.

MUNICH, Austin Francis. *The Beginnings of Roman Catholicism in Connecticut,* Tercentenary Commission of the State of Connecticut, XLI, New Haven 1935.

MURDOCK, Kenneth B. *Notes on the Magnalia,* in HOMES, Thomas James, ed., Cotton Mather; A Bibliography of His Works, vol. 2, Cambridge 1940.

NOONAN, John Carroll. *Nativism in Connecticut, 1829–1860,* Washington, D.C. 1938. (Unpublished dissertation.)

O'BRIEN, George F. *The Early Developments of the Roman Catholic Church in Danbury, 1838–1900,* Danbury 1967. (Unpublished dissertation.)

O'DONNELL, James H. *History of the Diocese of Hartford,* Boston 1900.

OSTERWEIS, Rollin G. *Three Centuries of New Haven, 1638–1938,* New Haven 1953.

PETERS, Samuel A. *General History of Connecticut,* Freeport, New York 1969.

PURCELL, Richard J. *Connecticut in Transition: 1775–1818,* Middletown, Connecticut 1963.

ORCUTT, Samuel. *A History of the Old Town of Stratford and the City of Bridgeport, Connecticut,* West Haven 1886.

O'REILLY, Mary Cecilia. *The Sisters of Mercy in the Diocese of Hartford,* Hartford 1931.

RILEY, Arthur J. *Catholicism in New England to 1788,* Washington, D.C. 1936.

RUMILLY, Robert. *Histoire Des Franco–Americains,* Lazard, Montreal 1958.

SCHENCK, Elizabeth Hubbell. *The History of Fairfield, Fairfield County, Connecticut,* vol. II, New York 1905.

SELLECK, Charles M. *Norwalk after Two Hundred & Fifty Years,* South Norwalk 1901.

SHAUGHNESSY, Gerald. *Has the Immigrant Kept the Faith?,* New York 1969.

SHEA, John Gilmary. *History of the Catholic Church in the United States, 1763–1815,* vol. II, New York 1886.

SIMPSON, Alan. *Puritanism in Old and New England,* Chicago 1961.

SOLOMON, Barbara Miller. *Ancestors and Immigrants, A Changing New England Tradition,* Cambridge 1956.

STEPHENS, William R.W. *Life and Letters of Edward A. Freeman,* London 1895.

ARTICLES

BOOTH, Antonia. *History as a Prologue to Genealogical Research: Irish Catholics in Connecticut, 1829–1870,* in The Connecticut Nutmegger, 17 (1984) vol. 17, 187–196.

Catholics in the American Revolution, in The American Catholic Historical Researches, 1 (1906) N.S. vol. II, 7–11.

CONKLIN, Edward Grant. *Some Biological Aspects of Immigration,* in Scribner's Magazine, 69 (1921) 358.

Connecticut Industry, Danbury, March (1937).

CULLEN, Thomas F. *William Barber Tyler (1806–1849) First Bishop of Hartford, Connecticut,* in Catholic Historical Review, 23 (1937), 17–30.

FURLONG, Philip. *The Constitution and the Church,* in Catholic Historical Records and Studies, 29 (1938) 9–24.

GALLAGHER, JOHN P, POHL, Frederick J. *1,000 Years Before Columbus there were Catholics in Connecticut,* in Catholic Digest, (August 1980) 49–53.

GELLER, Herbert, *Bridgeport, 'The Ethnic City,'* 1982.

GRIFFIN, Martin I.J., ed. *Change in the Sentiments of the Revolutionists Toward 'Popery' After the French Alliance,* in American Catholic Historical Researches, 1 (1909) N.S. vol. V, 57–60.

GURN, Joseph. *The Faith in Connecticut,* in Columbia (June 1935) 7–20.

LENHART, John M. *The Capuchin Prefecture of New England,* in Franciscan Studies, 1 (1943) vol. 24, 21–46; 180–195; 306–313.

———. *An Important Chapter in American Church History (1625–1650),* in The Catholic Historical Review, 4 (1929) N.S. vol. VIII, 500–524.

LORD, Robert, *The Organization of the Church in New England: Bishop Benedict Joseph Fenwick (1782–1846),* in Catholic Historical Review, 22 (1936) 173–184.

PURCELL, Richard J. *Missionaries from All Hallows (Dublin) to the United States, 1842–1865,* in Records of the American Catholic Historical Society of Philadelphia, 4 (1942) vol. LIII, 204–249.

ROONEY, James A. *Early Times in the Diocese of Hartford, Conn.,* in Catholic Historical Review, 1 (1915) 148–163.

SEITZ, Don C. *Connecticut: A Nation in Miniature,* in Nation 3015 (1923) vol. 116, 461–464.

SHAHAN, Thomas J. *The Catholic Church in Connecticut—The First Priest in the Commonwealth,* in United States Catholic Historical Magazine, 9 (1890), vol. III, 16–25.

_____. *Early Catholics in Connecticut,* in United States Catholic Historical Magazine, 7 (1888), vol. II, 274–294.

SHEA, John Gilmary. *The Blue Laws of Connecticut,* in The American Catholic Quarterly Review, (1877), vol. II, 475–497.

Booklets

Ave Maria—Gratia Plena. 50th Anniversary of St. Mary's Church, Ridgefield, Connecticut, 1896–1946.

Centennial Anniversary of Saint Rose Church, Newtown, Connecticut, A Pictorial History, 1859–1959.

Centennial Celebration of the First Mass in Connecticut, (June, 1781), Sunday, June 26, 1881, in St. Peter's Church, Hartford, (1881).

A Century of Faith—1876–1976: St. Thomas Aquinas Church in Fairfield.

Dedicated to Sacred Heart Parish: Its Founders, Priests and Parishioners, December 26, 1965: 1884–1965.

Diamond Jubilee 75th Anniversary of St. Anthony of Padua, Bridgeport, Connecticut, 1894–1969, La Paroisse de St. Antoine de Padoue. La Parroquia de San Antonio de Padua.

Fifty Golden Years of Saint Joseph's Parish, Danbury, Connecticut, 1905–1955.

Golden Jubilee 1903–1953 Holy Rosary Church, Bridgeport, Connecticut.

Hommage Reconnaissant des Filles du Saint–Esprit aux Etats–Unis, 1902–1912.

Jankola Book, Honoring the Centennial of the Birth of Father Matthew Jankola (1872–1916).

Jubilé d'Or de La Paroisse St. Antoine de Padove de Bridgeport, Connecticut le 12 Novembre 1944.

Magnificat, Anniversary Booklet of the Srs. of Ss. Cyril and Methodius, 1909–1959.

Notre Dame of Bridgeport Catholic High School Dedication, September 26, 1957.

St. Joseph Polish National Catholic Church Diamond Jubilee Booklet, 1907–1982.

St. Michael the Archangel Church, 75th Anniversary Booklet.

75th Anniversary: 1902–1977. The Parish of St. Charles Borromeo.

Silver Anniversary Book of St. Emery Church, Fairfield, 1957.

Souvenir Album of the Golden Jubilee of Saint Michael the Archangel Church, Bridgeport, Connecticut, 1899–1949.

Spomenica posvenčenja slovenske pim. kat. cerkve sv. križa die 28. nov. 1915. Souvenir of the Dedication of the R.C. Sloven. Church of the Holy Cross, Bridgeport, Conn.